Ex Libris

Melvin H. Burke

RHODODENDRON
INFORMATION

1967

THE AMERICAN RHODODENDRON SOCIETY

R. 2, Box 105

Sherwood, Oregon 97140

4

Publications Committee

Dr. Robert Ticknor, Chairman

Forrest E. Bump, M. D.

Milton A. Foland

Molly Grothaus

Editor

J. Harold Clarke, Ph. D.

THE AMERICAN RHODODENDRON SOCIETY

6

DIRECTORS
of The American Rhododendron Society

Charles H. Anderson, *Seattle, Wash.*
Mrs. Robert Berry, *Aberdeen, Wash.*
Merle E. Cisney, *Camas, Wash.*
R. E. Comerford, *Marion, Ore.*
Russel L. Coovert, *Tacoma, Wash.*
Louis Grothaus, *Lake Oswego, Ore.*

John Henny, *Brooks, Ore.*
Alfred S. Martin, *Ambler, Pa.*
Donald McClure, *Seattle, Wash.*
Merle Saunders, *Eugene, Ore.*
Cecil Smith, *Aurora, Ore.*
Thomas Wheeldon, M.D.
Richmond, Va.

Together with the Presidents of the Chapters as follows

ALBANY-MOHAWK—Ralph H. Smith, *Delmar, N. Y.*
CALIFORNIA—Mrs. Philip McCombs, *Berkeley, Cal.*
CONNECTICUT—Ludwig Hoffman, *Bloomfield, Conn.*
EUGENE—James Gossler, *Springfield, Ore.*
GRAYS HARBOR— Harley Adamson, *Montesano, Wash.*
GREAT LAKES—A. W. Hartman, *Mansfield, Ohio.*
INDIANAPOLIS—Paul N. Harris, M.D., *Indianapolis, Ind.*
MIDDLE ATLANTIC—Robert E. Lee, *Charlottesville, Va.*
MIDWEST—Ray Michel, *Oak Lawn, Ill.*
NEW JERSEY—Charles Kwitchoff, *Ramsey, N. J.*
NEW YORK—Henry A. Dumper, *Roslyn Estates, N. Y.*
NORTH KITSAP—Howard A. Short, *Bainbridge Island, Wash.*
OLYMPIA—Joe Wheat, *Olympia, Wash.*
OLYMPIC PENINSULA—Lee Boardman, *Sequim, Wash.*
PHILADELPHIA—Francis J. Sholomskas, *Norristown, Pa.*
PORTLAND—Robert Whalley, *Gresham, Ore.*
PRINCETON—C. C. Bahrenburg, *Belle Mead, N. J.*
SEATTLE—C. E. Simons, Jr., M.D., *Edmonds, Wash.*
SHELTON—L. Frank Maranville, *Shelton, Wash.*
SOUTHEASTERN—W. H. Thorne, *Asheville, N. C.*
SOUTHERN—Arthur I. Coyle, *Houston, Texas.*
TACOMA—Robert L. Badger, *Tacoma, Wash.*
TAPPAN ZEE—Richard Redfield, *Closter, N. J.*
TUALATIN VALLEY—Lloyd Baron, *Hillsboro, Ore.*
VALLEY FORGE—Charles Herbert, *Phoenixville, Pa.*
VANCOUVER, B. C.—J. G. Lofthouse, *Vancouver, B. C.*

FOREWORD

This is the eighth in a series of books published by The American Rhododendron Society. Five Yearbooks were printed, from 1945 to 1949 inclusive. Then, after several years without a book we had "Rhododendrons 1956," the first in a series which might be called "Yearbook Type" but designed to appear about every five years. The second in this series was "Rhododendrons for Your Garden," and now "Rhododendron Information."

We hope the title is reasonably descriptive. It is meant to indicate that there are many important facts and figures, recommendations, and discussions, but not put together as a complete book on the subject of Rhododendrons. As we look it over it does seem, however, that all the essential information that a beginner would need to succeed with this group of plants may be found in the following pages.

No book of this type can be completely new, nor should it be. Each book adds much that is new, brings up to date the items which needed revision, and reiterates some of the longstanding truths which constitute the fundamental basis, the foundation, of success with a group of plants. Each book in the series published by the Society has contained new material, and much that is of lasting value. But all are out of print and the person with fresh new interest who wants to read all about his new hobby may have considerable difficulty finding copies. So we must, to a certain extent, provide in each new book that which the beginner needs, as well as the new and revised facts for the member of long standing.

The Ratings Committee has provided, for this book, a mass of information about garden hybrids which is unique for its scope and its detail. Here will be found descriptions and ratings for over 400 different sorts. The descriptions are very brief but they cover the points that are important in determining a rhododendron's usefulness.

Some may be surprised to find many old and presumably outmoded varieties included and other new, highly publicized kinds omitted. There are reasons for this. The old varieties are still on the market, and the beginner may have no way to sort out the poor ones from the superior ones, as catalog descriptions seldom strive to bring out faults and poor qualities. It is a service to the public, therefore, to the beginner especially, to rate the old varieties even if they are inferior. The only reason any new varieties were omitted was lack of sufficient information on which to base ratings and to compile factual descriptions.

Many varieties were discussed but bypassed with the suggestion that the names and parentage be printed, with the idea that they be watched and evaluated for rating at a future date.

The members of the Ratings Committee were not Azalea specialists and they had their hands full covering the non-Azalea types of the genus. Accordingly the group in Philadelphia, under the able leadership of Dr. West, were invited to bring up to date the ratings of the evergreen azaleas which grow so well in that area. We believe this will be a valuable feature of the book, especially to the beginner who is often faced with a very large number of varieties from which to choose, each of which may be described in rather glowing terms.

Likewise when the Committee came to the native azalea species the comment was that they might rate a few but it would be better to turn the job over to someone who was acquainted with all of them. Dr. Henry Skinner has made a detailed study of this group and was the logical choice. He very kindly consented and his ratings appear in the book.

The article prepared by Dr. David Leach is the result of the expenditure of much time in research and travel and is done most thoroughly but in a style that is interesting as well as informative. It adds things we need to know about the genus rhododendron, things we may have heard about in a vague way but never in a complete story like this. We should know of the toxic properties of leaf tissues, and of nectar of certain species, although it should not affect our love for the plants or our familiar method of handling them.

The third section of the book, dealing with cultural methods, pest control, variety choice and the other items will, we hope, be useful to beginner and to the more advanced amateur as well. We are especially interested in the article on Rhododendrons as Bonsai, contributed by the group in Seattle. We have seen, at some of the Seattle Chapter Shows, exhibits of rhododendrons and azaleas trained as Bonsai which were outstanding. We know of no plants better adapted to this very interesting Japanese method of training, something which can be practiced and enjoyed by the gardener with very limited space.

Finally we would like to point out that there is much more interesting information about rhododendrons that appears regularly in the Quarterly Bulletin of the Society. You are invited to contact the Executive Secretary, whose address appears at the back of the book, about the activities of the society and its various Chapters, and about the rights, privileges and advantages of membership.

ACKNOWLEDGEMENTS

This, like most American Rhododendron Society projects, has been a group effort. We would like to thank everyone, and hereby express our thanks to everyone who helped in any way, for surely we shall miss some when we come to name them, for there were so many.

First to be mentioned by name should be the Publication Committee, chairmanned by Dr. Ticknor, the A.R.S. Secretary-Treasurer. Other members included Dr. Forrest Bump, Milton Foland, and Molly Grothaus. Beginning some three years ago this committee met several times and discussed all the problems connected with the publication of a book of this kind.

The Ratings Committee was slow to get started but once under way Chairman John Henny kept pushing, with meetings every two weeks, and various members had to drive long distances to attend. The members of the committee contributed a great deal of time and effort and should be commended individually. They included, in addition to the chairman, Merle Cisney, George Clarke, J. Harold Clarke, Bob Comerford, George Grace, Louis Grothaus, Howard Slonecker, Cecil Smith, Robert Ticknor, and Wales Wood.

We are indebted to Dr. F. H. West and his collaborators of the Philadelphia Chapter for a much appreciated job on the evergreen azaleas. Dr. Henry Skinner, Director of the National Arboretum, took time from a very busy schedule to provide ratings for the native azaleas.

Writings by Dr. David Leach is always interesting and appreciated by members of the Society and we thank him for an unusual story.

Mrs. Blogg and her associates wrote as a group in preparing the fine, and very useful, story on Rhododendrons for Bonsai and our appreciation goes to each one of them individually.

Dr. Breakey and Dr. Gould have each helped the Society with

contributions to previous books and Bulletins. Both are very busy men and we are grateful to them for taking the time to bring up to date the recommendations in their respective fields.

From a previous book we have brought forward, with very slight revisions, a Glossary of Terms which the rhododendron fan is likely to meet in his reading. This was prepared originally by C. T. Hansen and so we thank him for the material prepared a number of years ago and now being used again.

No rhododendron book would be complete without pictures and again Cecil Smith has contributed most generously with black and white pictures for inside the book, and with a fine colored shot of 'Captain Jack', one of the late Rudolph Henny's varieties, for the dust cover.

Printer and engraver have been most cooperative and we are grateful to them.

J. HAROLD CLARKE
Long Beach, Washington
Editor

CONTENTS

12

LIST OF ILLUSTRATIONS

Part I

RATINGS

AND

DESCRIPTIONS

VARIETY

RATINGS

The variety is the basis of all horticulture and nowhere more so than with rhododendrons. We do not plant just a rhododendron but a 'Jean Marie de Montague' or some other named variety because we want something for a particular use, climate, or location, or for a predictable size of plant, color of blossoms, season of blooming or other characteristics. Descriptions of individual varieties in books or catalogs are useful but usually do not indicate the *relative* merit of two or more varieties. .

A number of years ago the British set up a ratings system for rhododendrons, giving four asterisks **** for the "best" varieties down to none for very poor ones.

FIRST A.R.S. RATINGS

The American Rhododendron Society embarked on a project of developing variety ratings early in its existence and the first A.R.S. ratings were published in the Bulletin in October, 1950. These ratings were revised and brought up to date in "Rhododendrons 1956" and again in 1961 in "Rhododendrons For Your Garden". This latter book was the first to contain separate ratings for bloom and plant characters. Previously one symbol indicated quality of the entire plant and bloom, and probably, in most cases, it was based primarily on the bloom. Although we may plant a rhododendron primarily for its blossom characteristics, nevertheless most of the year it is out of bloom and its value in the landscape is then determined entirely by plant and leaf characters.

Previous A.R.S. ratings have been based on four plus marks ++++ for the best varieties to zero for the poorest. Recently the A.R.S. Board of Directors decided to revise the methods of rating, and so the ratings which follow are on a somewhat different basis from those employed in previous publications:

NEW QUALITY RATINGS

The new quality ratings involve five classes as follows:

5—Superior
4—Above Average
3—Average
2—Below Average
1—Poor

These ratings may be expressed as numbers or plus marks. Where numbers are used the blossom is rated first and is expressed as the numerator of a fraction and the plant rating is expressed as the denominator. A variety rating of 4/2, therefore, would indicate an above average bloom and a below average plant.

HARDINESS RATINGS

Hardiness ratings of the A.R.S. early departed from the British custom of indicating by letter in what part of the British Isles the variety could be successfully grown. The A.R.S. ratings have become well known and are frequently seen in catalogs and magazine articles.

THE NEW SYSTEM

The previous A.R.S. hardiness ratings were based on temperature with H-1 indicating hardy to −25° F. The present ratings simply give in degrees the minimum temperature which the plant will normally withstand, if well matured, and if the minimum temperature period is not preceded by a warm spell, without visible damage to bud, leaf, or twigs. These temperature ratings are given in five degree steps as it is obviously impossible to make such ratings accurate within one or two degrees.

There may be some question as to why the ratings were not based on the U.S.D.A. Hardiness Zone Map. As a matter of fact they can be transposed quite readily since the different zones indicate areas of definite minimum temperatures. For instance the average annual minimum temperature of zone 6a is −10° to −5° of zone 6b −5° to 0°, of zone 7a 0° to +5°. However, where the terrain is rather uneven there may be quite a temperature difference within a very small distance; too small to show on a zone map. This is especially true in mountainous country where different gardens within the same city might be in two or three different hardiness zones.

It has seemed to the A.R.S. ratings committees now, as it has in the past, that the most satisfactory system of rating is based on the minimum temperature that one can expect in his own garden. A little experimenting with a thermometer, and a study of local weather records, will give a pretty good idea as to whether a temperature of 0° or +10, or −10 for instance may be expected regularly or may be expected occasionally. With this figure in mind the gardener can make a choice of varieties based on their response to minimum temperature as indicated by the ratings.

It should be understood that even very hardy varieties may be damaged by early frosts in the fall, by late frosts in the spring, or by a sudden cold spell following an unusually warm period during mid-winter. In some cases the descriptions will indicate that a particular variety tends to start growth exceptionally early in the spring and so may be unusually subject to damage by spring frosts. This might be true of a variety which would withstand a very low temperature during midwinter.

SIZE OF PLANT

In previous publications a figure was given to indicate the probable height of the plant after ten years of growth. In this book the following terms are used:

Dwarf   —Under 1½ ft. high at maturity.
Semi-dwarf —Under 3 ft. at maturity.
Low   —Under 4½ ft. at maturity.
Medium   —Under 6 ft. at maturity.
Tall   —Over 6 ft. at maturity.

SEASON OF BLOOM

Previously the blooming date was indicated as early, medium, or late. In the following pages a month, or possibly part of a month, is indicated, as Early April, June, March, etc. These blooming dates indicate the average experience in the Portland, Oregon, area. Those living in other areas will have to make an adjustment to fit their own conditions which should not be difficult. In the Portland area mid-season would be considered as the early part of May.

HOW THE COMMITTEE WORKED

Various ways of rating plants have been practiced by other single plant societies. Some have test gardens and average up the scores submitted by various testers. In the case of rhododendrons which are large plants and which, in some cases, take several years to bloom, it seemed from the first that the most feasible way was to get the opinion of people who have grown a large number of varieties. Accordingly a Ratings Committee was appointed by the A.R.S. President, the members being chosen for knowledge of rhododendrons over many years. They were also selected from a fairly limited area so they would be close enough together to meet at weekly or bi-weekly periods over several month's time. This committee consisted of John Henny, Chairman; Merle Cisney; George Clarke; J. Harold Clarke; Robert Comerford; George Grace; Louis Grothaus; Robert Ticknor; Howard Slonecker; Cecil Smith; and Wales Wood. In all some 16 meetings of the Committee were held, mostly at the North Willamette Experiment Station, a few miles south of Portland, Ore.

The procedure was to go through an alphabetical list of varieties and, after discussion, determine ratings for bloom, plant and hardiness and indicate size of plant, and season of bloom. In some cases there was much discussion as to ratings, and sometimes disagreement which had to be settled by vote. In other cases a consensus was easily reached.

After the ratings themselves were completed, the variety cards were passed out to individual members of the committee to be filled with other descriptive material, which was later discussed and approved or amended by the full committee.

OTHERS HELPED

During the preceding months several notices in the Bulletin requested suggestions and criticisms from the members which could be useful to the Ratings Committee. There was not a great deal of individual response but lists of ratings of a fairly large number of varieties were received from the Olympia Chapter, the California Chapter, and the Philadelphia Chapter. These lists were consulted and considered as the committee's work progressed.

There were two categories which caused the committee some concern. One included the old hardy varieties long grown extensively in the East but relatively scarce in the Northwest. The cards for many of these varieties were sent to our eastern A.R.S. Director to be referred to Eastern Chapters for suggested ratings.

The other group which caused the committee some concern included the new varieties originating in areas at some distance from where most of the committee members lived. New varieties which were not known to be in commerce were left out even though some had been mentioned in the last A.R.S. book. Others were referred to Chapters in areas where the breeder worked to find out if they are available, and if so to get suggested ratings from those who should know them best.

It was the feeling that all varieties available to the public should be rated if at all possible. Some of the very old varieties are still listed and advertised and the beginner should have ratings available in order for him to evaluate the catalog descriptions. The advanced amateur is probably more interested in new varieties and as rapidly as possible new varieties should be rated and that information made available to all who are interested.

THE GROUP VARIETIES

The so-called "group" varieties or "grex" varieties always pose a problem. As most rhododendron growers know, there was a period when rhododendron breeders, especially those in England, were in the habit of giving group names to all the offspring of a particular cross. At one time R.H.S. procedure indicated that this was desirable and that seedlings of the same cross made at a later date by some other breeder should have the same name. In some cases a particular clone of such a cross might be selected and given a clonal name. We have, therefore, the name 'Naomi' which is a group name and includes plants of quite a range of size, color, and plant characters. A number of clones of this Naomi group have been named, such as 'Naomi Nautilus'. In other cases varieties like 'May Day' were group varieties but no individual clone was named although one 'May Day' form received an A.M. and therefore could be identified as a clone.

Varieties are marged in the following report with a "g" to indicate group and unmarked to indicate clone. This information is derived partly from the experience of the committee, and partly from the International Rhododendron Register. There are some group varieties, so indicated in the International Register which so far as the committee knows have been distributed in this country in only one clonal form. Where listed as a group name, however, it is possible that other forms are in existence in England and might eventually come to this country. There are others which were distributed in only two or three forms as, for instance, 'Vulcan'. For the most part that variety is being propagated in only one clonal form although at least one other, and quite different is in the trade.

These group varieties were so named by the breeders because that was considered to be the thing to do at that time. Botanists gave names to groups of natural hybrids occuring in the wild, and some of the early breeders being familiar with botanical practice followed the same method of naming. There have been other cases, however, where a variety was supposed to be a clone but mixtures have occurred. In some cases this may have been an accidental taking of cuttings from a sister seedling in the original seedling row. In other cases a variety originally introduced many years ago as a clone, as 'Roseum Elegans' for instance, has become somewhat mixed. This may have been due to similar seedlings being mixed in accidentally or, in some cases, similar seedlings might at the moment seem to be superior and so near to the variety in question that it was felt that a substitution could be made without being detected. It is the policy in this report to mark such varieties as clones but to indicate that there may be mixtures in the plants being sold under this name.

It is, of course, a difficult matter to establish a rating for a group variety which may be made up of several different clones. The ratings of such group varieties generally may be taken to indicate the quality, hardiness, etc. of the best form available.

MANY POINTS CONSIDERED

The bloom rating is based on a number of different characteristics including size, color, purity of color, lasting quality of the blossom, whether it fades or not, the character of the truss, whether or not flowers are borne freely, and the length of time required to start blooming. The plant characters involve the branching habit of the bush, whether it makes a neat attractive appearance, amount of training and pruning required, tendency for breakage, ability to hold the leaves for more than one season, and leaf size, color, glossiness, and the way they are displayed.

After the ratings, a brief description of flower and plant characters is given. Colors are for the most part described in common terms as most of the committee work was done during winter months and flowers were not available for accurate descriptions with use of color charts. More accurate descriptions are available for some of the newer varieties which have been registered and have a published description. Colors marked H.C.C., and expressed as whole numbers or two numbers as 620 or 32/2, are based on the R.H.S. color charts. Those indicated by combination of numbers and letters, as 7.5 Gy 4/4, are based on the Nickerson color fan.

It did seem practical to obtain measurements of leaf size as one character which might be of considerable value and available for study at any time. Accordingly many of the descriptions will include the length and width of leaf. This is based on the largest leaf on an average vigorous twig of a plant not growing in dense shade. Obviously size of leaf varies with age of plant, its vigor of growth as determined by soil fertility, whether it is in the shade or not and other environmental factors.

ACCURATE TECHNICAL DESCRIPTIONS NEEDED

It would be very desirable, of course, if these descriptions could be technical and give accurate leaf shapes, margins, character of scales and hairs if present, together with accurate color descriptions of the flowers. Such descriptions might make possible positive identification of plants in many cases but they would have required a great deal more time and effort than were available. Some members of the Ratings Committee are going ahead on their own, to make more technical descriptions for a future publication.

Other miscellaneous information given comes from the experience of committeemen and from the International Register. The cross and the name of the breeder are available in the Register and in other books, but it seemed worthwhile to put them in this publication for ready reference. In each case the female parent is mentioned first and the male parent second.

HEAT RESISTANCE

There is a rapidly increasing interest in heat resistance of varieties but this is complicated by root rots in hot climates, length of exposure to high temperatures, presence or absence of shade, sprinkling, and other factors so that about all we can do here is indicate that certain varieties have been reported as relatively resistant to heat. Quite often there is information as to whether the variety will stand full sun or need some shade in what might be considered a good average rhododendron climate.

The relative ease of rooting will be of interest to beginners who may want to try their hand at propagating. This information is not aimed at nurserymen who, for the most part, have that information already available.

It should be understood that all ratings are tentative and that these may well be changed at some future date as more information becomes available.

RHODODENDRON VARIETIES

AS GROWN IN

AMERICAN GARDENS

A. Bedford

E Hedge

Rating 4/3 — Mauve seedling X *R. ponticum;* Lowinsky. Vigorous, upright habit, leaves 6½" long, 2½" wide, dark glossy green. Flowers lavender blue, HCC 634/1, paler in throat, with dark blotch. Truss 6" in diameter, 6½" tall, compact, dome to conical shaped, 14 to 16 flowers per truss. Corolla 3¼" diameter, 2¼" long, funnel shaped, margins slightly frilled and waved. A. M. (RHS) 1936, F.C.C. (RHS) 1958.

Hardy to –5
Tall 6+
Late May

Adrastia g.

Rating 3/2 — *R. williamsianum* X *R. neriiflorum;* Aberconway in 1929. Possibly only one form extant in the U. S. Spreading, rounded bush, leaves roundish, 1¼" X 1". Flowers deep pink, bell-shaped, about 1½" in diameter, in clusters of 1 to 4. Not as vigorous as some other *R. williamsianum* hybrids. Not especially easy to propagate.

Hardy to 0
Semi-dwarf 3'
Late April

Aladdin g.

Rating 3/3 — *R. griersonianum* X R. auriculatum; Crosfield 1930. Habit, open, rangy, stiff, upright; leaves 7" X 2", auriculatum-like, glandular. Flowers, pink, open campanulate. To 4" across, 10 flowers in an open truss. Vigorous, easily grown. Needs shade for flowers, but plant does well in full sun. Heat tolerance is excellent. Roots easily. Resistant to pests. A. M. (RHS) 1935.

Hardy to 0
Tall 6+
June

Albatross g.

Rating 4/2
Hardy to –5
Tall 6 +
Early June

'Loderi' X *R. discolor;* Rothschild. Tall, vigorous plant with open habit, could hold foliage better. Leaves 6" X 2½". Flowers pink in bud, opening to white, very large, scented, good substance, in a tall open truss. Best results in part shade and out of strong winds. Two or more clones have been named, one received the A. M. (RHS) in 1934, A. M. (Wisley Trials) 1953.

Albert Close

Rating 3/2
Hardy to –5
Medium 6 '
Late May

R. maximum X *R. macrophyllum;* Gable. Somewhat straggly and open, with attractive blue-green foliage. Flowers bright rose pink with throat heavily spotted chocolate red. Compact conical truss. Shy bloomer when young.

Album Elegans

Rating 2/2
Hardy to –20
Tall 6 +
Late May

A *R. catawbiense* hybrid; H. Waterer, before 1876. Vigorous grower, somewhat open, good foliage. Flowers white, tinged lilac, in a medium sized, rounded truss.

Album Grandiflorum

Rating 3/3
Hardy to –15
Medium 6 '
Late May

A *R. catawbiense* hybrid; J. Waterer, before 1851. Flowers pale mauve, fading to white.

Alice

Rating 3/4
Hardy to –5
Medium 6 '
Mid-May

R. griffithianum hybrid; J. Waterer. Vigorous upright plant easily grown; leaves 6" X 2½". Flowers deep pink, fading to rose, large upright truss. Foliage stands sun but flowers best in some shade. A. M. (RHS) in 1910.

Alice Franklin

Rating 3/3
Hardy to 0
Medium 6 '
Late May

'Ole Olsen' X 'Loderi King George'; cross by Lem, raised and named by Larson. Plant habit sturdy and compact; leaves 5" X 2½", medium green. Flowers light yellow, throat uranium green, funnel campanulate, 7 to 10 in a rounded truss. P. A. (ARS) 1960.

America

Rating 2/2
Hardy to –25
Medium 6′
Late May

'Parson's Grandiflorum' X a dark red hybrid; M. Koster and sons, 1904. Low growing, sprawling plant habit, with dull green foliage. Leaves 4″ X 2″. Plant habit better in full sun. Flowers small, very dark red, in compact, ball type truss.

Americana

South side?

Rating 2/3
Hardy to –20
Low 4½
Early May

Graft hybrid (chimera? 'Britannia' grafted on a *R. discolor* hybrid); Lancaster. Plant a much branched, upright mound, leaves medium green, to 10″ X 2″. Flowers frilled bells, cherry red. Rounded truss of 12 to 15 flowers. Grows well in sun or shade, heat tolerant.

Amy

Rating 3/3
Hardy to –5
Medium 6′
Mid-May

A *R. griffithianum* hybrid; J. Waterer, Sons and Crisp. Sturdy plant with medium green foliage, leaves 6″ X 2½″. Very compact, upright truss of large rose pink flowers. Will grow in full sun.

Anah Kruschke

Rating 2/3
Hardy to –10
Medium 6′
June

A *R. ponticum* hybrid, introduced by Kruschke. Plant habit compact with dark green leaves 5″ X 2″. Flowers pale lavender blue in a tight conical truss. Does well in full sun.

Angelo g.

Rating 5/3
Hardy to –5
Tall 6+
Early June

R. griffithianum X *R. discolor;* Rothschild. Extremely vigorous grower, with leaves to 8″ X 3″, dark green. Flowers pale blush pink, fading to pure white, about 5″ to 6″ across, fragrant. Huge built-up truss of about 10 to 13 flowers. A. M. (RHS) 1935, F. C. C. (RHS) 1948.

Anna Rose Whitney   *7th choice in Seattle*

Award '54

Rating 4/3
Hardy to +5
Tall 6+
Late May

R. griersonianum X 'Countess of Derby'; Van Veen, raised and exhibited by Whitney. Plant upright, vigorous, taller than wide, requires much room. The leaves 8″ X 3″, dull olive green. The flowers are funnel-shaped, rose pink and 3″ to 4″ wide by 3″ long. The truss, of about 12 flowers is slightly open but not floppy. This grows well in full exposure but cold weather damages individual flowers in the bud, although rarely causing complete bud loss. It roots readily.

Anne Glass

Rating 3/2   'Catalgla' X *R. decorum;* Gable, exhibited in 1949.
Hardy to –15   Flowers white.
Medium 6'
Late May

Annie Dalton

Rating 3/2   (*R. decorum* X *R. griersonianum*) X 'America';
Hardy to –10   Gable. Leaves long and narrow with a slight
Medium 6'   twist. Some say poor foliage, bothered by pests.
Early May   Flowers large, a good pink, in a large lax truss.
   A. E. (ARS) 1960.

word '60

Annie E. Endtz

Rating 3/3   A 'Pink Pearl' hybrid; L. J. Endtz Co. in 1939.
Hardy to 0   Plant upright, spreading; leaves 6" X 2½", deep
Medium 6'   green, sinuate. Flowers medium pink, frilled mar-
Mid-May   gins, to about 3½" in diameter, 7 to 9 to a rounded truss. Vigorous, adaptable, reasonably heat
tolerant. Roots fairly easily. Fairly close resemblance in plant
and flower to 'Antoon Van Welie'.

Antoon van Welie

Rating 3/3   A 'Pink Pearl' hybrid; L. J. Endtz and Co. Stiff,
Hardy to –5   sturdy, vigorous plant which grows compact and
Tall 6+   spreading in full sun and more upright in part
Mid-May   shade. Foliage large, leaves 6" X 3", medium
   green. Flowers very large, deep pink in a tall
truss. Roots easily.

Arthur J. Ivens

Rating 3/3   *R. williamsianum* X *R. houlstonii;* Hillier and Son.
Hardy to –10   Dome shaped plant; leaves ovate 3¼" X 2". Flow-
Semi-Dwarf 3'   ers bell shaped and persian rose in color. Truss
Early May   lax, few flowers. Plant easily grown in full sun.
   Takes some time to start blooming. A.M. (RHS)
1944.

3'
E. side
of house

Arthur Osborn

Rating 3/2   *R. didymum* X *R. griersonianum;* Kew Gardens,
Hardy to +10 1929. Spreading to upright bush; leaves lanceolate
Semi-Dwarf   2¾ " X ¾ ". Flowers dark ruby red, trumpet-
Early June   shaped, to about 1½" in diameter, to 4 to a
              cluster. Medium vigor, not too easy to grow,
roots fairly easily, damps off easily. A. M. (RHS) 1933.

[handwritten left margin: Back walk 3']

Atrier g.

Rating 3/1   'Atrosanguineum' X *R. griersonianum;* Gable, ex-
Hardy to –10 hibited in 1945. Plant rather open, floppy, with
Medium 6   thin foliage. Flowers red, in a large truss. At least
Early May   two forms of the 'Atrier' group have been named.
              'William Montgomery', a clear scarlet, formerly
known as 'Atrier' var. 'William Montgomery', was exhibited in
1946. A selection known as 'Atrier' '#10, later named 'Redhead', is
said to be somewhat superior to other forms.

Atroflo g.

Rating 4/3   'Atrosanguineum' X *R. floccigerum;* Gable, ex-
Hardy to –5   hibited in 1940. Somewhat open habit, foliage dark
Medium 6'   green, suede-like above, heavy fawn indumentum
Mid-May   below. Flowers rose madder, fade rather rapidly
              but of very good substance, large, trumpet-
shaped, 10 to 12 in a lax, flat truss. Roots easily. Forms vary in
hardiness. One received the A.E. (ARS) 1960.

[handwritten left margin: Award '59]

Atrosanguineum

Rating 2/3   A *R. catawbiense* hybrid; H. Waterer, before 1851.
Hardy to –20 Foliage and plant habit good. Flowers dark red.
Medium 6'
Mid-May

Augfast g.

Rating 4/4   *R. augustinii* X *R. fastigiatum;* Magor, 1921. Very
Hardy to 0°   dense, dome shaped plant, new wood small in
Low 4½   diameter; leaves 1⅛" X ⅜", new growth usually
Mid-April   cream yellow. Flowers violet-blue, numerous,
              facing outward in a small truss. Grows in full sun.
Has, on occasion been sold as 'Blue Tit', which is lighter blue in
color.

Autumn Gold

Rating 4/3   *R. discolor* X 'Fabia'; Van Veen. Plant spreading,
Hardy to 0°   compact. Leaves 5" X 2". Flowers salmon apricot,
Medium 6'   in a ball type truss. Best results in some shade.
Late May

Avalanche g.

Rating 5/4   'Loder' g. X *R. calophytum;* Rothschild. Plant has
Hardy to 0°   thick shoots. Leaves 8½" x 2¾", held only one
Tall 6 +   year. Flowers fleshy white with magenta blotch.
March   Truss flat topped with many flowers. 'Alpine
Glow' is a named clone. There are at least two
named clones in England. One form received the A.M. (RHS)
in 1934, F.C.C. (RHS) in 1938.

Azma g.

Rating 3/2   *R. griersonianum* x *R. fortunei;* Stevenson, 1927.
Hardy to +10 Plant upright rounded, a bit open, with rather
Medium 6'   long narrow leaves. Flowers soft salmon pink,
Late May   to 4" across, in rounded, lax truss.

Azor g.

Rating 3/2   *R. griersonianum* X *R. discolor;* Stevenson. Up-
Hardy to +5   right to spreading, open plant with medium green
Medium 6'   leaves to 8" X 2½". Does not hold leaves well.
Early June   Flowers soft salmon pink, medium sized; rather
loose, open topped truss. Several poor forms are
in the trade. One form received A.M. (RHS) 1933.

Bacher's Gold

Rating 3/3   'Unknown Warrior' X 'Fabia'; grown by John
Hardy to 0°   Bacher. Leaves long, light green, yet a fairly
Medium 6'   dense habit of growth. Flowers 6 lobed, broad
Late May   funnel shaped, 4" X 2". Inside corolla venetian
pink, shading to saffron yellow at center, burnt
orange spots, shading to crimson in upper lobe. Outside
corolla same venetian pink with deeper shading on veins. Stamens
12, uneven, light cream with brown anthers. Plant does best in
some shade, but not required. Roots easily and does not seem to
be bothered by chewing insects. P.A. (ARS) 1955.

(handwritten: 6', ward '55)

(handwritten: Bovee : well in sun)

Bagshot Ruby

Rating 2/2   A *R. thomsonii* hybrid; J. Waterer, about 1900.
Hardy to –10   Good plant habit with dark, dull green foliage;
Medium   leaves 5″ X 2″. Flowers dark red, in compact
Early June   conical truss. Best results in partial shade.

Barclayi Helen Fox

Rating 4/2   *R. thomsonii* X 'Glory of Penjerrick'; Barclay
Hardy to +15   Fox. Upright habit, leaves medium green, narrow,
Medium   pointed, red streak in upper side of midrib, 5″
Early April   X 2″. Flowers deep blood red of heavy substance,
in a medium sized truss, rounded and rather loose.

Barclayi Robert Fox

Rating 5/3   *R. thomsonii* X 'Glory of Penjerrick'; Barclay
Hardy to +15   Fox. Upright, open habit; leaves flat, oval, round
Medium   at end, 4½″ X 2½″, with red streak in upper
Early April   side of midrib. Flowers deep blood red with a
waxy texture; slightly larger than above. Trusses
rounded and rather loose. Possibly the finest plant out of this
cross. A.M. (RHS) 1921.

Barto Blue

Rating 4/3   A form of *R. augustinii;* grown by James Barto,
Hardy to +5   selected by Phetteplace. Plant taller than wide,
Tall   sparse foliage. Leaves 3¼″ X 1⅜″. Flower color
April   a very good blue. Truss of three flowers, facing
outward. Grows in full sun. One of the better
blue augustiniis.

Beau Brummell g.

Rating 3/3   'Essex Scarlet' X *R. eriogynum;* Rothschild.
Hardy to –5   Plant habit rather open, foliage dull, dark green,
Medium   leaves 4″ X 1½″. Flowers waxy, very dark blood
June   red, speckled darker within, in a compact ball
type truss. One form received the A.M. (RHS)
1938.

Beaufort

Rating 2/3   'Boule de Neige' X *R. fortunei;* Gable. Plant com-
Hardy to –15   pact, large leaves. Flowers white, tinged mauve,
Medium   fragrant. Tends to be a shy bloomer.
Early May

Beauty of Littleworth

Rating 4/3   *R. griffithianum* X an unknown, probably *R. cam-*
Hardy to –5   *panulatum;* Mangles, about 1900. Extremely vigor-
Tall 6^1 ous, upright spreading habit with dark green,
Early May   slightly shiny leaves 7½" X 3½". Flowers white,
wth dark reddish purple spotting on upper part of
corolla, 4½" to 5" across. Buds when opening show mauve pink.
Highly built up, large truss of 16 to 19 flowers. F.C.C. (RHS) 1904,
F.C.C. Wisley Trials, 1953.

Belle Heller

Rating 3/3   'Catawbiense Album' X a white *R. catawbiense*
Hardy to –5   seedling; Shammarello. A vigorous grower of good
Medium $6'$ plant habit, with large dark green leaves. Flowers
Late May   large, white with a conspicuous golden blotch, in
a large, globular truss.

Betty Wormald

Rating 4/3   'George Hardy' X a red garden hybrid; M. Koster
Hardy to –5   and Sons before 1922. Plant upright, spreading;
Medium $6'$ leaves 5" X 3". Flowers pink, pale center, heavily
Mid-May   spotted on upper petal, very large, almost flat,
in a huge dome-shaped truss. Best in some shade.
Roots easily. A.M. (RHS) 1935.

Bibiani g.

Rating 4/4   'Moser's Maroon' X *R. arboreum;* Rothschild. A
Hardy to +10   full upright plant; leaves dark green, heavy tex-
Tall $6+$ ture, to 6" X 2", lanceolate. Flowers bright scarlet;
Late April   campanulate bells, 2¼" across in a conical truss
of up to 15 flowers. Easily grown, above average
vigor, but needs wind shelter. Roots easily. Loses leaves at +10 if
in wind, if not then good to 0°. Apparently only one form in this
country. A.M. (RHS) 1934.

Bluebird g.

Rating 5/3   *R. intricatum* X *R. augustinii;* Aberconway, 1930.
Hardy to 0   Plant habit compact and spreading. Leaves 1" X
Semi-dwarf   ½". Best results in a sunny location. Blue flowers
Mid-April   in profusion. A little slower in starting to bloom
than 'Blue Diamond'. Roots easily. One form re-
ceived the A.M. (RHS) 1943.

Blue Diamond g. *14ᵗʰ choice in Seattle*

Rating 5/4	'Intrifast' X *R. augustinii;* Crosfield. Plant habit
Hardy to 0	upright, compact, best results in a sunny
4½'✗ Low	location. Leaves 1" X ¾". Blue flowers in pro-
Mid-April	fusion on an upright plant. One of the best blues,

roots easily. A.M. (RHS) 1935, F.C.C. (RHS) 1939. Most 'Blue Diamond' plants in the U.S.A. are probably the award form.

Blue Ensign

Rating 4/4	Selected by W. C. Slocock in 1934, probably a
Hardy to –10	*R. ponticum* hybrid. Plant upright spreading;
Medium 6'	leaves 6" X 2", dark glossy green. Flowers pale
Late May	lavender blue with black spot, about 6 to 9 in a

rounded truss. Medium vigor, grows well, seems tolerant of sun. Roots easily. Resembles 'Blue Peter' but makes a better bush, leaves not as large or droopy.

Blue Jay

Rating 4/3	Probably a *R. ponticum* seedling; H. Larson. Com-
Hardy to –5	pact yet vigorous plant with bright green foliage
Medium 6'	that holds well for several years on the plant.
Early June	Leaves 5" X 1½". Flowers lavender blue with

brown blotch in upper petal. Very compact, tall, conical truss.

Blue Peter

Rating 4/3	Introduced by Waterer, Sons and Crisp, parentage
Hardy to –10	apparently unknown, possibly a *R. ponticum*
Medium 6'	hybrid. Plant as wide as tall of medium compact-
Early May	ness. Leaves 5½" X 2¼", dark, glossy green.

Flowers, frilled margins, light lavender blue, purple blotch, to 2¾" across; truss conical, compact. Plant easily grown in sun or shade. Foliage liked by leaf chewing insects. A.M. (RHS) 1933, F.C.C. (RHS) 1958.

Blue Tit g.

Rating 4/4	A lavender form of *R. impeditum* X *R. augustinii;*
Hardy to 0	J. C. Williams, 1933. Plant habit very compact.
3' ✗ Semi-dwarf	Leaves 1" X ¾". Will grow well in full sun.
Mid-April	Light greyish blue flowers abundantly pro-
	duced. Sometimes confused with 'Augfast' which

is violet blue.

Pot or Tub 3'
Top ✗
Patio

Bluette

Rating 3/4   *R. impeditum X R. augustinii* 'Lackamas Blue';
Hardy to –10   Lancaster. Plant twiggy, globe shaped, leaves
Semi-dwarf   1½" X ½", scaly. Flowers hyacinth blue, in an
Mid-April   8 flowered truss. Best in full sun, resistant to heat.

Bobolink g.

Rating 3/3   *R. discolor* x *R. neriiflorum;* Rothschild, 1934.
Hardy to 0   Flowers deep yellow or apricot.
Medium
Early June

Bonfire

Rating 3/3   *(R. discolor* X 'Mrs. R. T. Shaw') X *R. griersoni-*
Hardy to –5   *anum;* Waterer, Sons and Crisp, 1928. Plant habit
Medium   open and vigorous when young and grows com-
Late May   pact in open sunny location. Foliage dull green;
   leaves 6" X 2". Flowers fiery red in large, loose,
conical truss. A.M. (RHS) 1933.

Bonito g.

Rating 4/4   *R. discolor* X 'Luscombei'; Rothschild. Vigorous
Hardy to –5   upright habit with dark green leaves, 7" X 2¾".
Medium   Flowers pale blush pink, fading to white, with
Early June   heavy brown spotting in upper part of corolla,
   4½" to 5" across in a large, rounded truss. A.M.
(RHS) 1934.

Bo-peep g.

Rating 3/3   *R. lutescens* X *R. moupinense;* Rothschild 1934.
Hardy to +5   Low, open growing plant, scaly leaves 2⅛" X 1",
Low   light green. Flowers flat, 2" across, pale greenish
Late March   yellow, 2 to 3 per bud. A.M. (RHS) 1937.

Borde Hill

Rating 4/3   'Doncaster' X 'Mrs. A. M. Williams'; C. B. van Nes
Hardy to +5   and Sons. Upright, medium density, not particu-
Low   larly vigorous, dark green pointed leaves, 7" X 2".
Late May   Flowers dark red, waxy, 3" to 3½" across in a
   medium rounded truss. A. M. (RHS) Wisley
Trials 1948.

Boule de Neige

Rating 3/4   *R. caucasicum* X a hardy *R. catawbiense* hybrid;
Hardy to –25   Oudieu about 1878. Plant forms a dense, round
Low 4½   bush with rather upright leaves, 5½" X 1¾",
Early May   medium to light green. Flowers white in compact
               rounded trusses. Vigorous and rather easy to
grow. Roots easily. An old variety but still worth growing. Susceptible to Lace Wing bug.

Bow Bells g.   *6th choice in Seattle*

Rating 3/4   'Corona' X *R. williamsianum;* Rothschild. Rounded
Hardy to 0   ed spreading plant, with rounded, medium green
Pot or Tub Low 4½   leaves 2¼" X 1½", foliage on new growth copper
Side 4½' Early May   bronze. Cup shaped, medium sized, pink flowers
Top   in a lax truss of up to 7 flowers. One form received
the A.M. (RHS) 1935.   *Bovee: One of 10 Best*
                                   will stand considerable sun

Brandywine

Rating 4/2   *R. pubescens* X *R. keiskei;* Nearing. Leaves to 3"
Hardy to –10   X ½", dark bronze green, hairy. Flowers small,
Semi-dwarf 3'   cream, edged rose, in trusses the size of tennis
Late April   balls.

Bric-a-brac g.

Rating 4/4   *R. leucaspis* X *R. moupinense;* Rothschild in 1934.
Hardy to +5   Plant of A.M. form, spreading and dense; leaves
x Semi-dwarf 3' 1¼" X ¾", dark green. Flowers of the A. M. form
February   white with faint markings on upper petal, anthers
                chocolate. Blush pink form very similar except
for color. Truss with few flowers facing outward. Needs protection
from frost at blooming time. A. M. (RHS) 1945.

Brickdust

Rating 3/4   'Dido' X *R. williamsianum;* R. Henny 1962. Spread-
4½' Hardy to 0   ing habit, with dark green leaves 2" X 1". Flowers
x Low 4½   rose madder H.C.C. 32/2 shaded to red 22/3, 6 to
Early May   8 in a lax truss. *Bovee notes good, Roman Brick color*

Britannia

Rating 4/4   'Queen Wilhelmina' X 'Stanly Davies'; C. B. van
Hardy to –5   Nes and Sons, 1921. Spreading, fairly compact
Medium 6'   plant with light dull green leaves, 7" X 2½".
Late May   Flowers bright scarlet, bell-shaped in a medium
               rounded truss. Difficult to root, most plants are

grafted. Leaves tend to yellow in full sun. A.M. (RHS) 1921,
F. C. C. (RHS) 1937.

Brocade g.

Rating 4/4
Hardy to 0
Low 4½
Early May

'Vervaeniana' X *R. williamsianum;* Rothschild, 1934. Leaf color dark green, compact, medium dense habit. Flowers frilled, peach pink.

Broughtonii Aureum

Rating 3/2
Hardy to 0
Low 4½
Late May

An azaleodendron, *(R. maximum X R. ponticum)* X *R. molle,* probably made by W. Smith about 1830. Plant sprawly, especially in N. W., more upright where summers are hotter; leaves 4" X 1½", thin semi-deciduous. Flowers soft yellow with orange-yellow spots, to about 2½" in diameter, in small, rounded trusses, vigorous, reasonably heat tolerant. Roots fairly easily. Leaves, partly because of their texture, are susceptible to damage by pests and by wind. F. C .C. (RHS) 1935.

Buff Lady g.

Rating 3/3
Hardy to –10
Low 4½
June

'Nereid' X *R. discolor;* cross by Rose, raised and named by Lancaster. Plant rounded, leaves medium green, elliptic, 6" X 1½". Flowers egyptian buff, shaded coral pink, to 3½" across, 6 lobes, wide bell shaped, to 12 in a rounded truss. Heat tolerant. Two clones being propagated.

Bulstrode Park

Rating 3/2
Hardy to –5
Medium 6'
May

R. griffithianum hybrid X 'Sefton'; C. B. van Nes and Sons. Vigorous upright growth; dark green pointed leaves, 8" X 2". Flowers bright scarlet crimson, waxy, in a large, high, rather loose truss.

Bustard

Rating 3/3
Hardy to +5
Tall 6+
June

R. auriculatum X 'Penjerrick'; Rothschild, 1934. Tall, upright shrub with leaves 6" X 2". Extra large, white flowers, with a crimson spot in throat, good substance and borne in a tall truss.

Butterfly

Rating 3/3   *R. campylocarpum* X 'Mrs. Milner'; W. C. Slocock
Hardy to 0   about 1924. A rounded compact plant, appearing
6' Medium   more open because of small, 4" X 1½" leaves.
Mid-May   Flowers pale yellow, flecked red on upper lobe.
             Truss compact, rounded. Grows well in either sun
or shade, good heat tolerance, roots easily. A. M. (RHS) 1940.

Cadis

Rating 4/4   'Caroline' X *R. discolor;* Gable. Good habit, dense
Hardy to –15 foliage. Flowers light pink, large, very fragrant,
Award '59 Medium 6'   in a flat truss. Requires some sun to bloom well.
Late May   A. E. (ARS) 1960.

Calstocker g.

Rating 5/4   *R. calophytum* X 'Dr. Stocker'; Whitaker in 1935.
Hardy to 0   The form usually seen in the Northwest is the
Tall 6+   Exbury form, commonly known as 'Exbury Cal-
Mid-April   stocker'.

Captain Jack

Rating 4/3   'Mars' X *R. eriogynum;* R. Henny. Plant taller
Award '56 Hardy to +5   than wide, open growing. Leaves 6" X 2". Flowers
Tall 6 +   dark red, 3½" across; truss built up with about 15
Late May   flowers. Flowers are best when shaded from hot
             sun. P. A. (ARS) 1956.

Caractacus

Rating 1/3   A *R. catawbiense* hybrid; A. Waterer. Plant of
Hardy to –25 good compact habit but foliage tends to yellow in
Medium 6'   the sun. Flowers purplish red. F. C. C. (RHS)
June   1865.

Carita g.   *15th choice in Seattle*

Rating 4/4   'Naomi' X *R. campylocarpum;* Rothschild in 1935.
Hardy to +5 Habit dense with fine oval leaves 4½" X 2½".
Medium 6'   Flowers pale primrose. Truss with 12-13 flowers
Late April   is dome shaped, later slightly flat on top. Does not
             flower freely when young and requires shade from
hot sun. 'Carita Inchmery' and 'Golden Dream' are named clones.
One form received A. M. (RHS) in 1945.

Carmen g.

Rating 3/3 — *R. didymum* X *R. forrestii* var. *repens;* Rothschild,
Hardy to –5   1935. Plant spreading with attractive, dark green,
✗ Dwarf   obovate leaves 1¼" X ¾". Flowers deep, but
1½' Late April bright, red, bell-shaped, to about 1½" in dia., in
clusters of 2 to 5. Sturdy, but very slow growing.
Prefers at least partial sun. Roots easily. One of the best dwarfs.
Needs excellent drainage.

Caroline

Rating 3/3   Parentage unknown, probably a *R. decorum* or
Hardy to –15 *R. brachycarpum* hybrid; Gable. Plant vigorous,
Tall 6+   fairly upright, leaves large, wavy margins.
Mid-May   Flowers pale orchid, large, pleasantly scented.

Carolyn Grace

Rating 3/4   A *R. wardii* hybrid; George Grace. Fairly dense
ward '60 Hardy to +5 habit. Leaves 4½" X 2½", medium green, slightly
Medium 6'   shiny, red-brown petiole. Flowers wide, shallow
Early May   campanulate, 3½" across, good substance, pale
primrose, 7 to 10 in a medium, rounded truss.
A.E. (ARS) 1960.

Cary Ann

Rating 3/4   'Corona' x 'Vulcan'; Wright. Leaves 4½" x 1½",
Hardy to +5 dark green with sunken veins. Very floriferous.
ward'61 Low 4½'   Flowers 2" across, coral red, 17 in a conical truss.
Early May   Tolerant of full sun. P.A. (ARS) 1961.

Catalgla

Rating 4/2   A selection of *R. catawbiense* var. *album;* Gable.
Hardy to –25 Open habit, leaves dark green. Said to have poor
Medium 6   foliage under some conditions. Flowers white in
Late May   a tall many-flowered truss.

Catawbiense Album

Rating 3/3   A selection of *R. catawbiense;* A. Waterer. Plant
Hardy to –25 rather spreading. Leaves medium dark green, tend
Medium 6   to be convex. Flowers white, with greenish yellow
Late May   spotting, buds flushed lilac. A compact, rounded
truss. Very adaptable as to growing conditions.

Catawbiense Boursalt

Rating 2/3   A *R. catawbiense* selection; Boursalt. Good plant
Hardy to –20 habit. Flowers rose-lilac.
Tall 6+
Mid-May

Cavalier

Rating 3/3   'Pygmalion' X 'Tally Ho'; R. Henny. Low, mound-
Hardy to +5   ed habit. Leaves 4″ X 2″. Extra large flowers of
Medium 6′   flame red, spotted black in the throat. Small truss
Late May   but flowers cover entire shrub. There is another
              'Cavalier' g., an Aberconway cross of *R. eriogy-*
num X 'Radiance' introduced in 1950, described as a brilliant
scarlet. The name was also used by Noble in 1850 for a rosy lilac
variety.

C. B. van Nes

Rating 3/2   'Queen Wilhelmina' X 'Stanley Davies'; C. B. van
Hardy to +5   Nes and Sons. Plant upright, leaves 5½″ X 1¾″.
Medium 6′   Flowers scarlet to 3½″ across in a built-up truss.
Late April   Best results in partial shade. Easily rooted.

Chanticleer g.

Rating 4/3   *R. thomsonii* X *R. eriogynum;* Rothschild in 1935.
Hardy to +15 Plant rather upright; leaves bright medium green,
Tall 6+   rounded, 5½″ X 2″. Flowers scarlet, waxy, to
Late May   about 3″ in diameter, 6 to 9 in a rounded truss.
              Quite vigorous, fairly easy to grow, roots easily.
Attractive when not in bloom.

Charles Bagley

Rating 2/1   A *R. cawtawbiense* hybrid; A. Waterer, 1865. Plant
Hardy to –20 rather open, spreading. Flowers cherry red, in a
Tall 6+   large upright truss.
Late May

Charles Dickens

Rating 2/2   A *R. catawbiense* hybrid; A. Waterer. Slow grow-
Hardy to –25 er, leaves dark green. Flowers purplish crimson,
Medium 6′   in a full conical truss. Does not root very easily.
Mid-May   F. C. C. (RHS) 1865.

Chevalier Felix de Sauvage

Rating 2/2   *R. caucasicum* X a hardy hybrid; Sauvage, about
Hardy to –5   1870. Plant broadly spreading; leaves 5″ X 1¾″.
Low   4½   Flowers dark pink with blotch in upper petal,
Early April   to about 2½″ in diameter, 9 to 15 in a very tight,
upright conical truss. Medium vigor, and moder-
ately easy to grow. Roots fairly easily.

Cheer   3′, Shell pink, early April

Chief Paulina

Rating 4/3   A selection of *R. concinnum* var. *pseudoyanthi-*
Hardy to +5   *num;* James, and known as James' Purple
Medium 6′   form. Plant rounded upright, fairly compact with
April   2½″ X 1½″ leaves. Flowers royal purple, spotted
dark brown in 3 upper lobes, in a small truss of
3 to 6 flowers. P. A. (ARS) 1954.

ward 5⁴

China g.

Rating 3/4   *R. wightii* X *R. fortunei;* Slocock. Plant is open
Hardy to 0   growing with strong new growth. Leaves 7″ X
Tall   6 +   3½″. Flowers pale cream with small red basal
Mid-May   blotch, in a fine large truss, flat-topped or lax. Best
in open or light shade. Not easy to root. One form
selected by Slocock in 1936 received A. M. (RHS) in 1940.

Christmas Cheer

Rating 2/4   A *R. caucasicum* hybrid; Methven. Plant quite
Hardy to –5   compact, rounded; leaves narrowly obovate, 4″ X
Low   4¼   1¼″. Flowers light pink in bud, fading to very
Winter   light pink, to about 2″ in diameter in small upright trusses, moderately vigorous and easy to
grow. Will stand a considerable amount of sun. Roots easily.
Valued for its winter blooming in mild climate, often starting in
late fall and blooming sporadically until late spring. Much lighter
pink than 'Rosa Mundi', with which it is sometimes confused.

Cilpinense g.

Rating 4/4   *R. ciliatum* X *R. moupinense;* Aberconway, intro-
Hardy to +5   duced in 1927. Plant habit compact. Leaves shiny
Semi-dwarf   green, 2¼″ X 1¼″. Flowers white to blush pink,
March ¹⁶⁻⁶⁹   dark colored anthers. Pink form in N. W. probably
superior to very light pink form. Needs protection
from frost at blooming time. Partial sun or shade with some open
sky desirable. Roots very easily. Pale, shell pink form received
A. M. (RHS) in 1927. *Bovee: does well in full sun*

Top
x regront 3′

C. I. S.

Rating 4/2   'Loders White' X 'Fabia'; R. Henny. Plant open,
Hardy to +10   spreading, with medium green leaves, 6″ X 2¼″,
Medium 6′   leaves undulate, tips bent to right. Flowers biscuit
Mid-May   color, large showy calyx of same color, brilliant
                orange red throughout throat, 4″ across. Medium
sized, loose truss of 9 to 11 flowers. Requires light shade. P. A.
(ARS) 1952.

Award '52

Clementine Lemaire

Rating 2/2   From Moser and Fils. Flowers bright pink with
Hardy to 0   a yellow blotch, in a tight, rounded truss.
Medium 6′
Late May

Conemaugh g.

Rating 4/3   *R. racemosum* X *R. mucronulatum;* Gable, 1934.
Hardy to –15   Plant rather open when small, decumbent, usually
Low 4½   one or two stems shooting well above the rest of
Early April   the plant, semi-deciduous. Flowers lavender pink,
                star shaped in ball shaped truss about 2″ in
diameter. Varous clones quite similar.

Conewago g.

Rating 3/2   *R. carolinianum* X *R. mucronulatum;* Gable, 1934.
Hardy to –25   Plant fairly open, making long shoots from the
Low 4½   base. Leaves 2½″ X 1″. Flowers lavender rose. A
Early April   very floriferous form known as 'Conewago Im-
                proved' may rate slightly higher.

Confection

Rating 3/3   'Corona' X 'Dondis'; R. Henny. Plant is of medium
Hardy to 0   height with a fairly compact habit. Leaves oblong,
Medium 6′   6″ to 8″ X 2½″, with a good deep green color.
Mid May   Leaves are retained for 2 years or more. Flowers
                16 in an upright truss somewhat flat-topped to
dome shaped. Corolla is funnel campanulate, 3½″ wide, 2″ long,
5 lobes. Color is rose madder. Plant is a vigorous grower, roots
easily, and seems to resist most chewing insects. Blooms last about
three weeks under ideal conditions. Some shade is beneficial.
P. A. (ARS) 1956.

Award '56

1. 'Faggetter's Favorite' at the home of Art Wright, Milwaukie, Oregon.

2. 'Calstocker' in full bloom.

3. 'Bluebird' at Crystal Springs Island, Portland, Oregon. *Photo Cecil Smith*

4. 'Susan' in the Phetteplace garden, Eugene, Oregon.

Photo Carl Phetteplace, M.D.

5. Magnificent plant of 'Bow Bells' at the home of Art Wright, Milwaukie, Oregon.

Photo Cecil Smith

6. 'Lady Bligh' in the garden of Dr. Phetteplace, Eugene, Oregon.

Photo Carl Phetteplace, M.D.

7. Plant of 'Sir Charles Lemon' in Cecil Smith's garden near Newberg, Oregon.

Photo Cecil Smith

8. 'Carita', one of the better yellows.

Photo Cecil Smith

9. 'Ruby Bowman' P.A., *R. fortunei* X 'Lady Bligh', a deep rose pink.

Photo Carl Phetteplace, M.D.

10. 'Idealist', *R. wardii* X 'Naomi', a good grower and a good parent.

Photo Carl Phetteplace, M.D.

11. 'Countess of Haddington' in the cool house, Crystal Springs Park Test Garden, Portland, Oregon.
Photo Cecil Smith

12. 'Lucil', a hybrid of *R. leucaspis* X *R. ciliatum*.
Photo Cecil Smith

13. A twenty year old plant of 'Corona' that is 5 ft. tall.

Photo Carl Phetteplace, M.D.

14. 'Dora Amateis' A. E., *R. carolinianum* X *R. ciliatum*.

Photo Cecil Smith

15. A fine plant of 'Loderi King George' in the garden of Cecil Smith.

16. 'Cowslip', a pale primrose hybrid of R. williamsianum X *R. wardii.*

Cornish Cross g.

Rating 5/3   *R. thomsonii* X *R. griffithianum;* S. Smith. Upright
Hardy to +10   habit of growth with smooth maroon brown to
Tall (+   copper brown colored trunk. Leaves 6" X 3½",
Mid-April   oval, medium green, with red streak on upper
                surface of midrib. Flowers of good substance,
deep pink, nearly red, fading through rose pink to pale pink and
nearly white inside with a translucent quality, 4½" to 5" across.
Large, loose truss of 7 to 9 flowers. Some forms much superior to
others. 'Exbury Cornish Cross' (Rothschild) received A. M. (RHS)
1935. 'Pengaer' (Llewelyn) received the A. M. (RHS) in 1911.

Cornubia g.

Rating 4/3   *R. arboreum* X 'Shilsonii'; Barclay Fox. Upright
Hardy to +15   habit with leaves 5" X 2½", medium green slightly
Tall (+   bullate. Flowers blood red in a rather large coni-
Late Winter   cal truss. Roots easily. A. M. (RHS) 1912. A select-
                ed clone known as 'John McLaren' is grown in
the San Francisco area.

Corona

Rating 4/2   A J. Waterer seedling of unknown parentage.
Hardy to –5   Plant medium compact, stiff, roundish, upright,
6' X Medium   branches brittle. Leaves oval, oblong, 3½" X 2".
Late May   Flowers coral pink, 2" wide, open bells, in an up-
                right truss of 15 flowers. Easily grown, moderate-
ly vigorous, will take full exposure. Heat tolerance good. Roots
fairly easily. Good resistance to pests. A.M. (RHS) 1911.

Corry Koster

Rating 2/2   Parentage uncertain, grown by M. Koster and
Hardy to –5   Sons, 1909. Plant rather upright, medium compact
Medium 6'   with medium green leaves, 5" X 2½", which stand
Early May   upright. Flowers pale pink, heavily spotted red
                in throat, with frilled edges, in a large, rounded
truss. Roots easily.

Cotton Candy

Rating 4/4   'Marinus Koster' X 'Loderi Venus'; J. Henny.
Hardy to 0   Very sturdy plant habit with large, dark green
Medium 6'   foliage; leaves to 6" X 3". Flowers soft pink, very
Early May   large, in tall compact truss. Grows well in full
Vigorous   sun. Roots easily. Boyce ', 5' in 10yrs

Countess of Athlone

Rating 2/3   'Geoffry Millais' X 'Catawbiense Grandiflorum';
Hardy to –10   C. B. van Nes and Sons, 1923. Plant upright,
Tall 6 +   leaves glossy, dark green, 6" X 2". Flowers mauve,
Late May   quite large, in a tight upright truss. Very vigor-
                ous and easy to grow, fairly sun tolerant. Roots
easily, resistant to pests. A very good mauve color.

Countess of Derby

Rating 4/3   'Pink Pearl' X 'Cynthia'; White. Open spreading
Hardy to –5   habit with leaves of medium green, 5½" X 2¼".
Medium 6'   Flowers deep rose-pink fading to pale pink, light
Late May   reddish spotting in upper corolla. Large, rounded
                truss. Sometimes sold in the U. S. as 'Eureka
Maid'. A. M. (RHS) 1930.

Countess of Haddington

Rating 4/4   *R. ciliatum* X *R. dalhousiae;* breeder not known.
Hardy to +20   Plant spreading, with oblanceolate leaves, to 5" X
Medium 6'   2". Flowers funnel shaped, about 4" long X 3"
April   wide, pink in bud, opens white flushed rose, 3 to 4
                in a very lax truss. Should have about half shade.
Heat tolerant, roots with medium ease. Not as fragrant as others
of this group, but more ornamental as a garden plant. Once estab-
lished it is a prolific bloomer. F. C. C. (RHS) 1862.

Countess of Sefton

Rating 3/3   *R. edgeworthii* X 'Multiflorum'; Davies, 1877. Plant
Hardy to +20   bushy; leaves lanceolate, to 3" X 1". Flowers wide-
Medium 6'   ly funnel shaped, corolla invariably split longi-
Mid April   tudinally, about 3" long by 2½" wide, pink in
                bud, opening white, 2 to 3 in a lax truss. Should
have about half shade, roots easily. Said to be the poorest of the
so-called Himalayan hybrids. Partly because of the flowers splitting
the total effect of plant and flower is not as beautiful as the other
hybrids in this group.

County of York

Rating 3/3   'Catawbiense Album' X 'Loderi King George';
Hardy to –15   Gable, exhibited 1936 under name of 'Catalode'.
Tall 6 +   Plant rather open, with long, convex dark green
May   leaves. Flowers, of good substance, pale char-
                treuse in bud, opening white with an olive throat,
in a tall truss.

Cowslip g.

Rating 3/2   *R. williamsianum* X *R. wardii;* Aberconway in
Hardy to 0   1930. Plant a rounded mound; leaves 2½" X 1½",
4½' Low   oval. Flowers pale primrose to cream, flushed
Early April   <u>pink,</u> saucer to bell-shaped. Truss few flowered.
Very effective when loaded with hanging bells.
Best in partial shade. Roots fairly easily. One form received A. M.
(RHS) in 1937.   Bovee: 2'in 10yrs, well in full sun

C. P. Raffill g.

Rating 4/3   'Britannia' X *R. griersonianum* at Kew Royal
Hardy to 0   Botanic Garden. Spreading, fairly dense plant
Medium 6'   with pale green leaves, 6" X 2", with reddish-
Early June   brown petioles. Flowers deep orange-red in a
rather large, rounded, truss. This rating is for the
Kew form only. Some inferior seedlings sold under the same name.

Cream Crest, April, 2', light yellow, -5°
Crest

Rating 5/3   *R. wardii* X 'Lady Bessborough'; Rothschild. For-
Hardy to −5   merly known as 'Hawk', var. 'Crest'. Plant is up-
Tall 6+   right, open and holds leaves but one year.
Early May   Leaves 4¾" X 2½", oval, glossy. Flowers nearest
to true yellow, to 4" in diameter. Truss dome
shaped, flowers elegantly spaced. Roots with some difficulty. Received F. C. C. (RHS) in 1953.

Crimson Glory - May, deepred, 5'
Cunningham's Sulphur

Rating 2/2   A Cunningham introduction of about 100 years
Hardy to −5   ago. Probably *R. caucasicum.* <u>Plant compact,</u>
3' Semi-dwarf   round and bushy. Leaves medium green, glossy,
Late Winter   elliptic, 3" X 1¼". Flowers pale <u>yellow</u> 1½"
across, in a rounded truss of <u>up to 15</u> flowers.
Vigorous, easily grown, but <u>does best in some shade.</u> Heat tolerance good, roots easily. Not very resistant to pests.

Cunningham's White

Rating 2/3   *R. caucasicum* X *R. ponticum* var. *album;* Cun-
Hardy to −15   ningham, 1850. Spreading, medium compact plant,
3' Semi-dwarf   leaves 6" X 2¼", lanceolate, moderately dark
Late May   green. Flowers small, white, with <u>greenish yellow</u>
blotch. Truss, small, upright, many flowered.
Takes full exposure but <u>best in some shade.</u> Roots easily and has
been used to some extent as an understock in Europe. Reported
to grow in neutral to slightly alkaline soil.

Cutie

Rating 3/3 — Said to have been purchased as *R. calostrotum,*
Hardy to –15 — probably a hybrid of that species. Sold for a time
✗Semi-dwarf 3' — as 'Calostrotum Pink'. Plant upright, rounded,
Early May — taller than wide unless in full sun. Leaves 1" x
½". Flowers of average size for a dwarf, of pink shaded lilac. P.A. (ARS) 1960.

Award '59

Cynthia

Rating 3/3 — *R. catawbiense* X *R. griffithianum* (?); Standish
Hardy to –10 — and Noble before 1870. Plant habit, vigorous and
Tall — tall, compact in full sun but open in shade. Leaves
Early May — 6" X 2¼", oval lanceolate, medium dark green.
Flowers rosy crimson, fade readily; to 3" wide.
Truss upright, conical. Roots readily, resistant to pests. Synonym
'Lord Palmerston', probably never used in the U. S. A. Will grow
well in either sun or shade. Roots easily.

Back Side 6'+

Dairymaid

Rating 3/4 — A *R. campylocarpum* hybrid; Slocock. Upright
Hardy to –5 — compact habit with medium green leaves, 4" X 2".
Medium 6' — Flowers light lemon yellow, tinged pink, heavily
Early May — spotted pink in upper corolla. Small rounded
truss. A. M. (RHS) 1934.

Dame Nellie Melba

Rating 4/4 — 'Standishii' X *R. arboreum;* Loder. Plant upright,
Tall 6+ — spreading; leaves glossy dark green, 5½" X 2½".
Hardy to +10 — Flowers bright attractive pink with crimson dots,
Late April — about 4" in diameter in a rounded, large upright
truss. Vigorous and easy to grow, needs some
shade; does not bloom as a small plant. Roots fairly easily. A.M.
(RHS) 1926.

Damozel g.

Rating 4/2 — A *R. griersonianum* hybrid; Rothschild, 1936.
Hardy to 0 — Plant upright spreading, rather open; leaves nar-
Tall 6+ — row, dark green, 6" X 1½". Flowers of the clone
Late May — common in the N.W., are bright red with darker
spotting, to about 2½" in diameter; upright truss.
Vigorous and easy to grow. Roots easily. One form, described as
deep rose pink, received an A. M. (RHS) in 1948.

Daphnoides, May, 3', bright purple

David

Rating 4/3 Parentage reported as 'Hugh Koster' X *R. nerii-*
Hardy to +5 *florum;* Swathling. Said by some to be a chance
Tall seedling of 'Earl of Athlone'. Plant very upright
Early May when young, of medium compactness. Leaves are
5½" X 1¾" and dark green in color. Flowers deep blood red and campanulate. The truss is built up and loosely formed. Plant does well in full sun but flowers last much better in some shade. Roots very easily. F. C. C. (RHS) in 1939, A.M. (Wisley Trials) 1957.

David Gable

Rating 4/4 'Atrosanguineum' X *R. fortunei;* Gable. Good
Hardy to –15 plant habit, large leaves. Flowers pink with a red
Medium throat, in a large, dome shaped truss. Floriferous
Early May and easy to grow. Synonym, is 'Gable's Pink No. 1'. A. E. (ARS) 1960.

Dawn's Delight

Rating 3/3 A *R. griffithianum* hybrid; Mangles. Plant round-
Hardy to +5 ish, compact with 6" X 2" obovate leaves of medi-
Medium um dark green. Flowers pale pink, tinged with
Mid-May rose pink, light spotting of red in upper corolla and base bright crimson. Medium size, tall, open truss. A. M. (RHS) 1911.

Day Dream, Biscuit form

Rating 3/2 'Lady Bessborough' X *R. griersonianum;* Roth-
Hardy to +5 schild. Spreading, willowy plant habit, leaves
Medium light green, 5" X 1¾", with light brown petioles.
Late May Flowers deep orange pink with orange red in throat, outer portion of corolla fading to biscuit color. Medium size, loose, round truss. In England the usual type of the 'Day Dream' group appears to be a deep crimson which received an A. M. (RHS) in 1940. This latter form now rather scarce in the Northwest, probably more tender than the Biscuit form.

Devonshire Cream

Rating 3/4 A *R. campylocarpum* hybrid; Slocock about 1924.
Hardy to 0 Very slow growing, compact plant with dark
Semi-dwarf green foliage. Leaves 2" X 1". Flowers creamy
Early May yellow in a very compact, ball type truss. Best results in partial shade. Roots fairly easily. A. M. (RHS) 1940.

Diane

Rating 3/2	'Mrs. Lindsay Smith' X a *R. campylocarpum* hy-
Hardy to +5	brid; M. Koster and Sons, 1920. Upright open
Tall *6+*	habit, with leaves 4½" X 2½", medium green,
Late April	mottled with yellow, shiny. Flowers pale yellow,

flushed with primrose yellow, fading to creamy white. Medium, tight, round truss of 9 to 10 flowers. Must be grown in shade. A. M. (RHS) 1948.

Diane Titcomb

Award '58

Rating 3/3	'Marinus Koster' x 'Snow Queen'; Larson, exhibit-
Hardy to 0	ed 1942. Sturdy plant with leaves 5" x 2½".
Medium *6'*	Flowers white, edged pink. Best results in partial
Mid-May	shade. P.A. (ARS) 1958.

Dido g.

Rating 2/3	*R. dichroanthum* X *R. decorum;* Wilding, 1934.
Hardy to +5	Compact sturdy plant habit. Leaves, light green,
Low *4½*	3½" X 1½". Flowers orange yellow, widely tubu-
Late May	lar in a lax truss.

Disca

Rating 3/3	*R. discolor* X 'Caroline'; Gable, exhibited 1944.
Hardy to –5	Vigorous grower, with a good plant habit, leaves
Medium *6'*	light green. Flowers scented, white, tinged pink,
Late May	large, slightly frilled, in a large domed truss. Best

in light shade.

Diva g.

Rating 3/2	'Ladybird' X *R. griersonianum;* Rothschild. Open,
Hardy to 0	somewhat sprawly habit, with 7" X 1" medium
Medium *6'*	green, dull leaves. Flowers deep orange pink in
Late May	a medium, round, loose truss. One form of this

group received the A. M. (RHS) in 1937.

Doncaster

Rating 2/3	A *R. arboreum* hybrid; Anthony Waterer, in the
Hardy to –5	latter part of the 19th century. Plant rather
3' x Semi-dwarf	spreading and open; leaves dark green, 6" X 2".
Late May	Flowers crimson scarlet, to about 2½" in diameter,

in a rounded truss. Medium vigor, fairly easy to grow. Somewhat heat tolerant. Roots fairly easily.

Dora Amateis

Rating 4/4	*R. carolinianum* X *R. ciliatum;* Amateis. Plant
Hardy to –15	rather compact, rounded; leaves lanceolate,
Semi-dwarf	3" X 1". Flowers white, lightly spotted green, to
Late April	about 2" in diameter, in clusters of 3 to 5. Vigorous, easy to grow. Roots easily. Very free flowering. A. E. (ARS)

3' x *(handwritten)*

Dormouse g.

Rating 3/4	'Dawn's Delight' X *R. williamsianum;* Rothschild
Hardy to 0	1936. Compact, close growing habit. Leaves 3" X
Semi-dwarf	2¼", oval, auriculate, medium green. Flowers pale
Late April	pink, flushed with bright pink on outside and deepening at rim, light spotting in upper corolla.

3' x *(handwritten)*

Small loose truss. *Borec : Lower + slower than Bowbells* *(handwritten)*

Doubloons, May, 3', deep yellow *(handwritten)*

Dr. A. Blok

Rating 3/3	'Pink Pearl' X a *R. catawbiense* hybrid; L. Endtz
Hardy to –5	and Co. Quite good upright habit with leaves 6" X
Tall 6+	2½", medium green. Flowers pink, fading
Mid-May	to lighter at center, with touch of pale yellow in upper center, in a rather large round truss. Frequently sold as 'Dr. O. Blok'. A. M. (RHS) 1937.

Dr. H. C. Dresselhuys

Rating 1/2	'Atrosanguineum' X 'Doncaster'; H. den Ouden
Hardy to –15	and Son, 1920. Plant upright, fairly good foliage
Medium 6'	but not enough of it. Flowers aniline red with
Mid-May	a lighter blotch, in a tall truss.

Dr. Ross

Rating 3/2	*R. griersonianum* X 'Borde Hill'; R. Henny. Plant
Hardy to 0	spreading. Leaves 6" X 2", pointed and medium
Medium 6'	green. Flowers bright red, funnel shaped. Truss
Mid-May	dome shaped, later flat topped.

Dr. Stocker

Rating 3/2	*R. caucasicum* X *R. griffithianum;* North. Habit
Hardy to +5	upright, open; leaves 6" X 2½", elliptic, medium
Medium 6'	green. Flowers open campanulate, 3" across, waxy
Mid-April	ivory white, in an open, well rounded truss of 12 flowers. Roots easily. Resistant to pests. A.M. (RHS) 1900.

Dr. V. H. Rutgers

Rating 2/3   'Charles Dickens' X 'Lord Roberts'; H. den Ouden
Hardy to –15 and Son, 1925. Plant broad, dense, leaves dark
Medium 6'   green. Flowers aniline red, fringed.
Late May

Earl of Athlone

Rating 5/2   'Queen Wilhelmina' X 'Stanley Davies'; C. B.
Hardy to 0   van Nes and Sons. Plant is open and spreading.
Medium 6'   Leaves 5" X 2", dark green. Flowers bright blood
Late April   red, campanulate. Truss dome shaped, compact.
              One of the finest red trusses. Difficult to root, but
plant rates better than 2 if on own roots. F. C. C. (RHS) in 1933.

Edward Dunn

Rating 4/2   *(R. neriflorum* x *R. dichroanthum)* x *R. discolor;*
Hardy to +5   Ostbo. Plant medium spreading; leaves medium
Medium 6'   dark green, 5" X 2". Flowers apricot pink, 3"
Late May   across, in a dome shaped truss. Best in part shade,
              heat tolerant. P. A. (ARS) 1958.

Edward S. Rand

Rating 2/3   A *R. catawbiense hybrid;* A. Waterer, 1870. Plant
Hardy to –15 compact, foliage tends to be yellowish green.
Medium 6'   Flowers crimson red with a bronze eye. Does not
Late May   root easily.

El Alamein , May , blood red, 4' , -15°

Eldorado g.

Rating 4/3   *R. valentinianum* X *R. johnstoneanum;* Roth-
Hardy to +15 schild, 1937. Small, open growing plant with
Low 4½   scaly dark yellowish green leaves 1¾" X 1".
Mid April   Medium sized yellow, funnel-shaped flowers with
              brown scales on the outside, in clusters of 3-4.
Bud tender. Propagates easily.

Eleanore g.

Rating 3/3   *R. desquamatum* X *R. augustinii;* Rothschild, 1937.
Hardy to +10 Upright plant. Leaves dark green, 2" X 1". Will
Tall 6+   grow well in full sun. Lavender blue flowers in
Late April   profusion. A. M. (RHS) 1943.

Elie, April, deep pink, 4', -15°

Electra g.

Rating 5/4	*R. chasmanthum* X *R. augustinii;* Rothschild.
Hardy to +5	Plant upright; leaves 3¼" X 1¼", medium green.
Medium 6'	Does best in light shade. As *R. chasmanthum* is
Late April	now considered a variety of *R. augustinii,* 'Electra'

might be termed a selected form of the species. Perhaps the bluest of the augustiniis, although the flowers are smaller than those of some selections. A fine plant for the woodgarden. A.M. (RHS) in 1940.

Elizabeth g. *8th choice in Seattle*

Rating 4/4	*R. forrestii* var. *repens* X *R. griersonianum;* Aber-
Hardy to 0	conway. Plant compact, grows wider than tall,
4½ Low	leaves 2½" X 1", are dark green above, glaucous
Mid-April	below with a trace of indumentum, and are held

three or more years. The 3½" flowers are funnel campanulate, and bright red. The lax truss is made up of 6-8 flowers. Some blooms open occasionally in the fall. Does well in full exposure or light shade, roots readily. A. M. (RHS) 1939, F. C. C. (RHS) 1943. Several forms are in the trade.

Elizabeth Titcomb

Rating 4/4	'Marinus Koster' X 'Snow Queen'; H. L. Larson.
Hardy to 0	Good sturdy plant, with dark green foliage.
Medium 6'	Leaves 5" X 2½". Pale pink very large flowers
Late April	with dark pink margin, of much substance, in tall

ard '58

conical truss. Will grow well in full sun.

Ella

Rating 4/3	*R. dichroanthum* X *R. wardii;* R. Henny. Leaves
Hardy to +10	are 3" X 1½", shiny green, and are held about
Low 4½	three years. Apricot-copper buds open to 3", flat,
Late May	orange to yellow flowers. Plant covers itself with

numerous 3 to 4 flowered trusses. Does best in partial shade. It roots readily.

Elspeth

Rating 3/4	*R. campylocarpum* X hardy hybrid; Slocock. Up-
Hardy to 0	right compact plant with light green leaves 4½"
Low 4½	X 2¼". Flowers opening bright scarlet in bud,
Mid-May	deep pink-apricot in flower, fading to cream.

Small, rounded truss. A. M. (RHS) 1937. There is another 'Elspeth', a pure white hybrid of 'White Pearl' by R. Gill and Son, probably not being grown in the U. S. A.

Endre Ostbo

Rating 3/3   *R. souliei* X *R. discolor;* Ostbo. Upright habit with
Hardy to 0   leaves 4″ X 2½″, medium green, slightly auricu-
Medium *6′*   late. Flowers pale blush pink, fringed deeper pink
Late May   with red spotting in upper portion of corolla,
                 saucer-shaped to 4″ across. Medium rounded truss
of 6 to 8 flowers. P. A. (ARS) 1954.

Award '54

Ermine

Rating 4/4   'Britannia' X 'Mrs. A. T. de la Mare'; R. Henny.
Hardy to 0   Stiff sturdy plant with medium green leaves 6″
Medium *6′*   X 1½″. Flowers of good substance, pure white, in
Late May   a tall, well filled, truss. Grows well in full sun.

Esquire

Rating 4/3   Probably a *R. griersonianum* hybrid; Barto,
Hardy to +5   grown and introduced by James. An upright,
Medium *6′*   spreading shrub, which becomes fairly compact
Early May   at maturity. Leaves dark green, with red-brown
                 petiole. Flowers deep pink, to 4″ across in a some-
what loose, round truss. The flower buds are very long and sharp
pointed.

Ethel g.

Rating 3/3   'F. C. Puddle' X *R. forrestii* var. *repens;* Aber-
Hardy to +5   conway. Plant has a spreading, creeping habit.
1½′ ×Dwarf   Flowers crimson scarlet bells, 3 to 5 to a truss.
Early May   Best in half shade. One form received an F.C.C.
                 (RHS) 1940.

Europa g.

Rating 3/3   *R. ungernii* X *R. kyawi;* Rothschild 1937. Upright
Hardy to +5   spreading, rather open; holds foliage 2 years.
Tall *6+*   Leaves elliptic, glossy dark green with prominent
June   veining, light tan indumentum, to 8½″ X 3″.
                 Flowers lilac pink, open tubular, to 3″ across in
a dome shaped, open truss. A showy foliage plant.

Evening Glow

Rating 4/3   *R. discolor* X 'Fabia'; Van Veen. Compact plant
Hardy to +5   habit. Leaves light green, 5″ X 2″. Flowers with
Medium *6′*   prominent calyx, light yellow in a very lax truss.
Late May

Everestianum

Rating 2/3   A *R. catawbiense* hybrid; A. Waterer, before 1850.
Hardy to –15   Vigorous plant making a full rounded form, leaves
Tall 6+   5″ X 2″, oval-oblong and dark green. The 2″ wide,
Late May   rosy-lilac flowers, spotted in the throat, have
frilled edges. About 15 flowers make a full round-
ed truss. This is a heavy bloomer, does well in either sun or light
shade, roots readily and is resistant to pests.

Fabia g.

Rating 3/3   *R. dichroanthum* X *R. griersonianum;* Abercon-
Hardy to +10   way 1927. There are several named forms of this
Low 4½   group with 'Fabia Tangerine' having perhaps the
Mid-May   best plant habit. 'Fabia Tower Court' was raised
by Stevenson in 1937; 'Roman Pottery' by Cros-
field exhibited in 1934, and 'Exbury Fabia' by Rothschild.

Fabia Tangerine

Rating 3/4   *R. dichroanthum* X *R. griersonianum;* Abercon-
Hardy to +10   way. Low compact plant habit, leaves 4″ X 1½″
Low 4½   with a reddish brown indumentum. Flowers
Mid-May   tangerine orange in a lax truss, quite effective in
large plants. Will give best results in partial
shade, although plant will grow well in full sun. A.M. (RHS) 1940.

Faggetter's Favourite

Rating 5/4   A *R. fortunei* hybrid; Slocock. Plant is vigorous,
Hardy to 0   upright, spreading. Leaves 7″ X 2¾″, dark green.
Tall 6+   Flowers are flushed pink, speckled bronze in
Late April   throat, and scented. Truss, built up, with many
flowers. Both foliage and flowers are best out of
hot sun. Not too easily rooted. A. M. (RHS) 1933, A. M. (Wisley
Trials) 1955.

Fanfare

Rating 3/1   Red *R. catawbiense* hybrid x red *R. catawbiense*
Hardy to –20   hybrid; Shammarello, selection by Leach. Plant
Medium 6′   open, spreading, leaves oblanceolate-oblong, medi-
Mid-May   um green, undulate, 5¼″ x 1¾″. Flowers bright
red, do not fade; in a dome shaped truss. Tolerant
of sun or shade.

Fastuosum Flore Pleno

Rating 3/3
Hardy to –10
Tall 6+
Late May

R. catawbiense X *R. ponticum* by Francoisi, before 1846. Plant habit slightly open, rounded. Leaves 5½″ X 2″, dark matte green above, light green below, slightly convex. Flowers lavender blue, darker markings, semi-double, 2″ across in a slightly loose truss. Requires half shade for flowers to last. The plant will tolerate full exposure. Good grower, roots readily.

Fawn

Award '55 '59

Rating 4/3
Hardy to +5
Tall 6+
Early May

R. fortunei X 'Fabia'; James. Upright habit with 4″ X 1½″, medium green leaves. Flowers salmon pink, shaded with orange yellow in center, 4½″ to 5″ across. Very flat corolla. Cylindrical open top truss. P. A. (ARS) 1955.

Fayella, May, bright red, +5, 2'

F. C. Puddle g.

Rating 3/3
Hardy to +5
Medium 6'
Mid-April

R. neriiflorum X *R. griersonianum;* Aberconway. Fairly upright habit, leaves 4″ X 1½″, dull, dark green, with hairy petioles. Flowers brilliant orange scarlet, in a medium sized, lax, open top truss. A. M. (RHS) 1932.

F. D. Godman

Rating 2/3
Hardy to –10
Medium 6'
Mid-May

A *R. catawbiense* hybrid; A. Waterer 1888. Flowers dark magenta red with a black blotch.

Forsterianum

Pot or Tub
Fragrant
Not Hardy

Rating 5/4
Hardy to +20
6' Medium
Early May

R. veitchianum X *R. edgeworthii;* Forster in 1917. Plant compact, upright, with lanceolate leaves, to 3½″ X 1¼″. Flowers wide funnel shaped, to 5″ across, white, with a conspicuous yellow flare, fragrant, 3 to 4 in a lax truss. Best in half shade, roots easily. Not as fragrant as 'Fragrantissimum' but flowers earlier and, because of its upright, compact habit, it is considered to be a better garden plant.

Fragrantissimum

Fragrant
Not Hardy

Rating 4/3
6' Hardy to +20
Medium 6'
Early April

R. edgeworthii X *R. formosum;* Rollisson. Plants with arching type of growth, inclined to be leggy; leaves lanceolate, to 3½″ X 1½″. Flowers open funnel shaped, to 4″ wide, buds flushed carmine, open pure white, with nutmeg fragrance. Lax truss of 2 to 4 flowers. Best in half shade. Easy to root. One of the most fragrant of all shrubs. Plant may be trained against a wall, up a post, or over a bank. Growth should be pinched back in young plants to promote branching. Will break readily from older wood if pruned back. F. C. C. (RHS) 1868.

Full Moon

Rating 4/4   'Crest' X 'Harvest Moon'; J. Henny. Low, sturdy, Hardy to –5   compact plant with prominently veined bright Low 4½   shiny green foliage. Leaves 3½" X 2½". Flowers Mid-May   waxy, deep canary yellow in compact ball type truss. Best results in part shade. Roots with difficulty. P.A. (ARS) 1955.

award 55

Fusilier g.

Rating 4/3   *R. elliottii* X *R. griersonianum;* Rothschild. Up-Hardy to +15 right habit with dark green leaves, 5" X 1½" Medium 6'   with maroon colored petioles. Flower bud and Late May   leaf bud scales long and protruding. Flowers brilliant orange red in a medium sized, open top truss. A. M. (RHS) 1938; F. C. C. (RHS) 1942.

Garnet g.

Rating 3/4   *R. griffithianum* X 'Broughtonii'; P. D. Williams, Hardy to +5   1942. Upright spreading habit, medium compact, Medium 6'   with 5¼" X 1½", dark green, shiny leaves. Mid-May   Flowers deep salmon rose, flushed red, fading to a pale pink. Possibly only one form being grown in the U. S. A.

General Eisenhower

Rating 2/3   A *R. griffithianum* hybrid; A. Kluis, 1946. Compact Hardy to 0   bush. Flowers deep carmine red, large with Medium 6'   ruffled edge. Mid-May

Gill's Crimson

Rating 4/3   A *R. griffithianum* hybrid; R. Gill and Son. Plant Hardy to +10 upright of medium density. Leaves 5½" X 2", light Tall 6+   green. Flowers blood crimson with good sub-Early April   stance, rather long lasting. Truss tight, dome shaped, later flat topped. Early flowering, needs frost protection. Roots easily.

Gladys g.

Rating 3/3 — *R. campylocarpum* X *R. fortunei;* Clarke. Plant
Hardy to 0 — rounded, medium open, with 5" X 2" medium
Tall *b +* — green leaves. Flowers various shades of pale yel-
Late April — low, with one form a pale buff-yellow, 2" across.
Small, rounded truss of 9 to 11 flowers. One form
received the A.M. (RHS) in 1926, another in 1950. Several forms of
the 'Gladys' group have been named, as 'Mary Swaythling' and
others.

Glowing Embers

Rating 4/2 — 'Romany Chal' X *R. griersonianum;* J. Henny.
Hardy to +5 — Plant of average compactness. Leaves 4½" X 1½",
Low *4 %* — dark green. Flowers bright geranium scarlet,
June — stamens rudimentary. Plant easily grown and will
stand sun but flowers best in some shade. Roots
easily.

Goldbug

Rating 3/3 — 'Fabia' X *R. wardii;* R. Henny. Plant habit is low
Hardy to +5 — spreading, fairly compact. The dark green elliptic
3' ⨯ Semi-dwarf — leaves average 3" x 1¼". The orange yellow
Early May — flowers, flushed red in the throat and heavily
spotted with small dark maroon dots, mature to
a gold color, are 1½" across, tubular campanulate in shape, and
are borne in lax trusses of 4-6. This is a novelty type; the color
changing with maturity adds interest.

Golden Belle

Rating 4/4 — *R. discolor* X 'Fabia'; J. Henny. Low, spreading,
Hardy to 0 — compact plant habit. Leaves 4" X 1½". Flowers
Low *4½* — large, saucer-shaped, deep pink edges, yellow cen-
Late May — ters in a compact, ball type truss. Best results
in partial shade. Formerly called 'Margaret
Dunn' var. 'Golden Belle'.

Golden Dream

Rating 5/3 — 'Naomi' X *R. campylocarpum;* Rothschild. A sister
Hardy to +5 — plant to 'Carita' A. M., with plant taller and a
Medium *6'* — little more open. Leaves medium green, oval, 3½"
Late April — X 2½". Flowers large, deep cream yellow in a tall
truss. Must be planted in some shade for
best results. Formerly known as 'Carita' var. 'Golden Dream'.

Golden Horn g.

Rating 3/3   *R. dichroanthum* X *R. elliottii;* Rothschild, 1939.
Hardy to +10   Slow growing, medium compact and spreading
Low 4½   with leaves 3¾" X 1½", medium green, slightly
Late May   shiny. Flowers light orange red, long tubular,
                         trumpet shaped. Small open topped truss of 9 to
11 flowers. A.M. (RHS) 1945.

Goldfort

Rating 4/3   'Goldsworth Yellow' X *R. fortunei;* W. C. Slocock,
Hardy to -10   1937. Upright, open habit with 6" X 2¾" leaves of
Tall 6 +   medium green. Flowers clear pale yellow, pale
Mid May   green yellow in center, in a medium sized round
                        truss.

Goldsworth Crimson

Rating 2/3   *R. griffithianum* X a hardy hybrid; W. C. Slocock,
Hardy to 0   selected 1926. Plant upright rounded, medium com-
Medium 6'   pact. Leaves dark green, glossy, 6" X 1¾".
Mid May   Flowers crimson, in a medium sized, dome shaped
                        truss.

Goldsworth Orange

Rating 3/3   *R. dichroanthum* X *R. discolor;* W. C. Slocock,
Hardy to -5   1938. Plant open, spreading. Leaves 5½" X 1½".
Medium 6'   Flowers pale orange tinted pink, funnel-shaped.
Late May   Truss lax. Foliage and flowers best in shade. Used
                        extensively in crossing for yellow.

Goldsworth Yellow

Rating 1/2   *R. caucasicum* X *R. campylocarpum;* W. C. Slo-
Hardy to -15   cock, 1925. Plant taller than wide, quite dense,
Medium 6'   leaves 4" X 1½", are held about 4 years and are
Late May   yellowish, even in half shade. The flowers are
                        thin in texture, apricot in the bud, opening to a
buff yellow with bronze spots on the upper lobe, and become more
yellow the longer they are held. The truss is compact and of
medium size. The plant will not bloom well in the shade. It roots
poorly. A. M. (RHS) 1925.

Gomer Waterer

Rating 3/4   A *R. catawbiense* hybrid; J. Waterer before 1900.
Hardy to –15   Plant broadly upright, spreading, leaves glossy,
Medium 6'   dark green, 6" X 3". Flowers delicate rose tinged,
Late May   fading to a blush white, to about 3" in diameter,
               7 to 12 in a tight rounded truss. Vigorous easy
to grow, heat and sun tolerant. Roots easily. Floriferous. Plant
attractive all year. One of the best of the old hardy varieties
but not an "ironclad."

Graf Zeppelin May, bright pink, 5', -5°

Great Lakes

Rating 3/4   *R. catawbiense* var. *album* Glass x *R. yakusiman-*
Hardy to –25   um F.C.C.; Leach 1952. Plant very compact, leaves
x Semi-dwarf   medium green, oblanceolate-elliptic, with a thin
Mid-May   tan indumentum, 3½" 1½". Pink in bud, flowers
               white, 2¼" across, 14 or 15 in a dome shaped
truss. Very floriferous, tolerant of sun. P.A. (ARS) 1960.

Grenadier g.

Rating 4/3   'Moser's Maroon' X *R. elliottii;* Rothschild.
Hardy to +5   Fairly open, upright, spreading plant with 6" X
Tall 6+   2", dark, dull green, somewhat bullate leaves,
June   some forms with red-buff colored indumentum.
               Orange buff spherical flower buds. Flowers deep
blood red with dark spots, in a medium size, round, full truss.
F. C. C. (RHS) 1943.

Gretchen g.

Rating 4/4   *(R. decorum* X *R. griffithianum)* X 'Kettledrum';
Hardy to –15   Nearing and Gable. Good foliage and plant habit.
Medium 6'   Flowers pink with a red throat, in a large dome
Mid-May   shaped truss. Very floriferous, does not root easily.
               Above description is for 'Gretchen No. 1', other
forms not quite as good.

Grierosplendour g.

Rating 3/3   *R. griersonianum* X 'Purple Splendour'; Loder,
Hardy to 0   1937. Plant rather upright when young, later
Low 4½   round spreading, leaves 5½" X 1¼", light green.
Late May   Flowers red purple or plum color, about midway
               between the parents, of good size in a medium
sized, rounded truss. Plants bloom profusely at an early age.
Roots easily.

Grosclaude g.
Rating 4/4   *R. haematodes* X *R. eriogynum;* Rothschild. Slow
Hardy to +5   growing, compact plant, leaves 3" X 1", light
Low 4½   green, recurved, with brown indumentum.
Late May   Flowers waxy, heavy textured, bright scarlet,
                 bell-shaped. Flat topped, medium sized truss of
9 to 11 flowers. A. M. (RHS) 1945.

Gypsy Queen, May, +5°, bloodred, 3' Bowbells ✕Robert Fox

Harvest Moon
Rating 3/3   'Mrs. Lindsay Smith' by a *R. campylocarpum*
Hardy to 0   hybrid; M. Koster and Sons. Upright habit, leaves
Medium 6'   4" X 2", yellow-green, shiny, slightly bullate.
Early May   Flowers pale lemon yellow with reddish spotting,
                 3½" across. Medium size, rounded compact truss
of 10 to 12 flowers. A. M. (RHS) 1948.

Helene Schiffner
Rating 4/3   Parentage unknown; Seidel. Plant medium com-
Hardy to –5   pact. The deep green 5" X 2" leaves are folded
Low 4½   upward and pointed. Flowers pure white in bud
Mid-May   and when open, with no spotting, medium size, in
                 a compact, dome shaped truss. F. C. C. (RHS)
1893.

Holden April, rosy red, 3', –5°

Hollandia
Rating 3/3   'Pink Pearl' X 'Charles Dickens'; L. J. Endtz and
Hardy to 0   Co. Good foliage. Flowers red-carmine. A syno-
Medium 6'   nym is 'G. Streseman'.
Mid-May

Honeymoon, April, yellow, 3', –5°

Hugh Koster
Rating 2/3   'George Hardy' X a 'Doncaster' hybrid; M. Koster
Hardy to +5   and Sons, 1915. Upright spreading, leaves 5½" X
Medium 6'   1¾", channeled. Flowers medium size, crimson,
Mid-May   lighter at center, truss roundish upright. Medium
                 vigor, should have some shade. Roots easily.
A. M. (RHS) 1933 after trial at Exbury.

Humming Bird g.
Rating 3/3   *R. haematodes* X *R. williamsianum;* J. C. Wil-
Hardy to 0   liams, 1933. Plant very compact, leaves 2¾" X
✕Semi-dwarf   ¾". Flowers in a selected superior form are
Late April   medium red with very heavy substance. Truss
                 lax, few flowered. Plant slow growing, takes a
long time to bloom and needs some shade. Easy to root.

Bed 3'

Hurricane, May, 5', -05° pink

Hyperion

Rating 3/3   Parentage unknown; A. Waterer. Plant medium
Hardy to –10   spreading, rather open, leaves dark green, 6" X
Medium 6'   1¾". Flowers bluish white with large, dark purple
Early May   blotch.

Idealist g.

Rating 4/3   *R. wardii* X 'Naomi'; Rothschild. Upright vigorous
Hardy to +5   habit with leaves 4½" X 2", medium green.
Medium 6'   Flowers wide campanulate, pale yellow, slightly
Late April   tinged green. Should have some shade. A. M.
(RHS) 1945.

Ignatius Sargent

55 ?.

Rating 2/2   A *R. catawbiense* hybrid; A. Waterer. Plant has
Hardy to –25   open habit, large leaves. Flowers deep rose,
Medium 6'   slightly scented, large.
Late May

Impi g.

Rating 2/2   *R. didymum* x 'Moser's Maroon'; Rothschild. Plant
Hardy to +10   dome shaped, slow growing, leaves dark green.
Low 4½   Flowers rather small, bell shaped in a small truss.
Late May   The value of the variety is the novelty of the very
dark red color, which is somewhat translucent by
back lighting. One of the darkest reds, but not dull. A.M. (RHS)
1945.

Indiana g.

Rating 3/4   *R. scyphocalyx* X *R. kyawi;* Rothschild, 1941.
Hardy to +15   Slow growing, spreading habit, leaves 4½" X
Low 4½   1½", somewhat bullate, shining, dark green with
June   edges turned down sharply; end of leaf round.
Leaves stand very upright. Flowers orange red in
a medium sized, loose, lax, open topped truss.

Ivery's Scarlet

Rating 3/3   Parentage unknown. Plant upright, inclined to
Hardy to +10   be willowy, with medium to light green leaves
Tall 6+   5½" X 1¼". Flowers bright red in small, dome
Late April   shaped truss. Roots easily.

Jaipur g.

Rating 4/2   *R. forrestii* var. *repens* X *R. meddianum;* Roth-
Hardy to +5   schild, 1942. Low, open, habit. Nodding, medium
Dwarf   1'/~   sized flowers of good substance, deep crimson, in
March   a lax truss. This is a difficult plant to grow;
blooms as a small plant.

Jalisco g.

Rating 4/3   'Lady Bessborough' X 'Dido'; Rothschild, 1942.
Hardy to 0   Leaves medium green, 5" X 2½". Flowers prim-
Medium   4'   rose yellow, with dark red spotting near base of
Late May   upper portion of corolla, 3½" across. Medium
sized, loose, open topped truss of 8 to 10 flowers.
At least 5 clones of the 'Jalisco' group have been named by Roth-
schild, of which 4 have received RHS awards; namely, 'Jalisco
Eclipse', 'Jalisco Elect', 'Jalisco Emblem', and 'Jalisco Goshawk'.
Some of these may be in the U. S. A.

James Barto

Rating 3/4   Parentage not fully authenticated, but it is
Hardy to –5   thought to be *R. williamsianum* X *R. orbiculare,*
Medium   4'   raised by James Barto and introduced by Clarence
Early May   Prentice. Flowers about a week after 'Temple
Belle' and has a similar compact habit of growth.
Leaves are elliptic about 3" X 2", rounded at base and rounded to
sub-acute at apex, somewhat tough in texture. Petiole up to 1¼"
long. Flowers fuchsine pink HCC 627/3, 3 to 5 loosely arranged
on a short rachis. Corolla funnel form, 2" X 2½". Slightly fragrant.
Plant is a vigorous grower after a slow start, withstands some
sun. P.A. (ARS) 1953.

Jan Dekens

Rating 2/3   An introduction of J. Blaauw and Co., 1940.
Hardy to 0   Sturdy vigorous plant habit with bold foliage;
Tall   leaves to 6" X 3". Flowers large, ruffled, <u>bright</u>
Mid May   <u>pink</u> with deeper pink edges which quickly fade
to very pale pink. May be planted in sun. Truss
upright, compact.

Janet g.

Rating 4/3   'Avalanche' X 'Dr. Stocker'; Rothschild. Plant
Hardy to +5   semi-compact, leaves 8" X 3". Flowers extra large,
Tall   6+   of pure white, deep crimson staining in the
Early April   throat, in a flat-topped, many flowered truss.

Janet Blair

Rating 4/3   A Dexter hybrid x ?; Leach, 1948. Plant compact,
Hardy to –15 densely foliaged, spreading, leaves dark green,
Tall 6+   oval-elliptic, 4½″ X 2½″. Flowers pale pinkish
Early May   mauve, golden bronze rays on upper lobe, fimbri-
              ate, large, in a tall truss. Floriferous.

Jasper g.

Rating 2/3   *R. dichroanthum* X 'Lady Bessborough', Roth-
Hardy to –5   schild 1942. Sturdy compact plant. Leaves dark
Semi-dwarf 3′   green 5″ X 2″. Flowers bell-shaped pale orange
Late May   with red edges. Truss flat topped.

J. G. Millais

Rating 3/2   'Ascot Brilliant' X 'Pink Pearl'; J. Waterer. Vigor-
Hardy to +5   ous, open habit, with 5″ X 2″, medium green
Tall 6+   leaves. Flowers deep blood red, heavily spotted,
Early April   in medium, round trusses.

J. H. van Nes

Rating 3/3   'Monsieur Thiers' X *R. griffithianum* hybrid; C.
Hardy to 0   B. van Nes and Sons. Plant fairly compact, light
Medium 6′   green leaves, 5″ X 2″. Flowers soft red fading to
Mid May   pale at center, about 2½″ in diameter, pointed
              lobes, in a conical, compact truss. Must have some
shade, resents over fertilization. Roots easily.

Jock g.

Rating 2/4   *R. williamsianum* X *R. griersonianum;* Maxwell in
Hardy to –5   1939. The plant habit is dense and spreading. The
Low   broadly lanceolate, dark green leaves are 2½″ X
Late April   1″. Flowers about 3″ across, dark pink with
              some bluishness, slightly orange in the throat,
making up a few-flowered loose truss. The plant does best in full
sun, and cuttings root easily.

John Coutts g.

Rating 4/3   ('Grand Arab' X *R. griffithianum*) X *R. griersoni-*
Hardy to +5   *anum;* Royal Botanic Garden at Kew. Fairly dense
Medium 6′   habit of growth, a bit sprawly, leaves 6″ X 1½″,
Mid-May   pointed, medium green. Flowers very smooth,
              salmon pink, deeper colored in throat, in a large,
open truss.

John Walter

Rating 2/3   *R. catawbiense* X *R. arboreum;* J. Waterer, before
Hardy to –10   1860. Flowers red-crimson.
Medium 6′
Late May

Jutland g.

Rating 4/3   *R. elliottii* X 'Bellerophon'; Rothschild. Foliage
Hardy to +5   dull, dark green. Leaves 6″ X 1½″. Flowers bright
Medium 6′   blood red in ball type truss. One form received
June   A. M. (RHS) in 1947.

Kate Waterer

Rating 2/3   Parentage not known; J. Waterer, before 1890.
Hardy to –10   Plant medium compact, fairly upright. Flowers
Medium 6′   pink with a golden eye.
Late May

Kentucky Cardinal

Rating 2/2   *R. brachycarpum* X 'Essex Scarlet'; Gable, ex-
Hardy to –5   hibited in 1946. Plant with an open habit, leaves
Low 4½   dark green. Flowers very dark red.
Late May

Kettledrum

Rating 1/1   A *R. catawbiense* hybrid; A. Waterer in 1877.
Hardy to –20   Plant habit and foliage somewhat inferior.
Medium 6′   Flowers purplish crimson.
Late May

King of Shrubs

Rating 4/2   *R. discolor* X 'Fabia'; Endre Ostbo. Plant open.
Hardy to +5   wider than tall. Leaves 5½″ X 2″, light green.
Medium 6′   Flowers apricot yellow at base, inner margin
Late May   banded porcelain rose. Truss lax. Best in after-
            noon shade. P. A. (ARS) 1950.

King Tut, May, pink, 3′, –25°

Kluis Sensation

Rating 3/2   'Britannia' X an unnamed seedling; A. Kluis, 1946.
Hardy to 0   Rather compact plant with very dark green,
Medium 6′   crinkly leaves. Flowers dark red, faintly spotted,
Late May   in a small, tight truss.

Kluis Triumph

Rating 2/3   A *R. griffithianum* hybrid; A. Kluis. Plant erect,
Hardy to 0   medium compact, with leaves 6″ long. Flowers
Medium 6′   light red.
Late May

Lady Alice Fitzwilliam

Rating 4/4   Parentage not known, probably similar to that
Hardy to +20   of 'Fragrantissimum'. Plant upright, open; leaves
6′ Medium 6′   elliptic lanceolate, margins curve inwards, to
Mid April   3½″ X 1½″. Flowers wide funnel shaped, flaring,
                to 5″ wide, pink in bud, white when fully opened,
fragrant. Lax truss of 2 to 4 flowers. Heat tolerant, half shade best,
roots easily. Very similar in leaf and flower to 'Fragrantissimum'
but more bushy and erect; preferred by some because of this trait.
F. C. C. (RHS) 1881.

Lady Berry g.

Rating 5/4   'Rosy Bell' X 'Royal Flush'; Rothschild. Upright
Hardy to +5   open habit, with blue-green aromatic leaves,
Medium 6′   3″ X 1½″. Pendant trusses of 8 tubular flowers,
Late April   rose opal on the inside, and jasper red on the
                outside 3″ long and flaring to 2″ wide. A.M. (RHS)
1937, F. C. C. (RHS) 1949.

Lady Bessborough g.

Rating 4/3   *R. discolor* X *R. campylocarpum* var. *elatum;*
Hardy to –5   Rothschild. Upright habit, with medium green
Medium 6′   leaves, 5½″ X 2¼″. Flowers pale yellow to nearly
Late May   white with yellow toward base of throat. F.C.C.
                (RHS) 1933. Several clones of the 'Lady Bess-
borough' group have been named, as 'Roberte', (F. C. C. (RHS)
1936) and 'Montreal'.

Ladybird g.

Rating 4/4   *R. discolor* X 'Corona'; Rothschild. Medium com-
Hardy to –10   pact habit, leaves 7″ X 3″. Extra large ruffled
Medium 6′   flowers, in soft variations of light and darker
June   coral pink, in a well filled, dome shape truss.
                A. M. (RHS) 1933.

Lady Bligh

Rating 4/3   A *R. griffithianum* hybrid; C. B. van Nes and
Hardy to 0   Sons. Plant forms a spreading, rounded bush,
Medium *6'*   slightly wider than tall, holds its leaves for 2
Mid May   years. The medium green, elliptic shaped (base
rounded, tip acute) leaves average 6" X 2½".
The flowers are strawberry red, fading to pink; to 3" across,
wide campanulate, 10-12 in a full rounded truss. A. M. (RHS) 1934.

Lady Chamberlain g.

Rating 4/3   *R. cinnabarinum* var. *roylei* X 'Royal Flush'
Hardy to +10   orange form; Rothschild 1930. The plant is up-
Tall *6+*   right, taller than wide, with slender, willowy
Late April   branches. The leaves are slightly convex, smooth,
waxy, bluish green in new growth, maturing to
medium green, obovate elliptic, 3" X 1½", with reddish petioles
and scaly underside. The fleshy, bright orange to salmon pink
flowers are tubular flaring to long trumpet shaped, 1½" across
by 3" long, carried in a very lax truss of 3 to 6. Does best in a
sheltered location. At least 10 forms have been named of which at
least two have received the F. C. C. (RHS), the first in 1931.

Lady Clementine Mitford

Rating 2/3   A *R. maximum* hybrid; A. Waterer, exhibited in
Hardy to 0   1870. Plant medium compact broader than tall,
Low *4½*   with leaves 5" X 1¾", medium to dark green.
Late May   Flowers soft peach pink with a darker edge,
many in a dome-shaped truss.

Lady Eleanor Cathcart

Rating 2/2   *R. maximum* X *R. arboreum;* J. Waterer before
Hardy to –15   1850. Plant medium compact, rounded. Flowers
Tall *6+*   clear pink with a purplish blotch.
Late May

Lady Grey Egerton

Rating 2/2   A *R. catawbiense* hybrid; A. Waterer, before 1888.
Hardy to –15   Pale lilac flowers in a tight, conical truss.
Medium *6'*
Late May

Lady Longman, pink, -5, 4'

Lady Montagu

Rating 4/3   Probably *R. griffithianum* X *R. thomsonii;* Roth-
Hardy to +10   schild. Flowers of good substance, large, <u>dark</u>
Tall 6+   rose pink, darker outside, in a very large loose
Mid-April   truss. Leaves roundish oval A. M. (RHS) 1931.

See P 109
6+

Lady Primrose

Rating 3/3   A *R. campylocarpum* hybrid; Slocock. A compact,
Hardy to 0   dense plant, holding its leaves well. The 3" X 1½",
Medium 6'   rounded leaves are light green in the sun and bet-
Mid-May   ter in light shade. Flower buds, yellow, tinged
with pink, rather flat, and clear primrose yellow
with red spots. The ball-shaped truss is compact. This plant is
slow to start growing but does well when established; needs shade
for best results. It is difficult to root. A. M. (RHS) 1933.

Lady Roseberry g.

Rating 4/3   *R. cinnabarinum* var. *roylei* X 'Royal Flush' pink
Hardy to +5   form; Rothschild. Plant is upright, taller than
Tall 6+   wide, willowy in habit with slender branches.
Late April   The smooth, medium green (bluish green in new
               growth) leaves are 3" X 1¼", with red petioles
and scaly underside. The flowers are shell pink, shaded rose at
base, fleshy, tubular, flaring to funnel shadep, 1½" across by 2½"
long and held in very lax trusses of 4 to 6. Best in a sheltered
location. Several clones have been named. One form received the
A. M. (RHS) 1930 and F. C. C. (RHS) 1932.

Lady Stuart of Wortley

Rating 3/2   Parentage unknown, possibly a 'Coombe Royal' or
Hardy to 0   a *R. griffithianum* hybrid; M. Koster & Son
Medium 6'   cross, 1909. Plant upright, rather open; leaves 6"
Mid-May   x 1¾". Flowers large, a rather distinctive lumi-
               nous pink, in a large, upright truss. Flowers at-
tractive but not long lasting. Trusses tend to hang over instead of
remaining upright. A. M. (RHS) 1933.

Lake Labish

Rating 4/3   'Lady Bligh' X 'Loderi Venus'; R. Henny. Plant
Hardy to +5   open growing, wider than tall. Leaves 5" X 2½",
Medium 6'   medium green. Flowers neyron rose, bowl shaped.
Mid-May   Truss tall, flowers well spaced. Stamens not fully
               formed. P. A. (ARS) 1955.

Award '55

Lamplighter

Rating 4/3
Hardy to 0
Medium 6'
Early May

1955.

'Britannia' X 'Madame Fr. J. Chauvin'; M. Koster and Sons, 1955. Compact, rounded plant with medium green leaves 6" X 2". Conical truss of large, light bright red flowers HCC 724, with a salmon glow, 10 to 12 per truss. F. C. C. (Boskoop)

Langley Park

Rating 3/2
Hardy to 0
Low 4½
Mid-May

'Queen Wilhelmina' X 'Stanley Davies'; C. B. van Nes and Sons before 1922. Plant bushy, broader than tall. The leaves are about 6" X 2", pointed, dark green, folded along mid-rib, and do not turn yellow in full sun. The deep red flowers, 2½" wide, are somewhat thin textured and, to last, need protection from the sun. The large, dome-shaped truss has 12 to 15 flowers. Roots readily.

Laura Aberconway g.

Rating 2/2
Hardy to +10
Tall 6+
Early May

R. griersonianum X 'Barclayi'; Aberconway, 1933. Plant is of rather tall, open habit. Leaves dark green above, with a light green under surface, rather thick and leathery. Flower color is geranium lake, corolla is funnel-shaped, expanding at mouth, some 2½" long X 3½" across, margin frilled. Truss is loose and contains about 9 flowers. A. M. (RHS) 1944.

Lavender Girl

Rating 3/3
Hardy to –5
Medium 6'
Early May

R. fortunei X 'Lady Grey Egerton'; Slocock, 1950. Plant habit is compact. The light green leaves are 3½" X 1½", slightly cupped and are held about three years. The 3" flowers are pale lavender, with a rose margin and white center, and make up a small, dome-shaped truss. Takes full exposure. A. M. (RHS) 1950.

Lavender Queen

Rating 1/4
Hardy to –5
Medium 4½
Mid-May

A Shammarello hybrid. Plant a vigorous, bushy grower with shiny, dark green leaves. Flowers small, light bluish lavender, slightly ruffled, with faint brown blotch.

Leaburg

Rating 4/3   *R. dichroanthum* X 'Penjerrick'; Phetteplace.
Hardy to 0   Very compact plant habit. Foliage glossy dark,
Semi-dwarf   green, leaves 2½" X 1½". Flowers brilliant, waxy,
Mid April   blood red in a flat top truss. P. A. (ARS) 1956.

Award '56
3' x

Lenape

Rating 3/2   *R. pubescens* X *R. keiskei;* Nearing, exhibited
Hardy to –10 1950. Leaves to 3" X ½", dark bronze green, hairy.
Semi-dwarf   Flowers are small, light yellow, in tight trusses.
Early April   Floriferous and roots easily.

3' x

Leo g.

Rating 5/3   'Britannia' X *R. elliottii;* Rothschild. A dome
Hardy to –5   shaped plant, wide as tall, with foliage to the
Medium 6'   ground. The 7" x 3" dark green leaves, with traces
Mid-May   of indumentum on the underside, are oblong-
              elliptic in shape. The 2½" waxy flowers are cam-
panulate in shape, dark cranberry red in color, and are carried in
a full, tight dome-shaped truss of 20 to 24 flowers. This is a good
foliage plant with an excellent blossom—one of the finest reds.
A.M. (RHS) 1948. The A.M. form is the one being grown in the
Northwest.

Leona

Rating 4/3   'Corona' X 'Dondis'; R. Henny. Plant open grow-
Hardy to 0   ing. Leaves medium green, 5" X 2". Flowers large,
Medium 6'   open, a rich pink. Truss dome shaped. Roots
Mid-May   easily.

Letty Edwards g.

Rating 3/3   *R. campylocarpum* var. *elatum* X *R. fortunei;*
Hardy to 0   Clarke. Rounded, medium compact bush, with
Medium 6'   medium green leaves, 5" X 2", with red-brown
Early May   petiole. Flowers pale sulfur yellow. Round truss
              of 9 to 11 flowers. A.M. (RHS) 1946 and F.C.C.
(RHS) 1948. The form grown in the U.S.A. appears to be one clone.
Needs partial shade. Bovee; lovely

Little Ben g.

Rating 3/3   *R. neriiflorum* X *R. forrestii* var. *repens;* C. R.
Hardy to +10 Scrase-Dickins. Plant habit is dense, low grow-
Dwarf   ing. Leaves stiff and a good dark green, some 2½"
Late April   X 1¼". Deep scarlet cluster of bell shaped flowers.
              F. C. C. (RHS) 1937.

1½' x

Little Bert

Rating 3/3
Hardy to +10
¹/₂ x Dwarf
Late April

R. forrestii var. *repens* X *R. euchaites;* C. R. Scrase-Dickins. Leaves are elliptic-ovate, rounded at each end, and may be up to 3 inches long by 1½" wide. Shining, crimson scarlet flowers, bell shaped with spreading lobes, 2 inches across and 1½" long, are carried in clusters of 4 or 5 in a rather loose truss. A. M. (RHS) 1939.

Little Bill

Rating 2/3
Hardy to +5
3' x Semi-dwarf
Late April

R. williamsianum X 'Lady Stuart of Wortley'; Robert Wallace 1934. Plant medium compact, dome shaped; leaves with reddish petioles, narrower than most hybrids of *R. williamsianum*. Flowers somewhat trumpet shaped, deep rose pink, few, in a rather lax truss. Seldom blooms when very young.

Little Gem, may, red, +5, 1½'

Little Joe g.

Rating 3/3
Hardy to +5
1½' x Dwarf
Late April

R. forrestii var. *repens* X 'May Day'; Brandt 1951. Plant is compact, wider than tall, with elliptic, dark green leaves 1½" X 1". Flowers bright red, 3 to 4 to a truss. Requires some shade. Strikes easily from cuttings. A number of forms are on the market, some being dwarf, some spreading or creeping, while others may be quite vigorous, mostly bright red.

Little Pudding

Rating 3/3
Hardy to +5
ward '53 Medium 6'
Mid May

R. decorum X 'Fabia'; R. Henny. Leaves elliptic about 3½" long, upper surface dark green, slightly grooved, under surface covered with a thin indumentum. Flowers camellia rose on the outer lobes, shade to near chinese coral in the throat, usually 10-13 loosely held in a terminal umbel. Flowers campanulate, 4" wide, 2" long with 5 to 7 lobes. Stamens white, 10 in number and uneven in length. Plant is slow growing and somewhat irregular in habit. Rooting is accomplished with medium difficulty. P. A. (ARS) 1953.

Little Sheba

Rating 3/4
1½' Hardy to +5
x Dwarf
ward '54 Early May

('Earl of Athlone' X 'Fabia') X *R. forrestii* var. *repens;* R. Henny. Very low growing, prostrate. Leaves 2¼" x 1", dark green, somewhat lighter on the underside. Three blood red flowers, 2" wide, 1" long in a terminal umbel. Vigorous

grower after becoming established. Likes well drained spot with
afternoon shade, but does not mind wind. Roots easily. P. A. (ARS)
1954.

Lodauric g.

Rating 3/3   'Loderi' g. X *R. auriculatum;* G. Taylor for Sir J.
Hardy to –5   Ramsden, exhibited by Crosfield in 1939. Plant,
Tall ᏝᏛ   vigorous, broader than tall, with 9″ X 3″ pointed,
Late June   light green leaves, with texture like *R. auricula-
              tum.* The 3½″ wide by 2″ deep flowers are trumpet-
shaped, white, with yellowish throat, slightly crinkled and have a
spicy fragrance. They last relatively well in the sun. The truss is
loose but not floppy, about 7″ to 8″ wide. The clone 'Iceberg' has a
greenish throat and received an A. M. (RHS) 1958.

Loderi g.

Rating 5/4   *R. griffithianum* X *R. fortunei;* Loder, about 1901.
Hardy to 0   There are 32 named clones of this group in the
Tall ᏝᏛ   International Register, of which 'Loderi King
Early May   George', is the best known in this country. These
              are rounded, upright, rather open plants with
thick branches which need sun and wind protection to be at their
best. The smooth, moderately dark green leaves are up to 8″ x 3″.
The large flowers are very fragrant, and make up a very large,
tall, slightly open truss. 'Loderi King George' is pink in bud, opening to white. 'Loderi Venus' and 'Loderi Pink Diamond' are shell
pink. Several have received RHS awards, the first in 1914.

Loder's White   8 ᵗʰ Choice in Seattle

Rating 5/5   Probably *R. arboreum* var. *album* X *R. griffithia-
Hardy to 0   num;* Mangles. Plant compact, wider than tall.
ᏝᏛ Medium   Leaves 6″ X 2½″, bright green. Flowers large,
Late April   delicate pink in bud, changing to white, slightly
              scented. Vigorous, free blooming. An easy doer.
A. M. (RHS) 1911, A. G. M. (RHS) 1931.

              Boree: one of Best white's

Logan Damaris

Rating 4/3   'Dr. Stocker' X *R. campylocarpum;* Stevenson.
Hardy to +5   Upright habit, wtih 5″ X 2″, light green leaves.
Low ᏝᏛ   Flowers lemon yellow, 3″ across. Medium sized,
Late April   round, rather loose truss of 9 to 11 flowers. A. M.
              (RHS) 1948. Several other forms of the 'Damaris'
group have been named in England but it is not known if they are

in the U. S. A. They include 'Cornish Cracker', 'Cream Cracker', and 'Townhill Damaris'.

Lord Roberts

Rating 2/3 — Parentage unknown; Mason. A vigorous plant, Hardy to –10 rounded upright in sun; in shade it is leggy and Medium 6′ doesn't bloom well. The leaves are 5″ X 2″, pointed Late May and dark green with heavy veining. The 2″ flowers are dull red with black blotch in a ball-shaped truss. Roots readily.

Louis Pasteur

Rating 3/1 — 'Mrs. Tritton' X 'Viscount Powerscourt'; L. J. Hardy to –5 Endtz and Co., 1923. Plant spreading. Flowers bicolor, red and white in a solid, dome-shaped truss. Medium 6′ color, red and white in a solid, dome-shaped truss. Late May Hard to propagate.

Lucky Strike

Rating 4/2 — *R. griersonianum* X 'Countess of Derby'; Van Hardy to +5 Veen. Foliage dull green, leaves 6″ X 2″. For best Medium 6′ results, should be grown in partial shade. Large Late May funnel shaped flowers of deep salmon pink in good conical truss.

Luscombei Leonardslee—see Pride of Leonardslee

Madame Carvalho

Rating 1/3 — A *R. catawbiense* hybrid; J. Waterer 1866. Dark Hardy to –15 green foliage, leaves 5″ X 2½″. Ball type truss Medium 6′ of white flowers with greenish spots. June

Madame de Bruin

Rating 3/2 — 'Prometheus' X 'Doncaster'; M. Koster and Sons, Hardy to –10 1904. This is a vigorous plant, taller than wide, Medium 6′ twigs break off easily. The pointed, 5″ X 2″ leaves Late May turn yellow in the sun, but the plant will not bloom well in shade. The 2″ flowers are cerise red, thin, and do not hold up in the sun. The ball shaped truss is about 4″ X 5″. It roots easily.

Madame Fr. J. Chauvin

Rating 4/3   A *R. fortunei* hybrid; M. Koster and Sons, 1916.
Hardy to –10   Upright habit, vigorous, with light green leaves,
Medium *6'*   7" X 1¾". Flowers rosy pink, paler in the throat,
Mid-May   with a small red blotch. Round truss. A. M.
                         (RHS) 1933.

Marchioness of Lansdowne

Rating 3/3   A *R. maximum* hybrid; A. Waterer, before 1915.
Hardy to –15   Plant spreading, rather open, with 4" x 1½"
Medium *6'*   leaves. Flowers pale violet rose with an almost
June   black blotch, rather small, but in a neat dome
                         shaped truss.

Marcia

Rating 4/3   *R. campylocarpum* X 'Gladys'; Swaythling. Up-
Hardy to 0   right, slow growing, with medium green leaves,
Low *4½*   3½" X 1¾". Flowers bright primrose yellow.
Early May   Round truss of 8 to 10 flowers. Should be grown
                         in shade. F. C. C. (RHS) 1944.

Margaret Dunn Talisman

Rating 3/3   *R. discolor* X 'Fabia'; J. Henny. Medium green
Hardy to 0   leaves 6" X 1½". Flowers narrow, funnel shaped,
Medium *6'*   apricot colored. Flat topped truss.
June

Maricee

Award '60

Rating 4/4   A selected form of *R. sargentianum;* Caperci, 1959.
Hardy to 0   Dwarf, twiggy plant, with medium green leaves,
1½' X Dwarf   ¾" x ¼", densely scaly below, shiny above. Very
Early May   small, creamy white flowers, in a few-flowered
                         truss. This variety is easier and faster growing
than the usual *R. sargentianum,* very floriferous. A. E. (ARS)
1959.

Mariloo g.

Rating 4/2   'Dr. Stocker' X *R. lacteum;* Rothschild, 1941. Form
Hardy to +10   A—Slower not quite so vigorous, leaves 6" X 3",
Tall *6+*   flat, dark green. Flowers pale, clear yellow in a
Mid-April   round truss. Form B—Leaves 6½" X 4", recurved,
                         light green, heavy texture. First year stems are
quite thick. Flowers cream colored with crimson spotting, in a
large round truss.

Marine

Rating 3/3	A *R. augustinii* selection; Bovee. Plant typical-
Tall ↳+	ly slender until quite mature. Leaves 2″ X 1″,
Hardy to +10	medium green. Flowers lavender blue, flat. Truss
Late April	three flowered, outward facing. P.A. 1960.

Marinus Koster

Rating 4/3	A *R. griffithianum* hybrid; M. Koster and Sons,
Hardy to –5	1937. Plant habit, upright; leaves 7″ X 2½″, shiny,
Tall ↳+	dark green. Corolla pink with brown spotting.
Mid-May	Flowers to 5″ across X 3″ deep, campanulate,
	10 to 12 in a dome-shaped truss. Plant takes full

exposure. Roots easily. Resistant to pests. A. M. (RHS) 1937, F. C. C. (RHS) 1948.

Mars

Rating 4/3	*R. griffithianum* X (?); Waterer, Sons and Crisp
Hardy to –10	before 1875. Slow growing, rather compact, reach-
Low 4½	ing 4-5 ft. in 10 years. Flowers flat, deep true red
Late May	with light colored, outstanding stamens. Compact,
	conical to dome shaped truss. While the plant is

hardy it seems to prefer some protection from afternoon sun. Roots easily, requiring a bit of extra time in the bed. Awarded A. M. (RHS) in 1928 and F. C. C. in 1935 after trial at Exbury.

Maryke

Rating 4/3	*R. discolor* X 'Fabia'; Van Veen. Compact plant
Hardy to 0	habit. Foliage light green, leaves 6″ X 2½″. Flower
Medium ↳′	color a blend of pink and yellow; size large. Truss
Late May	upright, lax, leans toward the light. Prolific
	bloomer.

Max Sye

Rating 2/3	A 'Chevalier Felix de Sauvage' hybrid; C. Frets
Hardy to 0	& Son, about 1935. Plant rather open and spread-
Low 4½	ing; leaves to 6″ x 1¾″, somewhat channeled,
Mid-May	medium dark green. Flowers red with a dark
	blotch, in a dome shaped truss.

May Day

Rating 4/3	*R. haematodes* X *R. griersonianum*. This cross was
Hardy to +5	made by A. M. Williams, whose plant received the
Low 4½	A. M., Lord Aberconway (Bodnant Form) who
Late April	exhibited it in 1939, and Rothschild (Exbury May
	Day). The A. M. form, most prevalent in the

Northwest, tends to be a rapid grower with a good dark green leaf color. Leaves are oblanceolate with a tawny indumentum, 3 to 4″ long and 1¼″ wide. As the plant becomes older it tends to slow its growth and becomes broader than high. The bright orange scarlet flowers, in a lax truss, are borne in abundance. Roots easily. A. M. (RHS) 1932.

Meadowbrook

Rating 3/3   'Mrs. C. S. Sargent' X 'Everestianum'; Vossberg,
Hardy to –15 1928. Plant habit fair. Flowers deep pink, fimbri-
Medium 6′   ated.
Late May

Medusa g.

Rating 3/3   *R. scyphocalyx* x *R. griersonianum;* Aberconway,
Hardy to +5   cross in 1928. Plant upright, rounded, very dense
Low 4 ½   and compact. Leaves 3½″ x 1¼″, dark green, with
Mid-May   light colored indumentum. Flowers long bell
              shaped, pendant, in flat topped, lax trusses, color
buff-orange with fine vermilion network of lines overall.

Mevrouw P.A. Colijn

Rating 3/3   'Mrs. E. C. Stirling' X 'Madame de Bruin'; M.
Hardy to –10 Koster and Sons. Compact plant habit; leaves dark
Low 4 ½   green, 4½″ X 2″. Flowers clear pink in a compact,
Late May   conical truss.

Michael Waterer

Rating 2/3   A *R. ponticum* hybrid; J. Waterer before 1894.
Hardy to –15 Plant habit very compact. Leaves medium green,
Medium 6′   4″ X 1″. Small flowers of magenta red in a round-
June   ed, ball type truss. Roots easily.

Mission Bells

Rating 3/4   *R. williamsianum* X *R. orbiculare;* Lancaster.
4½′ Hardy to –5 Compact shrub; leaves 4″ X 1½″, shiny, held for
X Low   2 years. Flowers, pale pink, slightly fragrant,
Early May   2½″ wide, campanulate 6 to 8 in a lax truss.
              Takes full exposure. Roots easily.

Miss Olympia

Award 6 Rating 4/4   'Loderi King George' X *R. williamsianum;* cross
Hardy to 0   made by Endre Ostbo, raised and introduced by
Low 4 ½   Roy Clark. Flowers up to 4″ wide, blush pink with
Mid May   darker pink in throat.

Mohamet g.

Rating 3/3   *R. dichroanthum* X 'Tally Ho'; Rothschild. Plant
Hardy to +5   upright spreading, moderately open; dark green
Medium 6   leaves, 5" x 1¾", with thin indumentum. Flowers
Late May   bell shaped in rather lax truss. Described as red
in the International Register, the clones being
grown in the Northwest are a deep salmon pink and an orange
red. It often produces a fair crop of attractive flowers in the fall.
A. M. (RHS) 1945.

Monsieur Guillemot

Rating 2/3   Parentage unknown; Moser. Plant upright, fairly
Hardy to –10   compact, leaves 4½" X 2", dark green, recurved,
Medium 6'   slightly shiny. Flowers dark rose, in a compact
June   truss, holding good color in the sun. Has been sold
in the U. S. A. as 'Madame Guillemot'.

Montchanin

Rating 3/3   *R. pubescens* X *R. keiskei;* Nearing. Graceful
Hardy to –15   habit. Flowers small, white, profusely borne.
Semi-dwarf
Late April

Moonstone g.

Rating 4/4   *R. campylocarpum* X *R. williamsianum;* J. C. Wil-
Hardy to –5   liams, 1933. The plant forms a compact mound,
Semi-dwarf   wider than tall and well covered with foliage to
Mid April   the ground. The oval, smooth, flat, medium green
leaves are approximately 2½" X 1¾". The flowers
are pale cream yellow, to 2½" across, open bell shaped, in lax
trusses of 3 to 5, that cover the plant. Best with afternoon shade.
This is one of the best yellow flowered semi-dwarfs, being a good
foliage plant and a prolific bloomer.

Moontide

Rating 3/2   *R. wardii* X 'Loder's White'; R. Henny, 1955. Plant
Hardy to 0   is upright, rounded, slightly open. The flat, oblong
Low 4½   elliptic, medium green leaves are approximately
Late April   4" X 2". The flowers are white, to 3½" across, fun-
nel shaped and 14 to 16 in a full rounded truss.
Requires afternoon shade to be at its best. P. A. (ARS) 1955.

Moser's Maroon

Rating 2/3   Parentage unknown; Moser and Fils. A vigorous
Hardy to –10 grower, but tends to sprawl.the new leaves and
Medium *6'*   stems are rosy red; the stems change to wine
Late May   red and the leaves retain a red cast. The mature
              leaves are 5" X 2", heavily ribbed, blunt tipped
and slightly waved. The 1½" flowers are deep wine red, not
distinctive, and make a tight 5" X 4" truss. This grows well in
full sun but does not bud well until about 4' in height. It
roots readily. A. M. (RHS) 1932.

Mother of Pearl

Rating 4/3   Sport of 'Pink Pearl'; J. Waterer, 1925. Like 'Pink
Hardy to 0   Pearl' in all respects except flowers open shell
Medium *6'*   pink fading to pure white, with very faint brown-
Mid-May   ish green spots on upper lobe. A. M. (RHS) 1930.

Mrs. A. F. McEwan

Rating 3/3   A seedling of 'Loderi' g., received from H. G. Ihrig
Hardy to –5   in 1940, grown and exhibited by Univ. of Washing-
Tall *6 †*   ton Arboretum. Plant compact, round pyramidal;
Early May   leaves shiny green, glaucous below to 7" x 2½".
              Flowers fuchsine pink to persian rose, with a
white throat, to 5" in diameter, in a lax, dome shaped truss. Should
have some shade. A. E. (ARS) 1956.

Award '56

Mrs. A. T. de la Mare

Rating 3/4   'Sir Charles Butler' X 'Halopeanum'; C. B. van
Hardy to –10 Nes and Sons. Leaves dark green, 7" X 2½".
Medium *6'*   Flowers 3½" to 4" across, white, with greenish
Mid-May   spot, slightly fragrant, somewhat thin texture, 12
              to 14 flowers in a dome shaped truss about 7"
across. Plant takes full exposure. A. M. (RHS) 1958.

Mrs. Betty Robertson

Rating 3/3   'Mrs. Lindsay Smith' X a *R. campylocarpum* hy-
Hardy to +5   brid; M. Koster and Sons, cross made in 1920.
Low *4'½*   Compact growing, leaves 4" X 2", tapering to a
Early May   sharp tip, longitudinally convex. Flowers pale
              yellow with a red center, of medium size, in a
compact, dome-shaped truss. Best results in partial shade.

Mrs. C. B. van Nes

Rating 2/2   'Princess Juliana' X 'Florence Smith'; C. B. van
Hardy to +5   Nes and Sons. Plant medium to open habit, leaves
Medium   light green, 5" X 3". Rosy red buds, opening al-
Late April   most red and rapidly fading to light pink.

Mrs. Charles E. Pearson

Rating 4/4   'Coombe Royal' X 'Catawbiense Grandiflorum';
Hardy to –5   M. Koster and Sons 1909. Plant of medium com-
Tall   pactness. Leaves 6" X 2½", dark green. Flowers
Mid-May   pale blush pink, shaded orchid, light brown spots.
Truss dome shaped, large. Roots easily. A vigorous
grower, attractive the year round. A. M. (RHS) 1933, F. C. C.
(RHS) Wisley Trials 1955.

Mrs. Charles S. Sargent

Rating 3/3   A *R. catawbiense* hybrid; A. Waterer, 1888. Mod-
Hardy to –25 erately compact, rounded plant. Flowers car-
Tall   mine rose, yellow throat, margins waved, in a
Late May   compact, dome shaped truss. One of the best of
the ironclads.

Mrs. Donald Graham

Rating 3/2   ('Crona' X *R. grersonianum*) X 'Loderi' g. cross
Hardy to +5   by Rose, named by Ostbo. Upright, open grow-
Medium   ing plant with medium green leaves, 7" X 2¼".
Early June   Flowers deep salmon pink. Open, flat topped truss
of about 9 flowers. P. A. (ARS) 1954.

Mrs. E. C. Stirling

Rating 4/4   A *R. griffithianum* hybrid; J. Waterer. Plant up-
Hardy to –5   right at first, later spreading, fairly open; leaves
Tall   medium light green, 6" X 2". Flowers blush pink,
Early May   shaded orchid, slightly frilled, of medium size in
a tall conical truss. The stamens extend well out
and curve up giving an appearance of lightness to the truss.
A. M. (RHS) 1906.

Mrs. Furnival

Rating 5/5   *R. griffithianum* hybrid X *R. caucasicum* hybrid;
Hardy to –10 A. Waterer; named about 1920. Plant compact.
Medium   Leaves 4" X 1¾", dark green. Flowers widely
Late May   funnel-shaped, pink, sienna blotch. Truss dome-
shaped, nicely spaced. Does not root very easily.

Mrs. G. W. Leak

Rating 4/4 'Coombe Royal' X 'Chevalier Felix de Sauvage';
Hardy to +5 M. Koster and Sons, 1916. Tall vigorous plant with
Tall 6+ dull grayish olive green leaves. Clear light pink
Late April flowers, with brownish purple blotch; in a tall
   compact truss. Roots easily, will grow in sun or
shade. F. C. C. (RHS) 1934.

Mrs. Horace Fogg

Rating 4/4 *R. griersonianum* X 'Loderi Venus'; Larson. Plant
Hardy to 0 fairly compact, stands full sun. Flowers medium
Medium 6' pink, frosted, throat nearly red, very large, in an
May upright truss. P. A. (ARS) 1964.

Mrs. J. C. Williams

Rating 4/3 An A. Waterer introduction of unknown parent-
Medium 6' age. Plant upright spreading, dense, twiggy, with
Hardy to –15 leaves 6" x 1¾", that are slightly rough. Flowers
June white with small blotch of reddish dots, frilled,
   in compact dome shaped truss. Rather slow to
start blooming. Roots easily.

Mrs. Lindsay Smith

Rating 4/1 'George Hardy' X 'Duchess of Edinburgh'; M.
Hardy to 0 Koster and Sons, 1910. Plant, upright, open, some-
Medium 6' times pendant. Leaves 5½" X 2", light green.
Mid-May Flowers white, slightly spotted red on upper lobe,
   large, flat. Truss large, upright. A fine truss on a
poor plant. A. M. (RHS) 1933.

Mrs. Lionel de Rothschild

Rating 4/2 Raised by A. Waterer, and a bright pink, accord-
Hardy to 0 ing to the Rhododendron Register. The clone sold
Medium 6' under this name in the Northwest has a white
Mid-May flower with a blotch of carmine spots. This is the
   one rated here.

Mrs. Mary Ashley

Rating 3/3 A *R. campylocarpum* hybrid; W. C. Slocock. Plant
Hardy to +5 of medium vigor, compact. Leaves 3" X 1½", oval
Medium 6' and medium green. Flowers salmon pink, shaded
Late April cream, in a medium sized, dome shaped truss.
   Plant resembles 'Unique' but not quite as com-
   pact.

Mrs. P. D. Williams

Rating 3/2   Parentage unknown, introduced by A. Waterer.
Hardy to –10   Plant fairly upright when small, then inclined to
Medium 6'   sprawl, seems to have a weak trunk-root connec-
June   tion and may flop over unless staked when young,
becoming more sturdy later. Leaves very dark
green, smooth, base very narrow, to 5½″ X 1½″. Flowers ivory
white with large golden brown blotch, medium size, in a tight
rounded truss. A.M. (RHS) 1936. This variety has occasionally
been confused with 'Mrs. J. C. Williams' in some nurseries.

Mrs. Philip Martineau

Rating 4/2   Parentage unknown, introduced by Knap Hill
Hardy to –5   Nursery Co. Loose, sprawly habit, with medium
Tall 6+   green leaves 6″ X 2½″. Flowers rose pink fading
Early June   lighter, with pale yellow blotch in a fairly large
            round truss. A. M. (RHS) 1933, F. C. C. (RHS)
1936.

Mrs. R. S. Holford

Rating 3/3   Parentage unknown; A. Waterer, 1866. Plant up-
Hardy to –15   right, rounded, leaves medium green, 5″ X 2″.
Medium 6'   Flowers rosy salmon, to 2½″ across, in a tight
Late May   truss.

Mrs. Tom H. Lowinsky

Rating 3/4   *R. griffithianum* x 'White Pearl'; probably an A.
Hardy to –10   Waterer cross, raised by Lowinsky. Plant round-
Medium 6'   ish, medium compact with very dark green, lus-
June   trous leaves, to 6″ x 2½″, inclined to be convex.
            Flowers open blush, soon white, with large, red-
dish brown blotch, in a good rounded truss. Blooms early and regu-
larly, roots easily, quite heat tolerant and generally adaptable.
Listed by the International Register as a group but its origin
might indicate otherwise, at least there is presumably only one
clone in the U.S.A., from 2 plants brought here in 1947. A. M.
(RHS) 1919.

Mrs. Walter Burns

Rating 3/3   'Standishii' X *R. griffithianum;* Lowinsky. Vig-
Hardy to 0   orous, upright, with dark green leaves, 4½″ X
Tall 6+   1½″. Flowers light pink, slightly deeper along
Early May   edges of petals, deep pink blotch at base of upper
            petals. A. M. (RHS) 1931.

Mrs. W. R. Coe

Rating 3/3   Probably a *R. fortunei* hybrid; exhibited by Dex-
Hardy to –5   ter. Leaves glossy, dark green, flowers deep bril-
Medium 6'   liant pink, with crimson throat, over 4" across in
Mid-May   a very large dome shaped truss.

Naomi g.

'Aurora' X *R. fortunei;* Rothschild, 1926. Ten clones have been named according to the International Register. In addition to those described here, the following clones are known to be available in the Northwest: 'Naomi Carissima', 'Naomi Early Dawn', 'Naomi Hope', 'Naomi Nautilus', A. M. (RHS) 1938, 'Naomi Nereid', 'Naomi Pink Beauty', 'Naomi Stella Maris' F. C. C. (RHS) 1939.

Naomi Astarte

Rating 4/4   'Aurora' X *R. fortunei;* Rothschild. Medium com-
Hardy to –10   pact shrub habit, leaves 7" X 3", rounded at ends.
Tall 6+   Flowers light pink, shading inward to yellow,
Early May   deeper yellow in throat. Not easy to root.

Naomi Exbury

Rating 4/4   'Aurora' X *R. fortunei;* Rothschild. Medium com-
Hardy to –10   pact shrub, leaves to 7" X 3", rounded at both ends.
Tall 6+   Flowers with lilac edges, going to straw yellow in
Early May   throat, in a good truss. Good substance. A. M.
                (RHS) 1933.

Naomi Glow

Hardy to –10   'Aurora' X *R. fortunei;* Rothschild. Plant medium
Rating 4/4   compact, leaves to 7" X 3", rounded at both ends.
Tall 6+   Flowers large, glowing bright pink, in a dome-
Early May   shaped truss. Perhaps the only 'Naomi' producing
                near a clear single color.

Naomi Pixie

Rating 4/4   'Aurora' X *R. fortunei;* Rothschild. Plant medium
Hardy to –10   compact a bit more vigorous than the other
Tall 6+   'Naomis', leaves to 7" X 3", rounded at both ends.
Early May   Flowers large, of bright pink, stained deep crim-
                son in the throat, long lasting, in a dome shaped
truss.

Nereid g.

Rating 3/4   *R. neriiflorum* X *R. dichroanthum;* Wilding 1934.
Hardy to 0   Very compact plant habit. Leaves dark green,
Dwarf   roundish oblong, 1½″ X 1″. Bell-shaped, peach
Late May   colored flowers, about an inch wide and an inch
long. Flat-topped truss.

Nestucca

Rating 4/4   *R. fortunei* X *R. yakusimanum;* cross by F. Han-
Hardy to –10   ger, named by C. C. Smith. Plant very compact
Semi-dwarf   and rigid. Leaves 5″ X 1½″, dark green. Flowers
Early May   bowl shaped, white with brown traces in throat.
Truss done-shaped. No indumentum. P.A. (ARS)
1960.

Nobleanum Coccineum

Rating 2/2   *R. caucasicum* x *R. arboreum.* This cross, first
Hardy to 0   made, by A. Waterer in 1835 was later made by
Medium   others; source of this particular clone is not
March   known. Plant somewhat sprawling with upright
shoots; leaves to about 5″ x 1½″, tending to roll.
Flowers scarlet, medium size, in a small rounded truss.

Nobleanum Venustum

Rating 2/2   *R. caucasicum* x *R. arboreum;* Smith. Plant tends
Hardy to 0   to be open, somewhat spreading, leaves tend to
Medium   roll, 5″ x 1½″. Flowers rose pink, medium size,
March   in small rounded truss.

Norman Gill

Rating 5/3   'Beauty of Tremough' X *R. griffithianum;* R. Gill
Hardy to +5   and Son. Plant habit vigorous. Leaves 5″ X 2½″.
Tall   Best results in partial shade. Flowers, very large,
Late May   white, with red basal blotch, in a tall truss. A. M.
(RHS) 1922.

Nova Zembla

Rating 3/3   'Parson's Grandiflorum' X a hardy red hybrid; M.
Hardy to –20   Koster and Sons, 1902. Plant vigorous, upright.
Medium   Flowers dark red. Said to be heat tolerant.
Early May

Nymph g.

Rating 3/3   *R. forrestii* var. *repens* X 'Largo'; Aberconway,
1½' Hardy to +5   1936, introduced in 1946. Plant habit dwarf, spread-
X Dwarf   ing. Dark green leaves. Flowers deep red.
Early April

Old Port

Rating 2/2   A *R. catawbiense* hybrid; A. Waterer 1865. Open
Hardy to –15   plant habit, vigorous, leaves medium green, 5" X
Medium 6'   2½". Flowers deep plum color, not as dark as
Early May   'Purple Splendour', in a compact, ball shaped
                 truss.

Ole Olson

Rating 4/3   *R. campylocarpum* var. *elatum* X *R. discolor;*
Hardy to 0   named by Lem. Upright, open habit with leaves
Tall 6+   4" X 2", medium green. Flowers pale yellow in a
Mid-May   loose truss. This is the same cross as the 'Lady
                 Bessborough' group.

Olympic Lady g.

Rating 4/4   'Loderi King George' X *R. williamsianum;* Ostbo,
Hardy to 0   raised and introduced by Clark. The plant forms
4½' Low   a fairly compact, spreading mound, wider than
Early April   tall. The flat, smooth, medium dark green, ovate
                 leaves are approximately 3" X 2¼", light green
beneath and with a reddish petiole. The light pink flowers are open
cup shaped, to 4" across, in a lax truss of 4 - 5. They fade to almost
white as they mature. A nicely shaped foliage plant that covers
itself with bloom. Bovee : 3 ft in 10yrs, considerable sun.

Parsons Gloriosum

Rating 2/2   A *R. catawbiense* hybrid; raised by A. Waterer,
Hardy to –25   introduced by Parsons about 1860. Compact habit,
Medium 6'   dark green leaves 6" X 2½". Flowers lavender,
Late May   shaded pink, in a compact conical truss.

Parson's Grandiflorum

Rating 1/3   A *R. catawbiense* hybrid, raised by A. Waterer,
Hardy to –25   introduced by Parsons, 1875. Plant fair as to
Medium 6'   habit and foliage. Flowers purplish rose.
Late May

Peachblow

Rating 3/3　　Probably a species, may be from the collector's
Hardy to 0　　number KW5659 which is listed as *R. hirtipes;*
4 ½ Low　　　　Barto, named and introduced by Wright. Growth
Late April　　habit compact, leaves 3″ X 1½″, light green with
　　　　　　　pinkish yellow petiole and yellowish midrib.
Flowers apricot, fading to primrose yellow. Should have some
shade.

Peach Lady

Rating 3/3　　　'Nereid' X *R. discolor;* cross by Rose, raised and
Hardy to –10　named by Lancaster. Plant upright rounded,
Low 4 ½　　　leaves medium green, 6″ X 1½″. Flowers peach
Late May　　　colored, edged camellia rose, with yellow eye, to
　　　　　　　4″ across, 12 in a rounded truss. Heat and sun
tolerant. Roots easily.

PeeKsboo, red, May, 1½', +5°

Penjerrick g.

Rating 4/3　　*R. campylocarpum* var. *elatum* X *R. griffithianum;*
Hardy to +15　S. Smith. Upright habit, with 5″ X 2″, medium
Tall 6+　　　　green leaves. Large plants have smooth barked
Mid-April　　　trunk. Flowers tubular campanulate, good sub-
　　　　　　　stance, white, pale yellow or pink in a loose truss.
One form received the A. M. (RHS) 1923.

Pera g.

Rating 3/3　　　*R. pemakoense* x *R. racemosum;* Lem 1948. Plant
1½ · Hardy to –5　compact, twiggy. Leaves oblong, rounded. Flowers
X Dwarf　　　lilac-pink, 1½″-2″, 5 to 6 in a flat top truss. Vigor
April　　　　　good, a very heavy bloomer. Stands full sun.
　　　　　　　There is another variety of the same name by
Aberconway.

Peter Koster

Rating 2/3　　　'George Hardy' X a 'Doncaster' hybrid; M. Koster
Hardy to –5　　and Sons, 1895. Leaves flat. Flowers magenta red,
Medium 6′　　edged a lighter shade, in a good solid truss.
Mid-May

Pilgrim g.
Rating 4/3   R. *fortunei* X 'Gill's Triumph'; Johnston. Plant
Hardy to 0   fast growing, open and vigorous. Leaves 6" X 2",
Tall 6+   dark green. Flowers large, rich pink with few
Mid-May   dark markings. Truss very large, dome-shaped.
                  Not very easy to root. A. M. (RHS) 1926.

Pink Pearl
Rating 3/3   'George Hardy' X 'Broughtonii'. One of our older
Hardy to –5   and best known hybrids, produced by J. Waterer.
Tall 6+   The plant is a free and open grower, and its
Mid May   leaves, about 5" X 2", tend to be light green.
                  Flowers open a soft rose pink in a full upright
truss, then fade to a blush. Roots easily and does not seem to
mind a bit of sun. A. M. (RHS) 1897, F. C. C. (RHS) 1900.

Pink Perfection
Rating 3/3   'Duchess of Edinburgh' x 'Princess Alexandra';
Hardy to –15   Van Houtte. Plant resembles 'Pink Pearl' but
Medium 6'   slightly more compact, rounded, leaves 6" X
Early May   2½". Flowers pale pink with a lilac tinge.

Pink Twins
Rating 4/3   R. *catawbiense* X R. *haematodes;* Gable. Plant
Hardy to –15   slow growing, compact, broader than high, leaves
Low 4¼   ovate elliptic. Flowers hose in hose, light shrimp
Late May   pink, fleshy, of good substance, 15 or more per
                  dome shaped truss.

Pinnacle
Rating 4/3   A pink R. *catawbiense* seedling X a pink R.
Hardy to –15   *catawbiense* seedling, exhibited by Shammarello
Tall 6+   in 1955. Well formed plant with good foliage.
Late May   Flowers glowing pink, delicate citron yellow
                  blotch, in a cone shaped truss.

Pioneer
Rating 2/3   Said to be a chance hybrid between 'Conemaugh'
Hardy to –20   and R. *mucronulatum;* Gable. Plant habit upright,
Medium 6'   responds well to cutting; semi-deciduous, 1½" x
March   1" leaves which tend to turn brown and cling to
                  twigs during winter. Flowers light mauve pink
about 1" in diameter, profusely produced.

P. J. M. g.

Rating 3/4   *R. carolinianum* X *R. dauricum;* P. J. Mezitt,
Hardy to –20 introduced in 1959. Plant compact and bushy.
Low 4½   Leaves 1⅝" X ⅞", medium green, mahogany
Early April   color in winter. Flowers light lavender purple
              10P 6/9, in a small truss. Very little fading. Plant
tolerant of sun, shade or drought. Blooms long lasting. Roots
with medium ease.

Polar Bear g.

Rating 3/3   *R. diaprepes* X *R. auriculatum;* Stevenson 1926.
Hardy to –10 Plant rather open, eventually wider than tall.
Tall 6+   Leaves heavily veined above, glaucous below, 7"
June   X 2". The flowers are fragrant, white with green
              throat, large, and 8 to 10 make up a somewhat
loose truss. Grows well in full sun or half shade but flowers last
better in part shade. One clone received the F.C.C. (RHS) in 1946.

Praecox g.

Rating 3/3   *R. ciliatum* X *R. dauricum;* exhibited by Davis in
Hardy to –5   1860. Upright, compact habit, leaves medium
Medium 6'   green, 2" X 1", slightly shiny, thin, with incon-
March   spicuous scales. Flowers, rosy lilac, small, 3 to
              4 flowered truss. A. G. M. (RHS) 1926.

Pride of Leonardslee

Rating 3/4   *R. fortunei* X *R. thomsonii;* Loder. Plant vigorous,
Hardy to 0   rounded, upright with medium green slightly
Tall 6+   shiny leaves, 4½" X 2¼". Flowers deep pink,
Mid-April   shaded mauve, in a loose, open-topped truss.
              Rather slow to bloom. Usually sold in the U.
S. A. as 'Luscombei' var. 'Leonardslee'. 'Luscombei' cross first
made by Luscombe and exhibited in 1880.

Princess Elizabeth

Rating 4/3   A 'Bagshot Ruby' hybrid; Waterer, Sons & Crisp,
Hardy to –10 1928. Plant erect, few branched, usually asymetri-
Tall 6+   cal, giving a rather striking form; leaves dark
June   green on reddish, thick shoots, tending to hang
              down, somewhat convex and bullate. Flowers
deep crimson in a large perfectly shaped conical truss. A.M.
(RHS) 1933.

Princess Juliana
Rating 3/3   A *R. griffithianum* hybrid; Otto Schultz, 1890,
Hardy to +5   introduced by van Nes. Flowers rose pink, fad-
Tall *6 +*   ing to white, in a tight truss. Sensitive to fertil-
Late April   izer.

Prize, April, pink, -15°, 3'

Professor F. Bettex
Rating 3/2   'Doncaster' X Atrosanguineum'; H. den Ouden
Hardy to –15 and Son, cross made about 1912. Good foliage.
Medium *6'*   Flowers brilliant red.
Mid May

Professor Hugo de Vries
Rating 4/3   'Pink Pearl' X 'Doncaster'; L. J. Endtz and Co.
Medium *6'*   Good foliage. Flowers pink, deeper than 'Pink
Hardy to –5   Pearl', in a large truss. Plant resembles 'Pink
Late May   Pearl'.

Professor J. H. Zaayer
Rating 3/1   'Pink Pearl' X a red *R. catawbiense* hybrid; L.
Hardy to –5   J. Endtz and Co. Plant vigorous, very sprawly,
Medium *6'*   leaves large, twisted, light green. Flowers light
Late May   red in a dome shaped truss.

Puget Sound
Rating 4/4   'Loderi King George' X 'Van Nes Sensation'; R.
Hardy to –5   W. Clark. Good vigorous plant habit, leaves dark
Tall *6 +*   green 6" X 2½". Very large pink flowers, slightly
Early May   tinged lilac, in a tall, well built truss.

Purple Emperor
Rating 2/2   A hybrid of 'Moser's Maroon'; Knap Hill Nursery.
Hardy to –5   Plant tall, open, usually only a few long shoots;
Tall *6+*   leaves 5½" X 1¾". Flowers dark purple, lighter
Late May   in throat, upper petal with black dots. Roots
              easily. A.M. (RHS) 1953.

Purple Gem
Rating 3/4   *R. fastigiatum* X *R. carolinianum;* Hardgrove.
Hardy to –15 Rounded dwarf shrub with medium green, scaly
Dwarf   leaves ¾" X ½". Small light purple flowers in
Mid-April   a small truss. Will grow in full sun.

Purple Splendour /2ᵗʰ choice in Seattle

Rating 4/3	A *R. ponticum* hybrid; A. Waterer, before 1900.
Hardy to –10	Compact growing plant, with convex, dark green
Medium	leaves with depressed midrib, 5¾" X 1½".
Late May	Large, ruffled, dark purple flowers with a black
	blotch, in a many-flowered, dome shaped truss.

Will grow in sun or shade. Roots easily. A.M. (RHS) 1931.

Purpureum Elegans

Rating 2/3	A *R. catawbiense* hybrid; H. Waterer, before
Hardy to –25	1850. Good plant habit and good foliage. Flowers
Tall 6+	purple.
Late May	

Purpureum Grandiflorum

Rating 2/3	A *R. catawbiense* hybrid; H. Waterer, before
Hardy to –20	1850. Large, attractive, convex leaves. Flowers
Medium 6'	medium purple, with a golden orange blotch.
Late May	

Pygmy, May, red, -5°, 1'

Queen Mary

Rating 3/4	'Marion' X 'Mrs. C. S. Sargent'; Felix and Dijk-
Hardy to 0	houis. Foliage shiny, leathery. Flowers pink (ben-
Medium 6'	gal rose). F. C. C. (Boskoop) 1948.
Early May	

Queen of Hearts g.

Rating 4/3	*R. meddianum* X 'Moser's Maroon'; Edmund de
Hardy to 0	Rothschild. Leaves are dark green, elliptic-lan-
Medium 6'	ceolate, 4" long and 2" broad, covered beneath
Late April	with loose brown tomentum. The dome shaped
	truss is made up of 16 flowers, of very dark

red, spotted with black on the three upper lobes. Tends to have branches not sturdy enough to hold the good sized trusses upright. A.M. (RHS) 1949.

Queen Wilhelmina

Rating 4/3	A *R. griffithianum* hybrid; Schulz 1890, introduc-
Hardy to +10	ed by C. B. van Nes and Sons in 1896. Buds are
Tall 6+	scarlet, opening to a beautiful pink. Old, but
Late April	still beautiful for a mild climate.

Racil

Rating 3/2	*R. racemosum* X *R. ciliatum;* exhibited N. S. Hol-
Hardy to –5	land 1937. Plant open at first, eventually compact.
3' x Semi-dwarf	Leaves 1¾" X 1". Flowers shell pink, small.
Early April	Truss 3 to 4 flowered. The plant covers itself
	with flowers. Roots easily.

Radium g.

Rating 4/3	*R. griersonianum* X 'Earl of Athlone'; Crosfield
Hardy to +5	1936. Upright, rather open habit of growth with
Medium *6'*	leaves, slightly shiny, 5" X 1¾". Flowers, gerani-
Mid May	um scarlet in a round, rather loose truss. Roots

easily. The same cross was made by Bolitho, who named 'Penalverne', formerly known as 'Radium' var. 'Penalverne'.

Ramapo

Rating 3/4	*R. fastigiatum* X *R. carolinianum;* Nearing, ex-
Hardy to –25	hibited 1940. Plant spreading, compact, leaves
Dwarf *1½*	attractive grayish cast, 1" X ¼". Flowers bright
Mid-April	violet pink. Roots easily.

Ray

Rating 3/3	*R. fortunei* X 'Idealist'; James. Flowers pale yel-
Award '56 Hardy to 0	low, 10 to 12 in a lax, ball shaped truss. Roots
Medium *6'*	easily. P.A. (ARS) 1956.
Mid-May	

Red Cloud

Rating 3/2	'Tally Ho' X 'Corona'; R. Henny. Plant habit open.
Hardy to +5	Leaves 5½" X 2½", medium green. Flowers
Award 53 Medium *6'*	medium size, claret rose to scarlet inside. Truss
Mid-May	many flowered, open dome shaped. Roots easily.
	P.A. (ARS) 1953.

Redwax

Rating 3/4	*R. haematodes* X 'May Day'; R. Henny. Low
Award '58 Hardy to +5	growing, spreading habit. Leaves oblanceolate,
3' x Semi-dwarf	3 inches long, dark green with heavy indumen-
Mid-May	tum. Flowers orient red, unspotted, funnel, cam-
	panulate, 2¼" wide, 1" long, 3 to 5 flowers in

a loose truss. Plant is a slow, dense grower, at its best in some shade. Roots easily. P.A. (ARS) 1958.

Renhaven

Rating 4/3   'Umpqua Chief' X *R. elliotti;* James, cross made
Hardy to –5   1949. Medium compact habit, with lanceolate,
Low   4½   acute, very dark green leaves, 4" X 1½". Flowers
funnel campanulate with calyx ⅔ length of corolla, glowing dark red with slight speckling. Lax, flat top truss. Tolerant of sun, but best results in part shade. P.A. (ARS) 1955.

Robert Allison

Rating 4/3   'Caroline' X *R. discolor;* Gable. Plant rugged,
Hardy to –10   upright, leaves waxy green, large. Flowers pink
Medium 6'   with golden throat, scented, to 3½" across, in a
Late May   flat topped truss. Floriferous, roots easily.

Romany Chai g.

Rating 2/2   'Moser's Maroon' X *R. griersonianum;* Roths-
Hardy to 0   child. Upright, fairly dense growing toward ma-
Medium 6'   turity; leaves dark green, 6" X 2", with reddish
Late May   brown petioles. Flowers scarlet red, spotted, of
thin texture, in a loose truss. Roots easily. A.M. (RHS) 1932. The same cross was made by Knap Hill Nursery which named 'Empire Day', formerly known as 'Romany Chai' var. 'Empire Day'.

Romany Chal g.

Rating 4/3   'Moser's Maroon' X *R. eriogynum;* Rothschild.
Hardy to 0   Upright, vigorous, leaves 6½" X 2¾", dark green,
Medium 6'   recurved, retains slight amount of indumentum
June   especially on petiole. Round trusses of dark
scarlet red flowers. Needs shade. A.M. (RHS) 1932, F. C. C. (RHS) 1937.

Rosamundi *house above Ravensview Drive*

Rating 2/3   A *R. caucasicum* hybrid; Standish and Noble.
Hardy to –5   Flowers a fairly strong rose pink, deeper than
Low   4½   those of 'Christmas Cheer' with which it is
March   often confused.

Rose Elf

Rating 3/4   *R. racemosum* X *R. pemakoense;* Lancaster. Shrub
Hardy to 0   is compact, spreading; leaves ¾" X ½". Flowers,
Dwarf   white, flushed bluish pink. Heavy bloomers. Take
Late April   full exposure, but frosts may damage swelling
flowers buds. Roots readily. P.A. (ARS) 1954.

Rose of China

Rating 3/3	'Tally Ho' X *R. discolor;* named by Lancaster,
Hardy to 0	seedling from Lem. Plant upright rounded, open,
Low 4½	leaves 7″ X 2″, lanceolate, slightly glandular.
June	Flowers clear china rose, bell shaped, to 4″ across,

10 to 12 in a truss. Grows well in sun or shade, heat tolerant, roots easily.

Rose Splendour

Rating 4/3	*R. griersonianum* X 'Purple Splendour'; Lan-
Hardy to 0	caster. Plant medium compact, rounded upright,
Low 4½	leaves dark green, 5″ X 2″, slight indumentum.
Late May	Flowers magenta rose with geranium lake eye,

bell shaped, to 4″ across, 12 or more in an upright, rounded truss. Tolerant of sun or shade.

Roseum Elegans

Ratings 2/4	A *R. catawbiense* hybrid; A. Waterer, before
Hardy to –25	1851. Plant vigorous, upright when young, later
Tall 6⁻⁴	spreading, good foliage. Flowers rose lilac, rather
Late May	small, in a good dome-shaped truss. Roots and

grows very easily. Probably the most popular variety for general landscaping in the Eastern states. Presumably introduced as a single clone but there are several forms being sold under this name.

Rosy Bell

Rating 3/3	*R. ciliatum* X *R. glaucophyllum;* Davies. Spread-
Hardy to –5	ing, moderately open habit, leaves 2¾″ X 1¼″,
X Semi- Dwarf	pale green, sometimes flushed bronze by autumn,
March	conspicously and heavily scaly on top, scattered

scales below. Flowers bell shaped, about 1½″ across, old rose or rose pink, deeper color center. 4 to 5 in a small truss. A.M. (RHS) 1894.

Rubens

Rating 2/2	Parentage unknown; A. Waterer before 1865.
Hardy to –5	Plant broader than tall, sprawling. The leathery,
Low 4½	flat leaves are 5″ X 3″ and are held several years.
Late May	The average sized flowers are deep rich red,

with white stamens and dark spotting on upper lobe. The tight, dome-shaped truss is not large. Roots readily.

17. *R. crinigerum,* the Rock 57 form. *Photo Cecil Smith*

18. *R. vernicosum* in the garden of Dr. Phetteplace, Eugene, Oregon.
Photo Cecil Smith

19. *R. inopinum* of the Taliense Series, in the Bob
Bovee garden, Portland, Oregon.   *Photo Cecil Smith*

20. *R. anwheiense* in the garden of The Bovees, Portland, Oregon.   *Photo Cecil Smith*

21. A *R. yakusimanum* seedling raised by Dr. Phetteplace, Eugene, Oregon. It is 10 years old, 4½ ft. tall, a bit larger in all its parts than the Exbury form.   *Photo Carl Phetteplace, M.D.*

22. *R. metternichii.* Larson form in the garden of Milton Walker, M.D., near Eugene Oregon.   *Photo Cecil Smith*

23. *R. hyperythrum.*

Photo Cecil Smith

24. *R. reticulatum.*

Photo Cecil Smith

25. *R. wightii.*

Photo Cecil Smith

26. Azalea garden of Mrs. Elsie Wilson, Narberth, Pa., showing use of white in blending colors. *Photo F. H. West, M.D.*

27. Azaleas used in an informal, Japanese style garden. *Photo J. H. Clarke*

28. Large plants of Kurume azaleas at the Winterthur Estate of Mr. Henry Dupont.
Photo F. H. West, M.D.

29. Glenn Dale azalea 'Martha Hitchcock'.
Photo F. H. West, M.D.

30. *R. falconeri* blooming in the Phetteplace garden, Eugene, Oregon.

Photo Cecil Smith

31. *R. deliense,* Kingdon-Ward's No. 21000 from the 1951 expedition.

Photo Cecil Smith

32. *R. yunnanense.* Photo Cecil Smith

33. *R. hanceanum nanum,* an attractive dwarf with
light yellow flowers. Photo Cecil Smith

Ruby Bowman

Rating 5/4	*R. fortunei* X 'Lady Bligh'; Mrs. Bowman, raised
Hardy to 0	and introduced by Druecker. Plant upright spread-
Medium 6'	ing, tall as wide, well covered with foliage to
Early May	the ground. Holds leaves for three years. The

medium green leaves are as large as 8" X 2½",
slightly glossy, elliptic to oblanceolate, with red petioles. The
tyrian rose flowers with blood red throat are to 4½" across,
open campanulate with 6-7 undulate and recurving petals, 13-15
to a full, dome shaped truss. Striking in flower and an excellent
foliage plant. P.A. (ARS) 1951.

Ru by Hart, May, red, -5°, 2'

Russautinii g.

Rating 4/3	*R. russatum* X *R. augustinii;* Ramsden, 1937.
Hardy to –5	Leaves medium green, 1" X ¾". Flowers purplish
Medium 6'	lavender blue, about 1" across, borne profusely at
Mid-April	early age.

Ruth Lyons

Rating 4/3	Parentage unknown, presumably a form of *R.*
Hardy to 0	*davidsonianum;* Barto, grown and introduced by
Medium 6'	Lyons. Upright plant with leaves 2¼" X ¾",
Early May	which fold upwards sharply from the midrib to

give a V-shaped cross section. Flowers bright
pink, self colored, to 1¼" across, 6-7 in a rather
open, flat topped truss.

Saffron Queen

Rating 4/3	*R. xanthostephanum* X *R. burmanicum;* C. Will-
Hardy to +20	iams, 1948. Plant upright, with leaves lanceolate
Low 4½	to oblanceolate, to 3" X 1". Flowers widely fun-
Late April	nel shaped, sulfur yellow, 2½" long by 1½" wide.

Lax truss of 8 to 9 flowers. Holds color better
than average in partial shade which it should have. Roots with
medium ease. A.M. (RHS) 1948.

Sapphire

Rating 4/4	'Blue Tit' X *R. impeditum;* Knap Hill Nursery.
Hardy to 0	First plants brought to U.S.A. in 1947 so far as
Dwarf	known. Plant spreading, dense, compact if in
Mid-April	full sun, stretches up in shade. Leaves ¾" X ⅜".

1½" X

good Blue Flowers a good light blue, 3 or 4 to a cluster.
Very floriferous.

Bovee *Boxes front of garage*

Sappho

Rating 3/2   Parentage unknown; A. Waterer before 1867.
Hardy to −5   Plant vigorous, open growing, inclined to be
Tall   6+   leggy; leaves 4¼″ X 1½″, moderate olive green.
Mid-May   Flowers of medium size, white with large pur-
plish blotch, in a compact dome-shaped truss.
English descriptions read "White, heavily spotted maroon". The
blotch in the plant sold extensively in the Western U.S.A. as
'Sappho', is not maroon.

Sarita Loder g.

Rating 3/3   *R. griersonianum* X 'Loderi' g.; G. H. Loder.
Hardy to +10   Open upright habit. Flower deep crimson in bud,
Medium   6′   but opens to a deep rose or salmon. Plant requires
Late May   some protection from sun and frost. One form
received the A.M. (RHS) 1934. Some very poor
forms have been sold occasionally in the Northwest.

Scandinavia

Rating 3/2   'Betty Wormald' X 'Hugh Koster'; M. Koster &
Hardy to 0   Sons. Plant spreading, wider than tall, twigs
Low   4½   reddish, leaves medium green, convex, shiny, 7″
Late May   X 2″. Flowers open funnel shaped, red with a
black blotch, in dome shaped truss. A.M. (RHS)
1950.

Scarlet Wonder, April, red, -15°, 2′

Scintillation

Rating 4/4   A Dexter seedling of unknown parentage. Plant
Hardy to −10   medium compact, of good dome shaped habit,
Medium   6′   leaves lustrous, dark green, rather large. Flowers
Mid-May   light pink with bronze throat, large, of very good
substance, in a large, dome shaped truss. Should
have some shade.

Seattle Springtime

Rating 3/3   *R. leucaspis* X *R. mucronulatum;* Mulligan, 1954.
3′   Hardy to +5   Open growing plant. Leaves 1¾″ X ¾″, moderate
X   Semi- Dwarf   olive green 7.5GY 4/4. Small flowers, 1¼″ across,
March   white, flushed amaranth rose.

Sefton

Rating 3/2   A *R. catawbiense* hybrid; A. Waterer 1881. Plant
Hardy to −15   spreading, inclined to be straggly. Flowers are
Low   4½   plum maroon and both flowers and truss are
Late May   large for a *catawbiense* hybrid.

Sir Charles Lemon

Rating 3/5   *R. arboreum* X ?; exhibited by Aberconway 1937.
Hardy to +10   Plant fairly compact. Leaves very showy, 5" X
Medium *6'*   2", dark green, above and deep reddish brown
Mid-April   below. Flowers white with faint speckles in
                throat, campanulate. Truss dome-shaped rapidly
becoming flat topped. Roots fairly easily. Millais says it came
from seed sent by Sir J. Hooker.

Sir Fredrick Moore g.

Rating 4/2   *R. discolor* X 'St. Keverne'; Rothschild. Vigor-
Hardy to –5   ous, upright plant with dark green leaves, 8"
Medium *6'*   X 2¾". Flat top trusses of large, light pink
June   flowers, with heavy red spotting around the
                base inside. A.M. (RHS) 1937.

Skyglow

Rating 3/2   A Dexter seedling, formerly known as Dexter
Hardy to –5   No. 9. Rather poor plant habit and leaf color.
Medium *6'*   Flowers peach, tinged apricot, in a flat truss.
Mid-May

Snow Lady

Rating 4/4   *R. leucaspis* X *R. ciliatum?*; obtained from Roths-
Hardy to 0   child as *R. leucaspis* by W. G. Tucker, introduced
3' X Semi-dwarf   by Lancaster. Compact spreading shrub that takes
and '55 March   full exposure, but buds may be damaged, after
                swelling, by frost. Leaves medium green 3" X 1"
hairy, oval lanceolate. Flowers white, dark anthers, 2" wide, in
a lax truss. Roots easily. P.A. (ARS) in 1955.

Bovee : one of finest early whites

Snow Queen g.

Rating 5/2   'Halopeanum' X 'Loderi' g.; Loder, 1926. Vigorous,
Hardy to +5   open habit with leaves that will not withstand
Tall *6+*   sun. Leaves 8" X 2½", are medium green, in
Early May   shade. Fairly large truss of pure white flowers
                with very small red blotch at base. Flowers, be-
fore they are entirely open, are neyron rose. A.M. (RHS) 1934, A.M.
(Wisley Trials) 1946. The parent variety 'Halopeanum' is better
known in the U.S.A. as 'White Pearl'.

Souvenir of W. C. Slocock

Rating 3/3   A *R. campylocarpum* hybrid; W. C. Slocock and
Hardy to –5   Co. Compact, but upright to spreading, slow
Low 4½   growing shrub with leaves having a characteris-
Early May   tic slight twist. The leaves are medium green,
   4″ X 1½″. Compact, rounded trusses of primrose
yellow flowers, which open an apricot yellow. A.M. (RHS) 1935.

Sue

Rating 4/4   'Loderi King George' selfed; James. Reddish
Hardy to 0   brown petioles and buds. Vigorous habit, leaves,
Tall 6+   medium green, 7″ X 2½″. Flowers, deep pink,
Early May   5″ across, on an extremely tall, narrow truss.

Sugar Plum

Sunrise g.

Rating 4/2   *R. griffithianum* X *R. griersonianum;* Abercon-
Hardy to +5   way, cross made in 1926. Plant upright spreading,
Tall 6+   about same spread as height. Leaves 6½″ X
Late May   1¾″, medium green, matte surface. Flowers large,
   light, to a medium dark pink, in a rounded
truss. More than one form being sold in the Northwest. Easy to
root. One form received an F.C.C. (RHS) 1942.

Susan

Rating 3/4   *R. campanulatum* X *R. fortunei;* J. C. Williams.
Hardy to –5   Plant open growing. Leaves 5½″ X 2″, dark
Medium 6   green, firm and flat with purplish petioles and
Late April   trace of indumentum. Flowers amethyst violet
   spotted, dark purple on upper petal at throat.
Truss dome-shaped, loose. Very difficult to root. A.M. (RHS)
1930, A.M. (RHS, Wisley Trials) 1948, F.C.C. (RHS) 1954.

Sweet Simplicity

Rating 2/3   A *R. ponticum* hybrid; J. Waterer, Sons and
Hardy to –5   Crisp, before 1922. Habit bushy, about as broad
Medium 6'   as tall. The 5″ X 2″ leaves are shiny, dark green,
Mid-May   elliptic and slightly waved. Deep pink buds open
   to ruffled 2½″ flowers of flushed white edged
with pink. The truss is well filled, round, and of average size.
This is an easily grown plant of average vigor, a heavy bloomer,
and both flowers and leaves stand full exposure. It roots readily.

Tally Ho g.

Rating 4/3　　*R. griersonianum* X *R. eriogynum;* Crosfield. Up-
Hardy to +10　right, fairly dense habit with dull, medium green,
Medium 6'　　6" X 2", somewhat bullate leaves; margins of leaf
June　　　　 twisted. Flowers brilliant huntsman red in a lax
　　　　　　　truss. Roots easily F.C.C. (RHS) 1933.

Temple Belle g.

Hardy 3/4　　*R. orbiculare* X *R. williamsianum;* Royal Botani-
Hardy to –5　cal Garden, Kew 1916. Leaves light green, cordate-
Low 4½　　　oval. Plant medium compact. Flowers pink, bell
Eary April　　like, in a lax truss. Prefers partial shade. Rooting
　　　　　　　usually takes a little longer than the easier vari-
eties but is not difficult. It is not bothered much by pests.

Tessa g.

Rating 3/4　　'Praecox' X *R. moupinense;* Stevenson. Grows vig-
Hardy to –5　orously, taller than wide, but slower in full sun.
4½' Low　　　Lower stems are smooth reddish brown, leaves
Early April　　1½" X ¾", elliptic convex, matte green above with
　　　　　　　brown scales below. Flowers, outward-facing, deep
lilac pink, about 2" wide and flat, opening in groups of 3 to 4 along
the stem at the leaf axils. Grows and blooms well in sun or shade
but the leaves will be lighter and flowers not last as long in sun.
Roots readily. A clone received an A. M. (RHS) 1935.

Bovee: Best in group, 2-3 feet in 10 yrs

The Bride

Rating 2/3　　*R. caucasicum* var. *album,* inbred; Standish and
Hardy to –15　Noble before 1850. Good growth habit. Flowers
Medium 6'　　white with a yellow blotch, somewhat resembling
Late May　　 'Madame Masson'. F. C. C. (RHS) 1871.

The Hon. Jean Marie de Montgue

Rating 3/4　　A *R. griffithianum* hybrid; C. B. van Nes & Sons. 3rd choice
Hardy to 0　　Compact, spreading habit with concave, dark　　in Seattle
c K, 4½ Low　 green leaves, 5½" x 2". Large scarlet flowers in a
do　Early May　10-14 flowered, dome shaped truss. Easily grown
　　　　　　　in the Pacific Northwest, in sun or shade, but
flowers fade in sun. Roots easily. Currently one of the best selling
commercial varieties in the Northwest. Sold as 'Montague', 'Jean
Montague', 'Jean Marie', 'Jean Marie de Montague', etc.

Thomwilliams, g.

Rating 3/4   *R. thomsonii* X *R. williamsianum;* first cross by
Hardy to –5   Magor in 1921, introduced in 1927, described as a
Semi-dwarf   deep shade of rose pink. Aberconway made a later
Mid-April   cross and one of his plants received an A. M. from
the RHS in 1935. It is described as clear, waxy,
rose magenta. Plant compact, rounded, leaves resemble those of
R. williamsianum.

(handwritten: Front Bed) **Tidbit** *(handwritten: Tony, Ma, red, –25°, 3'; –15° sturdy, compact)*

(handwritten: Award '57)

Rating 3/4   *R. dichroanthum* X *R. wardii;* R. Henny. Low
Hardy to +5   growing, with dense foliage. Flowers are fleshy,
Low *(4½)*   campanulate 2″ wide and 2½″ long with 6 or 7
Early May   blooms in each loose truss. Flowers open a straw
yellow deepening and somewhat more intense
after a few days. It is somewhat difficult to root. Resents quickly
any degree of poor drainage. Prefers a shady location. P. A. (ARS)
1957. *(handwritten: Bovee rates rather high)*

Towhee

(handwritten: Award '65)

Rating 3/3   'C. P. Raffill' X ('Redcap' X 'Tally Ho'); James.
Hardy to +5   Flowers bright, waxy, scarlet in a medium sized,
Low *(4½)*   open top truss. P. A. (ARS) 1956.
Late May

Trilby

(handwritten: Side)

Rating 3/3   'Koningin Wilhelmina' X 'Stanley Davies'; C. B.
Hardy to –5   van Nes and Sons. Plant fairly full, yet upright,
Medium *(6')*   leaves gray green, to 7″ X 3″. Flowers deep crim-
Late May   son, almost black at the center with darker dots,
in ball shaped truss. Grows well in sun on Pacific
coast.

Tumalo

(handwritten: Award '55)

Rating 3/3   *R. decorum* X 'Loderi King George'; James.
Hardy to 0   Spreading habit with 6½″ X 2½″, light green
Medium *(6')*   leaves. Flowers frilled and fragrant, white, green
Early May   at base, suffused pale chartreuse before entirely
opening, 5″ to 6″ across. Large, round, rather loose
trusses. Tends to bloom so heavily it may need to be partially disbudded. P. A. (ARS) 1955.

Twinkles

Rating 3/2   *R. racemosum* X *R. spiciferum*, Wright. Vigorous
Hardy to 0   plant, putting up long shoots during growing sea-
Low 4½   son, tends to be decumbent, responds to pruning.
Mid-April   The leaves, dark green above and gray below,
are 1¼" X ¼". The small, light pink flowers are
borne along the stems. The plant blooms heavily, takes full exposure. Roots easily.

Unique

5th Choice in Seattle

Rating 3/5   A *R. campylocarpum* cross; W. C. Slocock, Ltd.
Hardy to +5   Plant very compact, symmetrical. Leaves 3" X
Low 4½   1½", oval and medium green. Flowers red in bud
Mid April   opening to pale yellow, slightly tinged peach.
Truss dome-shaped, medium sized. Easy to root.
A.M. (RHS) 1934, F.C.C. (RHS) 1935.

Unknown Warrior

Rating 3/2   'Queen Wilhelmina' X 'Stanley Davies'; C. B. van
Hardy to +5   Nes and Sons before 1922. A vigorous plant, grow-
Medium 1'   ing upright and open, and needs much early train-
Mid-April   ing to have good shape, grows well in the sun, but
in the shade is leggy. The pointed, dark green
leaves, 6" X 2" are folded upward along the mid-rib. About 12, rose
red flowers, to 3" broad, make up the large, dome-shaped truss. The
texture is thin and protection from full sun is desirable. Roots
readily.

Vanessa Pastel

Rating 4/3   'Soulbut' X *R. griersonianum;* Aberconway, cross
Hardy to +5   made in 1930. Plant rather upright, leaves medium
Medium 1'   green, 5" X 2". Flowers open brick red and change
Late May   to apricot and then to yellow. Compact ball truss.
A.M. (RHS) 1946.

Vanguard g.

Rating 3/2   *R. venator* X *R. griersonianum;* Headfort, 1940.
Hardy to +15   Plant open, spreading, wider than tall; leaves
Low 4½   dark green, 5½" x 1¼". Flowers bright red in a
Early May   rather lax, dome shaped truss. Blooms at an early
age and profusely. Roots easily.

Van Nes Sensation

Rating 3/4	'Sir Charles Butler' X 'White Pearl'; C. B. van Nes
Hardy to 0	and Sons. Plant somewhat spreading, of medium
Medium	compactness. Leaves 5" X 2½", medium green.
Early May	Flowers pale lilac, lighter center, scented, large,

widely funnel-shaped. Truss very large, dome-shaped. Roots fairly easily.

Van Veen, May, red, -5°, 5'

Victorianum

Rating 5/2	*R. dalhousiae* X *R. nuttallii;* Pince, before 1871.
Hardy to +20	Plant erect, inclined to be leggy. Leaves oblanceo-
Medium	late, to 5" X 2" veins impressed. Flowers creamy
Late April	yellow in bud, opening to pure white, funnel

shaped, flaring to 6" across, lobes reflexed, of good substance. Lax truss of 4 to 5 flowers. Should be grown in shade, roots with medium ease. Leggy and rather ungainly at times but the flower is magnificent, beautifully sculptured with the "mark of the potter's thumb" at the base of the corolla.

Vulcan g.

Rating 3/4	'Mars' X *R. griersonianum;* Waterer, Sons and
Hardy to –5	Crisp, exhibited in 1938. Plant medium compact.
Medium	Leaves 5½ X 2", dark green. Flowers bright red.
Late May	Truss dome-shaped. Flowers at an early age and

regularly thereafter. Roots very easily. Most plants in the Northwest are of one clone. There are some poor clones.

Vulcan's Flame

Rating 3/4	*R. griersonianum* X 'Mars'; Lancaster, from seed-
Hardy to –5	ling from Lem. Medium compact. Leaves 5" X
Medium	1¾", dark green, stiff, persistent. Flowers bright
Late May	red, to 3" in diameter. Truss of 12-15 flowers,

dome shaped, flat-topped later. Vigorous, roots easily. The reverse cross of 'Vulcan'.

Wheatley

Rating 4/3	Raised by H. Phipps. Plant compact, of good
Hardy to –15	habit, with very good foliage. Flowers delicate,
Medium	silvery pink, large, in a good, tall truss. Will stand
Mid-May	some sun.

White Olympic Lady

Rating 4/4
Hardy to 0
Low 4½
Early April

'Loderi King George' X *R. williamsianum;* Ostbo, raised and introduced by Clark. Plant a fairly compact, spreading mound, wider than tall. The flat, smooth, medium dark green ovate leaves, are 3" X 2¼". The white flowers are to 4" across, open cup shaped, 4-5 in a lax truss. P. A. (ARS) 1960.

handwritten: ward'66

White Pearl

Rating 3/3
Hardy to +5
Tall 6+
Mid-May

R. griffithianum X *R. maximum;* Halope, 1896. Vigorous, rather upright grower, with dark green slightly bullate leaves, 7" X 2½". Lower branches spreading. Flowers flushed with slight pink, fading to white, in a tall conical truss. A. M. (RHS) 1906. Synonym is 'Halopeanum'.

White Swan

Rating 4/3
Hardy to 0
Tall 6+
Mid-May

R. decorum x 'Pink Pearl'; Waterer, Sons & Crisp. Plant upright, medium compact, leaves tend to be rather stiffly erect, 6" x 2". Flowers a good white with a green eye at base of upper corolla, in a dome shaped truss. Roots fairly easily. A.M. (RHS) 1937, F.C.C. (RHS) 1957.

Wilbar g.

Rating 3/3
Hardy to +5
Low
Early April

R. williamsianum X 'Barclayi' Aberconway 1938. Leaves are a dark green, ovate with red petioles. Plant habit is quite compact, spreading further than its height. Flower color, deep rose pink.

handwritten: 4½'

handwritten: Wilgens Ruby, May, red, 4', -15°

Windbeam

Rating 4/3
Hardy to –25
Semi-dwarf
Late April

A 'Conestoga' hybrid; Nearing, exhibited 1943. Plant has long, willowy shoots arising from base of plant, a bit sprawly; leaves 2¾" x 1". Flowers apricot pink, changing to a light pink. Roots easily. Bovee: hardy

handwritten: 3'
handwritten: X

handwritten: Wilsoni, June, red, 3', -15°

Wyanokie

Rating 3/4
Hardy to –25
Low 4½
Early May

A 'Conestoga' hybrid; Nearing exhibited 1950. Good plant habit, leaves to 3" X ¾", dark and lustrous. Flowers white, small, in 2" trusses, ball like. Floriferous. Easy to root.

Yellow Creek

Rating 4/2
Hardy to +15
Award 58 Medium 6'
Early May

'Idealist' x 'Sarita Loder'; James. Plant medium open habit, with light green, oblong lanecolate, glabrous leaves, to 6" x 1¾". Flowers flat, and flaring to 4" across, primrose yellow HCC 601/2, in a lax, dome shaped truss. Best results in some shade. Roots easily. P.A. (ARS) 1958.

Yellow Hammer g.

Rating 4/3
Hardy to +10
Medium 6'
April

as spring.

R. sulfureum x *R. flavidum;* Williams. Upright open plant with scaly light green leaves, ¾" x ¼". Flowers small ½" x ½", tubular, exceptionally yellow, in three-flower trusses. Many buds produced. Will stand full sun. Blooms in fall as well

Zuyder Zee

Rating 3/2
Hardy to +5
Low 4½
Early May

1936.

'Mrs. Lindsay Smith' X a *R. campylocarpum* hybrid; M. Koster and Sons, 1936. Plant is compact wider than tall, leaves, 5" X 2½", very light green, burn easily. Flowers campanulate, pale yellow, with red spots at base. Needs shade. A.M. (RHS)

THE

RATING

OF

RHODODENDRON

SPECIES

The objective of the Society has been to maintain a continuous interest and activity in connection with the ratings of both species and varieties. All ratings must be considered as tentative and subject to revision for two reasons. In the first place they are derived by con-census of a group which is necessarily limited, based on personal experiences of the committee members, and another committee, at another time might, quite likely, have different opinions of certain plants. In the second place additional information accumulates over the years and, as time goes on, each new ratings committee has the benefit of the opinions of its predecessors, as well as its own.

The procedure has been to print a revised set of ratings about every five years, in the A.R.S. books which are printed at approximately five year intervals. Hopefully those members who are growing fairly large numbers of species will accumulate information each year which may be passed on to the ratings committee from time to time.

The symbols used in rating species are the same as those previously explained for rating varieties. However, varieties are clones, except for the "group" varieties, and even with those the ratings are usually based on one clone, the one which is being shown in the Northwest, hence a single figure can be arrived at to indicate quality of flower, and another to indicate the quality of plant and foliage.

Species, on the other hand, are usually grown from seed, and seedlings vary, and so in some classes the quality might range from 1 to 5, that is from inferior to superior, in the one lot of seedlings. Fortunately most species do not vary that much and so ratings might be 1-2 or 3-5, and in exceptionally uniform species a single figure might be sufficient to indicate quality, as *R. ferrugineum* has a plant rating of 3, although the flowers may vary somewhat more than the plant, so rate 2-3.

The question may be raised as to why only one figure is given describing the hardiness of a species. True, individual seedlings will differ considerably in hardiness, although usually not as greatly as they differ in general appearance and garden value. One can look at a batch of seedlings in bloom and immediately see that some are practically worthless whereas others may be well above average. It is much more difficult to make any meaningful separation based on hardiness. Quite frequently a cold snap will cause damage to all, or to none. The figures printed as hardiness ratings, that is "Hardy to—" reflect the experience of the members doing the rating as to the hardiness of the usual selected forms being grown in their gardens.

The more important species were both rated and described in the preceding book of the Society, "Rhododendrons for your Garden," and formed the main feature of that publication. In this book more attention, and space, is being given to varieties with only brief species information presented in table form.

It should be bore in mind that these ratings are based on a slightly different scale than those reported in previous books, and any comparisons should be made with that in mind. See the explanation of ratings preceding the section on Variety Ratings and Descriptions.

RHODODENDRON

SPECIES

RATINGS

Species	Hardy to	Ratings Flower	Plant	Season	Size
aberconwayi	0	3-5	3-4	May	semi-dwarf
adenopodum	−5	2-3	3-4	Apr.	low
albiflorum	−25	1-2	2-3	June	med.
albrechtii	−15	4-5	2-3	Apr.	low
amagianum	−15	2-3	2-4	June	med.
ambiguum	−5	1-2	2-3	Apr.	med.
anwheiense	−5	2-3	3-4	Apr.	semi-dwarf
arboreum	+15	3-5	3-5	Mar.	tall
argyrophyllum	−5	3-4	3-4	May	med.
arizelium	+10	3-4	3-4	Apr.	tall
augustinii	+5	1-5	2-4	Apr.	tall
auriculatum	−15	2-4	3-4	July	tall
auritum	+10	3-4	3-4	Apr.	low
barbatum	+10	3-5	2-4	Mar.	med.
bathyphyllum	−5	2-4	3-4	Apr.	dwarf
bauhiniiflorum	+5	2-4	2-4	May	med.

Species	Hardy to	Ratings Flower	Plant	Season	Size
beanianum	+10	3-5	3-4	Apr.	low
brachyanthum	-5	1-2	2-3	June	semi-dwarf
brachycarpum	-15	2-3	3-4	June	med.
bullatum	+15	3-5	3-4	Apr.	low
bureavii	0	1-3	3-5	May	low
burmanicum	+15	2-4	2-3	Apr.	low
(caeruleum) see rigidum					
callimorphum	0	2-4	2-4	Apr.	low
calophytum	-5	4-5	4-5	Mar.	tall
calostrotum	-5	2-3	2-4	May	dwarf
caloxanthum	+5	1-4	1-3	Apr.	low
campanulatum	0	1-4	2-5	Apr.	med.
campylocarpum	0	2-5	2-3	Apr.	med.
campylogynum	0	3-4	3-4	May	dwarf
camtschaticum	-25	3	2-3	May	dwarf
carolinianum	-25	1-3	2-4	May	low
catawbiense	-25	1-3	2-3	May	med.
caucasicum	-5	1-2	2-3	May	low
cephalanthum	0	2-3	2-3	May	semi-dwarf
chaetomallum	+10	3-5	2-4	May	low
chapmanii	0	2-3	2-3	Apr.	low
charitopes	0	3-4	2-4	May	semi-dwarf
chlorops	-5	2-3	3-4	May	med.
chrysanthum	-5	1-2	2-4	May	dwarf
chryseum	-10	1-4	2-3	Apr.	dwarf
ciliatum	+10	2-4	2-3	Mar.	semi-dwarf
ciliicalyx	+20	3-4	2-3	Apr.	low
cinnabarinum	0	1-4	3	May	med.
concatenans	+5	1-4	3-4	May	med.

Species	Hardy to	Ratings Flower	Plant	Season	Size
concinnum	+5	1-5	1-3	May	med.
crassum	+15	3-4	3-4	Apr.	med.
crinigerum	+5	3-4	1-4	Apr.	low
cuneatum	0	2-3	2-3	Apr.	low
dasycladum	+5	2-3	2-3	Apr.	low
dauricum	−15	2-4	3-4	Mar.	low
davidsonianum	+5	1-5	3-4	Apr.	med.
decorum	0	1-4	3-4	May	med.
degronianum	−10	2-4	2-4	Apr.	semi-dwarf
desquamatum	−5	1-3	2-3	Apr.	tall
diaprepes	+10	2-4	2-3	June	tall
dichroanthum	0	1-2	2-3	May	semi-dwarf
(didymum) see sanguineum					
discolor	−10	1-3	2-3	June	tall
drumonium	0	2-3	2-4	Apr.	dwarf
eclecteum	+5	1-3	2-3	Apr.	med.
edgeworthii	+15	3-5	3-4	Apr.	low
elliottii	+15	3-5	2-3	June	med.
eriogynum	+15	2-5	2-3	June	med.
falconeri	+10	2-5	3-5	Apr.	tall
fargesii	−5	3-5	3-4	Mar.	tall
fastigiatum	−10	1-4	3-5	Apr.	dwarf
ferrugineum	−15	2-3	3	June	semi-dwarf
fictolacteum	−5	1-3	2-4	Apr.	tall
flavidum	−5	1-3	1-3	Apr.	dwarf
fletcherianum	+10	2-3	2-3	Apr.	semi-dwarf
floccigrum	+10	1-4	1-4	Apr.	low
forrestii	+5	1-4	1-4	Apr.	dwarf
fortunei	−15	2-4	2-4	May	tall

Species	Hardy to	Ratings Flower	Plant	Season	Size
fulgens	+5	1-3	2-4	Apr.	low
fulvum	+5	1-4	1-4	Apr.	tall
galactinum	−10	1-2	3	Apr.	med.
glaucophyllum	−10	3-4	3	May	semi-dwarf
glischrum	+5	2-3	2-4	May	med.
glomerulatum	−5	2-3	2-3	Apr.	semi-dwarf
griersonianum	+10	1-4	1-3	June	low
griffithianum	+15	3-5	2-3	May	tall
gymnocarpum	−5	2-4	3-4	Apr.	semi-dwarf
habrotrichum	+10	2-4	2-4	Apr.	med.
haematodes	0	3-5	2-4	May	semi-dwarf
hanceanum (nanum)	+5	1-3	1-4	May	dwarf
heliolepis	−5	1-3	1-3	May	med.
hemitrichotum	+5	2-3	2-3	Apr.	semi-dwarf
hemsleyanum	+5	2-3	3-4	June	tall
hippophaeoides	−10	2-3	2-4	Apr.	semi-dwarf
hirsutum	−5	1-2	3	June	semi-dwarf
hodgsonii	0	2-3	3-4	Apr.	med.
hookeri	+15	3-4	3-4	Apr.	tall
houlstonii	−5	2-3	2-3	May	med.
hyperythrum	−10	3-4	2-3	May	med.
impeditum	−10	2-4	3-5	Apr.	dwarf
imperator	+5	3-4	2-3	May	dwarf
insigne	0	2-3	3-5	June	low
intricatum	−10	2-4	2-4	Apr.	semi-dwarf
irroratum	0	2-4	2-3	Apr.	med.
johnstoneanum	+15	2-3	1-3	Apr.	med.
kaempferi	−15	1-4	2-4	May	med.
keiskei	−15	2-3	2-5	Apr.	low

Species	Hardy to	Ratings Flower	Plant	Season	Size
keiskei (dwarf form)	−5	3	5	Apr.	dwarf
keleticum	−10	2-4	3-5	Apr.	dwarf
kotschyi	−15	3-4	2-4	June	dwarf
lacteum	+5	1-5	1-3	Apr.	med.
lanigerum	+5	3-4	3-4	Apr.	tall
lepidostylum	0	1-2	4-5	June	dwarf
lepidotum	0	2-3	1-3	May	semi-dwarf
leucaspis	0	3-4	2-4	Mar.	dwarf
litiense	0	2-5	3-4	May	med.
lutescens	0	1-5	3-5	Apr.	tall *10th choice in Seattle*
luteum	−15	2-3	3	May	med.
macabeanum	+15	4-5	4-5	Apr.	tall
macrophyllum	−5	1-3	3	June	tall
makinoi	−10	2-3	2-4	June	low
mallotum	+10	1-4	3-5	May	low
maximum	−25	1-2	2-3	June	tall
meddianum	+5	3-4	2-4	Apr.	med.
megeratum	+10	2-4	2-4	Mar.	dwarf
metternichii	−15	3-4	2-4	Apr.	low
micranthum	−20	1-2	1-2	May	low
microleucum	−5	3-4	3-4	Apr.	dwarf
minus	−15	1-2	1-2	June	med.
mollicomum	0	3-4	3	Apr.	low
morii	0	2-4	2-3	Apr.	tall
moupinense	0	3-5	2-3	Mar.	semi-dwarf
mucronatum	−10	3-5	3	May	low
mucronulatum	−25	2-4	1-3	Feb.	low
neriiflorum	+5	3-5	2-4	Apr.	low
nitens	−10	2-3	2-3	June	dwarf

Species	Hardy to	Ratings Flower	Plant	Season	Size
niveum	−5	2-3	2	Apr.	med.
nuttallii	+30	4-5	1-3	Apr.	tall
occidentale	0	2-4	3	June	med.
oleifolium	+10	2-4	2-3	Apr.	low
orbiculare	−5	2-4	2-5	Apr.	low
oreodoxa	0	2-3	2-3	Apr.	tall
oreotrephes	0	1-4	2-4	May	med.
orthocladum	−5	3	2-3	Apr.	low
pemakoense	0	2-3	2-4	Apr.	low
pentaphyllum	−5	3-4	3	Mar.	dwarf
ponticum	−5	1-3	3	May	tall
prostratum	0	2-3	2-4	Apr.	dwarf
proteoides	+5	3-5	2-5	Apr.	dwarf
(pseudoyanthinum) see concinnum					
pubescens	+5	2-4	2-3	Apr.	low
quinquefolium	−5	1-2	3-4	Apr.	semi-dwarf
racemosum	−5	1-4	1-4	Apr.	low
radicans	−5	2-4	3-5	Apr.	dwarf
recurvoides	0	2-4	3-4	Apr.	semi-dwarf
reticulatum	−15	2-3	3	Apr.	med.
rex	−5	3-4	3-4	Apr.	tall
rhabdotum	+30	3-5	1-2	May	med.
rigidum	+5	3-5	3	Apr.	med.
roxieanum	0	2-3	3-4	Apr.	low
rubiginosum	−5	1-3	2-4	Apr.	tall
rupicola	0	2-3	2-3	Apr.	dwarf
russatum	−10	2-5	3-4	Apr.	semi-dwarf
saluenense	−5	1-3	2-3	Apr.	semi-dwarf
sanguineum	+5	1-4	1-3	May	semi-dwarf

Species	Hardy to	Ratings Flower	Plant	Season	Size
sargentianum	–5	2-4	2-4	Apr.	dwarf
schlippenbachii	–25	3-5	3	Apr.	med.
sinogrande	+15	4-5	4-5	Apr.	tall
smirnowii	–15	2-3	3-4	May	med.
souliei	–5	3-5	2-4	May	med.
sperabile	+15	1-3	2-4	Apr.	low
spiciferum	+5	2-4	1-3	Apr.	semi-dwarf
spinuliferum	+10	1-3	1-3	Apr.	low
strigillosum	+10	1-5	2-4	Apr.	med.
sutchuenense	–15	3-4	3-4	Mar.	tall
telopeum	+5	2-4	2-4	Apr.	low
tephropeplum	+10	2-4	2-3	Apr.	semi-dwarf
thomsonii	+10	2-5	2-3	Apr.	med.
(timeteum) see oreotrephes					
trichanthum	–5	2-4	3-4	May	med.
trichostomum	–5	2-4	2-3	May	semi-dwarf
uniflorum	0	2-3	2-3	Apr.	dwarf
valentinianum	+10	2-4	2-3	Apr.	semi-dwarf
venator	+10	2-4	2-3	May	low
vernicosum	0	1-3	2-3	Apr.	tall
wardii	0	1-5	3-4	May	med.
wightii	+5	2-4	1-3	Apr.	med.
williamsianum	–5	2-4	3-5	Apr.	semi-dwarf
wiltonii	0	2-3	3-4	May	med.
xanthocodon	+5	1-4	3-4	May	med.
xanthostephanum	+15	2-3	1-3	Apr.	low
yakusimanum	–15	2-5	3-5	May	semi-dwarf
yunnanense	0	2-5	3	May	tall
zeylanicum	+15	3-4	3-4	Apr.	med.

Native American Azaleas, Ratings, *

Species	Hardy to	Ratings Bloom	Plant
alabamense	–5	3	3
arborescens	–5 to –20	1-3	2-3
atlanticum	–10	2-3	2-4
austrinum	0	2-3	3
bakeri	–15	3-4	2-3
calendulaceum	–20	3-5	3
canadense	–30	1-2	2-3
canescens	+5 to 0	1-4	2-4
nudiflorum	–15 to –25	1-3	2-4
oblongifolium	0	1	2
prunifolium	0	2-5	3-4
roseum	–10 to –25	3-4	3
serrulatum	+5 to 0	1-2	2-3
speciosum	0	3-4	3
vaseyi	–15	2-5	2-3
viscosum	–5 to –25	1-2	1-4

*The information on these two pages, including the ratings, was furnished by Dr. Henry Skinner, Director of the National Arboretum, Washington, D.C. Dr. Skinner has made a special study of these azaleas and is our best informed authority on their botanical relationship as well as their horticultural value.

Blooming Season and Plant Size

Bl. Season in Wild	Bl. Season in Wash., D.C.	Plant Size
4/20 - 5/6	early May	semi dwarf to low
5/25 - 7/15	mid-June - early July	medium
4/25 - 5/15	early May	semi dwarf to low
4/1 - 4/15	early May	medium
6/5 - 7/25	June - early July	low to medium
4/20 - 6/5	mid-May	medium
4/10 - 6/15	mid-April	semi-dwarf
3/15 - 4/25	late April	med. to tall
4/5 - 6/5	late April	low to medium
5/5 - 5/20	early June	low
7/8 - 7/25	July - early Aug.	med. to tall
5/13 - 6/15	early July	medium
6/25 - 8/20	mid-July - early Aug.	med. to tall
4/15 - 5/5	early May	medium
4/20 - 5/22	mid-April	medium
5/25 - 7/25	June - early July	semi-dwarf to med.

EVERGREEN AZALEA

RATINGS FOR

THE PHILADELPHIA REGION

FRANKLIN H. WEST, M.D.

This report brings up to date the ratings for evergreen azaleas published in the Quarterly Bulletin of the ARS in January, 1964. Twenty contributors have generously shared their experience with the writer to make this report possible. These new ratings reflect their greater experience and firmer opinions about the varieties they grow. The asterisk marking certain varieties in the table below signifies that they are widely grown as well as highly rated. These are "the cream of the crop."

The rating number scale used is the same as for rhododendrons: 1—poor, 2—fair, 3—average, 4—good, 5—excellent. Many factors are considered in selecting the final rating values. The first number (for the flower) reflects the color, form, size, substance, and fragrance; the second number (for the plant) reflects general garden value, foliage, form, vigor, and floriferousness. A rating of 3/3 would indicate an average, reliable, but unexceptional bloom and plant.

Individually, any azalea is beautiful. Occasionally a variety such as 'Amoenum' earned a low rating for flowers because of its garish incompatibility with any other colored variety, despite the fact that, when seen by itself, 'Amoenum' is a spectacular plant in full bloom.

We venture to assert that the greater Philadelphia region is the farthest north that so many evergreen varieties can be found growing successfully outdoors. It is quite possible that parts of Long Island would prove to be equally hospitable if an extensive testing program were to be undertaken. Generally speaking, azaleas are given very little attention and need very little pampering once established in a favorable location, and they continue to put on increasingly more spectacular displays year after year. For this reason, azaleas are grown here much more commonly than rhododendrons.

Since resistance to unfavorable conditions is only one of many factors contributing to the rating for the plant, the reader must understand that a high plant rating number does not necessarily mean iron-clad hardiness for that variety.

Specimen evergreen azaleas will start to perform best the second or third year after being planted under high shade, protected from wind and winter sun, with a permanent mulch. The hardiest variety can be damaged severely or killed if newly transplanted to a windy hilltop or a low-lying "frost pocket" in full sun without mulch. Special observations about hardiness are noted in many cases, in the comments after the variety name.

All but one of our 20 reporters gave their average minimum winter temperatures from minus 5°F. to plus 5°F., which agrees with the plant hardiness maps that place the Delaware Valley region in zones 6b (-5° to 0°) and 7a (0° to +5°). One reporter, with a minimum average of minus 10°F. (zone 6a), had only one of several thousand Glenn Dale plants survive, and this survivor "does flower occasionally." Reports from zone 7a are much more enthusiastic about the Glenn Dale varieties.

Many devotees of broad leafed evergreens complain of the aesthetic difficulty in planting azaleas with rhododendrons and conclude that they look better segregated. Other complaints about azaleas are:

1. Their vigorous growth makes them greedy consumers of real estate.

2. Some varieties in winter are barely evergreen and make too sharp a contrast with other broad leafed evergreen plants.

3. Their loud, bright colors require some segregation to prevent offensive disharmonies. Our most experienced landscape designers devote 50% or more of their azalea plantings to white varieties to minimize this problem.

4. Azalea petal blight, unmistakably identified and rather prevalent in this region in late spring eight years ago, is considered a threat, but fortunately has not reappeared in epidemic proportions as many feared it would.

The ratings that follow are a consensus. The values were arrived at by finding the median of the opinion submitted by the twenty contributors named at the end of this report. The varieties with the asterisk are clearly the best for this region, and might be expected to do well in zones 6b and 7a (minimum temperatures of -5° F. to +5° F.) elsewhere in the United States where similar cultural conditions can be provided.

I. Species and Variants (all dependably plant hardy)

*1. *R. mucronatum* ('Ledifolia Alba') 4/3. Hardy to 0°. Unequalled in protected sites, needs room.

*2. *R. mucronatum* 'Delaware Valley White' 5/4. Hardy to -5°. Excellent, distinctly hardier, midseason.

3. *R. mucronatum* 'Sekidera' ('Magnifica') 4/3. Hardy to +5°. Less floriferous than white form. Much greater fragrance.

4. *R. obtusum* 'Amoenum' 2/4. Hardy to -5°. Early, hardy, fine form; color clashes.

5. *R. pulchrum* var. 'Maxwelli' 4/3. Hardy to +5°. Best in zone 7b, irregular bloomer here.

*6. *R. indicum* var. 'Balsaminaeflorum' 5/3. Hardy to 0°. Very compact, late; rabbit bait.

7. *R. indicum* 'Hakatashiro' 4/3. Hardy to 0°. Nice frilly flower, needs protection.

8. *R. indicum* 'J. T. Lovett' 4/4. Hardy to 0°. One of latest singles.

*9. *R. indicum* 'Beni Kirishima' ('H12G'; 'Macrantha') 4/4. Hardy to 0°. Best late double, fine foliage.

10. *R. simsii* var. eriocarpum 'Gumpo White' 4/3. Hardy to +5°. Needs shade and rabbit protection.

11. *R. simsii* var. eriocarpum 'Gumpo Pink' 3/3. Hardy to +5°. Same as 'Gumpo White', but less bud hardy.

12. *R. poukhanense* (single) 3/3. Hardy to -5°. Leggy, fragrant, hardy, early.

13. *R. poukhanense* (double) 3/3. Hardy to -5°. Nearly deciduous, less dependable bloomer.

II. Kurume Hybrids (all do well in protected locations).

*1. Addy Wery 4/3. Hardy to -5°. Very good blood-red, medium-tall grower.

2. Christmas Cheer 3/3. Hardy to 0°. Hardy, profuse bloom, dependable.

3. Coral Bells 3/2. Hardy to 0°. Lovely, very popular, tender.

4. Eleanor Allen 4/4. Hardy to -5°. Early, profuse flowers; windburns.
5. Guy Yerkes 4/3. Hardy to 0°. Fine flower; more reliably bud hardy than 'Pink Pearl'.
6. Hatsushima 4/3. Hardy to +5°. Variegated flower much admired.
7. Hershey's Red 4/3. Hardy to +5°. Some find it tender; fine hose in hose bloom.
8. Hexe 2/3. Hardy to +5°. Best in zone 7b, poor performer here.
9. Hinodegiri 3/4. Hardy to 0°. Consistent bloomer, very popular; color clash.
*10. Hino-Crimson 4/4. Hardy to 0°. Better bloom and foliage than 'Hinodegiri'.
11. Hinomayo 4/3. Hardy to +5°. Spectacular at Winterthur.
12. Pink Pearl 3/2. Hardy to +5°. Especially fine pink, needs shade and protection.
13. Psyche 3/3. Hardy to +5°. Average, root system inadequate.
*14. Red Progress 5/4. Hardy to -5°. Excellent red, superior hardiness, best Hino form.
15. Salmon Beauty 3/3. Hardy to +5°. Fine color, not reliably hardy.
16. Sherwood-Orchid 3/3. Hardy to -5°. Good strong plant, superior hardiness.
17. Sherwood Red 4/3. Hardy to -5°. More compact plant than 'Addy Wery'.
*18. Snow 3/3. Hardy to 0°. Very popular, but fades fast, holds dead blooms.
19. Sweetbriar 3/3. Hardy to 0°. Dependably good bloomer.

III. Kaempferi Hybrids (a truly iron-clad group, hardy to -5° at least.)
1. Beethoven 4/3. Dependably hardy.
*2. Carmen 4/4. Dependable and vigorous, excellent hardiness.
3. Cleopatra 4/3. Very good pink, "lovely," hardy, mid-season bloom.
*4. Fedora 3/3. Popular, reliable bloomer every year.
5. Johann Strauss 4/3. Gets leggy, fine large flowers.
6. Mikado 3/3. An unusual red.
7. Othello 3/4. Hardy, color may clash. Fades in sun.

*8. Palestrina ('Wilhelmina Vuyk') 3/3. Hardy to 0°. Tall, vigorous, popular. Very attractive as hedge or screen.

IV. Pericat Hybrids (all too tender even with much protection)
   1. Mme. Pericat 4/2. Hardy to +10°. A beauty but much too tender.

V. Indicum-Satsuki Hybrids (well worth special pampering)
   1. Gyokushin 4/4. Hardy to 0°. Flowers late, large, flat-faced like Sekidera.
   2. Jindai 4/3. Hardy to 0°. Late white with variable red stripes.
   3. Kingetsu 4/4. Hardy to 0°. Best bloomer; white, pink blotch, and stripes.
   4. Mai-Hime 4/3. Hardy to +5°. Marked tendency to sport. Fades.

VI. Gable Hybrids (all dependably bud hardy except #4, 8, 9, 10 and 27, to -5°, some lower)
   *1. Big Joe 5/3. Big showy flowers entirely cover bush, dependable, early.
   2. Billy 3/3. Attractive blossom, dwarf.
   3. Boudoir 2/3. Doesn't live up to the name at all.
   4. Cameo 3/2. Hardy to 0°. Good pink double, poor bush form.
   *5. Campfire 5/3. Bright hose in hose, best red for some.
   6. Carol 3/3. Nice hose in hose, violet red, later than 'Campfire'.
   7. Caroline Gable 4/3. Very good late red.
   8. Charlotte 3/3. Hardy to 0°. Taller, paler than 'Viola', and earlier.
   9. Chinook 3/2. Hardy to 0°. A trifle paler than 'Mary Dalton'; fades.
   10. Corsage 4/2. Hardy to 0°. Leggy and showy, nearly deciduous.
   11. Elizabeth Gable 4/3. Very good late single red, frilled.
   *12. Herbert 3/3. Hardy to -10°. Best of the Gable purples. Most compact.
   *13. James Gable 4/4. A favorite early, hardy bright red.

14. Jessie Coover 4/3. A later, larger darker Rosebud.
15. Jimmy Coover 3/3. Bright, orange red. Late.
16. Kathleen 4/3. Like Kaempferi varieties, smaller flowers.
17. La Lumiere 3/3. An average orange red azalea.
18. Lorna 3/3. Larger plant, darker Rosebud bloom.
*19. Louise Gable 5/4. One of best of all azaleas, neat double.
20. Mary Ann 3/3. Fair late double, light pink.
21. Mary Dalton 3/3. Very good early hose in hose, orange red.
22. Mary Frances Hawkins 4/3. "Lovely" pink, hardy, tall.
*23. Mildred Mae 4/4. Very good, more compact than 'Viola'.
24. Polaris 4/3. Beautiful, compact, white, semidouble, deserves higher rating.
25. Purple Splendour 3/3. Hardy to $-10°$. A good, dependable, hardy purple.
*26. Rosebud 5/3. Hardy to $-10°$. Superb, "perfect for this area," compact.
*27. Rose Greely 4/3. Hardy to $0°$. Very good, white hose in hose, fine bush, very evergreen in winter.
28. Royalty 3/3. More leggy than 'Purple Splendour'. Same color.
*29. Springtime 5/3. Hardy to $-10°$. Very bright pink. First azalea to bloom here.
*30. Stewartstonian 4/4. Hardy to $-10°$. Fine fall foliage; bright red 'Hino' type bloom, no trace of blue.
31. Susan 3/3. Single pink, hardy.
32. Viola 3/3. Vigorous, hardy bush. Later than *R. poukhanense*.

VII. Glenn Dale Hybrids (generally reliable—zone 7a; borderline hardy 6b)

*1. Ambrosia 4/2. Hardy to $-5°$. Tall, needs room. Unique apricot pink.
2. Angela Place 4/3. Hardy to $-5°$. Lovely white, late, very good.
3. Anthem 3/3. Hardy to $0°$. Strong grower, rose pink single.
4. Antique 3/2. Hardy to $+5°$. 'Sekidera' type. Blooms before 'Gyokushin'.
*5. Aphrodite 4/3. Hardy to $-5°$. Dependable, light, pure pink, fine foliage.
6. Ballet Girl 3/3. Hardy to $0°$. Very showy. Light red, hose in hose.

7. Bishop 4/3. Hardy to 0°. Tall. Good, lively rose color.
8. Buccaneer 3/3. Hardy to 0°. Put in shade to avoid sunburn.
9. Carrara 3/3. Hardy to 0°. Low, midseason white. Not reliably hardy.
10. Cavalier 3/3. Hardy to +5°. Good Kurume style orange red.
*11. Copperman 4/3. Hardy to 0°. Excellent in shade. Large, orange red, late.
12. Cygnet 4/3. Hardy to 0°. Interesting, floriferous white.
*13. Dayspring 5/3. Hardy to −5°. Very good, very early—just after 'Springtime'.
14. Delos 4/3. Hardy to 0°. Best double pink Glenn Dale Azalea.
*15. Dragon 4/3. Hardy to 0°. Bright, loud red. Best red Glenn Dale.
*16. Dream 5/3. Hardy to −5°. Best of the *R. simsii* hybrids. Ruffled bloom.
17. Driven Snow 3/3. Hardy to 0°. Winter burns, not dependably bud hardy.
*18. Elizabeth 4/3. Hardy to −5°. Low, late orange red. Good foliage.
19. Eros 3/2. Hardy to +5°. Very fine foliage. Buds freeze.
20. Everest 4/3. Hardy to 0°. Large white bloom. Dense plant.
21. Fairy Bells 4/3. Hardy to 0°. Pink hose in hose pendant flowers.
22. Fashion 4/3. Hardy to +5°. Nice plant, one of best, Kurume hardiness.
23. Festive 4/3. Hardy to 0°. Early, 'Geisha' type. Rose stripes and sanding.
*24. Gaiety 4/4. Hardy to −5°. Very good, flashy bright late pink. Evergreen.
*25. Geisha 5/4. Hardy to −5°. Best striped Glenn Dale—"like this one."
*26. Glacier 4/4. Hardy to 0°. Hard to beat, superb foliage, needs protection for best performance.
*27. Glamour 4/4. Hardy to −5°. Very good, glowing pink, favorite.
28. Gorgeous 3/3. Hardy to 0°. Medium orange pink. Fine symmetrical plant.
29. Grace Freeman 4/3. Hardy to 0°. Paler than 'Antique' or 'Nobility'. Flesh tint.

30. Greeting 3/4. Hardy to 0°. Medium orange pink. Fine symmetrical plant.
31. Harlequin 3/3. Hardy to 0°. Leggy and showy striped variety.
*32. Helen Close 4/4. Hardy to 0°. Low, late white. Five stamens identify it.
33. Helen Gunning 4/4. Hardy to 0°. A pink 'Martha Hitchcock', very beautiful.
*34. Joya 4/3. Hardy to –5°. One of best, floriferous; large, spreading plant.
35. Kobold 4/3. Hardy to 0°. Dark, frilled, blackish red.
36. Lillie Maude, 5/3. Hardy to 0°. Excellent, frilled, lavender pink. So-so bush.
37. Louise Dowdle 4/3. Hardy to 0°. Large, bright pink flowers with white centers.
*38. Martha Hitchcock 4/3. Hardy to –5°. Vigorous plant, showy bloom. Succeeds at Martha's Vineyard! No white centers on young plants.
39. Moonbeam 4/3. Hardy to 0°. Large white flowers, ruffled, late.
40. Niagara 4/3. Hardy to 0°. Reliably good white, compact.
41. Pinkie 4/3. Hardy to 0°. Light pink variegated; often sports.
*42. Polar Sea 4/3. Hardy to –5°. Gigantic white flowers, late, very good.
43. Prudence 3/4. Hardy to –5°. Bright pink, excellent evergreen foliage.
44. Sagittarius 3/3. Hardy to +5°. Buds tender, superb foliage, like boxwood.
45. Sarabande 4/3. Hardy to 0°. Very good. Pale 'Martha Hitchcock' type.
46. Sebastian 3/3. Hardy to –5°. Early shrimp pink, hose in hose. Needs shade.
47. Snowclad 4/4. Hardy to 0°. Very good white.
48. Suwanee 3/3. Hardy to 0°. Sturdy, dependable lavender. Large plant.
*49. Swansong 4/3. Hardy to 0°. A favorite very late white. Fine form.
50. Tanager 3/3. Hardy to 0°. Color no match with the bird, very evergreen.

*51. Treasure 4/3. Hardy to 0°. Best white for some. Winterthur prefers *R. mucronatum.*

 52. Vestal 3/3. Hardy to 0°. Showy, white with pale magenta stripes.

*53. Wavelet 5/4. Hardy to –5°. Best of late whites. Blooms Memorial Day.

Many other varieties are under observation, but too few reports were received to assign a valid rating for them. No variances have been found between the plants grown and the published descriptions as to plant size, habit, and season of bloom. Consequently, by careful selection from the cream of the crop, the grower can have azaleas in bloom from April to June in this climate, with gratifyingly brilliant displays of color every year once the plants have reached full maturity.

CONTRIBUTORS

The following members assisted by providing information from which the above ratings were derived: Edward Ansell, Bryn Mawr, Pa.; George A. Arrington, Huntington Valley, Pa.; Ross Davis, Wayne, Pa.; Charles Herbert, Phoenixville, Pa.; Mrs. Julian W. Hill, Wilmington, Del.; Sylvester F. Hubbard, Mechanicsville, Pa.; Mrs. Raymond P. Jefferis, Media, Pa.; Arnold A. John, Springfield, Pa.; Mrs. W. A. Kelius, Levittown, Pa.; Walter Kern, Woodlyn, Pa.; Philip A. Livingston, Narberth, Pa.; Everitt L. Miller, Longwood Gardens, Pa.; Mrs. J. D. Otley, Narberth, Pa.; Lloyd E. Partain, Falls Church, Va.; John Schamenek, Willow Grove, Pa.; Francis J. Sholomskas, Norristown, Pa.; J. Russell Sonneborn, Willow Grove, Pa.; C. Gordon Tyrrell, Winterthur, Del.; Franklin H. West, Gladwyne, Pa.; Mrs. Elsie Wilson, Narberth, Pa.; John C. Wister, Swarthmore, Pa.

OTHER VARIETIES

The advanced rhododendron fancier would undoubtedly rather have ratings on the newest introductions than on those which have been around for awhile, although for the beginner and the average gardener, information about the older, standard varieties would be most valuable. Because rhododendrons are rather slow growing and slow to propagate a new introduction may appear in a show and receive a great deal of publicity when the only plant in existence is the original seedling in the breeder's garden. It would be several years before blooming size plants would be growing in the gardens of enough knowledgeable people who could get together and agree that the variety is ready for a quality and hardiness rating. Even then experiences may differ and it may seem best to defer rating until further information is at hand.

The American Rhododendron Society does encourage its members to get acquainted with the new originations. It does this by printing, in the A.R.S. Registry, the names and descriptions of all new varieties that are registered, and encourages registration by publicity, and by providing the service free of charge.

The description printed in the Registry are usually furnished by the breeder, and may be from the one original plant. Sometimes a seedling may appear to be outstanding the first two or three years it blooms, and then gradually lose its pristine vigor and quality as it encounters various unfavorable environmental factors. The Ratings Committee must base its official opinion on the experiences of several people who have seen a variety several seasons and under different growing conditions and have enough information to write its own description.

Realizing that many readers would like to have information about the newer sorts the Ratings Committee did suggest the printing of a brief list of a few of the newer names which are being seen and heard of in shows and appearing in lists of the new and promising. Actually this could make a very long list and require much research to compile. The practical thing seemed to be to restrict it primarily to those varieties which came up for discussion by the Committee but were omitted from the ratings table because of lack of sufficient information on which to base ratings, or a meaningful description, or both.

AWARD

PLANTS

It might seem that all those plants which have received an A.R.S. Award, either Preliminary Award, or Award of Excellence, should have been rated and described. However, for a number of years a P.A. could be given to a single truss brought in to a show. It may have been the first bloom for the plant, and such first blooms may excel anything produced thereafter. It is not strange that many Award Plants have not been heard from since the Award was given. In fact, perhaps a dozen awards were given to plants which the breeder eventually decided were not really superior and so were never even named.

In recent years the rules have been made more stringent and Awards can not be given to a single truss, they are given subject to being named with a name which conforms to the International Code of Nomenclature, and the date of the Award becomes an integral part of it, expressed for instance as P.A. 1967.

The A.R.S. Committee on Awards Policy has attempted to collect information about all the plants which have received Awards, as to whether they are still in existence, and if so, whether they have been considered worthy of propagation.

Those which received an Award several years ago, and are now unknown, or are not being distributed, must be considered as of relatively little value. At this writing not enough information has been received by the Awards Policy Committee to enable the sorting out of the promising from those best forgotten.

However, the granting of the Award does indicate that, at the time, a competent committee did believe that the plant was of superior quality and promise. Many Award plants have, of course, lived up to that promise and are now being distributed as important new varieties.

The following list of Award Plants is presented to provide information as to parentage, the name of the breeder, and the date the Award was given. A number of these appear in the Variety Ratings and Descriptions section but are also included here in alphabetical list.

PLANTS

WHICH HAVE

RECEIVED

A.R.S. AWARDS

Alice Franklin PA 1959 ('Ole Olsen' X 'Loderi King George'), Lem, Larson

Alley Cat PA 1960 (Parentage unknown), Ostbo

Anna PA 1952 ('Norman Gill' X 'Jean Marie de Montague'), Rose, Lem

Anna Rose Whitney PA 1954 *(griersonianum* X 'Countess of Derby'), Whitney

Ann Cary PA 1966 *(keiskei* X *spinuliferum)*, Anderson

Annie Dalton AE 1960 *(decorum* X *griersonianum* X 'America'), Gable

Atroflo AE 1959 ('Atrosanguineum' X *floccigerum)*, Gable

Bacher's Gold PA 1955 ('Unknown Warrior' X 'Fabia'), Bacher

Beechwood Pink AE 1960 ('Atrosanguineum' X *fortunei)*, Gable, Herbert

Bern PA 1955 *(decorum* X garden hybrid), Bacher

Blue River AE 1961 ('Van Nes Sensation' X 'Emperor de Maroc'), R. Lyons

Cadis AE 1959 ('Caroline' X *discolor)*, Gable

Captain Jack PA 1956 ('Mars' X *eriogynum)*, R. Henny

Captain Kidd PA 1960 ('Princess Elizabeth' X 'May Day'), R. Henny

Carol Jean PA 1957 ('Vulcan' X 'Robin Hood'), Klupenger

Carolyn Grace AE 1960 *(wardii* hybrid), Grace

Cary Ann PA 1961 ('Corona' X 'Vulcan'), A.Wright

Catalode AE 1960 ('Catawbiense Album' X 'Loderi'), Gable

Cathye Mayo PA 1959 (deciduous azalea), Bovee

Chief Paulina PA 1954 (clone of *concinnum* var. *pseudoyathinum)*, James

Confection PA 1956 ('Corona' X 'Dondis'), R. Henny

Coral PA 1956 *(neriiflorum* X *dichroanthum)* x *discolor*, F₂, Ostbo

Cutie PA 1959, AE 1962 *(calostrotum* hybrid), source unknown

David Gable AE 1960 ('Atrosanguineum' X *fortunei)*, Gable

Desiree PA 1960 (evergreen azalea, *poukhanense* X 'Ledifolia Alba'), Shammarello

Diane Titcomb PA 1958 ('Marinus Koster' X 'Snow Queen'), Larson

Dora Amateis AE *(carolinianum* X *ciliatum)*, Amateis

Doris Caroline PA 1960 ('Loderi' X 'Lady Bligh'), R. Henny

Edna McCarty PA 1959 ('Alice' X *auriculatum)* X *discolor*, Ostbo

Elizabeth Titcomb PA 1958 ('Marinus Koster' X 'Snow Queen'), Larsen

Endre Ostbo PA 1954 *(souliei* X *discolor)*, Magor, Ostbo

Eulalie Wagner PA 1963 ('J. H. van Nes' X 'Loderi King George'), Lem, Fawcett

Exotic PA 1961 ('Loderi King George' X Ostbo's #3), Bovee

Fair Lady PA 1959 *(arboreum* var. *roseum* X 'Loderi Venus'), R. Henny

Fawn PA 1959 *(fortunei* X 'Fabia'), James

Flatterer PA 1957 ('Corona' X 'Lady Bessborough'), R. Henny

Flora Markeeta PA 1967 *(thomsonii* X ('Unique' X 'Luscombei'), Beck

Full Moon PA 1955 ('Hawk' X 'Adriaan Koster'), John Henny

Geneva PA 1955 ('Unknown Warrior' X 'Fabia'), Bacher

George Grace PA 1952 ('Loderi' X 'Borde Hill'), R. Henny

Gladys Johnson PA 1958 ('Diva' X *fortunei)*, Johnson

Gold Mohur PA 1955 ('Day Dream' X 'Margaret Dunn'), Brandt

Golden Wit P.A. 1967 Scyphocalyx X (Moonstone X Adrastia) Michaud

Great Lakes PA 1960 ('Catawbiense Album' X *yakusimanum)*, Leach

Helen Johnson PA 1956 ('Mrs. Furnival' X 'Mrs. Donald Graham'), Ostbo

Hotei PA 1964 ('Goldsworth Orange' X *souliei-wardii)*, Sifferman

Idol PA 1957 ('Loderi King George' X 'Britannia'), R. Henny

Inca Gold PA 1961 *(chlorops* hybrid), Lancaster

James Barto PA 1953 (Parentage Unknown), Barto, Prentice

Julie Titcomb PA 1958 ('Marinus Koster' X 'Snow Queen'), Larson

Ken Janeck PA 1964 *(yakusimanum* seedling), Janeck

Kimberly PA 1963 *(williamsianum* X *fortunei)*, H. Greer

King of Shrubs PA 1950 *(discolor* X 'Fabia') ?, Ostbo
Lackamas Blue PA 1963 *(augustinii* clone), Lancaster
Lackamas Cream PA 1962 *(chlorops* clone), Lancaster
Lackamas Gold PA 1962 *(chlorops* X *wardii)*, Lancaster
Lackamas Spice PA 1962 *(chlorops* X *diaprepes)*, Lancaster
Lake Labish PA 1955 ('Lady Bligh' X 'Loderi Venus'), R. Henny
Last Chance PA 1957 ('Mars' X *eriogynum)*, R. Henny
Leaburg PA 1956 *(dichroanthum* X 'Penjerrick'), Phetteplace
Lem's Goal PA 1952 ('Lady Bessborough' X 'Azor'), Lem
Lisa PA 1962 ('Catalgla' X 'Madonna'), Gable
Little Lou PA 1963 ('Lucy Lu' X *valentinianum)*, M. Summer
Little Pudding PA 1953 *(decorum* X 'Fabia'), R. Henny
Little Sheba PA 1954 ('Earl of Athlone' X 'Fabia') X *repens*, R. Henny

March Sun PA 1963 ('Caucasicum Citrinum' X 'Moonstone'), Wyrens
Maricee AE 1960 *(sargentianum* sdlg.), Caperci
Marine PA 1960 *(augustinii* sdlg.), Bovee
Martha Isaacson PA 1956 *(occidentale* X 'Mrs. Donald Graham' PA), Ostbo
Mary Belle PA 1962 ('Atrier' X 'Dechaem'), Gable
Mary Harmon AE 1958 ('Mrs. Donald Graham' X *occidentale)*, Ostbo
Mary Mayo PA 1960 ('Loderi King George' X Ostbo Y3), Bovee
Merle Lee PA 1954 ('Azor' selfed), Esch
Mildred Fawcett PA 1960 ('Faggetter's Favorite' X 'Mrs. Donald Graham'), T. Fawcett
Miss Olympia PA 1960 ('Loderi King George' X *williamsianum)*, Ostbo, Clark
Miss Sausalito P.A. 1967 (Loderi Venus X Calophytum) Bovee
Moontide PA 1955 *(wardii* X 'Loder's White'), R. Henny
Mrs. A. F. McEwan AE 1956 ('Loderi' seedling), Univ. of Wash. Arboretum
Mrs. Donald Graham PA 1954, AE 1958 ('Corona' X *griersonianum)* X 'Loderi', Rose, Ostbo
Mrs. Horace Fogg PA 1963 *(griersonianum* X 'Loderi Venus'), Larson

Nestucca PA 1960 *(fortunei* X *yakusimanum)*, C. Smith

Odee Wright PA 1966 ('Mrs. Betty Robertson' X 'Idealist'), Wright
Opal Fawcett AE 1958 (azaleadendron, ?), Ostbo, Fawcett
Ostbo's Low Yellow PA 1960 (Parentage Unknown), E. Ostbo, O. Ostbo

Phyllis Ballard PA 1956 *(neriiflorum* X *dichroanthum)* X discolor, F₂, Ostbo

Pink Mermaid PA 1954 ('Azor' selfed), Esch

Pink Parfait PA 1961 (parentage unknown-azaleadendron), J. Senko

Ray PA 1956 *(fortunei* X 'Idealist'), James

Red Cloud PA 1953 ('Corona' X 'Tally Ho'), R. Henny

Redwax PA 1958 *(haematodes* X 'May Day'), R. Henny

Renhaven PA 1955 ('Umpqua Chief' X *elliottii),* James

Riplet PA 1961 *(forrestii* var. *repens* X 'Letty Edwards'), Lem

Roseann PA 1956 ('Britannia' X 'Loderi Venus'), R. Henny

Rose Elf PA 1954 *(racemosum* X *pemakoense),* Lancaster

Ruby F. Bowman PA 1951 *(fortunei* X 'Lady Bligh'), Bowman, Druecker

Ruth Lyons PA 1961 *(davidsonianum* seedling), Barto, Lyons

Sandra Marie PA 1959 (deciduous azalea), Bovee

Sharon PA 1955 *(souliei* X 'Loderi King George'), James

Snow Lady PA 1955 ('leucaspis' X 'ciliatum' ?), Rothschild, Lancaster

Souldis PA 1954 *(souliei* X *discolor),* Ostbo

Starlet PA 1963 ('Diva' X *williamsianum),* Lem, Fawcett

Stoplight PA 1951 *(griersonianum* X 'Cornubia'), R. Henny

Thelma PA 1958 *(griersonianum* X 'Armistice Day'), Lem

Tidbit PA 1957 *(dichroanthum* X *wardii),* R. Henny

Towhee PA 1965 ('C. P. Raffill' X 'Red Cap') X 'Tally Ho', James

Trude Webster PA 1963 ('Countess Of Derby' X ?), Greer

Tumalo PA 1955 *(decorum* X 'Loderi King George'), James

Tyee AE 1960 ('Esquire' X 'Idealist'), James

Vampire PA 1951 ('Britannia' X 'Fabia'), A. Wright

Voodoo PA 1952 ('Britannia' X 'May Day'), R. Henny

Warpaint PA 1956 *(elliottii* seedling), James

White Olympic Lady PA 1960 ('Loderi King George' X *williamsianum),* Clark

Wink PA 1960 ('Loderi' X 'Mrs. Mary Ashley'), R. Henny

Wizard AE 1959 ('Catawbiense Album' X 'Fabia'), Lem

Yellow Creek PA 1958 ('Sarita Loder' X 'Idealist'), James

P.A. 1967 (Thomsonii X Loderi Superlative) Pierce. Name submitted for verification.

ADDITIONAL VARIETIES

In addition to the varieties rated and described, and to those in the Awards Plant list, a number of others came up for discussion. Some were American varieties, many were from Great Britain. Most were relatively new, others, especially of English origin were introduced some years ago but were not well known to most of the committee members. The committee suggested that a number of these be printed, with the parentage, and the name of the breeder to indicate that they were left out of the ratings because of lack of information about them.

Akbar—*discolor* X 'Loderi King George', Rothschild.

Allegro—'Azor' X 'Loderi King George', Lancaster.

Anna Baldsiefen—'Pioneer' selfed, Baldsiefen.

Anna Hall—*catawbiense* var. *album* 'Glass' X *yakusimanum,* Leach.

Argosy—*discolor* X *auriculatum,* Rothschild.

Aries—*thomsonii* X *neriiflorum,* Ramsden.

Avita—*occidentale* X 'Margaret Dunn', Brandt.

Babylon—*calophytum* X *praevernum,* Reuthe.

Barbara—*campylocarpum* var. *elatum* X 'Loderi'.

Barto Rose—a selection of *R. fargesii,* Barto, James, Phetteplace.

Besse Howells—

Betty Breen—smirnowii X a Dexter hybrid, Leach.

Biskra—*cinnabarinum* var. *roylei* X *ambiguum,* Rothschild.

Blaze—'Mars' X *catawbiense* var. *rubrum,* Leach.

Blush Button—'C. O. D.' X 'Honeydew', Mrs. Knippenberg.

Boule de Rose—red *catawbiense* hybrid X 'Boule de Neige', Leach.

Break of Day—'Dawn's Delight' X *dichroanthum,* Rothschild.

Burgundy—'Britannia' X 'Purple Splendour', Lem.

Carex Blush—*irroratum* X *fargesii,* Rothschild.

Carex White—*irroratum* X *fargesii,* Rothschild.

Chesapeake—*pubescens* X *keiskei,* Nearing.

Chintz—parentage unknown, Waterer.

Cindy—*calostrotum* X *ciliatum* var. *bergii,* Larson.

C. O. D.—*fortunei* X ?, Dexter, Everitt.

Conestoga—*carolinianum* X *racemosum,* Gable.

Conewingo—*haematodes* X *diphrocalyx,* Gable.

Corinne—'Vulcan' selfed, Lem, McClure.

Darlene—*griersonianum* X 'Armistice Day', Lem.

Delaware—*pubescens* X *keiskei,* Nearing.

Doubloons—'Moonstone' X 'Carolyn Grace', Wright.

Dream Girl—'Day Dream' X 'Margaret Dunn', Brandt.

El Alamein—*griffithianum* hybrid, Kluis.

Estelle Gatke—'Loderi Venus' X 'Tally Ho', Gatke.

Eupheno—*sperabile* X *griersonianum,* Aberconway.

Evelyn—'Loderi Venus' X 'Britannia', R. Henny.

Fanfare—red *catawbiense* hybrid X red *catawbiense* hybrid, Shammarello, Leach.

Fascinator—*forrestii* var. *repens* X 'Hiraethlyn', Aberconway.

Fayetta—'Tally Ho' X 'Golden Horn', Whitney.

Finch—a selection of *R. desquamatum,* R. Henny.

Finesse—*souliei* X 'Bowbells', R. Henny.

Fireball—*barbatum* X 'Ascot Brilliant', Gill.

Fire Bird—'Norman Shaw' X *griersonianum,* Rothschild.

Firetail—'Britannia' X *eriogynum,* Crosfield.

Flame—'Corona' X 'Loderi', Lem.

Flare—'Mrs. R. S. Holford' X (*auriculatum* X *griersonianum*), Slocock.

Fortune—*falconeri* X *sinogrande,* Rothschild.

Francis Hanger—*dichroanthum* X 'Isabella', Rothschild.

G. A. Sims—parentage unknown, Waterer, Sons & Crisp.

Gaul—'Shilsonii' X *elliottii,* Rothschild.

Gene—*spiciferum* X *ciliatum,* Mulligan.

Gina—parentage unknown, Lowinsky.

Glow—*griersonianum* X 'Armistice Day', Bovee.

Golden West—*fortunei* X *campylocarpum*, James.

Halcyone—*souliei* X 'Lady Bessborough', Rothschild.

Helen—*decorum* X 'Souldis', Brandt.

Hiraethlyn—*haematodes* X *griffithianum*, Aberconway.

Hockessin—*pubescens* X *keiskei*, Nearing.

Hotshot—*eriogynum* X 'Mars', R. Henny.

Ibex—*griersonianum* X *pocophorum*, Rothschild.

Impeanum—*impeditum* X *hanceanum*, Kew.

Inamorata—*wardii* X *discolor*, Rothschild.

Isabella—*griffithianum* X *auriculatum*, Loder.

Jade—'Fabia' X 'Corona', R. Henny.

Jervis Bay—*wardii* X 'Lady Bessborough', Rothschild.

John McLaren—*arboreum* X 'Shilsonii'.

Karkov—*griersonianum* X 'Red Admiral', Rothschild.

Kiev—*elliottii* X 'Barclayi', Rothschild.

Kingcup—*dichroanthum* X 'Bustard', Rothschild.

Lori Eichelser—pink *forrestii* var. *repens* X 'Bow Bells'; Brandt, Janeck.

Kismet—'Grenadier' X 'Pygmalion', R. Henny.

Leda—*apodectum* X *griersonianum*, Aberconway.

Little Dragon—'Fabia' X *venator*, Lancaster.

Lucy Lou—*leucaspis* X (*ciliatum* X *leucaspis*), Larson.

Madonna—(*decorum* X *griersonianum*) X 'America', Gable.

Mandalay—*haematodes* X *venator*, Rothschild.

Mary Francis Hawkins—parentage unknown, Gable.

Mellow Gold—*wardii* X *campylocarpum*, Lancaster.

Moonglow—'Loderi Venus' X 'Lady Bessborough', Rothschild.

Mt. Mitchell—*maximum* X *catawbiense*, Gable.

Mucram—*mucronulatum* X *ambiguum*, Gable.

Nancy Read—*pemakoense* X 'Racil', Larson.

Nymph—*forrestii* var. *repens* X 'Largo', Aberconway.

Old Copper—'Vulcan' X 'Fabia', Van Veen.

Othello—'Carmen' X ('Armistice Day' X *griersonianum*), Brandt.

Pastel Star—(*catawbiense* var. *rubrum* X *discolor*) X 'Azor', Hardgrove.

Penny—'Sarita Loder' X 'Idealist', James.

Pink Petticoats—'Jan Dekens' selfed, Lofthouse.

Prelude—*wardii* X *fortunei*, Rothschild.

Quinella—'Britannia' X 'May Day', R. Henny.

Red Cap—*didymum* X *eriogynum*, Stevenson.

Red Riding Hood—'Atrosanguineum' X *griffithianum*, Slocock.

Rev Rose—pink *forestii* var. *repens* X 'Bow Bells', Brandt.

Ruby Hart—'Carmen' X 'Elizabeth' X *elliottii*, Whitney.

Seattle Gold—'Diva' X 'Lady Bessborough', Lem, McClure.

Seta—*spinuliferum* X *moupinense*, Aberconway.

Sir James—a *fortunei* hybrid, Gable.

Spring Song—(*racemosum* X *keiskei*) X *keiskei*, Hardgrove.

Starlight—*carolinianum* X *leucaspis*, Hardgrove.

Starry Eyed—(*catawbiense* var. *rubrum* X *discolor*) X 'Azor', Hardgrove.

The Don—'Doncaster' X *griffithianum*, Lowinsky.

The General—red *catawbiense* sdlg. X red *catawbiense* sdlg., Shammarello.

Tolo—'Sarita Loder' X (*lacteum* X 'Mary Swathling'), James.

Treasure—*forrestii* var. *repens* X *williamsianum*, Crosfield.

Umpqua Chief—'Fabia' X 'Azor', James.

Vernus—*catawbiense* hybrid X 'Cunningham's White', Leach.

Virginia Scott—a *souliei* hybrid, Larson.

Virginia Richards—(*wardii* X 'F. C. Puddle') X 'Mrs. Betty Robertson', Whitney.

War Paint—a selection of *R. elliottii*, James.

Whimsey—*souliei* X 'Bow Bells', R. Henny.

William Montgomery—'Atrosanguineum' X *griersonianum*, Gable.

William R. Coe—a *fortunei* hybrid, Dexter.

Part II

THE

TWO THOUSAND

YEAR CURSE

OF THE

RHODODENDRON

THE TWO THOUSAND

YEAR CURSE

OF THE RHODODENDRON

DAVID G. LEACH

INTRODUCTION

The green cloak of vegetation which beneficially mantles the earth has some painful traps for the unwary: poison ivy, stinging nettles, poison oak, the devil's walking stick and others similarly spined or daggered. These are the obvious malefactors in the generally benign world of plants. And then there are a few deceptive weeds and flowers of innocent appearance which are dangerously toxic if parts of them are eaten. Children are warned to avoid the beckoning blue blossoms like helmets with beaked visors on the venomous monkshood, and to shun the black berries which glitter invitingly on the notorious nightshade. But the Rhododendron, the dramatically beautiful springtime feature of surburban landscapes, without evil reputation, has the most lurid past of all.

Rhododendrons and Azaleas, both in the same genus of plants, contain one of the most deadly of the world's natural poisons. Its grim history coils back more than 2,400 years. In the ancient world the course of western civilization was affected by its lethal impact. In modern times victims of rheumatism and arthritis suffered appallingly for nearly a century after a German experimenter published an erroneous report that an infusion made from Rhododendron leaves would cure the diseases.

RHODODENDRON HONEY AND THE GREEK ARMY

Ironically, primitive peoples knew the poisonous properties of the Rhododendron. The pounded pulp of the leaves was thrown into a pool of water to paralyze fish so that they could be caught on the surface. But the first man in recorded pre-Christian history to be ensnared by the deceptive Rhododendron was Xenophon, the brilliant intimate of Socrates, author and military leader. His *Anabasis* describes the retreat from Babylon of 10,000 Greek soldiers of fortune in 401 B. C. following the slaughter of their officers by the treacherous Persians. Trapped deep inside Asia Minor, surrounded by the enemy, the despairing Greeks elected Xenophon to command. Taking a supreme gamble, he led them inland to the mountains of Kurdistan. In deep snows and bitter cold the starving soldiers fought their way through savage mountain tribes into Georgia and then Armenia.

Two days' march from Trebizond (Trabzon) on the Black Sea coast of Turkey, the army came near to disaster. In Xenophon's own words, ". . . there being great quantities of beehives in those villages, all the soldiers who ate of the honeycombs lost their senses, and were seized with vomiting and purging, none of them being able to stand on their legs. Those who ate but a little were like men very drunk, and those who ate much, like madmen, and some like dying persons. In this condition great numbers lay on the ground, as if there had been a defeat, and the sorrow was general. The next day, none of them died, but recovered their senses about the same hour they were seized; and the third and fourth day they got up as if they had taken a strong potion."

At no time in the retreat had the soldiers been so vulnerable. Had the harrassing Colchian enemy attacked, one of the epics of military history would have become an anticlimax of accident, an obscure textbook footnote, instead of the stirring account of bravery, endurance and ingenuity spurring a determined army of the lost through two thousand miles of hardship in hostile lands to final success and reunion with Greece.

Xenophon's anguish as he faced catastrophe with his soldiers unaccountably stricken after months of battle and privation was all because of a Rhododendron. The honey had been made from the poisonous nectar of the yellow flowered Pontic Azalea, *Rhododendron luteum*, which gilds the hillsides in springtime near Trebizond to this day, and brings harrowing illness and death to its peasants.

RHODODENDRON HONEY AND A ROMAN DEFEAT

History is full of curious coincidences, and the Roman Empire was later to falter for a time because of the same Rhododendron. In 67 B. C. Cicero had supported the transfer of army command from Lucullus to Pompey in perhaps the most skillful of his political speeches. And so Pompey, thirty-seven years old and the Alexander the Great of his day, embarked on a campaign to conquer Rome's ancient and inveterate enemy, the King of Pontus. His adversary was King Mithridates, one of the most formidable intellects and most dramatic personalities of the ancient world. Mithridates had mastered twenty-two languages. He was an art collector, a magician, a giant of a man, as famous for his strength, courage and skill with weapons as for his prodigious capacity for food and drink.

The campaign began auspiciously. Pompey's military genius steadily eroded the armed strength of Mithridates until the following year, when three of his armies camped near Trebizond, at almost exactly the same place where Xenophon's exhausted soldiers had stopped to forage for provisions three hundrd and thirty-five years earlier. The drama was repeated but with an ending far different, described a few years later by the native historian, Strabo, in his *Geography*. After eating the poisonous honey the disabled troops were massacred by the Pontic army and it was to take Pompey three years to defeat Rome's wily enemy. So, to a degree, was the flow of power of the Roman Empire dammed for a time by a Rhododendron.

Almost certainly Mithridates knew of the toxic honey produced from the golden flowered Azalea of the Armenian hills. By a coincidence still more curious, his personal physician was Krateuas, a Greek expert on plants and their medicinal uses, considered to be the first herbalist of record. His drawings are reproduced in the most famous of all manuscript herbals, the *Juliana Anicia Codex*.

The reason for Pompey's military reverse filtered back to Rome and became a part of the lore surrounding the legendary general. A hundred years later the renowned Roman naturalist, Pliny, was writing, "Another kind of honey there is in the same region of Pontus . . . which because it driveth folks into a rage and madness, they call in Greek *maenomenon*. Some attribute the occasion hereof to the flower of the Rhododendrons whereof the woods and forests there be full. The nation selleth no honey at all, because it is so venomous and deadly: notwithstanding they do pay for tribute a huge masse of wax unto the Romans every year."

RECORDS FROM EARLY HERBALS

Dioscorides, a Greek physician in the service of Nero and the greatest pharmacologist of all antiquity, whose *De materia medica* was the dominant herbal used by physicians for more than 1,500 years, wrote a half century after the birth of Christ, "About Heraclea Pontica, in certain seasons of the year, the honey makes those mad who eat of it; and this certainly proceeds from the quality of the flowers from which it is distill'd. They sweat abundantly, but they are eas'd by giving them rue, salt-meats and metheglin, in proportion as they vomit. This honey is very acid, and causes sneezing. It takes redness from the face, if pounded with costus. Mixed, with salt or aloes, it disperses the black spots that remain after bruises."

A millenium and a half passed. Through the hush of the dark ages and the brilliant clamor of the Renaissance few real advances were made in pharmacology. Following the invention of the printing press the most useful guide for doctors that could be produced was still Dioscorides' *De materia medica,* issued in two editions in 1478, about 1,500 years after it was first written.

The earliest Renaissance reference to Rhododendrons is in *Medendi Ratio* ("An Account of Healing"), by Paul Aeginetes, published in Latin in Basle is 1538. It is now in the library of the Palace of Rectors in Dubrovnik, Yugoslavia. "Concerning poisoned honey," he wrote, "which is produced in Heraclea, those who ate or drank the honey . . . suffered the same unpleasant after-effects as those who took aconite." He is proud to be able to offer an infallible antidote: "A very sound remedy exists in aqua mulsa which is swallowed, an undiluted drink mixed with the leaves of rue." Elsewhere he warned, "The bark of the Rhododaphne tears asunder; this taken internally is fatal."

By 1581 the Rhododendron itself was generally known to be dangerous, at least to herbalists. Maplet, in his *Diall of Destiny*, cautioned, "Rhododaphne which being taken inwardly, poysoneth."

In 1700 Joseph Pitton de Tournefort, the most eminent botanist in Europe before Linnaeus established the classification of flora still in use today, spent three years in Greece and Asia Minor collecting plants at the direction of Louis XIV.

Eighteen years after his journey to the Near East his *Relations d'un Voyage du Levant* was published, a vivid recital of his observations and a diary of suspense relating the perils of his journey. In it he weighed the writings of the ancient Greeks and Romans on Rhododendrons and added an anecdote of his own: "I thought it *(R. luteum,* the Pontic Azalea) so very fine that I made up great nosegays of it to put in the Bassa's tent: but I was told by the first officer of the household that this flower caus'd vapours and dizziness. I thought he rally'd very pleasantly, for the Bassa complain'd of those distempers. The first officer gave me to understand that he was in earnest, and assur'd me he had lately been inform'd by the natives that this flower was prejudicial to the brain. Those good people, from a very ancient tradition, grounded perhaps upon several observations, maintain also that the honey which the bees make after sucking that flower, stupifies those who eat it, and causes loathings."

MODERN REPORTS OF POISON HONEY

More than two hundred years later the honey produced in the lands surrounding the Black Sea was still an annual scourge. Dr. G. Mosolevsky of Sukhum in Transcaucascia, writing in 1929: "Cases of poisoning are very numerous, particularly among the villagers in the mountains. Three to four hours after consuming honey suddenly slight vertigo comes on and instantly disappears. It is the first warning of approaching danger. Experienced people usually at once . . . purify the stomach by causing vomiting. If this is not done, after about half an hour a fresh paroxysm of vertigo follows—a much more violent one this time. The succeeding intervals grow shorter and shorter, the paroxysms more and more violent, till you feel that you are deprived of the ability to stand and must hasten to lie down. At the same time one becomes almost blind; the whole field of sight fills with the most intense whirls of bright golden-yellow colour. Some individuals speak of dark whirls."

"The utmost weakening or derangement of the sense or sight is the outstanding characteristic of this process. Considerable weakening of the heart's action can be observed. In the worst cases convulsions occur, sometimes very violent ones; and a long swoon, resulting

—if not in death—in the utmost weakness for a long time. Fatal cases occur most frequently among children. As for medical assistance, it is—with our exceedingly impassable roads—merely a distant *pium desiderum.*" Twenty-three hundred years earlier Aristotle, with some justification, had imagined that honey made from the Pontic Azalea "depriv'd those of their Senses who eat of it, and were in health before; and that on the contrary, it cured those who were already mad."

RHODODENDRON LEAF TEA FOR ARTHRITIS

In 1768, in St. Petersburg of Imperial Russia, John George Gmelin, a German professor of chemistry and natural sciences who explored Siberia with Vitus Bering for ten years, published in Latin *Flora Sibirica,* which was to bring down upon the Europeans a curse lasting more than a century. He reported that a tea made from the leaves of the Siberian Snow Rose was used successfully by foresters in the East to alleviate rheumatic knee pains, and as a restorative after laboring at high altitudes. He was referring to *Rhododendron chrysanthum,* a dwarf species with white or yellow flowers which grows in the eastern reaches of Asiatic Russia. J. G. Gmelin's book was published posthumously but his notebooks had been inherited by his newphew, Samuel Gottlieb Gmelin, also a professor and botanist at St. Petersburg, who explored southeastern Russia with another famous botanist-author, Peter Simon Pallas from 1768 to 1773. The nephew passed on to the chief health officer of Stettin in Germany, Dr. Alexander Bernard Koelpin, the information of medical interest which he had found in his uncle's papers.

On October 10, 1776 Dr. Koelpin began treating fifteen of his arthritic patients with tea prepared from dried Rhododendron leaves which he had received through Professor Pallas from Siberia. With German thoroughness, he kept a daily diary. His first patient drank two ounces each morning for the first twelve days with no effect. On the thirteen day he was given four ounces without result. On the fourteenth day the amount was increased to eight ounces. Within two hours the sixty-eight year old patient was violently ill and in a short time he lost consciousness. His pulse was weak and slow; his heart skipped every fourth or fifth beat. Dr. Koelpin carefully noted that the body felt cold and clammy even though the room was overheated. He left instructions that he was to be notified of any change and then returned in late afternoon when no word was received. By that time the patient was normal except for a feeling of constriction in his chest.

The treatment was continued. On the fifteenth day the patient continued to complain of tightness in his chest and the following day he had severe diarrhea. By the seventeenth day the chest pain was so piercing that the wretched patient described it in terms of a wood-chopper flailing rhythmically with an axe beneath his breastbone. Koelpin noted that the pulse was weak and decided to reduce the daily morning tea to two ounces. Even so, the chest pain persisted.

For the next several days vomiting was so violent that Dr. Koelpin discontinued the medication, whether by necessity or out of consideration his diary does not note. After two days the patient was told to resume the morning tea at eight o'clock. By ten he was nauseated, the tightness in his chest was severe, breathing was painful and he went into convulsions as he was telling Dr. Koelpin of the pain in his arms and legs. A short time later he lost consciousness. The pulse was feeble. When he revived late in the afternoon the base of his palm was numb and remained so until the following day.

On October 27th, seventeen days after the treatment was started, the patient reported that his arthritic pain had disappeared and that he was comfortable except for the tightness in his chest. The morning tea was continued but a few days later his pulse slowed alarmingly. He felt intoxicated and by the end of November he was near unconsciousness again, with a halting, irregular pulse and excruciating pain beneath his breastbone. During December the patient's breathing became so slow that he was near suffocation and Dr. Koelpin prudently decided in early January, three months after it was begun, to stop the medication. The patient lived for nine months afterward, his arthritis somewhat improved.

Fourteen other suffering rheumatics were given the Rhododendron infusion with much the same hideous results, described in lurid, conscientious detail by the German doctor. Two of them died, but the physician thought that the tea was not responsible. Dr. Koelpin felt that the treatment in his eleventh case was particularly successful in relieving the pain of arthritis and so he published, in 1779, his treatise for the guidance of the medical profession, *Praktische Bemerkungen uber den Gabrauch der Sibirischen Schneerose* ("The Use of the Siberian Snow Rose in Arthritis"). In it he recorded his observations and reassured other doctors that, rumors to the contrary, they need not fear that their patients' mental condition

34. Plant of *R. impeditum*, trained as bonsai by the Seattle group which prepared the chapter in this book.   *Photo Don Normark*

35. Three plants of *R. serpyllifolium* of the Azalea Series, Obtusum Subseries, in a group bonsai.

Photo Don Normark

36. A piece of petrified wood, with a convenient hollow, holding a tiny *R. radicans.*

Photo Don Normark

37. 'Racil' trained to an attractive bonsai form. *Photo Don Normark*

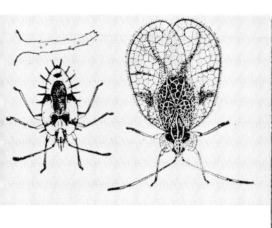

38. Upper left. Rhododendron lace bug, adult and nymph. From Insects and Diseases of Ornamental Trees and Shrubs, Felt and Rankin, Copyright 1932. The Macmillan Co. (By permission).

39. Upper right. Rhododendron whitefly adult on underside of leaf.
Photo Dr. E. P. Breakey

40. Lower left. Rhododendron whitefly. Adults congregating on new leaves. From U. S. D. A. Circular 429, 1937.

41. Lower right. Black vine weevil. Adult, pupa, and larva. Representative *Brachyrhinus* weevil.
Photo Dr. E. P. Breakey

42. Upper left. Woods weevil. Adult, dorsal view. *Photo Dr. E. P. Breakey*

43. Upper right. Obscure weevil. Adult, dorsal view.
Photo Dr. E. P. Breakey

44. Lower left. Rhododendron leaves notched by feeding of woods weevils.
Photo Dr. E. P. Breakey

45. Lower right. Rhododendron leaf showing injury to petiole by feeding of woods weevil. *Photo Dr. E. P. Breakey*

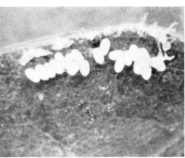

46. Upper left. Azalea girdled near surface of soil by feeding of root weevil grubs.
Photo Dr. E. P. Breakey

47. Upper right. Eggs of woods weevil fastened (cemented) to surface of rhododendron leaf near margin.
Photo Dr. E. P. Breakey

48. Lower left. Eggs of woods weevil cemented in fold near tip of azalea leaf.
Photo Dr. E. P. Breakey

49. Lower right. Rhododendron bud moth. Larva in bud.
Photo C. F. Doucette

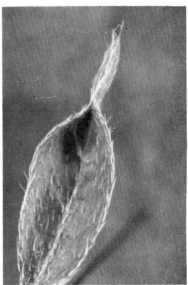

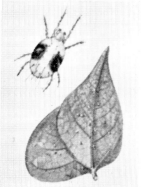

50. Upper left. Azalea leaf miner. Leaves folded by larvae.

Photo C. F. Doucette

51. Upper right. Two-spotted spider mite. Adult greatly enlarged, and infested bean leaves. From, Lawn and Garden Insect Control Manual. Copyright 1964. Geigy Chemical Corporation. (By permission).

52. Lower left. Cyclamen mite. Adult greatly enlarged, and injured cyclamen flower. From Lawn and Garden Insect Control Manual. Copyright 1964. Geigy Chemical Corporation. (By permission).

53. Lower right. Aphids infesting new growth of rhododendron.

Photo Dr. E. P. Breakey

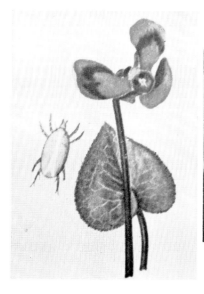

would be affected by the Snow Rose *(Rhododendron Chrysanthum)* tea. He also warned them against impatience with weak, old or long confined patients who took much longer to respond favorably, and he commented that sometimes temperamental persons were not improved at all.

The 1779 book by the German Dr. Alexander Kolpin recommending a tea made from the leaves of the poisonous Siberian Snow Rose *(Rhododendron chrysanthum)* for the treatment of arthritis had an almost hynotic effect upon the doctors of Europe, eager as they were for any remedy that might aid their afflicted patients. Eerily, it somehow persuaded them to ignore the grisley side effects which were dutifully documented and diverted their attention instead to the reported cure, however tenuous the evidence for it.

The medical profession at the time had not too long before struggled free from an arcane morass originating in sorcery and superstition. Within the century witches had been as knowledgeable as doctors in plant therapy. All medicine was derived from vegetable sources. The properties of plants had been described in books by the herbalist-physicians as "medicinal and occult." The science was yet to come. The well intentioned Dr. Koelpin doubtless had a vision of epiphany: opening the gates to heaven for the suffering. But he opened the gates to hell instead.

No one knows how many thousands, or tens of thousand of tormented arthritics were subjected to the appalling Rhododendron tea treatment as a result of the distribution of Dr. Koelpin's book to physicians throughout the continent. Rhododendron leaves were shortly included in the Pharmacopeia at Edinburgh. By 1793 Woodville remarked in his *Medical Botany* that they were "very generally employed in chronic rheumatism in various parts of Europe."

Certainly the prostrating therapy traveled quickly across the Atlantic because Professor B. S. Barton in his Collections, a compendium of information on medically useful plants published in 1794, mentions ". . . the *Rhododendron chrysanthum*, which has lately acquired much reputation in the cure of chronic rheumatism." Jacobs Bigelow, professor of Materia Medica at Harvard, published his *American Medical Botany* a few years later in which he refers to the familiar Rosebay Rhododendron of the Northeast, *R. maximum*, as possessing astringent properties, and to prove his belief that it was not poisonous described how he "swallowed a green leaf of the middle size, so large that it required some resolution to masticate so unpalatable a morsel, but have found no ill effect whatever to result from it."

The account of the determined, black garbed New England professor browsing soberly at his desk on a Rhododendron leaf evokes an entertaining mental image. But the brave Dr. Begelow was wrong. A single leaf of the American Rosebay would have produced no illness. As late as 1905 a British author, William Watson, was writing, "A decoction of *Rhododendron chrysanthum* . . . is now used in some European countries . . . in the treatment of rheumatism and other affections of the joints and muscles . . . and in the United States a decoction of the leaves of *R. maximum* is occasionally used for the same purpose." Dr. Koelpin's chamber of horrors had expanded into a corridor of suffering which extended for a hundred and fifteen years.

REPORTS OF
INTOXICATING EFFECTS OF RHODODENDRONS

In the long and venomous history of the pretty but pernicious Rhododendron its narcotic properties provided one note of comic relief. In 1768 Catherine the Great, a devoted student of human anatomy, employed a German botanist, Peter Simon Pallas, as a naturalist on a six-year expedition to explore the empire to the frontiers of China, and she subsequently underwrote the cost of publishing his book, *Flora Rossica,* in 1784. It was extraordinarily handsome for its time, bound in royal red Morocco leather with Catherine's coat of arms, the imperial double eagle, emblazoned in gold on the cover. Graceful, sophisticated colored drawings illustrated many of the plants described in Latin by Pallas, with Russian subtitles.

G. W. Steller, yet another botanist and explorer in the German colony which formed the scientific community in Russia in the eighteenth century, had edited the later volumes of J. G. Gmelin's *Flora Sibirica* after his death. Pallas described, in *Flora Rossica,* Steller's experience with a pet deer which ate about ten leaves of *Rhododendron chrysanthum.* "After a few minutes the animal began to beat the ground, to dash its head and to stagger. In a short time it fell on its knees, trying in vain to rise again, nor was it revived with milk, but overcome by a deep drunken sleep remained on the ground for several hours . . . and trembling from time to time in its sleep; however, after it awakened, it was as before—cheerful, nor did the Rhododendron ever affect it again."

But Steller's servants on the expedition had seen the cheerful deer too, and thereafter he had an exasperating time keeping them sober. They were "intoxicated very often because of the pleasure of the boiled down drink of leaves." Steller probably did not know that the Armenians had, for centuries, added small quantities of honey made from the Pontic Azalea *(R. luteum)* to alcoholic drinks to intensify their effect.

Dr. Steller later described, in his *Beschreibung von dem Lande Kamtschatka* ("A Description of Kamtschatka," 1774) how the local wild deer on the Siberian peninsula after eating Rhododendron leaves "become intoxicated, fell down and went to sleep. When the native people find an animal so affected they tie its legs together until the effect is over and then kill and eat it. But if they kill it while the animal is sleeping or mad, anyone who eats the meat will have the same symptoms of madness."

Professor Pallas, unhappily, furthered the legend of relief from arthritis by the drinking of Rhododendron tea. In his beautiful book he wrote ". . . the medicinal value of this Rhododendron has become especially famous. I have concluded that its use is harmless, because the inhabitants of the woods of Tatarus, near the ridge of Sajanense, are accustomed to use the ripened leaves continually after the manner of tea and praise them for assisting in health. I have observed that a great many inhabitants of Siberia, having been cured from very serious gouty ailments—rheumatism, nay even venereal diseases, by a boiled-down drink of the leaves—have readily returned to this excellent domestic remedy."

"I . . . when the opportunity was given, not only have proved its great usefulness, but also when an abundance of the Rhododendron (chrysanthum) leaves had been brought from eastern Siberia, gave the opportunity to my old friend Dr. Koelpin of confirming the values of this shrub by repeated experiments, nor did I stop until it might always be on hand in the future for the relief of sick people. It is now sold by public pharmacists everywhere for the price of a ruble a pound."

"Dr. Koelpin has explained the use and effects of Rhododendron in his own work. It confirmed to a very great extent what I previously reported; he explained that it is very beneficial for rheumatism and especially for chronic arthritis; that it also helps the pain of gout, even of the plague itself." Pallas overlooked Dr. Koelpin's report that the tea, held in the mouth, relieved toothache as well.

On August 15, 1796 Anthony Hove, a Polish born gardener

enroute to Bombay to obtain seeds of cotton for the West Indian colonies, at the direction of the Royal Botanic Gardens at Kew, wrote from Odessa a letter which is still in the Banks Correspondence at the famous botanic garden near London. In it he described the Pontic Azalea *(R. luteum)* notorious in antiquity and continued, "The inhabitants use the leafs & buds as Tea, especially after being fatigued with labour, they refresh themself with great and speedy surprise, it stupifyes them for an hour or so, and throws them into a sleep, on awakening they resume their work without the least appearance of bad effects."

"In Chronik Rheumatik disorders they use it with greater success of which I was not only an eye witness but have been self cured of a violent Rheumatik pain in Arms, and thighs which I had some time contracted by sleeping on the swampy grounds, and could not get rid of it until I dranck of this decoction."

"On drinking of it an English pint, I found myself quite restored in less than twenty-four hours, during the process I found myself in a kind of anxiety and great uneasiness, which lasted above an hour, recovered of the pain, much strengthened without the least symptom of headack."

"They likewise, use it in Syphylitic cases, with what success I had not so much opportunity as yet to determine, but as the disease is not very common amongst them, although they are frequently visited by the Russian Armys, I am led to credit their relation."

Two years later Hove sent a plant to Watson's Nursery in Islington which shortly flowered in a greenhouse and so, at last, the dangerous *R. luteum* was seen in bloom in the western world.

The use of the Pontic Azalea in the Ukraine and of the evergreen *R. chrysanthum* in eastern Siberia, 4,000 miles distant, to ease rheumatic pain seems an unlikely coincidence. But the buds and leaves of the Alpine Rose, *R. ferrugineum*, were gathered in the Alps and used in Italy for the same purpose. In Japan the older generation, even today, makes a tea from *Rhododendron brachycarpum*, which grows there, and dried leaves have been commonly sold for centuries in Chinese drug shops for the treatment of circulatory disorders, a remarkable prescience in view of later developments. The rolled-up leaves of another species are smoked for the relief of asthma. In China Rhododendron leaves are used to adulterate conventional tea. Southward, snuff is made in India from the powdered leaves of *Rhododendron campanulatum* which is common on the lower slopes of the Himalaya. Two other sorts are used as stimulants.

REPORTS OF LIVESTOCK POISONING

The world-wide use of Rhododendrons for medicinal purposes and as an intoxicant goes back many thousands of years but it was not fully explained until Dr. S. W. Hardikar of the Pharmacological Laboratory at the University of Edinburgh published, in 1921, an exhaustive study of Rhododendron poisoning. He reported that the active agent causes "a narcotic action upon the higher centers of the brain." Whether intoxicant, pain killer or deadly poison depends upon the size of the dose.

Dr. Hardikar began his massive study because, he said, "Some time ago some sheep in the neighborhood were reported to have shown symptoms of poisoning from eating Rhododendron leaves." In his published paper is a terse summary of the effect of injecting .28 milligrams of the Rhododendron extract into a female rabbit in his laboratory:

"May 2, 1921:

9:30 a. m. Respiration 30, heart 35, per 10 seconds

9:36 a. m. Subcutaneous injection

9:40 a. m. Respiration 20; uneasy

9:43 a. m. Respiration 11, heart 33; biting movements. Got out of tray.

9:48 a. m. Respiration, 6; laboured; mouth breathing; ears feel hot.

9:53 a. m. Tends to fall on the side, but recovers itself.

9:59 a. m. Heart 42; ran out of tray to a corner of the room.

10:00 a. m. Respiration 12; saliva dribbling from the mouth; head falls on its side, but occasionally tries to raise it.

10:05 a. m. Falls on side; pupils small and unequal in size; not responsive to light.

10:10 a. m. Respiration 10, heart 40.

10:26 a. m. Respiration 6; limbs give way when it tries to rise.

10:39 a. m. Respiration 4; heart 28.

11:07 a. m. Convulsion

11:10 a. m. Lying absolutely limp; no response on strongly pinching the skin; mouth breathing.

12:36 p. m. Convulsive tremor of limbs; mouth breathing; respiration 11, heart 19.

9:30 p. m. Respiration 7; heart 13.
9:20 a. m. Found dead and in rigor.

Domesticated animals have been scourged by Rhododendrons from pre-historic times. Those who wrote of their direct effect upon man also reported on the indirect effect through the loss of livestock by poisoning.

An issue of *The Botanical Magazine* in 1799 quotes the same Professor Pallas who extolled a tea made from the Siberian *Rhododendron Chrysanthum* as a cure for arthritis: ". . . goats, kine and sheep on eating its leaves have been poisoned thereby." In his description of the Pontic *(R. luteum)* Azalea Pallas had written, "The leaves, which smell pleasant and are bitter at first, when the pastures are not yet green, are often eaten by goats with an intoxicating effect: even the intoxicated cattle and sheep die thereupon." His contemporary colleague, G. S. Steller, across the continent at the Pacific limit of Asia, saw "a goat, which, by eating . . . the plant, was seized in a few minutes with tremblings, sopor, etc." related Woodville in his *Medical Botany* of 1792. Forty-six years later John Lindley published in London his *Flora Medica* and included in the directions for medicinal use of the Siberian Rhododendron a comment on the Pontic Azalea that "goats which browse on the leaves . . . suffer in consequence, and that . . . cattle and sheep perish."

In mid-century Sir Joseph Hooker led a plant hunting expedition to Sikkim which resulted in the publication in 1849 of *Rhododendrons of the Sikkim Himalaya*. He described one of his discoveries, the beautiful bell-flowered Cinnabar Rhododendron *(R. cinnabarinum)*, as being "universally considered poisonous to cattle and goats." J. G. Millais produced a notable volume on Rhododendrons in 1917 in which he commented ". . . the leaves of many species are poisonous to animals. *R. ferrugineum* causes losses in the Alps; sheep, goats and cattle are poisoned and sometimes killed by *R. ponticum*." He describes the near-fatal effect on a baker's horse which had nibbled two shoots of *R. ciliatum* "in a gentleman's drive." "In England," wrote Watson in 1905, "Rhododendrons are not usually eaten by animals, not even by rabbits and hares, but when they have been eaten by accident their effect has been noxious."

Half a world away the sole species which is found in Afghanistan *(R. afghanicum)* is notoriously virulent. It has been a curse of shepherds for centuries. In 1965 an explorer in New Guinea, Michael Black, wrote of an orange flowered Rhododendron common in the

Central Highlands, "It has a reputation through the country of being exceedingly poisonous to livestock, and I was told of three mules which had recently expired after eating small quantities of the foliage."

In the United States, Chesnut's *Preliminary Catalogue of Plants Poisonous to Stock* lists the common West Coast Rhododendron *(R. macrophyllum)*, as being injurious to sheep in Oregon, and the only western native Azalea *(R. occidentale)*, is indicted by Professor Pommel of Iowa State College as being toxic to livestock in California. In the East, the famous Catawba Rhododendron, *R. catawbiense*, of the North Carolina mountains is equally guilty. So the toll of domestic animals by the deceptively beautiful Rhododendron has been worldwide and all but unknown to millions of homeowners who treasure them in their gardens.

But perhaps the strangest application of the Rhododendron to animals was proposed by a Japanese nurseryman in the Royal Horticultural Society's *Lily Yearbook for 1964*. He suggested that lilies would not be devoured if they were planted among Rhododendrons, thus turning to advantage the usual aversion of animals to the shrub.

ISOLATION OF THE TOXIC PRINCIPLE OF RHODODENDRONS

The discovery of the effect of digitalis upon the heart stimulated a great wave of scientific investigations into medicinal plants in the latter half of the nineteenth century. In 1882 von Eykman isolated the active principle in Rhododendrons from a related Japanese plant and named it asebotoxin. Five years later Plugge found it in Rhododendrons and gave it the name andromedotoxin. Finally, in 1899, Dr. Konstantin Archangelsky at the Laboratory for Experimental Pharmacology in Strassburg isolated andromedotoxin, along with rhododendrin and rhododendrol from the leaves of *R. chrysanthum*, the infamous Snow Rose of Dr. Koelpin's book. It was a classic investigation. Methods for the segregation of the compounds were given, their physical and chemical properties defined. Andromedotoxin was shown to produce in dogs paralysis, vomiting, dyspnoea, convulsions and, finally, death from respiratory failure. But most important of all, he observed the profound depression of blood pressure in a dog after being given small doses of andromedotoxin.

In a high voltage industrial society where hypertension has been a major medical problem, Dr. Archangelsky's challenging observations were inexplicably ignored. For nearly a quarter of a century no further investigations were carried out, and then a study was made by Dr. S. W. Hardikar at the Pharmacological Laboratory of the University of Edinburgh only to determine the action of the toxin which had poisoned livestock in Scotland. Dr. Hardikar was the first to isolate pure crystalline andromedotoxin. He described in detail how it depressed respiration, slowed the heart with an accompanying toxic action on it, paralyzed the skeletal muscles and caused vomiting. Again, the provocative reduction in blood pressure was noted in his published report.

RECENT INVESTIGATON WITH ANDROMEDOTOXIN

In 1953 a group of investigators at Emory University School of Medicine, in cooperation with The National Heart Institute, repeated the Hardikar experiments, this time largely on dogs. The results were much the same but the techniques used were more sophisticated and they were able to show that some of the effects were not caused in the manner suggested by Hardikar. The depression of blood pressure was studied intensively and the discovery was made that the fall in pressure was by no means due entirely to the slowing of the heart action. Thus, after a strange hiatus of sixty years, Dr. Archangelsky's observations of 1899 were at last on the threshold of contributing to mankind's welfare.

The door was now open and a brilliant group of researchers at The National Institutes of Health entered it eagerly. Their first publication, *Andromedotoxin: A Potent Hypotensive Agent from Rhododendron Maximum*, described how a dose as small as one part in ten million of andromedotoxin lowered the blood pressure of dogs by as much as forty percent. The next paper showed exactly the site of effect in the circulatory system and proved that the action was entirely reflex in nature. At the same time, the structure of the andromedotoxin molecule was partially determined.

Two groups of researchers at Nagoya University and Okayama University in Japan made a critical contribution when they provided, in 1961, a structural formula for acetylandromedol, as it is now called. And finally, in 1962, an American investigator completed the long search when he determined in detail the stereochemical structure of the acetylandromedol molecule.

So a final, paradoxical chapter is about to be added to conclude one of the strangest stories in the annals of medicine. At last, after twenty-four centuries of vicious afflication, the beautiful but baleful Rhododendron can be converted from a bane to a benefit for mankind. With a model from nature of the acetylandromedol molecule research chemists can now modify it for the relief of one of the world's most pernicious illnesses, high blood pressure.

But there is yet a footnote to this curious history. In 1949 a Turkish investigator discovered a method of detecting acetylandromedol in honey made from Rhododendron nectar. Extracts of suspect honey are injected into mice and guinea pigs. Their response to the poison confirms, in modern terms, the observations of Pliny, the great naturalist of the Roman Empire. The research was done in Northern Turkey, near the shores of the Black Sea, at almost exactly the same place where the armies of Xenophon and Pompey had come to grief two thousand years and more before.

ADDENDUM

Not all Rhododendrons contain acetylandromedol, at least in their nectar, and, as a practical matter, the hazard to humans from any source but honey is infinitesimal. There are some authentic reports of bees being poisoned by Rhododendrons, which I find puzzling, and I believe that toxic honey must be extremely rare in western Pennsylvania because I seldom see honey bees "working" the flowers of the evergreen species and hybrids despite the presence of an apiary nearby. Bumble bees visit the Rhododendrons in such large numbers that the flowers are bruised by them, but the honey bees largely confine their attention to fragrant deciduous Azaleas in my plantings. Almost no scented evergreen Rhododendrons can be grown in the cold climate at Brookville. However, honey bees will consume the nectar of evergreen Rhododendrons in a laboratory as they evidently do in nature in other climates. Some strains of honey bees are presumably immune to the toxic nectar whereas others are not.

It is obviously prudent for growers of Rhododendrons, and especially for those with sizeable plantings of *R. luteum* or other fragrant deciduous Azaleas to be wary of honey produced in nearby hives. In a report published in the *Journal of Pharmacy and Pharmacology* in 1959, researchers at the University of Glasgow and the West of Scotland College of Agriculture found that *R. thomsonii* and its hybrids secrete nectar which is especially and virulently poisonous. Their findings can be summarized as follows:

Highly Toxic	Intermediate	Non-Toxic
thomsonii	barbatum	fictolacteum
arboreum	sinogrande	sperabile
niveum	fulvum	neriiflorum
pratti	macabeanum	sperabiloides
Red Admiral	Abbott	scyphocalyx
Fiery Cross		haematodes
Barclayi		Dicharb
Red Star		Redwing
R. J. G. Millais		May Day
Ascot Brilliant		

The parentage does not necessarily indicate whether a hybrid will be toxic. 'Redwing', for example, derived from three poisonous species out of the four in its ancestry, is innocuous.

In western Pennsylvania animals generally avoid browsing on Rhododendrons if there are alternate plant food sources available, but the literature cites many cases of poisoning of ruminants, and there can be little doubt that Rhododendrons are a hazard to livestock.

Part III

CARE

AND

CULTURE

OF

RHODODENDRONS

RHODODENDRONS

AS BONSAI

This material was prepared by The Kelly Nishitani Bonsai Unit #73 of The University of Washington Arboretum Foundation, Seattle, Washington. Primary responsibility was in the hands of Mrs. Ainsworth Blogg, assisted by Mrs. Joseph Butler and Mrs. Charles Hayter.

With Americans becoming increasingly interested in bonsai it is only natural that rhododendron enthusiasts ask the question "Can rhododendrons be trained as bonsai?" The answer is "Yes!" The Japanese have trained them for many years, and although most of them fall into the *R. obtusum* or Kurume classifications, they have produced some beautiful specimens. Bonsai is a truly Japanese art brought to perfection over a period of five hundred years. Only in the past few years, however, have the techniques of this art become known outside of Japan.

Perhaps the greatest error in the Western mind regarding these dwarf trees is that they must be grotesquely twisted and deformed. Aside from material collected in the wild where wind, snow and the struggle to live have shaped the trees in unusual forms, the trees are grown and trained to a natural form, and therein lies the need for knowledge of how to obtain this form. Branch and root pruning, wiring, trimming, fertilizing and watering are all factors in producing healthy, beautiful miniature trees growing in containers.

Since this article mainly relates rhododendrons to bonsai, only brief instructions on technique are included. For a detailed account of all the steps necessary to obtain the results sought, it is best to refer to books on "how to". An outstanding and complete book from both a horticultural and esthetic approach is *Miniature Trees and Landscapes* by Yoshimura and Halford. An excellent companion book of advanced information is *Bonsai: Trees and Shrubs* by Lynn

Perry. To this may be added a good book on rhododendron culture such as David Leach's *Rhododendrons of the World* and one can proceed toward the development of a successful rhododendron bonsai.

Suitability of material is of primary importance in developing a bonsai. Trees grown in containers will, over a period of time, slow down in growth. Leaves will reduce in size to a degree. Flowers will not; thus it is well to consider these points when selecting material to be used. Numerous species rhododendrons, some hybrids, and some azaleas naturally have very small leaves and flowers and low growth patterns. It is in this area one will find plants that will produce beautiful effects without the many years generally required to obtain a successful bonsai. The plant's tenderness rating and the way in which it reacts to sun and exposure are also points which must be taken into consideration in choosing material suitable for bonsai culture. Additionally, some rhododendrons resent being moved; hence survival is doubtful since they must be root pruned and repotted periodically. Others are sensitive to drainage; consideration of this must be given in determining the style and manner in which they are potted.

Bonsai vary in size and style. There are four size categories for a bonsai: miniature—less than two inches in height, small— from two to four inches, medium—six to twelve inches, and large —twelve to twenty-four inches. Size of leaf and flower will determine which species will fit the classification. Similarly, a bonsai may be one of six style categories: formal, informal, upright, slanting, cascade or group planting. The shape and growth pattern of the plant will determine the style in which the tree is to be planted.

After selecting suitable material, one must select a suitable pot or container. To create a pleasing bonsai, the pot should be related to the tree. It must also have drainage holes. While the dark brown unglazed pot is most frequently found, a flowering tree is better displayed in a glazed, colored container which harmonizes with the color of the flower, but, overall, is subordinated to the tree. Pots vary in size, shape and depth. The type of material being used, the style of bonsai being created, and the esthetic eye of the individual determine the type of pot to be used. Probably the greatest error is to overpot. A general rule, however, is that round, square and octagonal pots are one-third the height of the tree. In pots of this shape the tree is always planted in the center of the container. The formula for rectangular or oval pots is that the length of the pot plus the depth equals the height of the tree. For this shape pot, the tree is potted toward the back, to the right or left of center with the longer branches extending toward the far ends of the pot visually creating a triangle. The shorter branches may extend slightly over the near end of the pot.

Since it is not always possible to obtain the Japanese bonsai pots, substitutions must be made. Low flower bowls, glazed flower pots, even cereal bowls have been adapted. In such substitutions drainage holes must be created. The process is tricky since the glaze must first be scored deeply, then the hole gradually drilled. If done with power tools, the pot must be placed in a larger container of water to offset the heat generated. Be prepared for disaster! But it can be done.

In creating a rhododendron bonsai, probably one of the most important aspects to be considered is the root system. The tiny fibrous growth can become so compact in a pot that the plant literally strangles itself to death. Hence root pruning becomes important. It is always done *after* flowering. When the blossoms are spent, they should be removed entirely and the repotting procedure begun. Two rather unorthodox methods not found in books have proved helpful in preparing a rhododendron for potting when it is necessary to prune considerable root growth. To prevent injury and to loosen the root ball, a hose is turned on it, full force. This loosens the tight ball; the roots can then be spread out and pruned, reducing them by one-half to two-thirds.

Another method, useful particularly for trees that have been potted for some time and are well established, is to cut pie-shaped wedges in several places about the roots. The tight root ball left is loosened a bit with chop sticks and then fresh soil is filled in where the wedges of root have been removed. This allows new root growth to reach out for nourishment but doesn't disturb the entire root system of the plant. Some rhododendrons will send out long, strong roots with fibrous growth at the tips. Some of these may be cut back, but several should be retained. In planting, these should be spread in as balanced a pattern as possible within the container, but not curled under and constricted. Regardless of the method used, there still must be an area into which new roots can grow. The Japanese provide precise formulas for soil, but it has been found that a soil mixture in which rhododendrons are normally happy, with the addition of a small amount of sand, is satisfactory.

Proper preparation of the container and the method of potting are important for the healthy development of the material chosen. Before planting, the holes in the pot are covered with a piece of plastic screen. Then a thin layer of soil is spread over the bottom of the pot. The soil must be in not-quite-dry condition. The tree is then placed in position with ample room for the roots to spread and grow. More soil is added and gently worked into the roots with pointed chop sticks to alleviate any chance of air pockets. This is a slow process but necessary for a healthy tree. More soil is added as needed until the tree is firmly held and the pot is filled to within one-half inch of the top. Moss may be laid on top and gently pressed in. In all cases after repotting, the plant is soaked in a transplanting solution to reduce shock and stimulate growth.

Rhododendron growth is such that shaping is better accomplished by branch pruning than by wiring. As new shoots appear all but two of them should be removed, and the remaining shoots reduced to two or three leaves. This should be done over a period of time rather than at one sitting. Branch pruning presents problems in that some species will form new growth at a dormant node, while others will not. Much of the pleasure of developing a bonsai is the horticultural experimentation that must go on to learn how to make the plant respond to the shape desired. The books previously mentioned give clear instructions that will prevent many frustrations and costly errors in pruning and shaping.

Fertilizing and general maintenance, which includes watering, are important aspects of healthy bonsai. Contrary to the myth that bonsai are starved to keep them small, they must be fertilized. This is done in the spring after flowering and again in the fall, twice a month. A liquid fertilizer in weak solution is used. Weather determines the watering schedule. During the hot months of the year this may have to be done twice a day, generally in the morning, when the sun is not on them, and again in the afternoon. It must be remembered that bonsai are not house plants. They can be brought inside for a few days at a time, but to live and grow well they must be kept outdoors. Azaleas like full sun; some rhododendrons do not, and this determines the spot in which they will live outdoors. After a plant is newly potted it is always kept in the shade for at least a week, and sheltered from wind and rain.

Following is a list of species and varieties of rhododendrons, including azaleas, that have proved satisfactory when trained as bonsai.

Campylogynum—reduce the number of flower heads for restrained beauty. Var. myrtilloides is excellent.

canadense

cephalanthum—must have good drainage; mound high when planting.

chryseum—difficult to train as a subject with a single trunk.

fastigiatum—deep purple flower outstanding.

ferrugineum

forrestii—slow to bloom; can be used in cascade style

glaucophyllum

hanceanum nanum

hippophaeoides—needs considerable moisture.

hirsutum

impeditum—locate variety inclined toward a single trunk in growth.

imperator

intricatum

kaempferi azalea

keiskei—dwarf form.

keleticum

lepidostylum

megeratum

microleucum

nitens

obtusum—variety Mystery Japonica excellent for miniature and group planting.

prostratum

pumilum—a bit touchy on pruning.

racemosum—dwarf forms best.

'Racil'

radicans

sargentianum—touchy about repotting; variety 'Maricee', fine material.

schlippenbachii—fine for large bonsai; beautiful trunk patterns.

serpyllifolium—both pink and white excellent as single specimen or in group plantings.

spiciferum

tephropeplum

trichostomum

uniflorum

williamsianum

Undoubtedly there are other species and hybrids which fit all requirements of a fine bonsai, but it is just a matter of locating the lesser known plants. Field grown plants which have been exposed to the vagaries of the seasons give one a head start on the appearance of age. Mr. and Mrs. Caperci of Rainier Mt. Alpine Gardens have made a particular effort to raise species suitable for bonsai and their stock is all field grown after leaving the propagating beds. On rare occasions it is possible to find a rhododendron which naturally has grown with all the characteristics of a finished bonsai. However, the greatest pleasure is watching the response of a plant in the hands of a patient enthusiast who may spend several years in guiding it into the shape and refinement of an outstanding bonsai.

The highest compliment to a rhododendron bonsai came in reverse at a recent Rhododendron Show where bonsai were on display. An *obtusum* owned by a local doctor was at the peak of perfection, completely covered with lavender pink blossoms. One visitor turned to her companion and asked "Is it real?" Her friend answered with a twist of the mouth, "No, plastic!"

54. *Septoria* leaf spot on azalea.   *Photo Dr. Chas. Gould*

55. *Phyllosticta* leaf spot on rhododendron.   *Photo Dr. Chas. Gould*

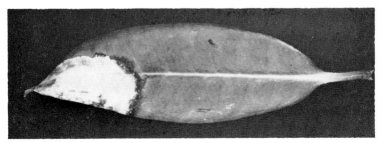

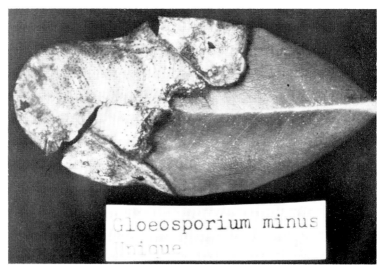

56. *Gloesporium* leaf spot on rhododendron.   *Photo Dr. Chas. Gould*

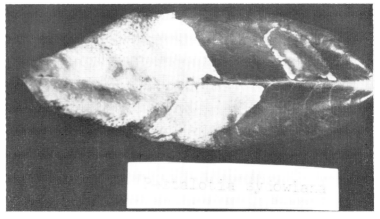

57. *Pestalotia* leaf spot on rhododendron.   *Photo Dr. Chas. Gould*

58. Upper left. *Exobasidium* leaf gall on *R. macrophyllum.*

59. Upper right. *Exobasidium* leaf blister on evergreen azalea.

60. Lower left. Rhododendron rust on spruce.

61. Lower right. Rhododendron rust on azalea leaf.

62. Mrs. Cecil Smith inspects a tall plant of *R. rubiginosum*, a Dr. Rock introduction.

Photo Cecil Smith

63. 'Loder's White' in a semi-formal garden.

Photo J. H. Clarke

64. An informal path in the rhododendron garden at Crystal Springs Lake Park in Portland, Oregon.   *Photo J. H. Clarke*

65. Water makes a good background for rhododendrons, at the Rhododendron Island, Portland, Oregon.   *Photo J. H. Clarke*

66. Light colored azaleas show well against a dark background.

67. Looking over the rock garden on Crystal Springs Lake Island towards the entrance bridge.

68.   Seedlings of deciduous azaleas being carried over winter in a green-house. *Photo J. H. Clarke*

69.   Rhododendron cuttings in the cutting bench. *Photo J. H. Clarke*

70.   Rhododendron cuttings rooted and replanted in peat.

Photo J. H. Clarke

71.   Young rhododendron plants in semi-shade in a lath house.

Photo J. H. Clarke

INSECT PESTS

OF RHODODENDRONS

AND AZALEAS

E. P. BREAKEY*

The growing of rhododendrons and azaleas can be and should be an enjoyable avocation. Unfortunately, rhododedrons and azaleas may be injured by insects and related pests. It is advisable, therefore, to be forewarned and prepared, and it is hoped the information given here will assist those who may have an insect control problem.

A few general observations may help evaluate the problems as they arise. Plants grown in considerable shade and in soil with adequate humus and mulch seldom suffer extensive damage from such insects as lace bugs. It has also been noted that such plants usually escape appreciable injury by the Japanese beetle in those areas where the insect is presently established. Moisture and shade also tend to discourage spider mites. The azalea whitefly, *Aleyrodes azalae* D. & M., injures *Rhododendron mucronatum* and related species and their derivatives but is rarely injurious to the Kurumes. A heavy infestation may spill over into other nearby species and varieties, but the insects probably will not breed on them. The rhododendron whitefly, *Dialeurodes chittendeni* Laing, is restricted primarily to those species and varieties whose leaves are relatively free of scales or tomentum on the under surfaces. Leaves with thick or leathery epidermis are also partially or wholly immune to attack.

---

*Entomologist, Washington Agricultural Experiment Stations, Washington State University.

Rhododendron Lace Bug (*Stephanitis rhododendri* How.)

The rhododendron lace bug (Fig. 38), when present, may be found on the undersides of the leaves of rhododendrons, azaleas and mountain laurel. The name lace bug alludes to the gauze-like reticulated wings, the peculiar hood-like structure over the head, and the broad lateral expansions of the prothorax, suggestive of an exaggerated Elizabethan collar. The nymphs or larvae are relatively small and spiny. It is a native of eastern United States and was introduced from there into Europe and the Pacific Northwest. It was and still is a much more serious pest in the east and south than it is in the Pacific Northwest.

Eggs are inserted in the lower surfaces of the new leaves along the midribs and larger veins in late summer and early fall. Nymphs hatch from these eggs the following spring and become fully grown by June or early July. A second generation of adults often appears in late summer or early fall.

Injury results from the insects sucking the juices from the undersides of the leaves. When feeding, they remove or destroy the chlorophyll, causing the leaves to take on a mottled grayish discoloration. Later these leaves may turn brown and leathery and cease to grow. The lower surfaces of infested leaves are further disfigured with numerous small dark varnish-like spots of excrement and sometimes with cast nymphal skins.

Azalea Lace Bug (*Stephanitis pyriodes* Scott)

The azalea lace bug apparently does not occur in the Pacific Northwest. It is one of the worst pests of azaleas in certain areas where these plants are grown and prized, and will also attack rhododendrons and mountain laurel. Its life history is very similar to that of the rhododendron lace bug and since the eggs are laid in the bark of new growth and in the midribs of the leaves, there is always danger of introducing it. Those who bring azaleas into the Pacific Northwest from other sections would do well to pick off and burn all of last season's leaves as an added precaution against introducing it.

Control

Lace bugs are readily controlled by the timely application of a good contact insecticide. Malathion is one of the most effective of the new insecticides and its use will not encourage the development of a spider mite population. Diazinon is also very effective. Both are available in emulsifiable concentrates. Prepare the spray according to the manufacturer's directions. The application of the spray should be timed to kill the nymphs before they have developed into adults and have laid eggs, i.e., about the middle of May in most areas. It is usually advisable to make a second application about a week or 10 days after the first, particularly where the foliage is dense. Spray thoroughly and direct the spray upward against the lower surfaces of the leaves.

Rhododendron Whitefly (*Dialeurodes chittendeni* Laing.)

The rhododendron whitefly (Fig. 39 and 40) may be found on the undersides of the leaves of rhododendrons. These small white moth-like insects are related to the scale insects. Like the scale insects, the immature stages are sedentary, with the exception of the newly hatched larvae which move about until they begin feeding. Adults of both sexes are winged and quite small, measuring about one-tenth of an inch across the fully expanded wings.

In 1933 the insect was found in Seattle, Washington, on rhododendrons that had been imported from England. This chance discovery prompted a survey of the Puget Sound country and disclosed well established populations in Seattle and Tacoma, in the Fraser River Valley east of Vancouver, British Columbia, and on Vancouver Island near Victoria. Fortunately, the insect has not been a serious problem in this area.

There is but one generation each year in the Pacific Northwest. The rather large eggs are laid on the undersides of the new leaves during the months of May, June and July. Development during the winter months is very slow and second- and third-stage larvae are present in about equal numbers. A few pupae may be found as early as November, but the peak development of this stage occurs in April and May.

The insects are found on the undersides of the terminal leaves where the larvae feed by sucking the plant juices. When present in numbers, the feeding of the larvae causes a yellowing and mottling of the leaves. The rate of development of the population is so slow that feeding is not deleterious to leaf growth or appearance until spring. Then the consumption of plant juices may be sufficient to give the leaves a mottled appearance. Considerable loss in ornamental value of the plant also results from the growth of sooty mold fungus on the lower leaves which catch the honeydew dropped by the larvae above them.

Azalea Whitefly (*Aleyrodes azaleae* B. & M.)

The azalea whitefly is another insect pest that apparently does not occur in the Pacific Northwest. It is very similar to the rhododendron whitefly in appearance and feeding habits. It is not a major pest of azaleas in those areas where it does occur for it may infest only a few bushes even in extensive plantings, being limited apparently to *Rhododendron mucronatum* and related species and their progeny. The Kurumes are seldom injured.

Control

Diazinon and malathion are some of the most effective of the new insecticides used to date. The best time to apply sprays for the control of whiteflies is early in the fall. The terminal leaves are still erect (Fig. 40), making effective spraying easier, and the whitefly larvae have not developed to a point where their feeding has done serious injury.

Root Weevils

Root weevils are probably the most important insect pests attacking rhododendrons and azaleas in the Pacific Northwest and are also a serious problem in other parts of the country. They destroy many valuable plants each season, and usually belong to one of three species: the strawberry root weevil, *Brachyrhinus ovatus* (L.); the rough strawberry weevil, *B. rughostriatus* (Goeze); and the black vine weevil, *B. sulcatus* (Fab.). Adults and larval forms are similar in appearance except for size. They are known collectively as the *Brachyrhinus* weevils (Fig. 41).

Life histories of all root weevils are somewhat similar. Most of them pass the winter as white to pinkish-colored legless grubs in the soil around the roots of the host plants. In the milder sections, however, some adult weevils overwinter around the bases of the plants. The over-wintering adults usually become active during the latter part of March or the first part of April.

The search for a practical control for root weevils has claimed the attention of entomologists and others for nearly a century in the United States and for a much longer time in Europe. For many years cultural practices and such impractical measures as the collecting of adults, flooding to drown the larvae, and the erecting of barriers against the migrating weevils, were the extent of our defense against these pests. As our knowledge of chemicals increased, fumigants, repellants, poisoned sprays, and poisoned baits were developed and put to test.

The development of poisoned baits has taken place in fairly recent years. Melander and Spuler (1926) of the Washington State University staff were the first to publish on the use of poisoned baits for the control of root weevils. Their work was inspired by the investigations of M. J. Forsell of Seattle who patented a bait (1927) that was known by the trade name "Go West." Forsell's investigations led to the development of the first practical and effective method of root weevil control. After the first year's baiting, the N. W. Cannerymen's Association reported an increase of 90,000 barrels of strawberries here in the Pacific Northwest.

Then came the great advance in the development and use of pesticides following the second World War. Insecticides led this advance and before long Eide (1952), also of the Washington State University staff, was able to report his success in controlling *Brachyrhinus* weevils in strawberry plantings by mixing certain new insecticides with the soil before setting the plants. After many years of failures, partial successes and frustrations, it appeared that we had a method of weevil control within our grasp that was not subject to the uncertainties of baiting.

Eide (1955) also showed that aldrin, dieldrin, heptachlor, and chlordane each gave effective control of *Brachyrhinus* weevils for two years or more when incorporated in the soil in suitable amounts, while DDT, BHC, Toxaphene and methoxychlor failed to control at any of the dosages tested. Breakey (1959) found that aldrin and heptachlor were still giving excellent control five years after application. Chlordane was still giving good control and lindane only partial control when tested under the same conditions.

Control

Incorporating either aldrin or heptachlor with the soil before setting the transplants became standard procedure for the control of *Brachyrhinus* weevils in strawberry plantings. Growers of other crops, i.e., raspberries, blueberries, azaleas, primulas, etc., where root weevils are a problem, were quick to adopt the practice.

While most growers were satisfied with the control they obtained, there were a few who reported failures. Eide (1955) was the first to report such a failure. This proved to be due to an entirely different species of weevil; one that does not belong to the Brachyrhinus group. The weevils were identified by R. E. Warner of the Entomology Research Division of the U.S.D.A., Beltsville, Maryland, and assigned to the species, *Nemocestes* (*Geoderces*) *incomptus* (Horn.), (Fig. 42.).

Eide (1959) named it the 'woods weevil', "since the strawberry fields attacked are nearly always located in brushy areas." The name is appropriate, also, for the known natural distribution of the insect is limited to the milder and more humid portions of western boreal North America.

Until quite recently, the woods weevil was so seldom encountered as to be of interest primarily as a collector's item. Presently, it is a hazard to the production of such crops as strawberries, raspberries, blueberries, azaleas, rhododendrons and primulas throughout the Pacific Coast. It has often been found in pure populations where soil treatments had eliminated the Brachyrhinus weevils. Aldrin, dieldrin, heptachlor and chlordane, have no apparent effect on either the grubs or adults of the woods weevil. Occasionally, it has been found associated with another, though smaller, native species, *Scioptes obscurus* (Horn.), the obscure root weevil (Fig. 43). By eliminating the woods weevil's chief competitors, we have enabled it to move into and occupy the areas once held by the Brachyrhinus weevils.

The adults of *N. incomptus* (Horn.) are voracious feeders (Figs. 44 and 45). The larvae or grubs not only destroy the roots of azaleas, rhododendrons, and blueberries, but girdle the plants by eating the bark from the stem immediately below the surface of the soil (Fig. 46) and often include the bark of the larger roots. Both adults and larvae of the woods weevil are much more active than those of the *Brachyrhinus* weevils and readily move about. Doubtless the larvae are capable of moving from plant to plant, providing the distance is not too great.

Life history—The *Brachyrhinus* root weevils are known to have fairly well defined life history patterns, even in western Washington where the climate seems to mitigate against an insect maintainig the same predictable development it would have in an area where the seasons are better defined. The woods weevil seems to have lost any life history pattern it may once presumably have had. Development is continuous throughout the year. When sifting the soil under azaleas in December, 1964, larvae of all sizes were found together with pupae and recently formed adults. Some of the larvae were not much larger than the eggs. Many adults were found when sifting the mulch of leaves under and around the plants. As soon as they were brought into the insectary, some began laying eggs. When recently emerged adults were taken from the soil under infested plants and placed in the insectary where they could be fed and watched, it was approximately three months before they began egg laying. Only those adults still bearing mandibulary cusps were included in this test.

The eggs have been found in neat rows near the margins on the undersides of rhododendron leaves where they had been placed side by side and firmly cemented to the leaf surface (Fig. 47). The eggs were white, kidney shaped, and about twice as long as their greatest diameter. When thinner leaves were available, such as azalea leaves, the eggs were found firmly cemented in a fold near the tip of the leaf (Fig. 48). This habit is quite different from that of the *Brachyrhinus* weevils who scatter their eggs indiscriminately through the soil and debris under the plants.

Control

Adults of the woods weevil were completely destroyed by single applications of a weevil bait containing sodium fluosilicate and dried apple pomace. Since the emergence of the adults from the soil is practically continuous throughout the year, control with poisoned baits would be very expensive and impractical.

DDT, parathion, and diazinon each gave excellent control of the adults of the woods weevil, when applied as drenching sprays to the mulch and soil surface under infested azalea plants. Aldrin, endrin, dieldrin, and cygon were ineffective when applied in the same way. DDT was slower in action than parathion or diazinon. However, DDT has a long residual life, is inexpensive and relatively safer to use. Larvae were present in the soil in large numbers and of all ages, together with pupae and adults, and adults continued to emerge for many months. No method for killing the larvae in the soil without killing the azaleas is known at present.

Rhododendron Bud Moth (*Eucordylea huntella* Keifer)

The rhododendron bud moth injures the flower buds of the native rhododendron, *Rhododendron macrophyllum* Don, along the west coast. The buds are killed and eaten by the pinkish-white larvae of a small moth. The larva partly girdles the stem at the base of the bud before eating its way up inside the bud (Fig. 49). Infested buds die and turn brown in color. Moths appear in April and May and buds containing small larvae have been found in September.

Control

Potentially, this insect could be a serious pest of rhododendrons. At the present time it seems to be confined to the native rhododendron along the coast and is apparently heavily parasitized. There are reports of some damage to plantings in the Portland area. Injured buds can be detected during the winter months and early spring. The alert grower can watch for these and remove and destroy them immediately before the larvae can escape.

Azalea Leaf Miner (*Gracilaria azaleella* Brants)

The azalea leaf miner is the larva of a tiny yellowish moth. It is primarily a greenhouse pest but may be carried into the field and is often established outside in the Pacific Northwest. Feeding of the larvae makes the plants very unsightly, injuring the leaves and reducing their activities. The small moth lays her eggs on the leaves. Tiny carterpillars hatch from these and mine the tissues of the leaves, producing irregularly shaped tunnels and blotches. When about half grown they leave these mines and fold back the edges or tips of the leaves, making shelters in which to live and feed while completing their development (Fig. 50).

The azalea leaf miner has been difficult to control because the larvae are protected by the tunnels and shelters in which they feed and because there are several overlapping generations each year. However, some of the newer insecticides have given very good control, particularly DDT, lindane, diazinon, and malathion. Follow the manufacturer's directions when preparing the spray and observe the precautions. The use of DDT may encourage the development of a spider mite population while the use of diazinon or malathion will help control these pests.

Rhododendron Leaf Miners

Two leaf miners are present on the west coast, neither of which appears to be a serious pest of rhododendrons.

The larvae of the moth, *Lyonetia candida* Braun form winding mines ending in large blotches on the leaves of rhododendrons in California, Oregon and Washington.

The larvae of the moth *Gracilaria ferruginella* Braun make tentiform mines on the undersides of the leaves of rhododendrons and roll the tips into cones throughout California. Controls that are effective against the azalea leaf miner should be effective against these insects.

Red Spiders - Spider Mites

Spider mites are small and almost invisible to any but the sharpest eyes. The average gardener can satisfy himself as to whether or not his plants are infested by jarring the leaves over a sheet of white paper. The mites will fall off and appear as specks on the paper. If these specks move, then the gardener can be quite sure he has an infestation of spider mites. There are several generations each year, the generations overlapping so that all stages can usually be found at any one time. Development in the greenhouse is practically continuous throughout the year.

Spider mites feed by sucking the juices from the undersides of the leaves. The damage appears first as small white stippling on the upper surface of the leaves. As the injury progresses the stipplings coalesce and the leaves take on a dried or burnt appearance. A heavy infestation is usually accompanied by considerable webbing.

The two-spotted mite, *Tetranychus bimaculatus* Harvey, (Fig. 51) is distributed throughout the United States. It is often a pest of azaleas, particularly when they are grown in the greenhouse. This is the mite that is known as the yellow mite in parts of the south. It does not injure azaleas so severely in the south as the southern red mite, *Paratetranychus ilicis* (McG.), but infestations of both may occur on the same plant. Infestations of the two-spotted mite are usually accompanied by a webbing on the undersides of the leaves and the mites tend to restrict their activities to the area covered by the web. Feeding within this area may be severe, the effect showing as reddish spots on the upper surface of the leaf. The mites are hairy creatures, yellowish in coloration, with dark brown areas on the sides toward the rear of the body, hence the name "two-spotted mite." The spherical eggs are yellowish and are usually laid on the undersides of the leaves.

The southern red mite is a major pest of azaleas in the south.

Heavily infested leaves appear as if sprinkled with red pepper. The mites feed on both surfaces, causing the upper surfaces to become reddish brown. Severe infestations may discolor all of the leaves and cause some of them to drop. Adult females may be nearly black, but males and nymphs are usually light red. The body of the mite is covered with spiny hairs which curve backwards. Most of the red spherical eggs are deposited on the lower surfaces of the leaves. Infestations build up during the winter months and reach the greatest population density in the spring.

Control

Spider mites can be controlled by dusting or spraying with an acaracide such as aramite, ovex, diazinon or malathion. Aramite is an effective acaracide. Ovex is also effective against most spider mites and will kill the eggs as well as the active stages. Malathion and diazinon are two of the safest of the organic phosphate insecticides but should be used with care. Prepare the spray according to the manufacturer's directions and apply to the lower surfaces of the leaves. If the infestation is well established and much webbing has been done, the grower may have difficulty in applying the spray effectively. It may be advisable to make a second application 10 days following the first to kill any mites not killed with the first application and to kill those hatching from eggs.

Soft Scales - Scale Insects

Two scale insects are known to be injurious to azaleas in the east, from Maryland southward. There have been instances when these pests have been extremely destructive.

One of these is the azalea bark louse or mealy bug, *Eriococcus azaleae* Comst. This mealy bug over winters in the south in the nymphal stage and may do the same in the more northern limits of its distribution. Eggs are deposited in a cottony sack from which the young emerge on hatching. The young crawlers disperse over the plant and attach themselves to the twigs where they remain for the rest of their lives. As the nymphs grow they produce long waxy filaments that partially cover their bodies. On maturing, these filaments become matted and form the cottony sack in which the eggs are laid. These sacks will remain on the plant for some time, and help give it an unsightly appearance. Infested plants become unthrifty and this condition together with the accumulation of dirt and old egg sacks rapidly destroys their ornamental value.

Pulvinaria ericieola McC. is the other scale insect that attacks azaleas in the east. It was described from specimens collected from the native azalea, *Rhododendron nudiflorum*, and has also been taken on *R. viscosum* in the woods and on various cultivated hybrids. The insect is usually found near the base of the plant, but if the infestation is heavy, the white egg sacks may be so numerous as to make the stems appear white for their entire length. The pest overwinters as fertile though immature females. Eggs are laid in June and the young, on hatching, establish themselves on the twigs.

The peony scale, *Pseudaonidia paeoniae* Ckll., is common in the south, but has been found occasionally as far north as Washington, D. C. Foliage of infested plants becomes thin and the twigs and entire branches may be killed. The insect apparently desposits a toxin in the plant as it feeds, killing or stunting the tissues immediately beneath it so that the outer bark of the twigs tends to overgrow the insect, more or less concealing it, and producing a globular swelling or nodule. As a result, badly infested twigs have a bumpy appearance. Eggs are deposited underneath the insect and remain over winter, hatching in late March to early May, and like the newly hatched crawlers of other species these scatter over the plant where they settle down and feed. There is only one generation each year.

Control

Summer oil emulsion has been used effectively against these pests and is usually applied at the rate of 2 per cent, 2 gallons of the emulsified oil, making 100 gallons of spray. In smaller amounts this is roughly 2 tablespoonsful to the gallon. The oil spray can be made even more effective by adding lindane to it at the rate of 1 pound of the 25 per cent wettable spray powder to each 100 gallons. In smaller amounts this would be approximately 1 teaspoonful to the gallon. Diazinon and malathion have given very good results against these insects. DDT in the emulsifiable form has also been effective against many scale insects. Prepare these sprays as directed by the manufacturer and observe the precautions.

Control measures should be directed against the nymphs or crawlers. Sprays applied soon after the eggs begin hatching usually produce best results. Oil sprays have one advantage over most others in that they will penetrate the protective covering of most scale insects.

Asiatic Beetles

The Japanese beetle, *Popillia japonica* Newm., and the brown garden beetle, *Antoserica castanea* Arrow, feed upon the foliage, eating irregular holes in it. Fortunately, neither are known to be present in the west. Japanese beetles are about ⅜ inch long, bright metallic green in color with bronze wings. They are active during the day and are often present in considerable numbers. Brown garden beetles are about ¼ inch long and of velvety chestnut-brown in color. They are active at night, hiding among the trash and rubbish on the ground during the day.

Control

Both of these beetles may be prevented from feeding upon rhododendrons and azaleas by keeping the foliage covered with a stomach poison such as DDT from the first of July until the middle of August. Unfortunately, a DDT spray prepared from the wettable spray powder may leave an unsightly residue. Many of the new insecticides can be obtained in the emulsifiable form and would doubtless be preferable since they would not leave a noticeable residue. DDT, chlordane, and aldrin are available in emulsifiable concentrates and are stable enough to provide a protective covering for several weeks. Use according to the manufacturer's directions.

Azalea or Rhododendron Stem Borer (*Obera myops* Hald.)

The stem borer is the larva of a beetle that girdles the tips of azaleas, rhododendrons, and mountain laurel in the east. The beetle places an egg below the girdle and the larva bores downward toward the crown of the plant, expelling frass from holes cut at intervals through the stem. The yellowish larva is nearly one inch long when fully grown. After constructing a pupal chamber in the crown of the plant just below the surface of the soil, the larva nearly cuts off the stem several inches above the ground line. Such weakened stems are easily broken off by the wind or by the gardener when working among the plants. Pupation takes place in the spring and the beetles emerge in June.

Control

Dead or dying tips noticed in summer or early fall should be cut out and destroyed. Cut below the point reached by the larva and immediately burn all twigs so removed.

Cyclamen Mite (*Tarsonemus pallidus*, Banks)

The cyclamen mite is often a serious pest of azaleas, particularly in greenhouses. These small mites are practically invisible to the unaided eye. They prefer the tenderest growing parts and are able to enter the buds, both flower and vegetative. Injury consists in stunted and badly distorted growth (Fig. 52), and discolored and distorted flowers.

Control

Insecticide control of the cyclamen mite has been difficult. Some of the newer insecticides have been more effective than were the older. There are a number that will kill the mites on contact. Summer oil emulsion at 2 per cent will do that and diazinon has given good control when properly applied. The difficulty is due to our inability to penetrate the buds with the insecticide. Unfortunately, many organic phosphate insecticides, such as TEPP, parathion and malathion, that were so effective against the spider mites, gave disappointing results against the cyclamen mite. The "systemics" belong to this last group and they, too, were disappointing.

Fumigation with methyl bromide is the most dependable way to clean out an infestation. Many commercial growers use methyl bromide fumigation as a routine measure in the production of their stock. This involves the construction of a gas-tight fumigation chamber equipped with a fan for circulating the gases, heating elements, and temperature contol, suitable dispensing equipment, and an exhaust fan for quickly and safely removing the poisonous fumes. None of this equipment need be costly or elaborate, but it is all essential. The methyl bromide should be used at the rate of 2 pounds per 1000 cubic feet, and the plants exposed to the gases in the fumigating chamber for 2 hours at a temperature of 70° F.

Aphids

Aphids, various species, often infest the new growth of rhododendrons (Fig. 53). They feed on the tender young leaves, causing them to curl and become badly distorted. Since many rhododendrons hold their leaves for several years, these injured leaves remain to detract from the appearance of the plant until shed several years later.

Control

The timely use of a good contact insecticide will give control. Diazinon and malathion have both given excellent control. Prepare according to the manufacturers directions and observe the precautions. Watch the development of the new growth and apply as soon as the presence of aphids is noted.

Other Insect and Mite Pests

It would be unrealistic and impractical to attempt to include all of the insects and mites that are known to attack rhododendrons and azaleas in various parts of the country. Several have been omitted from this discussion and, perhaps, others should have been. An attempt has been made to include those that are of most general interest. Also included are recent advances in our knowledge of certain pests and their control. An exception to the latter is a shoot miner in rhododendron. The writer expects to publish on the life history and control of this insect in the near future.

LITERATURE CITED

Melander, A. L. and A. Spuler. 1926. Poisoned Baits for Root Weevil. Wash. Agric. Exp. Sta. Bul. 199.

Forsell, M. J. 1927. A Composition of Matter. United States Patent No. 1,618,702, February, 22.

Eide, P. M. 1952. Soil Treatments for Strawberry Weevil Control. Proceedings of the Western Washington Horticultural Association. Jan., 1952. 43:7.

Eide, P. M. 1955. Soil Treatments for *Brachyrhinus* Control in Strawberries. Jour. Econ. Ent. 48:207-8.

Breakey, E. P. 1959. Control of Root Weevils in Strawberry Plantings. Jour. Econ. Ent. 52:1117-1119.

Eide, P. M. 1959. Ethylene Dibromide for Strawberry Weevil Control. Down to Earth, Fall, 1959 Issue, The Dow Chemical Company.

RECENT ADVANCES

IN OUR KNOWLEDGE

AND CONTROL OF

RHODODENDRON DISEASES

CHARLES J. GOULD*

Rhododendrons are one of our most disease-resistant evergreen ornamental plants, particularly in the Pacific Northwest. However, the more any crop is grown and investigated, the more fungus diseases are usually found on it (often diseases that were previously attributed to climate, poor culture or some other physiological factor). This is also true of rhododendrons. The present article attempts to bring up to date discussions on diseases and recommendations for control published in the 1961 Proceedings of the International Conference (3). Detailed descriptions of diseases are not included unless they are new. If rates of fungicides are not listed, the manufacturer's recommendations for general use should be followed.

GENERAL PROBLEMS

Over three-fourths of the specimens received from home owners in Washington state have been affected, not by pathogens, but by such physiological factors as sunburn, dessication (especially in

*Plant Pathologist, Washington State University, Western Washington Research and Extension Center, Puyallup, Washington. Particular thanks are due Dr. Maksis Eglitis for identifying certain fungi; Mr. Worth Vassey, Experimental Aide, for his assistance in propagating plants used in our experiments; Mr. Wm. Scheer, Experimental Aide, for his assistance in the rust investigation; and several members of the American Rhododendron Society for donations of seeds or plants.

winter in exposed locations or under eaves), freezing, and planting in too heavy soil or soil too high in lime. Home owners need more education on cultural practices that will prevent or reduce such injury. Recent articles by Pridham and Lieberman (14) and Raabe (15) discuss some of these factors in detail.

SEED DECAY AND DAMPING OFF

This is perhaps the most common "problem" encountered by hobbyists, particularly those whose greenhouses have poor air circulation. We have obtained very good stands of seedlings at the Western Washington Experiment Station when thiram-treated-seeds are sprinkled over a seed bed composed of a 50:50 mixture of new sand and peat with a one-fourth inch layer of shredded sphagnum moss on top. To reduce the chance of damping off, the seedlings are sprayed with thiram (at 2 lbs/100 gal) every two or three weeks, or more frequently, if damping off develops. The usual sanitation procedures are also followed: new or disinfested flats are used; flats are placed on disinfested soil or benches and we avoid splashing soil into flats. Good air circulation is also maintained, particularly after the seedlings have emerged.

ROT OF CUTTINGS

Several fungi can rot cuttings, particularly if the cuttings are quite soft, or are placed under unfavorable conditions (poor drainage, insufficient light, poor air circulation, non-sterilized soil, etc.). We usually use a mixture of new sand and peat for the cuttings. Drenches with thiram or Morsodren (methyl mercury dicyandiamide) have usually given us good results. In California (8) and other areas where *Rhizoctonia* causes considerable trouble, drenches with PCNB (pentachloronitrobenzene) at 1½ lbs/100 gal or ¼ oz/gal of water are recommended.

Another fungus, *Cylindrocladium scoparium*, has caused a damping off, cutting rot, leaf drop, leaf blight, and crown rot of azaleas in Alabama and Colorado (13,18). Self (18) obtained good control of this disease by soaking cuttings for 30 minutes in solutions of one of the following fungicides (given in lbs/100 gal water) with a spreader-sticker added:

    a. Thylate (4 lbs) = thiram

    b. Phaltan 75 (2 lbs) = folpet

    c. Tersan OM (3 lbs) = thiram + hydroxymercuri chlorophenol

    d. Actidione + Thiram (2 lbs) = cycloheximide + thiram

    e. Sunox ($1\frac{1}{4}$ lbs) = oxyquinoline sulfate

    f. Mycostatin ($\frac{1}{2}$ lb) = nystatin (antibiotic)

Phillips (13) found that in addition to treating cuttings the control was improved by supplemental weekly sprays of fungicides containing captan or maneb. Proper sanitation practices, as outlined under damping off, should also be followed.

NEMATODE ROOT ROT

Research during the last 10 years indicates that dieback, or stunting, of azaleas in the South or in greenhouses in the North, can be caused by nematodes. Symptoms include root rot, chlorosis, leaf tipburn, and mild to severe leaf drop. Losses seem to be most common outdoors in the southern U.S. and in greenhouses in the North. Normal outdoor winter temperatures in Wisconsin (1) killed the most common nematodes, *Tylenchorhynchus claytoni* and *Trichodorus christiei*. Barker, et al (1) reported that these nematodes are often re-introduced into greenhouses on planting stock imported from the South. These studies have show that:

    a. Good sanitation is extremely important,

    b. Treating the soil with nematocide, Nemagon, was very promising. The root knot (*Meloidogyne*) and some other nematodes have also been found on azaleas (6).

AZALEA ROOT ROT

Certain fungi (especially species of *Pythium*) have been found on stunted and root-rotted azaleas in California, particularly during cold, wet weather (12). Controls recommended there (8) consist of:

    a. Sterilization of the media with methyl bromide.

    b. Good sanitation procedures.

    c. Drenching plants with Dexon (= p-dimethyl aminobenzenediazo sodium sulfonate) at 1 oz (70%) in 100 gal water every 7 or 14 days.

PHYTOPHTHORA ROOT ROT

The soil-borne fungus *Phytophthora cinnamomi* frequently causes stunting, wilting and dieback of rhododendrons in several areas of the world. It is usually worse in warm climates and in waterlogged soil. The fungus attacks over 100 different types of plants, ranging from pines to snapdragons; consequently, rotation is seldom a practical control measure. However, grasses are resistant and can be planted where rhododendrons are removed. Diseased plants should be eliminated in order to reduce spread of the fungus. Good drainage is essential. In fact, partially infected plants may recover to some extent if drainage is improved by use of tile or replanting in raised beds. This should be attempted only with very choice specimens, if at all, since the fungus may spread to other plants. Spores of the fungus swim and, therefore, easily spread downhill in drainage water.

The new fungicide, Dexon, has given excellent results against this fungus on avocados and certain other plants. McCain (8) recommends drenching azaleas at 7 to 14 day intervals with Dexon at 50 ppm (1 oz of 70% formulation in 100 gal water). Cuttings should also be taken from the highest branches of stock plants and the rooting medium should be treated with methyl bromide before planting.

ARMILLARIA ROOT ROT

The root rot or shoestring mushroom, *Armillaria mellea*, periodically causes trouble to rhododendrons. It has a very wide host range. In 1962, Raabe (16) published a list of 40 pages of hosts. As yet there is no simple control. Plants that are definitely infected, and ones adjacent to them, should be removed and the area replanted to grass or fumigated with methyl bromide, steam, or carbon bisulfide. The fungus spreads faster in heavy, moist soils, so these should be avoided.

STEM CANKERS AND GALLS

In 1964 Schreiber (17) described a dieback and canker disease of rhododendrons caused by *Botryosphaeria ribis* in nurseries in northern Ohio. This fungus has also been reported in other areas and on other hosts. Schreiber showed that the fungus penetrated through wounds and that it could be spread from diseased to healthy plants on pruning tools and by pinching old flowers. Even such natural wounds as leaf scars served as infection sites. Several other canker-producing fungi have been isolated by us and by others. Also, Crown Gall, caused by the bacterium, *Agrobacterium tumefaciens*, has been reported on rhododendrons in Ohio (2).

When working with diseased plants, disinfest pruning tools often in some material such as 70% denatured alcohol. Also, until research on sprays for cankers has been done, it might be good insurance to try spraying infected stocks in the spring with one of the fungicides used against leaf spots, such as zineb.

AZALEA FLOWER BLIGHT

This disease, caused by the fungus *Ovulinia azalea*, is mostly confined to warm climates. PCNB is recommended in California (8) for control of the soil-borne phase. It should be applied to the soil several weeks in advance of the rainy season at the rate of 3 lbs of 75% w.p. to 1000 sq ft. Zineb, at 12 oz in 75% w.p., in 100 gal of water is frequently recommended for control of the blossom blight (8). Other materials that have given promising results are Thylate, Phaltan, and formulations containing Actidione. The latter have sometimes caused injury, particularly to white flowering varieties (5,11,18).

BOTRYTIS PETAL BLIGHT

Petals of azaleas in Alabama have been blighted by the ordinary gray mold, *Botrytis cinerea*. Thylate at 2 lb/100 gal gave better control than any other compound tested (18). This disease also occurs on rhododendrons and azaleas in the Pacific Northwest. Spraying has not been considered practical in the latter area because of the numerous applications necessary and the disfiguring spray deposit. The problem is most serious in heavily shaded locations. Satisfactory control can usually be achieved by eliminating part of the shade, and improving air circulation.

BUD BLAST

This disease, caused by *Sporocybe* (*Pycnostysanus* or *Briosia*) *azaleae*, is common in the Pacific Northwest only on the native rhododendron (*R. macrophyllum*). It normally destroys 25% or more of the rhododendron buds. There is increasing evidence that the fungus enters buds through wounds made by insects laying eggs. Howell and Wood (7) significantly reduced infection by three sprays of colloidal sulfur between July and October. Other promising compounds in their tests were DDT, captan and Bordeaux, but the latter material was somewhat phytotoxic.

LEAF AND FLOWER GALLS

Leaf galls, caused by species of *Exobasidium*, were unusually common in Washington in 1964, perhaps because the summer was unusually cool. Research in the Netherlands (4) has shown that azalea leaves are apparently susceptible to infection while still enclosed in the bud and remain susceptible until the leaves are about one-third of an inch long. The spores of the fungus remained viable in dormant buds for at least 6 months in their tests. Zineb (8) is frequently recommended for control of this group of fungi. Ferbam, Bordeaux and Puratized Agricultural Spray are also recommended in Oregon (10). Sprays should be applied at bud break and repeated every 2 weeks as long as young leaves are present.

LEAF SPOTS

Azaleas are more susceptible to leaf spotting fungi than are rhododendrons. The most common problem on azaleas is one called Scorch, caused by *Septoria azaleae*. This fungus is particularly troublesome in greenhouses, but may also do damage in outdoor plantings. Zineb, at 1½ lbs per 100 gals, or 1 oz in 4 gals, plus a spreader-sticker is most often recommended as a fungicide (8). Tribasic copper sulfate (10) is also sometimes recommended but, unless used carefully, such copper compounds may burn azaleas and rhododendrons. Sprays should be applied every two weeks in the spring and fall (10). For the best control, fungicidal spraying must be supplemented by the removal and destruction of fallen leaves to eliminate as many spores as possible.

Varieties resistant to Septoria are also available. McCain and Humphrey (9) recently published a list of these, based upon observations in California. Their ratings are as follows:

Very Susceptible—Hexe, Rose Queen, Paul Schame, and Sweet Sixteen.

Susceptible—Dorothy Gish, Firelight, Lentengroet, Pink Pearl, Red Wing and Adrian Steyeart.

Slightly Susceptible—White Orchid, Vervaneana alba, Vervaneana Variegated and Professor Walters.

Not Susceptible or Just a Trace of Infection—Alaska, L. J. Bobbink, Brilliant, California Sunset, Duc de Rohan, Fielders White, Hybrid Salmon Dbl., Iveryana, Jean Haerrens, Laughing Waters, Mamie, Memoire de Sanders, Memoire John Hearrens, Orchid Flora, Phoenicia, Pink Charm, Pride of Dorking, G. L. Tabor and Variegated Phoenicia.

Many other fungi are also found in leaf spots on azaleas and rhododendrons. A few of these are strong parasites, but most are weak and can only develop in leaves injured by over-heating, freezing, alkalinity, etc. Control is often achieved by changing the location of the plant, avoiding over-fertilizing and similar measures. Diseased leaves should be removed and destroyed. Copper or zineb sprays are often recommended for spraying for general leaf spot control.

RUSTS

Rust fungi cause sporadic trouble on rhododendrons throughout the world. The rust, *Pucciniastrum myrtilli,* has been known for many years, mostly in the Eastern United States, where it does most direct damage to young seedlings. It is not usually serious on older plants, but other fungi such as species of *Pestalotia* are reported able to enter leaves through rust lesions and progressively kill the tissues. *R. ponticum* is apparently one of the most susceptible species. This fungus may spend part of its life on hemlock (Tsuga) returning to rhododendrons in the next season. However, on evergreen azaleas and rhododendrons the repeating spore (uredospore) stage of the rust may reinfect rhododendrons without the use of hemlock.

Species of *Chrysomyxa* rusts also attack rhododendrons. Their alternate host is spruce *(Picea)*. *C. roanensis* occurs on rhododendrons in the Appalachian mountains. *C. piperiana* is very widespread on the native *Rhododendron macrophyllum* on the Pacific coast, but fortunately does not attack many cultivated varieties.

The European rhododendron rust (*C. ledi* v. *rhododendri*) has a much greater host range, but is much more restricted geographically. It has been found in California, Oregon, Washington and British Columbia, but surveys indicate that it seldom persists more than a mile or two inland from the Pacific Ocean. The few exceptions have occurred with very susceptible infected varieties planted in shaded, moist locations with very little air movement.

Certain nurseries have reported promising control of rust by spraying with Actidione, but this fungicide may burn certain varieties such as 'Jock'. Highly susceptible infected varieties should be discarded, or at least separated by several hundred yards from other varieties.

We have been studying factors affecting the life history of the *Chrysomyxa* rusts since 1961 under a special grant from Initiative 171 funds for Medical and Biological Research at Washington State University. Much useful information has been obtained, but certain investigations must be completed before the information can be released. A summary of our results will be presented at a later date.

STUDIES ON DISEASE RESISTANCE

Interest in growing and hybridizing rhododendrons is increasing rapidly. It is hoped that resistance to the most serious pathogens can be incorporated into plants with desirable horticultural features. Adequate knowledge of sources of resistance is lacking, however. Therefore, we are building up a collection of the most important species in order to test their resistance, first to the *Chrysomyxa* rust fungi and later to other pathogens. Thanks to the assistance of several hobbyists and government agencies, we now have over 150 species under propagation. Certain additional species are needed.

Literature Cited:

1. BARKER, K. R., G. L. WORF, AND A.H. EPSTEIN. 1965. Nematodes associated with the decline of azaleas in Wisconsin. Plant Disease Reptr. 49:47-49.

2. BART, G. J. 1963. Crown gall on rhododendron. Phytopathology 53:870.

3. GOULD, C. J. AND MAKSIS EGLITIS. 1961. Diseases of rhododendrons in the Pacific Northwest. Proc. Intern. Rhododendron Conf. 1961:48-53.

4. GRAAFLAND, W. 1960. The parasitism of Exobasidium japonicum Shir. on azalea. Acta Botan. Neerl. 9(4):347-379. (Biol. Abst. 36:2239. 1961.

5. HAASIS, F. A., AND R. AYCOCK. 1963. Control azalea petal blight. Res. and Fmg., North Carolina, 1963. 22(2):7.

6. HAASIS, F. A., J. C. WELLS AND C. J. NUSBAUM. 1961. Plant parasitic nematodes associated with decline of woody ornamentals in North Carolina and their control by soil treatment. Plant Disease Reptr. 45:492.

7. HOWELL, P. J., AND R. K. S. WOOD. 1962. Some factors affecting rhododendron bud blast and its control. Ann. Appl. Biol. 50:723-733.

8. McCAIN, A. H. 1964. Azalea disease control. Calif. Plant Diseases -19. Univ. of Calif. Agr. Ext. Serv. Pub. AXT-147.

9. McCAIN, A. H. AND W. A. HUMPHREY. 1965. Susceptibility of azalea varieties to leaf spot. Pacific Coast Nurseryman 24(3):16. March, 1965.

10. McSWAN, I. C., AND R. L. POWELSON. 1964. Oregon Plant Disease Control Handbook. Coop. Ext. Serv. Oregon State Univ., Corvallis, Oregon.

11. MILLER, H. N. 1963. Fungicidal sprays for control of azalea flower blight. Ann. Rep. Orn. Res. (Florida). (So. Nurs. Assn.) p. 20.

12. MUNNECKE, D. E., P. A. CHANDLER, AND J.L. GIVINS. 1960. Investigations show azalea root rot can be controlled by soil treatment. Calif. Agr. 14(9):9.

13. PHILLIPS, D. J. 1962. A brief report on azalea cutting disease. Colo. Flower Growers Assoc. Bull. No. 146:2-3.

14. PRIDHAM, A. M. S., AND A. S. LIEBERMAN. 1962. Solving cultural troubles of rhododendrons and other Ericaceous plants. Cornell Ext. Bull. 1091. 8 p.

15. RAABE, R. D. 1961. Diseases of rhododendron. J. Calif. Hort. Soc. 22:52-57.

16. RAABE, R. D. 1962. Host list of the root rot fungus, Armillaria mellea. Hilgardia 33(2): 88 p.

17. SCHREIBER, L. R. 1964. Stem canker and die-back of rhododendron caused by Botryosphaeria ribis Gross & Dug. Plant Disease Reptr. 48:207-210.

18. SELF, R. L. 1963. Disease control studies. Ann. Rep. Orn. Res. (Alabama) (So. Nurs. Assn.) p. 9.

RHODODENDRON

AND

AZALEA CULTURE

J. HAROLD CLARKE

Under some conditions of soil and climate rhododendrons grow very freely and, as in parts of the British Isles, certain species may run wild and almost be considered as weeds. In other places they can be grown only with careful attention to cultural requirements. They do differ in their requirements from most other groups of plants and even the good gardener sometimes has difficulty if he does not provide the cultural treatments necessary for his particular soil and climate. The following is written primarily for the novice in this field, with apologies to the experienced rhododendron or azalea grower who may feel that it is over-simplified.

BOTANICAL CLASSIFICATION

Rhododendrons and azaleas belong to the genus Rhododendron of the family Ericaceae, or heath family. This family also includes the heaths and heathers as the name implies, and also blueberries, cranberries, pernettya, kalmia, andromeda and a number of other less well known ornamental plants. The members of this family in general require a rather acid soil and good drainage, but some are much more fastidious than others about their special requirements.

The genus Rhododendron is a very large one with more than a thousand species which have been described. As might be expected in such a large genus, there is some argument as to whether all of the species now considered as such are good valid species, and even whether some should be put into a different genus, and as a matter of fact some species now called Rhododendron have been considered by certain botanists as belonging to other genera. Scientific studies of chromosomes, breeding results, and classification of scales and hairs on the leaves have all given new insight into the relationship between groups within the genus. The trend has been towards consolidation of species, putting two or more closely related groups into one species rather than considering them as separate species. Much of this study has gone on at the Royal Botanic Garden in Edinburgh, Scotland and reviews of classification have appeared from time to time in the Royal Horticultural Society Rhododendron Yearbooks.

Because of the extreme complexity of the genus, the species known at the time were grouped some time ago into series, each including a number of species which have points of similarity. In the last R.H.S. Handbook, "Rhododendron Species In General Cultivation," forty-four different Series were listed.

All the species of rhododendron known as azaleas are included in one group, the Azalea Series, which includes some seventy or more different species. These are distinguished by botanical characters but it is not easy to give a simple distinction separating all those rhododendrons which belong to the Azalea Series from those which belong to the other Series. There are evergreen rhododendrons and azaleas and also deciduous rhododendrons and azaleas.

Used botanically, therefore, the word "rhododendron" includes azaleas. Horticulturally we usually speak of rhododendrons *and* azaleas, the former including all the non-azalea members of the genus, and that is the way the terms are used in this book.

NATIVE HABITAT

The many rhododendron species have come from a wide range of native habitats. A large number of our cultivated rhododendrons, especially those grown in the milder parts of the country, are derived from species coming from Asia, especially the foothills of the Himalaya Mountains, western China, northern India, Burma and Assam. Others come from Japan, some from Europe and some from North America. From the eastern United States we have *R. catawbiense,* the source of hardiness of most of the hardy hybrids which have been grown for many years on the east coast. Two other very hardy species from the eastern United States are *R. maximum* and *R. carolinianum.* They have not been used as extensively in breeding as *R. catawbiense* but there are fairly well known varieties now being grown which are hybrids between one of these two species and others, usually Asiatic species.

Azaleas native to the U.S.A. include several deciduous species, *R. occidentale* on the west coast and several in the East and Southeast. It was thought for a time that rhododendrons were rather strictly a northern hemisphere plant and that a lone species in Australia was about the only representative in the southern hemisphere. More recently a rather large group of species is being studied and named in the East Indies, especially New Guinea. Most of these are probably too tender for use in any except the mildest parts of the United States, but they will undoubtedly be useful as breeding material, especially to broaden the color range.

Up to the present time some ten thousand horticultural varieties of rhododendrons and azaleas have been named although many of these are probably not now in existence and certainly are not available in the nursery trade. Many new varieties are being named each year.

CLIMATE

Rhododendron species are found in the wild from the Arctic regions to the tropics spanning a wide range of climate. The factors which limit the growing of rhododendrons in the garden are primarily temperature, soil acidity and rainfall, with many other modifying factors such as prevalence of certain root diseases. In the United States a large number of varieties and species can be grown in the Pacific Northwest, especially between the Cascades and the Pacific Ocean. Favorable climate extends down the Pacific Coast, the area becoming narrower as it goes south, with the San Francisco Bay area, so far, being about the southern limit of easy rhododendron culture. Further south they may be grown but more care has to be given to cultural requirements and special treatment. Azaleas, however, can be grown successfully further south, a situation which holds true across the country. We find azaleas being grown in great numbers along the Gulf Coast, and other places in the South and Southeast, where so far rhododendrons have been considered difficult. However the culture of rhododendrons is moving southward as more is learned about their special requirements and interested gardeners are experimenting with varieties and culture.

Rhododendrons and azaleas grow well in the milder parts of the Middle Atlantic States and down into the Carolinas. Further inland, both toward the west and toward the north, where minimum temperatures reach −20° or lower, only the very hardy varieties will thrive. Most of the very hardy varieties have been hybrids of *R. catawbiense* or *R. maximum,* primarily the former, with certain Asiatic or European species. They began to become available about a hundred year ago and have been known as the "Old Hardies", "Ironclads" and other group names. Although hardiness varies within this group, some were able to withstand temperatures of −30° with no apparent injury if they were well matured plants. In recent years a great deal of attention has been given to the breeding of very hardy varieties and the range of types on the market is certainly on the increase. Some of the deciduous azaleas are extremely hardy and are becoming more popular in the north.

Throughout most of the Middle West and the Great Plains area, rhododendrons can be grown only with special care, and attention to the hardiness of the varieties planted, and to some winter protection, especially from very cold winds.

The range over which rhododendrons can be successfully grown is being increased fairly rapidly by the introduction of varieties that are more resistant to low temperature and to high temperature, and the development of cultural methods which tend to offset unfavorable conditions. In general the northern limit is determined by minimum temperature and it has sometimes been assumed that the southern limit is determined by maximum temperature. More recently there seems to be good evidence that temperature is only one factor and that the southern limit may be determined to a large extent by the prevalence of certain root rot organisms.

It might be assumed that rhododendron species native to very high elevations, or to northern latitudes might be most satisfactory for growing in very cold areas in this country. This, however, has not proven entirely true. Some species from elevations above ten thousand feet in the Himalayas have proven to be disappointingly tender. Presumably they have survived at those elevations because they were protected by heavy snows during the period of very low temperature. On the other hand certain species from relatively warm climates have exhibited a remarkable degree of hardiness.

SOILS

In general we consider rhododendrons and azaleas to have approximately the same cultural requirements, with azaleas being somewhat "less fussy" hence "easier to grow". Both prefer rather light soils although they can be grown in heavy soils if special precautions are taken as will be mentioned later. They do need good drainage, good soil aeration, and an ample supply of moisture during the summer. The term "good drainage" is somewhat more explicit than it would be as used for other garden plants. What might be considered as good drainage for roses or lilacs, for instance, might not be satisfactory for rhododendrons. One of the reasons for this is that rhododendrons are susceptible, in some areas, and under some climatic conditions, to root rot fungi which thrive in soil that is not exceptionally well drained.

A high content of organic matter is almost essential in most garden soils. In fact in unfavorable areas, rhododendrons are often grown in straight peat moss, or a mixture of peat moss and soil. It is true, however, that where other conditions are very good, rhododendrons can be grown in very sandy soil with a minimum of organic matter.

There may be exceptions with respect to a few odd rhododendron species but practically all species and varieties prefer an acid soil, the optimum degree of acidity being around pH 4.5 to pH 5.5. There are soils, mostly below pH 4, where it may be helpful to add lime, but this is the exception rather than the rule. In many areas soils are too high in the pH reading and need to be acidified.

WHAT TO START WITH

There are occasional advertisements offering rhododendrons, not by name, but in "pink, red and white colors." Usually these are seedlings of unknown quality and frequently inferior. As with all other horticultural groups of plants, it is advisable to start with named varieties which are clones, that is they are grown from cuttings of plants with known qualities.

Unfortunately there are a few "group" varieties, so called because breeders have given a name to a group of sister seedlings, and not to one single plant from which propagation has been by cuttings. This practice of naming group varieties is contrary to usual custom in this country and has caused confusion at times when different plants of a variety had obviously different characteristics. Plants which belong to such group varieties are designated by the letter "g" in the section on variety descriptions. In many cases only one clone of such a variety is available in a particular area but the letter "g" is a warning that other forms may be met with. This practice of naming group varieties has been discouraged by all rhododendron organizations for some time and very few breeders are now doing it.

RHODODENDRON SPECIES FOR THE GARDEN

As might be expected, many of the rhododendron species from which our cultivated varieties have been produced by the breeders are in themselves excellent ornamental garden plants. They are simply the wild type just as they exist in their native habitat. Usually they have been collected as seed and come relatively true from seed, although in some cases there is extreme variations within a species, especially in color of flower. In some species superior individuals have been selected out and grown from cuttings. Where such selected forms are available it would be preferable to use them unless you are especially interested in growing seedlings and doing your own selecting.

Named clones of species should be distinguished from certain "forms" being grown under a collector's number. A good example is *R. racemosum*, Forrest 19404, which is frequently mentioned in the literature as being a good dwarf form. The lot of seed collected by Forrest under this number undoubtedly did produce a very desirable dwarf type of plant. However, as open pollinated seed from a few of these original seedlings is distributed over the world, and then open pollinated seed from the resulting seedlings further distributed, the type is quite likely to be modified by cross pollination with other perhaps less desirable forms. With this species, for instance, it would seem preferable to specify the type of form desired rather than the collector's number, under which one might get some quite undesirable plants.

Although most rhododendron fans eventually grow some species and become quite interested in them, the beginner would probably do well to start with named horticultural varieties whose behavior is relatively well known.

TYPE OF PLANT TO PURCHASE

Rhododendron plants from a nursery are available as very small plants, without flower buds, or as larger sizes with flower buds already formed. In the South many growers feel that fairly large plants, possibly three to four feet in height, and with a rather large root ball, are most likely to survive. Smaller plants seem more susceptible to root rots, and the losses correspondingly heavy. As our knowledge about cultural requirements in this area increases, it may be possible to work out methods which will insure better survival of small plants. The larger sizes, of course, are more expensive and, if they are purchased from a distance the transportation costs are considerable.

In some areas plants collected from the wild are sometimes offered at various markets or peddled from a truck along the roadside. Prices may be rather attractive but survival rate in general is not very good. In most stands of native rhododendrons there are not a great many small plants which have had adequate space to develop, and which can be dug with a good part of the root system intact. Too often the small plants are sprouts which have grown up from older roots where plants were burned off or broken off in some way. With these heavier stumps it is difficult to get enough of a root system to make a good transplant. Of course the resulting flower will be the native species, and usually not comparable in size or color of flower to the better cultivated varieties.

WHEN TO PLANT

Rhododendrons and azaleas should always be moved with a ball of soil, either in a container or with the ball of soil wrapped with burlap. In favorable climates they may be transplanted almost any time of the year with reasonable success as all of the root system, or almost all of it, is moved with the plant and with no root damage. In most cases, however, it will be better to transplant in the fall or early in the spring. In the South fall planting is apparently much superior because the plant has a chance to make roots and become established before the long, hot summer. This is particularly true with large plants. Where winters are severe, spring planting is usually favored, so the plant will not be exposed to drying cold winds of winter before it has made new root growth. By fall planting we usually mean late September, October and early November. Spring planting is usually considered as satisfactory as soon as the soil can be gotten into good condition, and continuing until hot, dry weather begins. Within reason the earlier in the spring the transplanting can be done the better off the plant will be because it will form new roots, and be ready to take full advantage of what moisture there is in the soil when the warm, dry weather begins.

In the Northwest more rhododendrons are moved by far in the spring than the fall. This does not necessarily indicate that people feel spring planting to be superior, but rather that most of them have the urge to work in the garden in the spring to a much greater extent than they do in the autumn.

HOW TO PLANT

One should first consider the nature of the soil and, if it is not ideal, then prepare or modify it if necessary. This may mean working in peat moss or other organic matter, or possibly acidifying the soil if it is too alkaline. Ordinarily if it is more alkaline than pH 6 it would probably be advisable to add some agricultural sulfur unless the soil is going to be modified by using a large amount of acid peat moss. By large amount I would mean at least half of the planting soil. The amount of sulfur to add would depend on local Agricultural Extension Agent. Although aluminum sulfate has often been recommended to acidify the soil, the modern trend is to recommend against it as aluminum residue may be harmful to the plants. If the soil is in need of only a moderate amount of acidification, this may be obtained by the use of ammonium sulfate as a source of nitrogen. As the plants use up the nitrogen the sulfate is left in the soil and a considerable amount of acidification achieved. Of course if the soil does not need additional nitrogen, then this method would not be advisable.

As the plants will come wrapped in burlap, or in tin or plastic can, they must be unwrapped or removed from the container before planting. Where plants are heeled in for some time in sawdust bins in the nursery the roots will grow out through the burlap and the burlap eventually will decay. Where the roots are going through the burlap it should be left on. Simply open it up around the trunk and lay it back, or pull off the top part that has rotted loose.

One very common reason for poor results with rhododendrons is deep planting. The top of the root ball should be at the surface of the ground or a little above it. Never plant "an inch or two deeper than the plant was in the nursery" as is sometime recommended for other types of plants.

PROVIDE GOOD DRAINAGE

We used to see directions for digging a large hole and filling it with organic refuse, peat moss, sawdust, and soil, especially where soil conditions are somewhat unfavorable. This would be satisfactory under conditions of very good drainage. However, where the soil is heavy the large hole, filled with porous material, becomes a "tub" holding water to the height of the water table in the surrounding soil which may be high, during rainy weather, or periods of prolonged watering. In very light, sandy, acid soils which are ideal for rhododendrons, they may simply be planted in a hole a little larger than the root ball.

At the opposite extreme are the areas where the soil is alkaline, heavy, inclined to be waterlogged in winter, and probably deficient in organic matter. Under these conditions it is advisable to plant on top of the ground, that is a mound, of a mixture of peat moss or other organic matter and soil, or sand, or perlite is made and the plant is set in that mound entirely above the ground. In some cases it might rest on the normal soil surface, in others it would be desirable to build up two or three inches of gravel above the normal soil surface so that the root ball is completely out of contact with the normal soil of the area. The mound of soil may taper off at the edges, or be confined by planks or logs in the form of a planter. Such raised bed require special attention to watering during the summer.

PLANTERS AND TUBS

In areas where soil conditions are reasonably good rhododendrons will enjoy being planted in the open ground rather than in a planter, and will spread their root systems quite widely. However, where conditions are relatively unfavorable the planter is well worth considering. It may be better to set the plant on top of the ground and then fill in around it rather than construct a restricted trough of brick or other material in which the plants are to be set. In other words for best results the planter should be constructed with the plant requirements in mind rather than the plant being made to fit what may be a very restricted planter area. Planters are quite useful in formal or semi-formal gardens, provided they are made large enough, and rhododendrons, if properly treated, will do quite well in them. Unfortunately planters are often constructed as an integral part of a new house and very often are entirely too small to be satisfactory for any but very dwarf rhododendrons or azaleas.

Going a step further rhododendrons may be grown quite satisfactorily in large tubs made of redwood or asbestos cement, provided the tubs are large enough, the soil mixture is adequate, drainage is good and fertilization and watering are carried out intelligently. In some cities large tubbed rhododendrons are used quite successfully around public buildings or hotels, or in small city parks. Rhododendrons for planting in tubs should be selected to some extent for their pleasing branching pattern and bark texture and color. One would not call them bonsai, but nevertheless, pleasing form of the plant as a whole should be kept in mind and may often be achieved by a little judicious training and pruning.

SOME PROBLEMS IN THE SOUTH

In those areas in the South where rhododendrons frequently have died a short while after planting, there is considerable evidence that death is usually due to root rot organisms prevalent in those areas. During warm weather, and with plentiful moisture, the fungi flourish and the plant succumbs. Using a fungicidal drench at planting time in these soils may be helpful, especially one considered to be successful against Phytophthora root rot.

If a root ball is really dry it should be thoroughly soaked in a tub of water before planting. Under normal conditions it is not necessary or desirable to break apart the root ball unless it has been growing too long in a small container, in which case some breaking up of the root ball would be advisable. If there is a mat of roots around the outside of the container this mat shoud be broken up to encourage the roots to grow out into the surrounding soil. Where it is difficult to get rhododendron roots to grow out of the root ball it may be helpful to hose off the outer part of the ball until the ends of the roots are exposed. In some cases, where plants have been grown in rather tight clay soil, gardeners have found it desirable to soak the root ball and hose off nearly all of the soil and work a good soil mixture in around the roots. Where the plants have been grown in sandy soil, roots grow out of the root ball into the surrounding area somewhat more readily. Young plants which had been grown in pure peat moss sometimes are slower to grow out of the root ball than those which have been grown in a mixture of peat moss with soil, sand, sawdust or other material.

The newly set plant, with the soil carefully filled in around it, should always be well watered in.

SUBSEQUENT CARE

Although rhododendrons object to too much soil moisture, they are shallow rooted and the roots may dry out during the summer when deeper rooted plants show no ill effects. This means that they should be well watered during the summer, especially in the case of newly set plants. However, the watering must be adjusted to the conditions under which the plant is growing. If the soil is very light and the drainage good, and the temperature not too high, it is pretty difficult to over-water. However, if the soil is rather heavy, frequent watering may get the soil below the surface saturated with bad effects on the plant. If the soil is rather heavy and the summer temperatures high, and especially in areas where root rot organisms are known to be prevalent, summer watering must be done very carefully. The objective under such conditions is to keep the plants from wilting, except perhaps during the hottest part of the day, without putting on an excess of water. It is remarkable how rhododendrons can wilt during a very hot, dry day and come up again at night, or when water is applied.

With most other garden plants it is recommended that watering not be too frequent but that when water is given it should penetrate deeply into the soil and saturate the whole root system. With rhododendrons this advice, at least under some conditions, probably should be changed to indicate that frequent watering should be given but not enough to really saturate the soil. Most rhododendron roots are close to the surface, and even if the soil is saturated deeply the plant will depend mostly on the roots within a few inches of the surface. The plant can thrive if these surface roots are moist enough, even though the soil a few inches deeper may be quite dry. Possibly a condition such as this might be less conducive to root rot than where the soil is uniformly moist to a greater depth.

MULCHING

It is highly desirable to use some kind of a mulch which will help conserve moisture and eliminate the need for cultivation. Normally no cultivating should be done around rhododendrons. Weeds should be pulled, or in extreme cases shaved off with a sharp hoe.

Modern research with some of the newer herbicides indicates that weeds may be controlled, to a very large extent at least, by using chemical weed killers. However, such chemicals need to be used with extreme caution, and usually do not do a one hundred percent job. Mulches should be used for other reasons than weed control even if herbicides are used.

A fairly deep mulch of sawdust or shavings will be reasonably effective in keeping down weeds. Leaves are all right although they tend to blow away during the winter, if dry, and to mat down too tightly if wet. Peat moss as a mulch is not too satisfactory, because it is so difficult to wet once it gets thoroughly dried out, although it would be much better than leaving the soil bare. Other good mulching materials are pine needles, wood chips, peanut hulls, ground corn cobs and probably other similar materials which may be available only in limited localities. Any material which prevents the sun's rays from striking the ground directly, and the drying winds from actually hitting the soil surface, may be used.

FERTILIZATION

In very fertile soils rhododendrons may sometimes be grown well without addition of any fertilizers. In fact I have heard know-ledgeable rhododendron growers say that rhododendrons should not be fertilized. That is certainly not true on soils that are very sandy or of low fertility. Except where soils are very fertile it is my feeling that an application of a complete fertilizer, spread thinly on top of the soil at planting time and before the mulch is applied, would be desirable. The amount to use would depend on the normal fertility of the soil, which the gardener may be able to judge by his experience with other plants. Usually there will be need for some fertilizer and so on soils of what might be called low to average fertility, about half a teacupful for a small plant to a teacupful for a large plant, of 5-10-5, or similar material, might be used.

Where rhododendrons are mulched with organic material, such as sawdust, there will be a tie up of nitrogen, the plants are likely to show yellowish leaves and short growth, and some additional nitrogen should be applied. The nitrogen used on rhododendrons should be of the ammonium or urea forms. Most ericaceous plants for some reason do not seem to thrive with nitrate fertilizers. Ammonium sulfate is a very satisfactory material to use as it is in the form rhododendrons like and the residue has an acidifying effect. Urea is satisfactory but does not have the acidifying effect of ammonium sulfate. It is quite soluble, very readily available and suitable for using in solution. In most soils nitrogen is the element most likely to be needed, probably every spring, especially where there is an organic mulch. Need for nitrogen is indicated by leaves which are yellowish or pale green but otherwise normal. Scatter ammonium sulfate over the mulch and water in, late winter to mid-summer if needed.

It is understood by most gardeners that heavy applications of nitrogen fertilizers in late summer are likely to stimulate soft growth which will be susceptible to winter injury. However, on poor soils the application of enough nitrogen to bring them up to the amount naturally present in a soil of good fertility should not cause any difficulty. Some gardeners carry to extreme this matter of no summer fertilizing, and their plants become semi-starved during fall and winter. Recent research indicates that plants reasonably well supplied with nutrients, including nitrogen, are more resistant to low temperatures than those that are starved. If a plant is really starved for nitrogen so that the leaves are yellow and somewhat small in size, a moderate application might be given most any time without causing any harm. In most areas applications up to the first of June, if they cause new growth, would cause it early enough so that it would mature before frost. Applications after late August would usually not stimulate growth because of the oncoming of cooler weather.

All plants require potassium but in many cases there is a sufficient amount of this element in the soil. Your local Extension Agent can tell you whether soils in your area are likely to be deficient in this element. Many people use a complete fertilizer for all garden purposes just to be on the safe side. A so-called complete fertilizer contains nitrogen, phosphorous and potassium.

All plants require phosphorous and, although phosphorous may be present in rather large quantities in the soil, it is sometimes fixed in compounds unavailable to the plants. Recent fertilizer experiments carried on by the late Arthur Myhre of the Western Washington Experiment Station at Puyallup, Washington, indicated that with young rhododendron plants heavy, early phosphorous fertilization tended to favor heavy production of flower buds. The efficacy of this treatment would depend on the amount of phosphorous naturally occurring in a particular soil and, of course, it would depend on the available phosphorous rather than the total amount. Phosphorous does not readily move down into or through the soil, hence it is desirable to see that there is a reasonable amount present at planting time.

One frequently hears that epsom salts is good for rhododendrons. As this material is magnesium sulfate, when magnesium is deficient in the soil the application of epsom salts is helpful. Magnesium is an essential element for all plant growth and lack of it will cause yellowish areas between the leaf veins. If the leaves of rhododendrons are a good dark green the addition of epsom salts would presumably not be helpful.

PROTECT AGAINST LOW TEMPERATURE

For those who live in areas where winter temperatures are rather low, the first thing to consider is the planting of varieties hardy enough to do well under the normal winter conditions. The A.R.S. Hardiness Ratings indicate the minimum temperature that a well matured plant can be expected to survive without damage to buds, leaves or woody tissues. It is not too difficult to find from the Weather Bureau, or a neighbor, or from your own experience, the approximate minimum temperature which may be expected in your garden.

Even with the hardy varieties it will usually be worthwhile to plant in a reasonably protected place, where they will not be subject to cold, drying winds during the winter. In some northern areas gardeners protect rhododendron plants by building a windbreak around them, or covering them with burlap, or other protective material during the worst part of the winter. The average home owner a little further south may prefer to occasionally experience slight damage to the plants rather than go to the trouble of winter protection, unless a particular plant is considered to be especially valuable. Very good winter protection may be provided by a covering of snow. The only problem is that the snow may not come early enough, or it may recede enough during the winter so that a subsequent cold spell will cause damage to parts projecting above the snow.

A mulch around the plants will give considerable protection against freezing damage to the roots which, because they are quite shallow, may be susceptible to cold injury. It has been found with azaleas, under certain conditions, however, that there may be more damage from spring frosts on mulched plants than on unmulched plants. Apparently the mulch prevents radiation of heat from the soil, which may occur, with unmulched plants, to a sufficient extent to provide some protection against frost damage.

Even in the so-called ideal rhododendron areas there may occasionally be damage by early fall frosts or by late spring frosts. In the Pacific Northwest, for instance, there are early varieties such as 'Cilpinense' which will start blooming in late February, and others will follow soon after. These early varieties may be quite hardy in bud but the open flowers will be damaged if there is frost. It is advisable to plant such varieties in a protected place and they may even be covered during a frosty night. These very early varieties, although susceptible to frost damage, have a special value in providing color and beauty in the garden when nearly everything else is still dormant.

It is possible, under certain conditions, to keep a garden sprinkler running during brief freezing periods, and if the flowers are continuously coated with water they will be protected from several degrees of frost. Many commercial strawberry growers, and nearly all commercial cranberry growers use water to prevent freezing damage after growth starts in the spring. There are certain problems involved where this method of frost protection is used in the garden. If the soil is heavy, or easily waterlogged, the water from sprinkling, plus that which is normally present at that time in the spring, may so saturate the soil that the rhododendron roots will be short of oxygen and sustain injury. If very low temperature is expected sprinkling should not be attempted as heavy ice formation could cause considerable breakage of the branches. If one wishes to try sprinkling for frost protection it would be advisable to obtain equipment which will put on a minimum of water. As long as the plant tissues can be kept covered with free water protection will be secured as it comes from the heat of fusion released when the water turns to ice. The temperature of the water itself is of little importance as the tiny droplets will be cooled to air temperature, or close to it, before they hit the leaves.

SHADE

Shade affects soil and air temperature and moisture, and so is an important factor in rhododendron growth. In most cases partial shade is desirable, and in hot, dry areas it is essential. In good rhododendron growing areas the plants may survive quite well in full sun but when they are in bloom the flowers will last longer if in partial shade. There are a few varieties, such as 'Snow Queen', which simply will not tolerate full sun, having quite yellowish leaves under such conditions. There are many others, however, which, in a reasonably favorable climate, will make better growth, a better shaped plant, and will set many more flower buds if grown in almost full sun. Full shade, on the other hand, is undesirable except possibly in extremely hot climates. Under full shade plants grow tall and leggy, the lower branches tend to die off, and flower bud formation is much less than in partial shade or full sun.

The beginner, without definite knowledge as to the requirements of a variety he may have purchased, would do well to plant it where it will receive some shade during the middle part of the day. Nurseries frequently keep their rhododendron plants under lath shade in order to keep the foliage in good condition. Gardeners in warm areas occasionally build a small ornamental lath house for their rhododendrons and certain other plants which require shade. Such a structure may be quite useful for some plants and for other purposes than protecting the rhododendrons. Lath houses are frequently built to give about fifty percent shade. If the slats are one inch thick they would need to be spaced further apart than their own width as the thickness of the wood will cast a shadow. For those gardeners who rely on a shade tree, or a building, to provide partial shade, it would be desirable to plant rhododendrons where they will be protected from the sun during the middle of the day and the early part of the afternoon. Morning or evening sun will, in most cases, not be undesirable.

PRUNING

Pruning of the young rhododendron or azalea plant normally begins in the cutting bench, or soon after the rooted cuttings are spaced out in greenhouse bench or plastic house. The pruning at this stage consists of rubbing out the terminal bud which can be easily done when it has started to expand and is approximately one-half to three-quarters inches in length. A little pressure at one size will cause the bud to separate easily from the plant. If the plant is not disbudded it will very likely make a straight growth and might eventually reach two or three feet in height with a single stem. Most people want plants that are branched near the ground, and disbudding stops the central axis and stimulates lateral buds to grow providing a plant with several stems originating close to the ground. If this disbudding is attempted too early it is difficult to do and if too late the plant has wasted some of its energy by making shoot growth which is later broken off. This method of shaping the plant by breaking out the terminal bud when it starts to grow may also be used on larger plants to make them branch. If the terminal bud on an older plant is a flower bud, disbudding is not necessary as the flower bud stops the single stem type of growth and will cause lateral shoots to grow out just below when the flower develops.

Normally very little pruning of the standard type, that is the cutting out of branches of various sizes will be needed. If a plant grows out over a walk or needs to be restricted for some reason, it may be pruned back moderately without fear that the plant as a whole will be damaged. The time of cutting is not particularly important. It is often possible to do the pruning during the blooming season and have some flowers for the house.

Sometimes a gardener has an old, leggy rhododendron plant which has grown out of all relation to its surroundings. Such a plant may be pruned back and rejuvenated but it must be done with some care. Usually about a third of the taller branches might be removed one year, half of the remaining branches removed the next, and the rest of them removed the third year, cutting back to two or three feet from the ground or wherever smaller side branches are available for starting the new framework.

The question is often asked about the possibility of moving an old rhododendron. These old plants may be of a poor variety and it would be better to replace them with a smaller plant of a superior type, although moving an old plant is possible provided a large ball of soil is dug with it. Very commonly the cost of moving an old plant is more than it would cost to purchase a younger plant and set in the desired location.

There are some species and varieties which can be cut back almost to the ground and which will make new growth from adventitious buds. There are others, however, which do not make such growth easily, and one may lose a plant unless it is known that it is the type which will rejuvenate readily.

DEAD-HEADING

It is usually desirable, with the large flowered rhododendrons, to remove the withered flower clusters after the blooming season. This is fairly easily done as the central axis of the cluster, or truss as it is usually called, will break free from the plant with a quick snap of the thumb pushing on the side. With the smaller flowered rhododendrons and azaleas, dead-heading is hardly feasible and generally unnecessary.

The reasons for dead-heading are to make the bush look more attractive, to prevent mold setting in on the flower petals and going down into the stems, and to prevent a heavy set of seed. Some varieties in some areas will set seed heavily, to an extent where it will weaken the plant and so they really need dead-heading. Others practically never set seed and so dead-heading with them is important primarily from the standpoint of appearance. In moist areas such as along the coast in the Northwest, high humidity at blossom time will sometimes be accompanied by an outbreak of Botrytis or gray mold on the petals of wilted flowers. This gives them an unattractive, soggy appearance and may even kill back the stem for a few inches.

Immediately after the flowers wither will be the best time for dead-heading from the standpoint of appearance, and from the standpoint of preventing mold infection of the petals. However, from the standpoint of preventing seed production, it may be done somewhat later, and even removing the developing seed pods when they are partially grown may be helpful if there is a very heavy seed crop. If, for some reason, one finds it impossible to take off the old flowers it will usually not be extremely serious.

PEST CONTROL

The control of most of the common insects and diseases has been discussed by Dr. Breakey and Dr. Gould. It is often advisable to secure some local advice from the County Agricultural Extension Agent or someone else who has experience in the immediate locality. In some areas there are no pests on rhododendrons or azaleas serious enough to warrant control measures.

It is true that control of insects and diseases is usually preventative rather than curative, and producers of many crops follow rigorous spray schedules to prevent infestation. There are some conditions under which regular spray schedules for rhododendrons and azaleas are probably advisable, but in many other areas one need not worry until some evidence of damage is visible. The perfectionist, of course, will carry on control measures designed to take care of pests prevalent in his locality and so may produce practically perfect plants. As indicated, certain diseases may to a large extent be prevented by care in planting, with good drainage, and with moisture conditions as nearly ideal as possible.

There is a great deal of varietal variability in susceptibility to both insects and diseases, although there is a great deal more research to be done before extensive lists of varieties resistant to particular pests can be published. Very often the experience of other growers in an area will enable one to select varieties with some resistance to pests that are serious locally.

WEED CONTROL

The removal of weeds by pulling, or by scraping with a sharp hoe, has been mentioned, together with suggestions as to weed suppression by the use of a mulch. Gardeners who mulch carefully will usually find no really serious problem with weeds unless they happen to have some of the undesirable perennial sorts such as horse tail, quack grass, Canada thistle, or some forms of morning glory. It would be advisable to eliminate such perennial weeds before planting if at all possible. There are now chemical weed killers which will eliminate these weeds if carefully and thoroughly used. However, this is tricky business with perennial weeds and it would be advisable to secure local advice from the County Extension Office before attempting it.

Commercial rhododendron growers use chemicals such as Casoron, Simazine and others, usually with good results. However when using chemical weed killers in the garden one must think not only about the rhododendrons but also other plants which may be close enough to be damaged. In any case where chemicals are used for pest control the directions of the manufacturer printed on the label should be carefully followed in order to get the most satisfactory control and the least likelihood of damage to ornamental plants.

PROPAGATION

In a general discussion of rhododendron cuture propagation is usually covered. In this case it seems of sufficient importance to be treated under a separate heading.

USE IN THE LANDSCAPE

Perhaps it is a tribute to the rhododendron that so many people, at least with their first plant, will set it out in the middle of the yard as a specimen to be admired by itself. Actually it is nearly always better to consider the rhododendron as part of the landscape and plant it in a border, or a foundation, or island planting with other shrubs. The other plant material may include small trees which will provide some shade, and add height to the planting. In a border planting there is considerable protection against wind and to some extent against frost.

Rhododendrons should be grouped to achieve certain effects, considering size, color, season of blooming and other characters. Usually the taller growing plants should be towards the back of the planting, medium sized ones in front, and low growing rhododendrons or other plants around the edges. Some of the tall growing varieties tend to become rather leggy and the lower plants in front of them hide the bare trunks and make for a much more pleasing picture. Most rhododendron varieties make a rather thick umbrella of leaves and lower branches and foliage tend to die off because of the shade.

Rhododendrons and azaleas go together very well in a landscape planting. With the deciduous azaleas thought should be given to the fact that there will be bare spots during the winter when the leaves have fallen. With a little forethought this situation can be pictured and the planting laid out in such a way that this lack of foliage will not be unsightly. As a matter of fact many of the deciduous azaleas have beautiful autumn colors and the bareness is not visible until winter when most gardens are supposed to be rather bare looking anyway.

Evergreen azaleas have very bright colors and it is usually better to plant them in masses with considerable care as to color harmony. This can be done very effectively with a little forethought. Somewhat the same may be said for deciduous azaleas and rhododendrons which should be grouped carefully in order to avoid too "spotty" a picture.

PLANT FOR THE FUTURE

In laying out a planting thought should be given to the ultimate size of the plant. It would seem that the size of the plant in about ten years is a good criterion to use as most of us are not concerned as to how large a rhododendron may ultimately grow, after fifty or a hundred years. The A.R.S. ratings in this book do not use the ten year scale but roughly indicate the relative size "at maturity." This may seem rather indefinite but perhaps one might think of most varieties attaining reasonably mature size in about ten or fifteen years. Actually some of the dwarfs reach a mature size, as to height, within four or five years or even less. They may spread out after that time but increase in height very little if at all.

Some of the larger growing varieties might continue to grow in height more or less indefinitely, depending on growing conditions and particularly whether or not they are in the shade. There are some rhododendron plants in England, for instance, which are over sixty feet in height and, in their native habitat, some which have been measured at eighty feet or higher. Some of the so-called dwarfs, if in a shady place and crowded a little, may grow up to several feet in height within a few years. However, if they are planted in full sun or almost full sun, under good growing conditions, they will bloom so heavily that they will not increase in height to any extent after the first few years.

SIZES VARY

There is really a great difference in the ultimate size of rhododendron and azalea varieties and plantings should be laid out with this in mind or else the rapid growing ones will soon crowd and shade out the slow growing ones. This poses a somewhat difficult problem to the gardener who must decide how far apart to plant his rhododendrons or azaleas. There are a few which make a very upright growth or a very spreading growth, but most, if given full space, will grow approximately as wide as they are tall. Thus one could determine planting distance by the indicated height at maturity.

But the gardener has to determine when he wants the planting to look its best. If he is thinking about fifteen or twenty years after planting, the plants should be widely spaced, and presumably filled in between with other low growing ornamental plant material. The present tendency of the American family is to move rather frequently rather than to set up a home which will be inhabited by future generations of the family which built it. Perhaps the appearance of the landscape in five to ten years should be the criterion affecting plant distance. Many rhododendron lovers set their plants quite close together, so that within three or four years they are touching and the border may look as if it is a continuous blanket of green. That is beautiful at the time but the larger growing varieties or species will begin to crowd, shed their lower leaves and twigs, and thrust up toward greater light. Even though some plants are badly crowded the overall effect may be reasonably good, as, when looking at the border as a whole, one will see only the foliage at the top of the plant which may look quite normal and blooming may be quite satisfactory. One may let such crowded plants go until they either die out or become so spindly that they may as well be removed.

Others may wish to dig the plants and move them before they are of moderate size. The roots are rather compact and fibrous, and a good sized root ball will include enough of the root system so that moving can be done without seriously shocking the plant. As a matter of fact many growers dig plants from their garden and take them to rhododendron shows, and then set them back in the garden without serious injury to them. The alternative to close planting, with eventual moving, of course, is spacing the plants so far apart when they are small that they look rather isolated. If they are inter-planted with annuals or other shrubs they may be crowded by the inter-plants and if so the effect is the same as if they were planted too close together.

Rhododendrons are friendly plants and seem to do better if planted in groups than if set out singly. Each plant will fill up its own area and help to make the border a solid mass of foliage.

COMPANION PLANTS

It is true that there are hundreds of varieties and species of azaleas and rhododendrons to choose from and a planting made up from this genus alone need not be monotonous. There may be great variation in size of plant, leaf texture and color, in addition to great differences in flower color, size, and season of bloom. However, most rhododendron lovers are also interested in other plants and feel that some other, may well be grown along with rhododendrons to give variety, accent, and possibly color when rhododendrons are out of season. The choice of such companion plants depends on their own beauty and desirability, of course, but also their cultural requirements.

Since rhododendrons so often need at least partial shade, some of the companion plants will usually be trees, in which case three things should be considered. One is whether the tree is shallow rooted, for if it is the shallow rooted rhododendrons may suffer from competition for plant food and water. A second thing to be considered is the density of the shade. There are some trees, like Norway maple for instance, which produce too dense a shade for best results with under plantings which prefer only partial shade. The third point is the attractiveness and desirability of the tree for its own good quality. There are some rather small growing trees, such as some of the Magnolias, which work out very well on the basis of all three points mentioned.

The use of deciduous shrubs among evergreen rhododendrons poses the same problem as mixing rhododendrons and deciduous azaleas. There will be gaps in the mass of foliage during the winter which should be carefully planned.

As rhododendrons are rather specific in their cultural requirements it would seem desirable to combine with them other plants which need similar conditions. This would include many of the genera within the family Ericaceae. A number of these were mentioned at the beginning of this section. When one goes to special effort to provide soil conditions suitable for rhododendrons it seems that it offers a good opportunity to try out some of the other acid loving plants such as heathers, pieris, andromeda, kalmia, and others.

In many cases it is somewhat undesirable to try to grow annual plants among small rhododendrons while they are becoming established. The annuals will probably require cultivation, at least when they are set out, which may be somewhat undesirable for the rhododendrons. Various types of bulbs, seem to fit in better as, once established, they seem to appreciate mulch culture and will grow up through the rhododendrons and provide color when the rhododendrons are not in bloom. This may include a number of types of low growing bulbous plants and also some of the lilies which will grow up through the rhododendron even after they have reached considerable height. A little forethought in choosing companion plants will give a more beautiful picture and avoid difficulties later.

VARIETIES TO PLANT

One of the most important requisites to success with rhododendrons is getting the right varieties to start with. It is somewhat difficult to specify particular varieties without going into a long discussion, but some lists can be suggested, based on various characters and requirements. For the beginner's first plant the advice of a local nurseryman should be as good as any. He will probably have several varieties, including some which might be called old standard popular types, perhaps a little outmoded. However the ones usually available on the market have attained that status by being good growers, adaptable to a fairly wide range of conditions, reasonably hardy and perhaps more able than others to take a little abuse and neglect. Some of the varieties still being planted, and still winning occasional prizes in the shows, are ones which were introduced fifty to a hundred years ago. Many of them are still beautiful and their staying power is worthy of consideration.

If one becomes biten by the rhododendron bug and wants to increase his collection he should study variety lists and read variety descriptions. If possible he should visit rhododendron shows, test gardens or nursery plantings where a number of varieties may be seen in bloom. Study the A.R.S. ratings and the experiences of your neighbors. There is one consolation, that you are unlikely to purchase a rhododendron which will not grow into a beautiful plant.

RHODODENDRON

PROPAGATION

The principles of propagation are the same for azaleas as for rhododendrons, with some differences in timing and minor details. The following is written especially for rhododendrons with side references to azaleas.

PROPAGATION BY SEED

The natural way for rhododendrons to increase, as with most other plants, is by seed. This is sexual as opposed to asexual methods such as layering, grafting and by cuttings. With asexual methods the plants produced are genetically identical with the one from which the cuttings or scions were taken. All such plants propagated from one original plant, and having identical characteristics, constitute a clone, and clones are what the gardener usualy wants. If he buys a plant of 'Cynthia' he wants it to be identical with one he saw in a Show or in a neighbor's garden.

With sexual propagation, on the other hand, every plant grown from seed will be a little bit, or possibly a great deal, different from every other plant. If the parents are hybrids between two species the offspring may be quite variable, so a clone like 'Pink Pearl' cannot be reproduced from seed; seedlings would be a mixture of types, sizes and colors, mostly inferior to the seed parent. This variability, however, is just what the breeder wants, in order to find new combinations of characters, and so the raising of seedlings is important to the breeder.

Seed propagation is also very commonly used to increase a species, and most species do tend to come true from seed, although always with minute variations. Most species plants available from nurseries are seedlings although superior forms of some have been selected out and grown from cuttings and are usually so indicated.

Rhododendron and azaleas seeds usually germinate quite readily if sown on top of moist peat moss, without covering. Results will be better if the peat is covered with half an inch of ground up sphagnum moss. This should be thoroughly wet, pressed flat, and the seed scattered thinly on top, after which the container should be covered tightly with a sheet of glass, or enclosed in a polyethylene bag. The container should be set in a place with plenty of light but not in direct sunlight. The containers used may be standard greenhouse flats or other small boxes, or plastic icebox dishes with tight fitting lids. No additional watering should be needed until after the seeds have germinated, which should be in 3 or 4 weeks for most kinds. As soon as the seedlings are big enough to take hold of, perhaps ¼ to ½ in. in height they should be spotted off into sphagnum peat, in flats or pots. Later they may be put into larger pots or lined out in a lath house or specially prepared nursery bed in partial shade.

PROPAGATION BY LAYERS

Rhododendrons may be propagated rather easily by layering but it is a very slow method, usually used in this country only infrequently to increase an old plant which has some low branches which may easily be bent down into a shallow trench. Usually the branch is notched on the under side and pegged down with soil or peat moss to a depth of 3 or 4 inches, kept moist, and left in that position for several months. After the branch roots, at or near the notch, it may be dug, severed from the old plant, and put into a nursery row for a couple of years to develop side branches.

PROPAGATION BY GRAFTING

Not so many years ago practically all the rhododendrons grown in this country were grafted, but now that most varieties can be grown from cuttings, more cheaply and satisfactorily, very little grafting is done except for special purposes. These would include propagation of those varieties that are especially difficult to root, to propagate out of season, or to save valuable plant material that is in poor condition. Seedlings of *R. ponticum* were commonly used as understock but any easily rooted variety, or species seedlings, that are fairly closely related to the scion material, may be used.

Many different kinds of grafts have been used but, for the occasional graft, the cleft or saddle graft is probably best for the amateur. These grafts are known at least by name, to most gardeners, the cleft graft being the one usually used for top working fruit trees. In this graft the understock is split and a long wedge shaped scion inserted in the cleft so that the cambium layers are in contact. In the saddle graft the stump of the understock is trimmed to a long, 1 to 2 inches, wedge and the scion has a long notch, of the same length, cut into its base, so it can be fitted snugly over the wedge. The graft may be tied with a rubber strip and a polyethylene bag fitted over the scion and graft to keep the union from drying out.

PROPAGATION BY CUTTINGS

Grafting and layering were treated very briefly because nearly all rhododendrons and azaleas are now grown from cuttings. This has come about since the development of mist propagation and the availability of chemical root-inducing hormones. Bottom heat is important too, now mostly from electric cables, but also available years ago from steam pipes.

Cuttings of azaleas are usually taken quite early in the growing season, as soon as the new shoots have firmed up so they can be handled without wilting. Rhododendrons are usually taken in late summer or early fall, the wood being in the best condition just before it hardens up and becomes woody. Most nurseries probably take their cuttings by the time of year, rather than by the condition of the individual shoot.

Cuttings are made from healthy, medium vigorous shoots of the current season's growth. Four or five inches is the usual length; some leaves may be removed, leaving 4 to 6 at the tip. If the leaves are quite large it is the usual custom to trim them back by $\frac{1}{4}$ or $\frac{1}{2}$ so they do not take up so much room in the bench. Most propagators wound the cutting by slicing an inch or so of the bark from one side of the base to stimulate root formation. The cuttings is then ready to dip into one of the hormone powders or liquid formulations, and insert into the rooting medium.

The medium may be of peat, sand, perlite or other inert material, or a combination of two or more of them. Some successful propagators use straight peat, others mixtures of various kinds. The bench, or box in which the cuttings are placed should be deep enough so the medium will not dry out too rapidly, and so cuttings may be inserted to a depth of about 2 inches, less for very small cuttings.

Most propagators in the Northwest use electric cable bottom

heat, and intermittent overhead mist. The amateur may easily rig up a propagating bed with a short electric cable but the mist will require a little more construction, ingenuity and money. Many amateurs get good results by having a tight frame which can be tightly covered with polyethylene sheeting to maintain high humidity. With frequent attention to watering very satisfactory results may be obtained with such a plastic covered frame, with electric cable heat, but no mist. Such frames may be constructed in a basement, with fluorescent lights, especially if the gardener wants to work during severe weather.

Some years ago Guy Nearing of New Jersey worked out a carefully planned propagating frame to be used outdoors, with no bottom heat and no mist. It involved a carefully prepared rooting medium, in layers, a glass covered frame shaded by a slanting, white painted board frame which kept off the direct sun but reflected a maximum of north light into the frame. Many amateurs, and some commercial propagators found the Nearing frame to be very satisfactory and it is still being used to some extent in the East. It has never been used to any extent in the Northwest, partly because the time required for rooting was quite long. Directions for making the frame were published in a New Jersey Experiment Station Circular.

After cuttings are rooted they are commonly "weaned" from mist, the bottom heat is decreased or cut off, and the rooted cuttings potted or lined out in a plastic house or in a specially prepared nursery bed.

All through the propagation process care should be taken to keep things clean, moist enough, but not too moist, and not overcrowded, in order to keep the danger of fungus attack, damping off, at a minimum. This may come in spite of everything, in which case give more ventilation if the cuttings are rooted and can stand it, plus a light dusting with Captan.

GLOSSARY

There have been frequent requests for a reprinting of a glossary of terms similar to that appearing in "Rhododendrons 1956", long out of print. It is reproduced herewith, with a few additions and minor changes, and with Mr. Hansen's introductory paragraph.—Ed.

The study of Rhododendrons, especially the species, is fairly complex for the amateur who does not have the proper background. The descriptive terms used in the "Species" book are usually beyond the scope of the ordinary layman. In trying to track down a species, I usually arm myself with a dictionary and two or three other horticultural books having glossaries. Finding this too cumbersome when I wanted to track down a single leaf, I finally started my own glossary.

One day, not so long ago, I happened to tell the editor of this book about my project. He thought such a glossary might be useful to others and asked to use it, so here it is. Remember—it is not intended as a scientific treatise but only as a layman's help for other laymen.

C. T. Hansen

Aberrant. Differing from the common type.
Aborted. Said of parts which have imperfectly developed, as stamens consisting of filaments only.
Acuminate. Tapered to a long point.
Acute. Sharply pointed but not long tapered.
Adpressed. Growing in contact with a stem but not adhering to it.
Adventitious. Occurring in unusual places.
Agglutinate. Joined by adhesion.
Alveolate. Full of hollow cells; honeycombed.
Annular. Ring shaped; marked with rings.
Anther. The part of the stamen that bears pollen.
Anthesis. The time of opening or expansion of a flower.
Apex. Tip or free end.
Apices. Plural of apex.
Apiculate. Having a short sharp point.
Appressed. Pressed closely against.

Aristate. Having a bead-like or bristled appendage; awned.
Attenuate. Thin; small or fine; slenderly tapering.
Auricle. An ear-shaped appendage.
Auriculate. Bearing auricles.
Axil. The angle between a leaf and a stem.
Axillary. Borne in an axil.
Basal. Pertaining to or at the base.
Bistrate. Two-layered.
Bloom. A waxy coating.
Bract. A modified, reduced leaf.
Bracteole. A little bract, on a pedicel.
Bullate. Having a blistered or puckered appearance.

Callus. The undifferentiated growth that forms over cut or wounded area on a plant stem.
Calyx. The outer set of parts (sepals) of a complete flower at the base of, and external to the corolla.
Campanulate. Bell-shaped; cup shaped.
Candelabroid. Shaped like a candelabra.
Canescent. With gray pubescence.
Capitate. Collected into a head or dense cluster.
Capsule. A dry seed vessel splitting at maturity.
Carpel. A single simple pistil, or a single unit of a compound pistil. The number of carpels can generally be determined by the number of placentae, or the number of compartments in a pistil, or the number of styles and stigmas. The blending of parts in a compound pistil tends to obscure this point.
Cartilaginous. Gristly.
Cespitose. Growing in tufts.
Chartaceous. Writing paper texture.
Cilia. Small, sometimes microscopic, hair-like processes.
Ciliate. Fringed with hairs.
Ciliolate. Minutely ciliate.
Clavate. Club-shaped.
Clone. A horticultural variety propagated asexually, by cuttings, grafts, or layers, and not by seed.
Cm. Abbreviation for centimeter, approximately two-fifths of an inch.
Conic. Cone-shaped; conical.
Conoid. Nearly conic.
Contiguous. Adjacent; joined at the edge.
Convex. Curved outward, as the outer surface of a sphere; opposed to concave.
Cordate. Heart-shaped, with two rounded lobes at the base.
Coriaceous. Leathery in texture.
Corolla. The part of the flower just outside the stamens, usually colored, and consisting of separate or more or less united petals.
Corymb. Cluster of flowers, flat-topped due to unequal length of pedicels and flowering from the margin inward.
Corymbose. Borne in a corymb.
Crenate. Dentate with rounded teeth.

Crenulate. Minutely crenate.
Crispate. Having a crisp or curled appearance.
Crustaceous. Of hard and brittle texture.
Cultivar. Horticultural variety.
Cuneate. Wedge-shaped.
Cupular. Cup-shaped.
Cuspidate. Tipped with a sharp, stiff point.
Cylindric. Shaped like a cylinder.

Deciduous. Falling off at maturity; not evergreen.
Declinate. Curved downward.
Decumbent. Reclining, with tip ascending.
Decurrent. Applied to a sessile leaf having its base extended downward along the stem.
Dehiscing. Gaping or opening, as of a seed capsule.
Deltoid. Triangular; shaped like the Greek letter Delta.
Dendroid. Treelike in form.
Dentate. Having teeth that point outward rather than upward.
Denticulate. With minute teeth pointing outward.
Dimorphic. Occurring in two forms.
Discoid. Having the form of a disc.
Dissected. Cut deeply into many segments.
Dorsal. Pertaining to the upper surface of a leaf.
Double. Having more than one set of petals.

Eglandular. Without glands.
Elepidote. Without scales.
Ellipsoid. A solid figure having every plane an ellipse or circle.
Elliptic. Oval; oblong narrowed to rounded ends.
Emarginate. Having the margin notched or indented at the apex.
Entire. Not cut or toothed.
Epidermis. Outer layer of cells on leaf or other plant organ.
Epiphyte. A plant growing non-parasitically upon another.
Erose. Having an irregular toothed margin, as if gnawed.
Evanescent. Fleeting or liable to disappear.
Exserted. Protruding from surrounding parts.

Farina. White, powder-like material on surface of leaf or flower.
Farinose. Covered with a white, meal-like powder.
Fasciate. Characterized by a flat or ribbon-like growth.
Fasciculate. Growing in bundles or clusters.
Fastigiate (branches). Erect and near together; narrowly upright.
Ferruginous. Rust colored.
Fertile. Capable of performing its functions, as a stamen or pistil.
Filament. The stalk or support of an anther.
Filiform. Thread-like; filamentous.
Fimbriate. Fringed.
Flexuous. Bending alternately in opposite directions; slightly wavy.
Floccose. Having tufts of soft hairs or wool.

Floret. Any of the small flowers making up the head of a composite flower.

Floriferous. Bearing flowers.

Flower. A single blossom, consisting usually of pistil, stamens, corolla and calyx.

Foliaceous. Leaf-like; having leaves.

Foveolate. Having foveola or little pits.

Fulvous. Tawny.

Gamete. A mature male or female sex cell.

Genus (pl. Genera). A group of species which are similar in many respects and presumably more closely related to each other than to other species.

Gibbous. Irregularly rounded; lumped or swollen on one side.

Glabrescent. Shedding hair; becoming glabrous.

Glabrous. Not rough or hairy; smooth.

Gland. A small secreting body, or a similar body which does not secrete.

Glandular. Bearing glands.

Glaucous. Covered with a whitish waxy or powderly substance.

Globose. Spherical.

Glomerate. Compactly clustered.

Glutinous. Besmeared with sticky or slippery moisture.

Grex. A group variety including more than one seedling of a given cross.

Heterozygous. That condition of an individual in which any given factor has been derived from only one parent, so that half the gametes will contain this particular factor, half will lack it; such an individual will not breed true with respect to this particular character.

Hirsute. Covered with rather coarse, straight hairs.

Hispid. Rough, with stiff hairs or bristles.

Homomorphic. Having the same form.

Homozygous. That condition of an individual in which any given genetic factor is doubly present, hence such an individual produces gametes of only one kind and breeds true with respect to the given character.

Hose-in-hose. Flowers in which the sepals are petal-like as to size and color, so the flowers appear to have two complete cycles of petals, one within the other.

Hyaline. Glassy surfaced; translucent.

Hybrid. Offspring of a cross between two species; used of rhododendrons of mixed origin, that is not pure species.

Imbricate. Overlapping like shingles.

Indumentum. Felt-like hairy covering on the under side of a leaf.

Inflorescence. The flower cluster or flower arrangement.

Internode. The part of a stem between nodes or joints.

Involute. Rolled inward.

Laciniate. Slashed into narrow lobes.
Lacunose. Furrowed or pitted.
Lamina. The blade or flat expanded portion of a leaf.
Laneolate. Tapering like the head of a lance.
Lepidote. Bearing scales.
Ligulate. Strap-shaped.
Linear. Very narrow and elongate with margins parallel.
Lobate. Divided into lobes.
Lobe. A rounded projection or division.
Lobulate. Having small lobes.

Mealy. Having the appearance of being covered with meal.
Membraneous. Thin and more or less transparent.
-merous. A suffix indicating division into parts, as 5-merous.
Mucro. Small, abrupt tip of a leaf.
Mucronate. Terminating in a short straight point.
Murconulate. Minutely mucronate.
Mutation. A sudden variation in an inheritable characteristic; may occur in a seedling (seed mutation) or as part of a growing plant (bud mutation).

Nectary. Nectar producing organ.
Node. The place on a stem which normally bears a leaf.
Nodular. Containing nodules; lumpy.
Nomenclature. A system of naming plants or animals.

Oblanceolate. Widest near apex, tapering gradually to base; several times longer than wide.
Oblong. More or less rectangular and longer than broad.
Obovate. Egg-shaped, widest near apex.
Obtuse. Blunt or rounded at the end.
Orbicular. Circular.
Oval. Elliptical.
Ovary. Seed bearing part of pistil.
Ovate. Egg-shaped; broadest near base narrowing abruptly at tip.
Ovoid. Egg-shaped solid; with ovate outline.
Ovule. An immature seed.

Papillae. Nipple-shaped projections of the outer walls of epidermal cells.
Papillose. Bearing papillae.
Papyraceous. Papery.
Partite. Cleft nearly to the base, as a leaf.
Pedicel. The stalk of a single flower.
Peduncle. The stalk of a flower cluster.
Pellicle. A thin skin, film of layer.
Peltate. Having the stalk attached on the under side near the middle.
Perfect. Having both stamens and pistils in the same flower.
Perianth. The floral envelope consisting of calyx and corolla.
Persistent. Remaining attached, not falling off.

Perulae. Leaf bud scales.
Petal. A division of the corolla.
Petaloid. Petal-like.
Petiole. The stalk of a leaf.
Phylogenetic. Pertaining to the history of the evolution of a series or group.
Pilose. Covered with fine soft hair.
Pistil. The central seed-bearing organ, consisting of ovary, style and stigma.
Pistillate. Bearing pistils but no stamens.
Placenta. That part of the ovary to which the seeds are attached.
Pollen. Powdery substance borne in the anthers; the male element.
Procumbent. Lying flat; trailing.
Prostrate. Lying against the ground.
Puberulent. Covered with very fine hair or pubescence.
Pubescent. Covered with fine, soft, short hair.
Punctate. Covered with dots or depressions; dotted.
Punctulate. Minutely punctate.

Raceme. Inflorescence with flowers arranged along a stem, with the terminal flowers blooming last.
Racemose. In racemes.
Rachis. The axis of a flower cluster.
Receptacle. That part of the stem to which a flower is attached.
Recurved. Bent back or down.
Regular. Said of a flower when all the petals or all the sepals are of the same size and shape.
Reticulate. In the form of a network; net-veined.
Retuse. Having a rounded apex in which there is a slight notch.
Revolute. Rolled backward or downward from the margins.
Rhizome. An underground (or under water) perennial stem which is generally prostrate, and sends new shoots above ground each year, and roots below.
Rhombic. Four-sided with the sides oblique.
Rhomboid. Having oblique angles; diamond-shaped.
Rostrate. Beaked.
Rotate. Wheel-shaped; flat and circular in outline.
Rufous. Dull red; rust colored.
Rugose. Covered with, or full of wrinkles.
Rugulose. Sightly wrinkled.

Saprophyte. A plant which secures its food from dead plant or animal substances.
Scabrid. Roughened with minutely scurfy points.
Scabrous. Rough to the touch.
Scale. Tiny plate-like structure appearing on leaves and other organs of certain rhododendron species.
Scaly. Having a covering of scales.
Scurfy. With scaly matter adhering to the surface.
Sebaceous. Fatty; waxy.

Sepal. A division of a calyx.
Series. Rhododendron groups of species which have somewhat similar characteristics.
Serrate. Having sharp teeth pointing forward.
Serrulate. Finely serrate.
Sessile. Attached at the base without a stalk.
Seta. A slender spine or prickle; a bristle.
Setose. Bristly.
Setulose. Clothed with minute bristles.
Shrub. A woody plant smaller than a tree, and generally without a pronounced trunk.
Solitary. Only one in a place.
Spathe. A large bract enclosing a flower cluster.
Spatulate. Shaped like a spatula.
Species (pl. Species). Each recognizable kind of wild plant (or animal), consisting of individuals which are very much alike, most of the differences being due to external conditions and not inherited; hence a plant species essentially breeds true and may be propagated by seed.
Sport. Mutation; to mutate.
Stamen. The pollen-bearing organ of a flower, consisting of anther and filament.
Stellate. Star-shaped.
Sterile. Not capable of performing its normal function, as a stamen or pistil; not producing flowers, as a shoot.
Stigma. The pollen-receiving part of the pistil.
Stipitate. Elevated on a stipe or stalk.
Stolon. A trailing branch or runner which strikes root where it touches the ground.
Stoloniferous. Bearing stolons.
Stratum. Layer.
Strigillose. Minutely strigose.
Strigose. Rough with short, sharp appressed hairs.
Stud Book. The R.H.S. record of rhododendron crosses.
Style. The portion of the pistil connecting the stigma and ovary.
Sub-. A prefix meaning slightly, nearly, or below.
Subacuminate. Somewhat acuminate.
Subacute. Not as pointed as acute.
Subchartaceous. Less paper-like than chartaceous.
Subcordate. Modified heart-shaped.
Subcoriaceous. Somewhat less leathery than coriaceous.
Subdecumbent. Somewhat more upright than decumbent.
Subdiscoid. Modified disc form.
Subfoliaceous. Somewhat foliaceous.
Subglobose. Not quite globular in shape.
Suborbicular. Not quite circular.
Subprocumbent. Somewhat less than prostrate.
Subretuse. Modified retuse.
Subsessile. Attached with almost no stalk.
Subterminal. Below the terminal.

Subtriangular. Modified triangular form.
Subtruncate. Nearly truncate.
Subumbellate. Not quite umbellate.
Subverticillate. Somewhat less than verticillate.
Succulent. Fleshy, full of water.
Suffruticose. Diminutively shrubby.
Superior. Said of an ovary which is borne above the attachment of the calyx.

Terminal. At the end.
Throat. The upper expanded portion of a corolla tube.
Tomentose. Covered with matted, wooly hair.
Tomentum. A form of pubescence composed of matted, wooly hairs.
Trailing. Lying on the ground or over other plants, but not rooting at the nodes.
Translucent. Nearly transparent.
Truncate. Appearing as if cut or broken off squarely.
Truss. A flower cluster.
Tuberculate. Nodular; beset with small, pimple-like tubercles.
Turbinate. Top-shaped; inversely conical.
Trichomes. Minute structures which have grown from epidermal cells of the leaves and consisting of papillae, hairs and scales.

Umbel. A flat topped flower cluster with pedicels springing from the same point.
Undulate. With a wavy surface.
Unicellular. Single-celled.
Unilateral. One sided; growing chiefly to one side.
Unistrate. Single-layered.

Vein. A bundle of vascular tissue in the framework of a leaf usually appearing as a ridge.
Venation. Arrangement of veins as in a leaf.
Ventricose. Inflated on one side.
Verruculose. Beset with minute, wart-like projections.
Verticillate. Arranged in a whorl.
Vesicular. Bearing or containing air cavities or vesicles.
Vesitigial. Having become small or degenerate.
Villous. Covered with long, close, soft hairs.
Virgate. Long, straight and slender, like a wand.
Viscid. Sticky; adhesive; viscous.

Whorl. A set of leaves distributed in a circle round the stem.

Leaf Shapes—drawn by C. T. Hansen

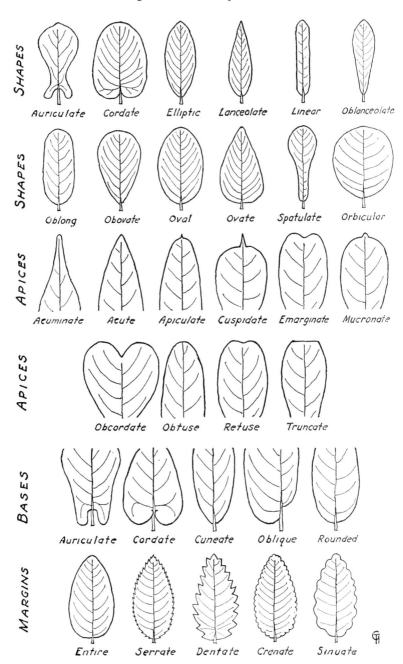

Flower Shapes—drawn by C. T. Hansen

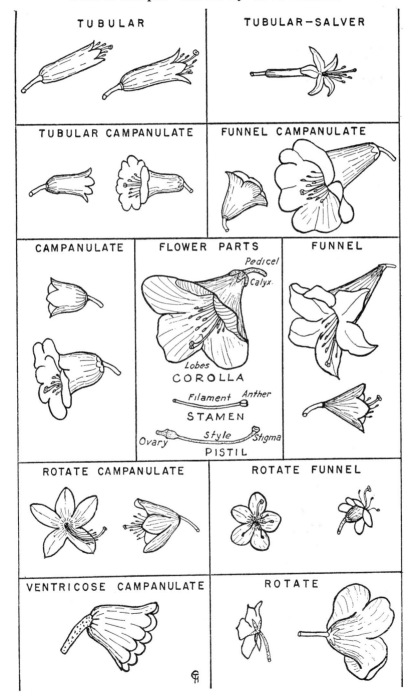

TUBULAR

TUBULAR—SALVER

TUBULAR CAMPANULATE

FUNNEL CAMPANULATE

CAMPANULATE

FLOWER PARTS

FUNNEL

Pedicel

Calyx

Lobes

COROLLA

Filament *Anther*

STAMEN

Ovary *Style* *Stigma*

PISTIL

ROTATE CAMPANULATE

ROTATE FUNNEL

VENTRICOSE CAMPANULATE

ROTATE

SOURCES OF

RHODODENDRON

AND AZALEA PLANTS

The following are, or have recently been, advertisers in the American Rhododendron Society Bulletin, and are suggested as sources of plant material.

A. M. SHAMMARELLO & SON NURSERY, 4590 Monticello Blvd., South Euclid, Ohio. Wholesale and retail.

COMERFORD'S, P. O. Box 100, Marion, Oregon 97359. Retail—Mail Order.

GEORGE W. CLARKE, 11740 N.E. Marine Drive, Portland, Oregon 97220. Retail and wholesale.

GILBERT AND JUNE ZOLLING, 6750 S. W. Oleson Road, Portland, Oregon. Retail.

HENNY & WENNEKAMP, INC., Box 212, Brooks, Oregon 97305. Wholesale and retail.

INDIAN RUN NURSERY, Robbinsville, New Jersey 08691. Retail.

ISLAND GARDENS, 701 Goodpasture Island Road, Eugene, Oregon 97401. Retail and wholesale.

J. B. WHALLEY NURSERY, R. 2, Box 683, Troutdale, Oregon 97060. Wholesale.

J. HAROLD CLARKE, Long Beach, Washington. Wholesale and Retail.

KAMMER'S, 403 - 49th Avenue N.E., Puyallup, Washington. Retail.

RAINIER MT. ALPINE GARDENS, 2007 - South 126 St., Seattle, Washington 98168. Wholesale and retail.

REDBARN NURSERY, 579 Main Street, Pennsburg, Pa. Retail.

ROYER GREENHOUSES, West Street, Doylestown, Pennsylvania 18901. Wholesale and Retail.

THE BOVEES, 1737 Southwest Coronado, Portland, Oregon 97219. Retail.

TUMBLE BROOK RHODODENDRON NURSERY, 365 Simsbury Road, Bloomfield, Connecticut 06002. Wholesale and retail.

VAN VEEN NURSERY, 3127 S. E. 43rd Avenue, Portland, Oregon 97206. Wholesale.

DEVELOPMENT OF

THE AMERICAN

RHODODENDRON SOCIETY

In 1944, in Portland, Oregon, several people interested in rhododendrons got together to discuss the possible formation of a Society where kindred spirits could get together from time to time to discuss their favorite group of plants. The result was the organization we now have, or rather the beginning of it. The next year, 1945, it was incorporated under the laws of Oregon.

From the beginning the emphasis was on activity and service. The first rhododendron show was held in Portland in May 1945. In 1950 the Portland Test Garden was established, the first ratings system was set up, and a system of awards to superior plants was started. The following year a key for the classification of varieties at shows was worked out so that competition would be between similar kinds.

The name American Rhododendron Society had been chosen advisedly as it was anticipated that rhododendron lovers in other areas would be interested in joining, but activities were more or less centered in Portland until 1951 at which time the Bylaws were amended to provide for Chapters. Almost immediately Chapters were formed in New York, Seattle, Eugene, San Francisco and Richmond. Growth has been steady and at this writing there are 26 active Chapters, centered in various areas throughout the U.S.A. and British Columbia.

The first A.R.S. Code of Nomenclature was set up in 1951 and by 1956 there was a registration service through which breeders could check to determine if the names they wanted to use had already been used, or were for some other reason not desirable.

A seed exchange has been started and thousands of packets of seed of many different species have been distributed at a nominal price to members.

All of the 26 Chapters have meetings where topics of interest are discussed by competent speakers. Most of them have annual rhododendron shows, and several have established test or display gardens. These are often in public parks where the public may see, enjoy and become more interested.

The Society sponsored an International Conference on Rhododendrons in Portland in 1961. It was so well attended that, since that time, two or three day Annual Meetings have been held in various parts of the country, on the east coast in odd years and on the west coast in even years.

CONCERNING

MEMBERSHIP

IN THE AMERICAN

RHODODENDRON SOCIETY

This is a non-profit organization whose objectives are to encourage interest in and knowledge of the genus Rhododendron, including Azaleas, and to provide a medium through which persons who are interested in this genus may communicate and cooperate with others of like interests through educational and scientific studies, meetings, publications and other activities.

A Quarterly Bulletin is issued and distributed to all members, test gardens are encouraged and supervised, new varieties are registered, activities of the various Chapters are encouraged and correlated, and other activities, usually associated with a national plant society are carried on.

Membership is open to anyone interested in these plants.

For additional information about THE AMERICAN RHODODENDRON SOCIETY write to

The Executive Secretary,

Mrs. W. J. Curtis,

R. 2, Box 105,

Sherwood, Oregon 97140

INDEX

Ancient Peoples and Places

NORWAY

General Editor

DR. GLYN DANIEL

ABOUT THE AUTHOR

Anders Hagen studied archaeology, ethnography, and ethnology at the University of Oslo, obtaining his M.A. degree in Scandinavian archaeology in 1945. His research into Iron Age farming communities earned him a doctorate in 1954. From 1945 to 1960, he was Curator at the University Museum of Northern Antiquities in Oslo. In 1960, he was elected to the Chair of Scandinavian Archaeology at the University of Bergen and became director of the Historical Museum there. Professor Hagen has excavated many sites, mainly from the Iron Age, and in recent years has been organizing salvage archaeology in Norway. He is the author of several books on Scandinavian archaeology and a frequent contributor to scientific journals.

Ancient Peoples and Places

NORWAY

Anders Hagen

75 PHOTOGRAPHS
68 LINE DRAWINGS
7 MAPS

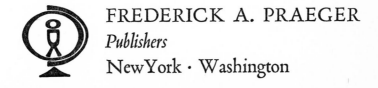

FREDERICK A. PRAEGER
Publishers
New York · Washington

THIS IS VOLUME FIFTY-SIX IN THE SERIES
Ancient Peoples and Places
GENERAL EDITOR: DR. GLYN DANIEL

Translated from the Norwegian by Elizabeth Seeberg

BOOKS THAT MATTER

Published in the United States of America in 1967
by Frederick A. Praeger, Inc., Publishers,
111 Fourth Avenue. New York, N.Y. 10003
Library of Congress Catalog Card Number: 67–17568
Printed in Holland

CONTENTS

ILLUSTRATIONS

7

8

9

To COMPREHEND the richly varied pattern of Norwegian cultural history – whether in the Stone Age or in modern times – it is essential to know what the country is like. Even the elementary fact that Norway is longer and narrower than any other European country is significant. From Kirkenes near the Russian border to Halden close to the west coast of Sweden, the coastline stretches over 12,500 miles.

Fig. 1

Obviously people could not live the same kind of lives, or in the same kind of house, by the bleak coast of Finnmark as by the more temperate waters of the Oslo Fjord; nor would they be likely, at any given time, to share the same kind of beliefs, customs or habits. The coast of Finnmark faces the open Arctic, and to the east lie the immeasurable expanses of the Russian tundra and taiga. The Oslo Fjord, on the other hand, is near to the Continent of Europe, and access is easy.

To some extent modern communications have neutralized the difficulties created by distance. Contrasts are growing less marked. But even to-day it is quicker to travel from the Norwegian capital to Rome than to Kirkenes.

The various parts of Norway are no longer separated by thousands of trackless miles, creating contrasts and nuances in culture; but it is not long since they did. Local traditions and the peculiar geographical structure of the country still make for considerable variation as between one area and another; thus, nomadic Lapps continue their habitual way of life in the North while the Oslo Fjord region is entering the Atomic Age. Power plants provide a basis for modern industry, deriving their energy from the extensive rivers and lakes of the mountain areas; on those same mountains Europe's last remaining herds of wild reindeer roam. Such contrasts add depth to the picture. Each year nearly 8000 reindeer are shot in the southern Norwegian mountain areas: the animal which the tundra tribes sought above all others at a time when the ice had not yet loosened its grip on the North still plays a part in the economy of the mountain hamlets.

In the inland forests, too, the fauna of the Stone Age and the cultural patterns of the industrial era meet. Here Norway's wood-pulp industry gets its raw materials; and here large numbers of elk still live. Of these animals, long extinct on the West European continent, nearly 10,000 are shot in Norway during the open season each autumn.

Modern times and prehistory draw perhaps still closer to one another in coastal waters and on the high sea. From time immemorial, Norwegians have found most of their food along the extensive coast. Whaling and sealing vessels of the most modern design operate to-day in the Arctic and the Antarctic, using echo-sounding, radar, asdic and other intricate technical devices. In the home waters, where fishing carries on a primeval tradition, it retains many of its primitive methods: the hook, line and sinker are still the important implements they were in the Stone Age. Fish has always been so plentiful along the Norwegian coast that the simplest methods sufficed, and they made it possible to find a livelihood even in the northern and the most remote parts of the coast.

Ocean and fjord, mountains and lowland forest, arctic air, midnight sun and the Gulf Stream – these are among the characteristic features of the Norwegian environment which have always been decisive factors in determining ways of livelihood and settlement. At the time when man's only sources of subsistence were hunting and fishing, this was a rich country. The arctic and sub-arctic coast, with its fjords and its surrounding belt of rocks and islets, was teeming with life, particularly during the summer when the midnight sun gives 'daylight' even at night. Whales, seals, salmon and other large fish had their best

Fig. 1. Norway is divided into four groups of counties: eastern Norway (Østfold, Vestfold, Hedmark, Opland, Buskerud, Telemark, East Agder and West Agder); western Norway (Rogaland, Hordaland, Sogn and Fjordane, Møre and Romsdal); Trøndelag (South Trøndelag and North Trøndelag); northern Norway (Nordland, Troms and Finnmark)

breeding grounds and spawning beds in these northern waters. On thousands of islets and skerries there were huge colonies of birds, providing an abundance of easily obtainable food; to this day, there are cliffs galore where bird-life abounds. From inland forests, mountains and plains, flocks of reindeer and red deer made for the coast each year, and the bear was a fairly frequent visitor even right by the sea. When farmers in other countries had ploughed the land and changed the nature of the fauna and the countryside, many parts of Norway still provided the same conditions as of old for fishermen, hunters and wild animals.

We should remember these basic facts when assessing the prehistory of Norway in relation to that of the rest of Europe. Consider, for instance, how at the close of the Ice Age forests grew and spread over the once open plains between the Elbe and the Vistula, with the result that hunting tribes of those areas saw their reindeer trek to other parts, while their living-conditions altered and their culture disintegrated under the impact of new climatic conditions. In the mountains of Norway, on the other hand, nature was still for thousands of years to provide opportunities for the old way of life. Natural resources were unchanged; so, therefore, taken by and large, was the daily existence of man.

In Norway a flora and a fauna extinct in most other parts of Europe still survive in considerable quantities. But we must not lose sight of the fact that varied agriculture and the keeping of livestock have gained ground right up to the Russian border. Though the Arctic Circle cuts off the northernmost third of the country, and though powerful mountain ranges account for much of it and the coasts are bare, yet conditions are not unfavourable for either stock-rearing or corn-growing, on a larger scale and over a longer period than one would tend to think. True, only a little more than 3% of Norway's soil is cultivated. But if we bear in mind the size of the country, and compare the acreage of arable land to the number of inhabitants, it becomes evident that agriculture, too, is more important than the percentage figure would suggest.

Norwegian agriculture has its roots in the Stone Age, and it has shown itself adaptable to the methods of the machine age. By far the most important factor making for favourable conditions is, of course, the Gulf Stream. This enormous, temperate mass of water that impinges upon its whole long coast has enabled this country, which lies on the same latitude as southern Greenland, to live at least partially on corn-growing and stock-rearing from the Stone Age onwards.

There are few parts of Europe where the farmer has found it harder to settle and maintain his way of life, and where he has been more dependent on geographical conditions and on climate, than in Norway. Great variations occur even over short distances. Along the fjords of western Norway, fruit trees blossom in their thousands while the snow still lies upon the mountain slopes beyond.

Oak, ash and beech, barley, wheat and other plants requiring warmth do well in parts of southern Norway, but a few miles away, in the hamlets on the mountain slopes where summer is short and winter severe, they cannot grow. Nor do such plants thrive in our day by the western coast, where the Atlantic climate and the stormy winters are limiting factors. But by the sea the winter is not too cold for sheep and other animals to graze for the greater part of the year. Near the Arctic Circle, in the archipelago of Lofoten, where our most important fishing grounds are, horses and sheep were pastured throughout the winter within living memory.

As a contrast to conditions by the sea, let us consider the mountain hamlets of eastern Norway, where the cattle must be fed in the shippon for at least nine months of the year, and where, during the coldest part of the winter, the temperature may sink to minus forty degrees Fahrenheit.

Not only agricultural but also cultural developments are de pendent upon the climatic, topographical and geological con ditions prevailing in the different regions. Nowadays the tilling of the soil is entirely mechanized in most places, especially in the Silurian districts; but those who farm steep slopes in the fjord and valley districts employ to this day implements and methods of work that have virtually not changed since pre historic times. Together with tractors and combine harvesters, a primitive plough and the scythe, the curved knife and the sickle from the Iron Age are still in use. Natural conditions in Norway have both preserved and promoted culture in this sphere as in others; and widely different usages could at all times be found existing within a short distance of each other. The fact that old ways and new have always been able to live side by side – in agriculture, in hunting and in industry – is a pecu liarity of Norwegian culture. Another, equally characteristic, feature is that each means of livelihood, and the culture associat ed with it, has generally been thoroughly intermingled with others – overlaid in varying degrees by the traditions and prac tices of other occupations which have sometimes included con tradictory elements. In only a few places was the farmer a farmer only, and the farm as such rich enough to allow of specializa tion. Thus fishing, hunting, stock rearing and corn growing were combined in all manner of ways. While the fisherman in the north would possess a few animals and a patch of land, the farmer by the coast farther south, though richer in fields and animals, would often resort to small time fishing and hunting as a profitable sideline. In the districts of the deep fjords and the long valleys, freshwater fishing, catching and hunting of every kind in the mountains and the forest were also of great impor tance. Of fundamental economic significance was the utilization of the vast tracts of uncultivated land by the farmers who owned them, for summer grazing; this in turn imparted special cultural characteristics to the settlements in the areas in question. The picture which we get of the occupational culture of Norway is complex, and it is not always easy to draw a line between the various pursuits, for we find all shades of transition from self-supporting farming to pure fishing.

The size of Norway, the way resources differ from region to region, and the decisive variations in climate and in flora between coast, mountain, valley and lowland – all these factors not only created problems of livelihood and a wide range of occupations, they also explain why Norway's prehistory was more varied than that of most countries, and full of contrasts and problems. Where their prehistory is concerned the coast of Finnmark, for example, differs very appreciably from the area around the Oslo Fjord. Nor did the 'ages' and the 'periods' coincide in the vast forests of eastern Norway and on the islands along the outer coast of western Norway. The schematic division into Stone Age, Bronze Age and Iron Age does not apply equally to all parts of this long, narrow land. Dividing lines of chronology and of cultures must be drawn separately for each of the contrasting geographical and economic environments of the north, the west and the south. While farming began early in Neolithic times in the lowlands around the Oslo Fjord, the ancient tribes of hunters found ample opportunity to live as before along the coast and on the open reindeer mountains, quite close to the villages of the pioneer farmers. Thus a Mesolithic and a Neolithic culture met and co-existed.

A Bronze Age chieftain class with metal weapons, with set burial rites and a form of culture according with southern Scandinavian custom, established itself on the coast of southern Norway, whilst in other parts of the country – particularly in the north – men continued to lead a typical Stone Age existence. Metal Age and Stone Age – two main stages of culture could occur in the same chronological period.

By the Early Iron Age, the big farmers and merchants of Norway were in close contact with those parts of Europe which were influenced by the Roman Empire, and they fashioned their weapons, their clothes and their household utensils according to the models set on the continent; yet there were still groups who hardly knew of the existence of iron, and whose daily round followed an ancient pattern. Officially, Norway became Christian during the first half of the eleventh century, but many Norwegian Lapps remained uninfluenced by Christianity for hundreds of years. While Norwegian agriculture uses thou-sands of tractors, the tools of the Viking Age have not yet dis-appeared entirely.

To sum up, the facts we must bear in mind when trying to understand Norwegian culture and history are: the great varia-tions in the setting and the parallel existence of different cultural groups.

CHAPTER I

The First Inhabitants

WHEN DID MAN first make his appearance in Norway?
No definite answer is possible, but we have reason to believe that he arrived as soon as open coasts and ice-free land
were to be found, and arctic vegetation and animal life had a
chance of survival. Small stretches of the coast in the west and
the north were open even during the last Ice Age, and certain
plants and small animals could, in fact, exist there. But even the
most frugal of hunters could hardly have found a livelihood on
these narrow, remote patches of land. There has been talk of a
'glacial' population on the Norwegian coast; this is merely wish-
ful thinking – though it is possible that human beings came to
Norway *before* the last Ice Age. In that event, however, we cannot expect to find any traces, for whatever they might have left
behind, the ice and the water must inevitably have washed away.

If we disregard all fanciful notions of people living here before or during the last Ice Age, we can set the upper date limit
of the earliest settlement in the period *c.* 10,000 – 8000 BC. During that time the ice was receding from large tracts of land in
the north of Norway and from coastal areas further south. Inland in eastern Norway the glaciers were slower to loosen their
hold on the land. By about 7000 BC, however, practically all
of the country was free of ice, offering life to man and beast.

These first millennia saw tremendous natural changes. New
land appeared from under the ice or out of the sea. Melting glaciers turned into rivers and channelled new beds; new coasts
and islands emerged. This rapidly changing land soon supported a fauna that must have tempted arctic hunters.

Whether we adopt a date of *c.* 10,000 BC for the first immigration, or consider the period around the year 7000 more likely
– either way, the land could support human life. Nevertheless

we must take a stand on the questions of dating, for they are closely connected with fundamental problems of culture. It is important to know where the first groups came from, and what their traditions of livelihood were when they arrived.

Were the first settlers descended from the Ice Age hunters, were their tools and their methods of hunting adapted to open land and to an arctic fauna? If they were, we must date the first appearance of man to pre-boreal times. Or did the first people come when southern Scandinavia was already covered with forests – forests that had forced the wild reindeer to quit, and man to change his pattern of life? If the latter was the case, even the very earliest traces of man must be comparatively late.

So we can see the importance of finding out whether the traces of the reindeer hunters of the mountain areas and of the fisher/hunters' settlements on the coast are those of the northern European Ice Age hunters, or of people who lived in more recent times, and had to learn anew how to hunt the reindeer and to fish in arctic waters. Or is there, perhaps, yet a third possibility? Do the Norwegian finds represent a coastal people who found shelter in Norway when the North Sea region was flooded? This bald statement of simplified alternatives still shows how necessary it is to study the chronological problems.

Important in this connection too is the question of the geographical origin of the earliest settlers and their culture. Did immigrations and impulses come exclusively from the south, or do even the earliest finds provide some indication of an origin in circumpolar areas or in Finno/Russian lands? The border between the north of Norway and Russia linked Europe with Asia, and communications between east and west seem to have been as easy and natural as the way south. We know for certain that during the Neolithic and later periods parts of northern Norway were in contact with the east. But did these routes to the east already exist during the earliest phase of the settlement of northern Scandinavia?

Finds and observations made in the forests east of the Oslo Fjord can apparently throw new light on the important and difficult problems of chronology and culture relating to the earliest Norwegian finds. Settlements that have come to light here during the last few years are, to all appearances, preboreal.

So far, three small sites have been found, close to each other. They are on the borders of small bogs that were once inlets of the sea, but the present coastline is twelve miles away. If we are right in thinking that these camps lay close to what was then the coast, they must be very ancient indeed. The local topography certainly suggests that the settlements 'hugged the shore'. The surrounding country is rugged, and long, narrow bogs alternate with steep hillocks. The soil is arid and the rock poor. Consequently, there is little variation in the vegetation, and game is very scarce. There is no fresh water, there being no rivers in the vicinity. Anyone trying to live by hunting in these parts today would soon starve.

But if we visualize a coastline traversing this landscape, we shall see a different land, well able to support life. Where there are bogs now, there would be inlets and straits. The highest points, sparsely wooded today, were once the islets, skerries and islands sheltering a coast where an arctic fauna thrived. A landscape like this makes the existence of the settlements reasonable: they lay on the shore, on a coast providing excellent fishing and hunting.

However, in order to find conditions like this – in fact, to find any natural explanation for the settlements and the finds – we must look far back in time, to an era when Norway was not yet covered by forests, and when the ice had barely disappeared from most of the land. Even if these hunters did not live right down by the shore, the sea level must have been at least 500 feet higher than it is today. We know that in this part of Norway the sea lay about 600 feet above its present level at the end of the

Ice Age; assuming that the land rose rapidly during the first centuries of the melting of the ice, the settlements must inevitably date from before 7000 BC.

The sites are small, each covering about 120 square yards. There are no traces of huts or tents, but remnants of paving have been found, and rows of sloping posts seem to indicate that there was a wind-break with an opening towards the sea.

As in all Norwegian excavations from the Early Stone Age, organic material is lacking here. What is remarkable about the inorganic material from Høgnipen is that the people who lived there used none of the local rock as raw material – they kept to flint, and that does not occur naturally in this district. The form the tools take and their craftsmanship show that these people had thoroughly mastered the art of working flint. In other words, this group of finds does not give an impression of isolation; its technology shows a close connection with that of the flint-using areas in the south.

The clearly defined tools are few but characteristic. The arrow and the scraper were the most important implements. A series of distinctive tanged points are typical; they are small, with a retouch on one working edge. This is a form characteristic of the beginning of the Mesolithic period from Poland in the east to

Fig. 2, 3

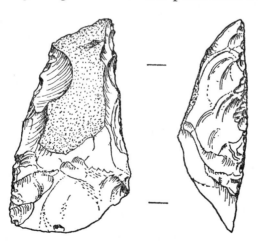

Fig. 2. *Flint flake-axe, Høgnipen, Østfold. Length 9 cm.*

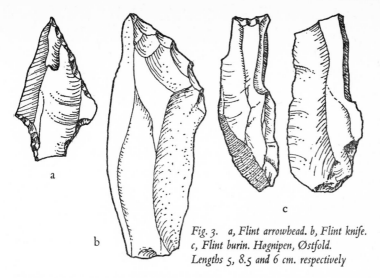

*Fig. 3.   a, Flint arrowhead. b, Flint knife.
c, Flint burin. Høgnipen, Østfold.
Lengths 5, 8.5 and 6 cm. respectively*

Belgium in the west, and it occurs frequently on western Swedish and Norwegian sites. No points of this type have, however, been found in southern Scandinavian settlements of the
forest period. Another type of point found at Høgnipen is characteristic of the pre-boreal Lyngby culture (Denmark): this
also would seem to indicate an early date. Great age is suggested
by the series of burins too. They are large, and well made. The
tools also include a number of blade knives, borers, blade scrapers, flake scrapers, and a few microliths – equipment common
in very many settlements of the Early Stone Age, regardless of
their date or cultural background. But it should be noted that
the primitive flake axe, though an insignificant part of the equipment, is archaeologically important. It is a recurrent item in
finds of hunting/fishing cultures, such as that of the Norwegian
west coast during the Fosna period, and that of the arctic Finnmark coast during Komsa times, a characteristic tool of both
these cultures. The Høgnipen finds show that this edged implement was fully developed before the onset of the forest period.

The above is a brief description of a group of finds made during the last few years. It presents a picture of roving bands of hunt-ers who lived close by the sea-shore but who, judging from their selection of tools, must have hunted big game on land as well. They still kept closely in touch with their southern back-ground, and they had not yet discovered a way of using the local raw materials for making tools. We have good reason to believe that these hunters were the pioneers who introduced the Fosna phase. It is an open question whether their technique of working the flint, and their characteristic series of arrowheads, burins, knives and scrapers, show that these people were the descendants of hunters who had roamed the open land that stretched from Poland to the North Sea before the forests came. But it is a very tempting notion – and not at all unlikely – that the herds of reindeer and the arctic hunters trekked north to Norway together, to seek a place where they might continue to live as they had done before – on the plains and by the treeless shores, where arctic conditions still prevailed. Certain it is that here in the North were districts where the old way of life, the old traditions of hunting and the old modes of settling could go on unchanged throughout the Stone Age. This knowledge may well be the key to the solution of many problems connected with the Fosna and Komsa cultures. However that may be, it is reasonable to assume that there were people in Norway in pre-boreal times, and that they came from the south.

THE FOSNA COMPLEX

While the finds from Høgnipen hardly show us more than an episode of the earliest history of man in Norway, the Fosna complex comprises a lengthy, composite part of the hunting/fishing culture. We have hundreds of settlements, widely spread in both time and space; they occur to the east of the Oslo Fjord, on the mountains dividing south-eastern from south-western

Fig. 4

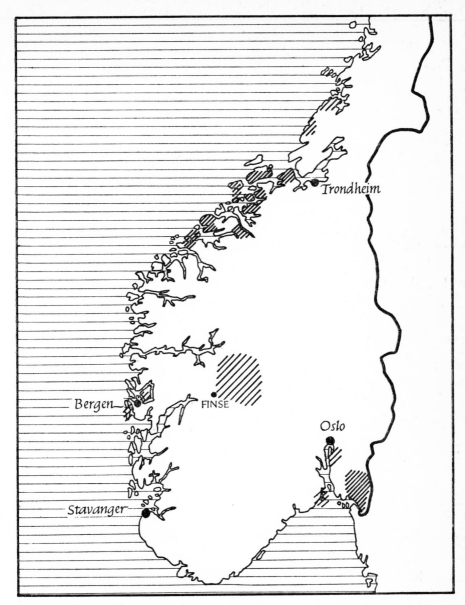

Fig. 4.   Distribution of the Fosna complex

27

Norway, and along the stormy west coast south of Trondheim. Their situation makes it clear that the Fosna people lived by fishing and hunting by the sea-shore, and by hunting the rein-deer in the mountains; forest hunting and fresh-water fishing apparently did not appeal to them.

Plates 2, 5

The Fosna people lived in open country, often in exposed places. They never made use of caves or rock-shelters, nor have any traces of huts, tents or of any other form of shelter been found. As a rule, their settlements are small. Those that have been surveyed vary in size from 1000 to 2000 square feet. The Fosna hunters obviously revisited many of their camps for season after season. From the size of the sites, and the number of finds, we may gather that they roamed around in small bands.

Fig. 5

All that remains of the Fosna settlements are objects of flint and local stone. The local flint of western Norway is poor, and the hunters who lived there made much use of stone from shore deposits. Those who lived in eastern Norway, on the other hand, had better sources of flint. Their use of raw materials reflects more clearly their contacts, both geographical and eth-nical, with people living further south.

Naturally, the form of the artifacts and the techniques em-ployed in fashioning them vary somewhat according to what raw material was used. The details of a knife, an arrowhead or a scraper of quartz will tend to differ from those of similar tools made from good flint. It would therefore be wrong to judge Fosna finds and forms solely by the standard of tools from the good flint districts of southern Scandinavia. Considered from the point of view of basic techniques, the tools are of three types – flakes, cores and blades. The selection is small, and the tools do not reflect these people's means of subsistence in much de-tail.

The most common tool is the scraper. Various forms and sizes have been found: core scrapers, blade scrapers, flake scrap-ers and all kinds of scrapers made from chippings. Most sites

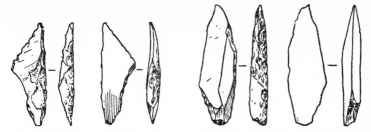

Fig. 5. Flint arrowheads of the Fosna group. Gyrinos, Hemsedal, Buskerud. Lengths about 2.5 and 3 cm. respectively

have yielded specimens of all these types. This tool was particularly useful in the mountains, where it was used for preparing the reindeerhides late in summer.

The bowandarrow played an important part. A popular form of arrowhead was a small tanged arrow, with a retouch on one edge. The transverse arrow, however, which is characteristic of certain Early Stone Age groups of southern Scandinavia, is rare in the Fosna culture. Heavy arrows such as, for example, the preboreal Lyngby folk in Denmark used are also rare. One may well be surprised that the light and thin arrowheads preferred by the Fosna hunters could be sufficiently effective for slaying reindeer, but the fact that they occur on the mountain sites proves their efficacy.

The burin is well represented among Fosna finds. This specialized tool, which was used for working antler and bone, is usually fairly small. Specimens have been found on eastern and on western sites. Oddly enough, the mountain hunters seem hardly ever to have used the burin. The explanation must be that the Fosna people spent the summer mainly in the mountains, the season when the antlers of neither reindeer nor elk are fully grown. Microliths have also been found: the most common type is lancet–shaped. These tiny flints with retouch, used as points and fixed to tools made of other materials – usually of

Fig. 5

antler or bone , – give us some idea, however vague, of the importance of the latter. The blade knife (usually with a curved
back with retouch) is common in the Fosna finds, but that is
no more than one would expect. A very different matter is that
of the flake axes, which are common in coastal settlements both
east of the Oslo Fjord and in the entire western Norwegian/
Trondheim Fjord area; for some unknown reason, no chopping
tools of this or any other type occur in the mountain camps.
Such implements apparently formed no part of the reindeer-
hunter's kit. It is interesting to note that the pre–boreal and later
reindeer-hunters of the northern European plain were apparently also unfamiliar with the axe.

This axe had already acquired its shape at the time of the
Høgnipen group; it forms a regular part of the Fosna assortment
of tools in the coastal settlements. It occurs even in the highest,
and therefore presumably most ancient sites – which should,
according to the current chronology of Swedish and Norwegian
prehistory, be pre–boreal. This is remarkable; for in Denmark, it
would seem, it did not become common until far later, and
when it does appear there, it is mainly in an ecological environment differing essentially from that of the Fosna group, whose
shores were far more exposed. Could it be that the flake axe,
occurring as it does along a Norwegian and western Swedish
coast-line several thousands of miles long, was invented in these
sub-arctic regions, to be later adopted and further developed by
younger hunting cultures farther south? The equipment found
is so mixed and varied, and studies of the chronological and
cultural problems have resulted in such apparently conflicting
views, that practically every known northern European Stone
Age culture, from Ahrensburg to Ertebølle, has been adduced
for comparison. But it may be that this surfeit of comparative
material reflects actual conditions, for it seems probable that the
earliest elements of the Fosna culture had their roots in traditions
that were shaped by the late glacial reindeer-hunting cultures of

continental northern Europe. A late Palaeolithic/early Mesolithic environment may naturally be expected to provide the
background for a culture in which series of tanged points, knives,
burins and microliths are important items. It also seems natural
that impulses from the new groups making their appearance
during the climatic and ecological changes in the south, gradually affected the Fosna culture. Such later influences are probably responsible for the arrowheads with oblique edges and
the transverse arrows, and for certain types of scraper and axe.
But these impulses do not seem to have been strong enough to
change the actual level of culture and equipment. The conserv-
atism of the Fosna complex can only be explained in terms of
the stable and uniform conditions which persisted in large parts
of Norway for many thousands of years.

But even if the oldest elements of the Fosna culture were a
heritage from tribes living on the northern European plain before the forest changed the scene, we cannot connect this Norwegian culture directly with any of the groups living on this
great plain which were discussed above. There is, in fact, a mis-
sing link. The explanation may be that the Norwegian groups
are descended from bands that originally roamed the ancient
shores of the North Sea, later to be submerged. We have no
positive proof of the existence of such groups of pre-boreal hunters, with cultures differing but little from those of the Fosna and
Komsa folk, but it is certainly feasible.

Be that as it may, the Fosna culture covered a very long period
of time during which old types of tool and new were in use
simultaneously. We do not know how much of their equipment was still in use during Neolithic times – this problem
awaits full investigation. What is certain is that the Fosna culture was still continuing when the first farmers were already
established in favourable areas.

It is, as we have seen, difficult to regard the Fosna group as
simply a branch of the later Mesolithic hunting groups of the

southern Scandinavian forests. For this, there are several sound reasons – for instance, the Fosna hunters' choice of hunting grounds, and the sites which they selected for settlement. This dogged preference for a particular type of natural environment is a basic and distinctive factor of their culture; we cannot assess their place in a wider context of European prehistory without a glance at the milieu in which they lived.

The mountain settlements are the most typically Norwegian. Here the vegetation and animal life were, and still are, arctic. In other words, conditions were very similar to those which prevailed in large parts of northern Europe during the late phases of the Ice Age.

The mountain plateau of southern Norway covers several thousand square miles. It consists of open moorland, is practically treeless, and situated some 2500 to 4000 feet above sea level. The undulating moorland is broken here and there by mountains 6000–8000 feet in height. Many parts of the area offer sufficiently favourable conditions to support a fairly numerous fauna – in particular, herds of reindeer. To-day, there are about 40,000 reindeer in these parts, 10,000 on the average being shot during the hunt each year; these figures give a good indication of the value of the hunting grounds in the past. The same applies to fishing; countless rivers and lakes join to form big and small watercourses, mostly well stocked with fish. There is no reason to suppose that conditions were different in prehistoric times.

Hunting the large herds of reindeer, and fishing in the bounteous waters, must have formed a good basis for seasonal camping. Life cannot have differed substantially from that in pre–boreal seasonal camps in other parts of Europe.

So far, archaeologists have investigated only limited areas of the Norwegian mountain moorland; but even so, more than two hundred settlements of Stone Age character have been located – and in part excavated – during the past eight years.

Of these, only a few are Mesolithic, but the material from them is so plentiful that a distinctive pattern emerges. The settlements are situated by good fishing grounds or in the best reindeer areas. Many of them are, furthermore, close to the treks of the reindeer.

The settlements lie on open land, many of them on dry head‐lands projecting into the water. Sites on islands are relatively scarce, but their very existence shows that boats were in use in the mountains during this phase of the Stone Age – or else that people also wintered here. Some of these places are wintry even in midsummer, especially those whose altitude exceeds 4000 feet. Ice and snow never disappear entirely – Ice Age conditions prevail to this day.

Plate 5

The tools associated with these arctic mountain sites differ little from those used by the hunters from the coast, with two important exceptions: the mountain folk lacked the axe, and the burin is extremely rare. But their choice of raw materials sets them clearly apart from their coastal colleagues: in the moun‐tains, about 90 per cent of the tools, and of the chippings, are of quartz or quartzite, excellent raw materials of which there was an unlimited supply. Apparently the mountain hunters did not often make the journey to the coast where flint could be obtained.

These archaic mountain settlements are as difficult to date as many of the Fosna settlements by the sea. Arrowheads, micro‐liths, knives, scrapers, etc. – all are types that belong to the Early Stone Age. As such types might very well have survived for longer here than further south in Scandinavia, any dating based on the nature of the tools must be uncertain. But radio‐carbon dating give readings varying from 7600 years ± 150, to 6200 years ± 140. If we accept these figures at their face value, they confirm the impression given by the finds: the reindeer‐hunters exploited these extensive moorlands for a very long time indeed.

Viewed in a European context, the mountain settlements de/
note an extreme, at least from a climatic and an ecological point
of view. The same is true, to some extent, of the west coast Fos/
na group. Here, too, natural conditions are harsher than in the
rest of northern Europe, but the yield from fishing and catching
on the open sea and by the coast was far from meagre. Fosna
hunters seem consistently to have avoided the inner, more tem/
perate fjords that cut their way inland between massive moun/
tains. They preferred the outer, open stretches – it was the coast
facing the ocean that was inhabited. We find the settlements on
headlands and islands, by sounds and creeks; and we may be
quite sure that good boats were indispensable for travel along
the stormy coast. Many of the inhabited sites are close together,
and regardless of their age, their size and lay/out remain un/
changed. Altogether, the Fosna group might almost be said to
be immune to change. Ecological conditions were stable, the
yield was rich, the hunting and fishing grounds almost in/
exhaustible.

This partiality for the outer coast through all phases of the
Early Stone Age seems to imply that the people had, at an early
date, developed a specialized form of hunting economy. Pre/
sumably the archaic features of the Fosna culture can be inter/
preted to mean that this specialization of life on a sub/arctic
coast had been completed before the Fosna hunters came to
Norway. If this reasoning is correct, it inevitably leads us back
to pre/boreal times.

If we think in such terms, and then turn again to the hunters
of the mountain plateau, it becomes very tempting to indulge
in wider speculation. Was Fosna a last flowering of the cul/
tures of northern Europe's arctic hunters? Those camps on the
wild mountain moors, those settlements on the rough outer
coast, could certainly offer refuge for hundreds of years to hunt/
ing/groups, to forms of social organization and culture, that
had melted away long since from other regions of Scandinavia

together with the snows and the glaciers. Viewed in such a light the culture of the Fosna group is by no means an uninteresting phenomenon.

We know the Komsa complex from a number of finds from the coast of Finnmark; a few other settlements have been found on the arctic coast of Russia, west of Murmansk, so that nearly a hundred are known, all told. All lie in open country either by the ancient coast-line or very close to it; many of the sites were islands or headlands in the past. No traces of huts, houses, tents or other forms of man-made shelter have as yet been discovered, which may seem strange in so weather-beaten a landscape.

Plate 3

There is no doubt that the settlements which have so far been found represent a mere fraction of the habitations of the Komsa hunters. This is mainly due to insufficient investigation. The known material seems, however, to represent a sound cross-section of the various phases of the Komsa complex.

To judge by present-day evidence, the Komsa culture was entirely coastal. The moors with their great rivers, so typical of the interior of Finnmark, of northern Finland and Sweden, do not seem to have been exploited by the Komsa hunters, for extensive field-work in these parts has been without result.

Fig. 7

No traces of organic material have been found at Komsa sites. The top-soil forms only a thin layer, and in many places implements and chippings can be picked up on the surface. As a rule, the Komsa hunters used the local stone which they found by the shore where they settled. The most usual are quartz and quartzite, but other fine-grained stones and greenstone also occur. These types of stone vary in texture, a fact which may have influenced the techniques that were employed and the types of tool produced.

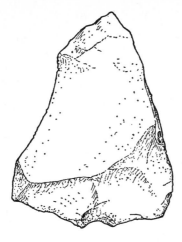

Fig. 6. Flake-axe of stone, Komsa. Length 9.5 cm.

The equipment from the Komsa sites is not uniform. Here we find large, coarse implements side by side with small tools of finer workmanship – part of the equipment is macrolithic, part microlithic. We are hardly in a position to decide whether this difference is due to the raw material employed, or whether it is dictated by cultural factors.

The Komsa hunters employed several basic techniques. Tools made from blades and chippings were important. Among the blade implements found there are knives, scrapers, burins and various small tools. Further, many of the Komsa sites have yielded coarse flake tools. Not infrequently these are hewn on both sides, and the shapes very considerably. They include hand-axes, flake axes and large scrapers.

Core tools have also been found, many of them worked into scrapers or pointed implements. There are also some hand-axes made from cores. The large tools of the Komsa group tend to overshadow the microliths, but these are of great importance. They include, for instance, entire series of arrowheads, some with a curved side with retouch, others single-edged, while yet others are lancet-shaped with a tang. This variety – large tools

Fig. 6

Fig. 8

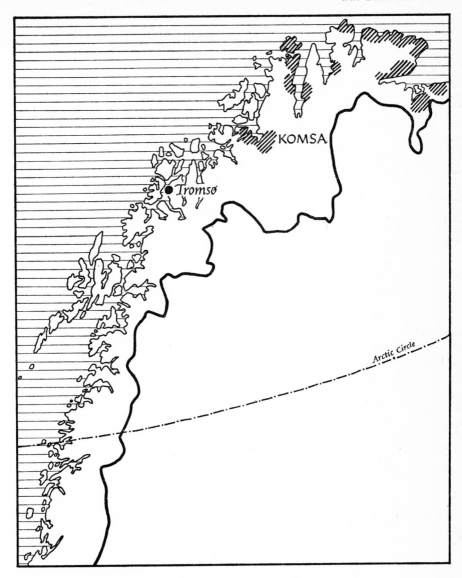

Fig. 7. Distribution of Komsa settlements

and small, old types and more recent ones – makes the Komsa group difficult to place in a plausible chronological and cultural context. Moreover, the centre of this culture lies in the northern, most part of Scandinavia, by the open Arctic Ocean, and far from all earlier hunting cultures of which we know. This has invited dramatic theories and fanciful speculations concerning the enigmatic Komsa folk. Some have supposed that this cul, ture represents the survivors of a people who 'wintered' here during the last Ice Age, on an ice,free strip of land. Others see in the culture a proto,Lappish group, the first sign of human life in northern Scandinavia. One hypothesis that has found much favour postulates an eastern origin: the Komsa culture, it is claimed, originated in the late Palaeolithic groups that lived on the plains of Russia and Poland. From there, as the ice be, gan to recede, they must have followed the rivers and made for the Arctic Ocean. Once they had reached the coast, they spe, cialized in seal catching. Then the climate became warmer, the drift,ice melted, the seal disappeared, and the Komsa folk left; and the land lay waste until the Late Stone Age.

The Ahrensburg group has also been drawn into the dis, cussion; a possible connection with the Swiderian of Poland has been suggested, and the hypothetical Pinneberg/Lyngby group has been considered too. Some scholars, we must add, regard the Komsa culture as identical with the Fosna culture, that is, late Mesolithic, contemporary with the Danish Ertebølle culture.

The Komsa material certainly contains elements that can be fitted to a number of different cultures – some Palaeolithic, others Mesolithic, and from regions that lie far apart. This is certainly problematic, and the discussion on this matter has tended to concentrate on certain details only, to base parallels and comparisons on these. And we must allow for a certain romantic tendency to push this culture of the arctic coast of Finnmark far back in time, and its origin to distant horizons.

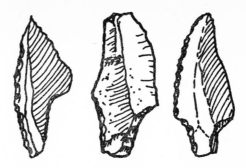

Fig. 8. Quartzite arrow-heads, Komsa. Lengths 2 and 2.5 cm. respectively

Sober analysis of the recognizable Komsa tools shows, however, that very archaic types and more recent ones are commonly found together. Some of the forms must be Palaeolithic in origin, others are unmistakably Mesolithic. It is also clear that certain of the simpler tools, as well as the primitive form of many of the finds, may often be explained in terms of the coarse raw materials at the disposal of the Komsa hunters.

In tackling the difficult problem of dating the Komsa culture, its final phase seems to offer the most promising angle of attack. Recent investigations show that these arctic tribes did not die out or trek away during the Atlantic period, as had previously been thought. It now seems that they still lived here at the beginning of the Late Stone Age. The 'old' single-edged points, the little blade arrow, the knife with a curved back with retouch – these and other archaic tools were in use by the coast of Finnmark at the time when polished axes, new types of arrowhead and pottery first appeared. The implements of the Komsa culture did not disappear completely until the second millennium BC.

The problems posed by the earlier phases of the culture are more involved. We must remember that this is not one homogeneous group, and assume that even here, new impulses arrived at different times and from different parts. The chronological problems, one must realize, are inextricably bound up with the

39

question of where new impulses and possible immigrations originated.

From the coast of Finnmark, it is natural to look for connec, tions with the east and the south-east. We have already seen that, in consequence, many scholars look eastwards for the ori, gin of the Komsa culture; as far east as central Russia and China, parallels are sought in the local Palaeolithic cultures. However, until fairly recently it was not possible either to prove or dis, prove these theories of an eastern origin.

To-day, things look different. In recent years, very consider, able investigations have been carried out in northern Scandina, via as well as in the arctic and sub-arctic areas of Russia. If the Komsa group was connected with cultures from these districts, the results of these investigations should furnish some proof of the fact.

Let us consider the nearest regions first. Neither the interior of Finnmark, northern Finland, nor the forests or mountains of northern Sweden have yielded a single trace of the Komsa or any other Mesolithic culture. Traces of the Komsa group have been long known on the Kola peninsula, as far east as the Kola Bay, but Mesolithic sites have yet to be discovered farther east than that. The coast of the White Sea – much of which has now been investigated – seems to have been waste land until the second millennium BC. So the assumption that the Komsa hunters were definitely not interested in fishing or catching off the coast east of the Kola Bay seems justified.

The picture becomes even more complicated when we leave the coast of the Arctic Ocean and the northern parts of Fenno, Scandinavia, and turn towards southern Finland and Karelia – a region where one should expect Komsa-type finds on the theory of an immigration/impulse route from the Baltic/Polish areas.

Karelia has yielded no material even distantly related to the coastal finds from Finnmark – on the contrary, the earliest dated settlement here seems to be from the third millennium BC, when the 'comb-pottery' culture came to these parts.

But turning to southern Finland we get a somewhat different picture. Traces of an apparently Mesolithic population, somewhat sparse it is true, have recently come to light here. This, the 'Askola culture', is represented by a group of settlements most of which lie east of Helsinki. The settlements are small, the repertoire of tools modest, and the forms often difficult to define. Coarse quartz was almost the only raw material used, a fact which made for tools rather haphazard in shape. But certain features of this culture must be Mesolithic, and are similar to what we see in some of the Komsa finds.

These few settlements with their haphazard repertoire of rough implements have led some Finnish archaeologists to sweeping conclusions. It has been supposed, for instance, that these finds reflect the earliest habitations of Finland; and the Askola culture, it is claimed, owed its origin to the late Palaeolithic cultures of northern Germany, which spread to Finland by way of immigration. The tribes are thought to have adapted their culture to local conditions on their way to Finland, starting to use quartz instead of flint. Moreover, it is claimed that Askola and Komsa represent two related tribes, the Finnish tribe stopping here on their way west from the Ladoga district, while the Komsa tribe trekked farther north to the coast of the Arctic Ocean.

Such theories can be no more than conjecture as yet. The large area which separated Finnmark from southern Finland has not yet yielded any finds of the type under consideration here. Nor have investigations in Karelia and Estonia brought to light any traces of a hunting culture resembling either Askola or Komsa. Add to this the fact that the connection with the late Palaeolithic groups in northern Germany is neither direct nor indisputable, and it appears that the background of the Askola culture is still more obscure than that of the Komsa group.

Among the more distant regions that have been considered in connection with the origin of the Komsa culture, we find both central Russia and Siberia. It is true that traces of Palaeo‑lithic and Mesolithic steppe and tundra hunters have been found there, but it seems that these hunters neither penetrated the forests nor migrated along the arctic coast. We must also note that a number of the Komsa industries are not identical with those of Russo‑Siberia. A really decisive factor is that the two areas are divided by thousands of miles of land completely devoid of finds. Thus, by and large we shall do well to disre‑gard bold and dramatic theories of tribes trekking over endless moors, along mighty rivers and through vast forests, finally to reach the distant coast of Finnmark.

The last remaining possible explanation for the chronology and the cultural background of the coastal culture of Finnmark in the Early Stone Age is this: that the origin of this culture lay further south on the Norwegian coast, and that impulses may have come from several sources, but mainly from the Fosna group. This would make the geographical connections easy, compared to those with other, more distant and hypothetical areas of origin. Moreover, we are here dealing with a form of life and settlement which is, on the whole, common to both these Norwegian cultures. Many of their tools are identical, such as all the characteristic types of arrowheads, their microliths, burins and whole series of scrapers, and not least the flaked axe, which occurs in both, Komsa and Fosna. Both cultures work‑ed their tools from the same basic shapes – in both, blade, flake and core techniques were employed.

But since the two cultures differ on certain points, a con‑clusion that the Komsa culture formed an integral part of the Fosna complex is unwarranted. Most of the Komsa industry is much coarser; tools such as discoid nodules, large, heavy scrapers made from boulders, hand‑axes and certain types of knife do not occur in Fosna. This difference can be explained partly in terms of the coarse raw material available in Finnmark, but local forms may also have been developed.

The connection between Komsa and Fosna is of vital im-portance to the problem of dating the earliest Komsa phase. This must be pre-boreal, and its cultural background must lie with the ancient tribes of hunters who roamed the coasts and moorlands, and whose culture had spread before forest and ocean had changed their conditions of life and their hunting grounds.

Purely geological investigations carried out in Finnmark would seem to confirm so early a dating of the oldest finds. It has, for instance, been established that the material from one of the typical, high-lying coastal settlements had undoubtedly been subjected to the eroding action of water. This settlement lies close to the late glacial limit, a fact which clearly indicates an early date. The earliest traces of hunters on the coast of Finn-mark must date from before 7000 BC, taking a conservative estimate.

Summing up our impressions of the Komsa culture, we may infer the following: it is most unlikely that the bearers of this culture were a people who reached the Arctic Ocean at a time when Palaeolithic reindeer-hunters were still roaming the north-ern German plain, nor were they a branch of a large, Asiatic group of hunters. No direct connection with any Late Palaeo-lithic culture can, in fact, be demonstrated. It seems evident, rather, that these tribes of Finnmark were the most northerly of all the known groups of the Early Stone Age. Furthermore, for thousands of years their lives were determined by a climate, a fauna and a flora very similar to those experienced by the tundra hunters who lived in more southern parts during Late Palaeo-lithic times. The archaic character typical of the Komsa cul-ture is apparently the result of these arctic conditions and Palaeolithic traditions, which persisted by the coast of the Arctic Ocean.

The third coastal hunting culture from the Early Stone Age in Norway is known as the Nøstvet complex. It owes its name to a locality east of the Oslo Fjord, about 12 miles south of Oslo.

The Nøstvet culture does not appeal to the imagination in the same way as the Komsa and Fosna groups. Nothing has been found here which would make one think of Ice Age hunters trekking north, nor has anyone thought to seek the origin and cultural background of these people in far distant lands. For this reason, the Nøstvet culture has not formed the object either of so much discussion, or of such detailed study.

Most traces of this culture come from the eastern Norwegian and western Swedish coastal districts. But it also occurs along the outer coast of western Norway, and certain finds unearthed in northern Norway must apparently also be classed as Nøstvet. The Nøstvet hunters do not, however, seem to have been in the habit of following the waterways inland. These people, like the bearers of the Fosna and Komsa cultures, based their lives on fishing and catching in the sea. Their choice of sites for settlements, too, resembles that of the Fosna and Komsa groups. With only a few exceptions, the settlements found lie on open land, within easy reach of the prehistoric coast-line.

Most of the Nøstvet finds seem to lie somewhat lower than the earliest Fosna settlements, yet Nøstvet traces have been found at a level higher than is compatible with a Neolithic dating. In other words, the Nøstvet culture must have originated later than the Fosna group but, like the latter, falls mainly within the Mesolithic Age. One thing seems certain – the western Norwegian branch continued in existence into the Neolithic Age, and was then gradually absorbed by the new groups of hunters. But it is impossible to say at this stage whether or not the eastern Norwegian and western Swedish fjord landscape lay waste, deserted by the Nøstvet hunters, when the first pioneer peasants arrived at the time of transition to the Late Stone Age.

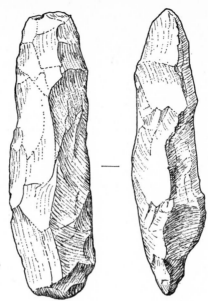

Fig. 9. Core axe of greenstone, Østfold. Length 14.5 cm.

No organic material has been found on the Nøstvet sites, but many of them have yielded finds far richer than either Fosna or Komsa encampments. We do not know whether this is due to a more settled way of life or to larger groups living together. Or were the camps perhaps in use more often?

The Nøstvet people used flint as well as the local stone. On the whole, they preferred to make their tools from fine-grained stone which they obtained from either gravel banks or moraines, though they sometimes quarried it from the rock face. The typi-cal tool of the Nøstvet culture, unknown in the Fosna or Kom-sa, is a pick-like core axe, and it was normally made from stone of this kind. This tool has a characteristic shape, long, and triangular or trapezoidal in section. The edge is strong, slightly curved, and sometimes carefully ground, a feature that is not found either in Fosna or in Komsa. Flake axes also occur, but they are comparatively unimportant. Far more typical is a third

Fig. 9

45

type of cutting tool, a long, ground axe with a rounded edge and oval cross-section. Thousands of specimens have been found, mainly in the south-eastern coastal areas. Even if this tool continued in use for a long time, it undoubtedly originated during the Nøstvet phase.

Another point on which the Nøstvet complex differs from the Fosna group is that blades and chippings were apparently not used much for the manufacture of small tools. Burins are rare, and no microliths have been found. In some respects the scrapers differ from earlier types. Flake and chip scrapers are the most numerous, and the heavy keeled scraper seems to have been in frequent use. Borers, too, are common. But it is odd that so few arrows have been found; it seems that these people did not make much use of either the little single-edged point or of other Fosna types.

The Nøstvet culture requires more study, but it seems safe to say that it differs from the Komsa culture in several decisive respects, and also significantly from the Fosna group. Nøstvet, in fact, allows us to see the Norwegian Mesolithic not only as an age of many unsolved problems, but also as one richer in contrast than one would, perhaps, have thought. This appears clearly when we consider two areas which differ geographically, climatically and, to some extent, also ecologically – both of them have yielded finds which we have chosen to group to-gether as the Nøstvet culture.

The place that has given the culture its name – Nøstvet in Ås, south of Oslo – provides a classic example of the type of settle-ment and the landscape favoured by the eastern Norwegian branch of the Nøstvet group. On this site, more than 250 typi-cal core axes were found in an area covering less than 2000 square feet. The land is full of bare, rocky knolls, allowing of but a poor vegetation and fauna. This craggy terrain slopes fairly steeply towards the west, towards the sea. But there are also many sheltered hill-sides sloping towards the south and south-west, with rich, warm soil, where oak and ash can thrive. It is these fertile spots, where knolls and hillocks provide shelter from wind and weather, that have yielded traces of habitation, in an area whose lower limit lies 180 feet above the present shore.

Near by and a little lower down there is a small lake. In the distance and at a still lower level one can just glimpse part of a narrow arm of the Oslo Fjord; the nearest open, navigable water is thus about two miles away. But it is certain that at the time when the settlement was in use, the sea must have been much closer – its situation would not make sense on any other assumption. If we visualize a sea-level some 160–180 feet higher than that of to-day, the land takes on a different aspect, and the location of the settlement becomes ideal: a coast with islets, skerries and sheltered inlets. Close by the camp would be the sea, with beds of shell-fish, bird cliffs and fishing grounds; and one would not need to paddle far to get to rich fishing out at sea. These two facts – that no finds occur below a level of 180 feet, and that the situation of the site would only make sense if the sea were close by – provide a fairly secure basis for dating. The movements of the coast-line of the inner Oslo Fjord have been studied in some detail. Pollen analyses and other investigations have established that the shore by which the Nøstvet site must have lain is that of between 5000 and 4000 BC. This, then, is a culture of the Atlantic period, when the weather here by the fjord was comparatively warm and moist, and when primeval forests covered the whole land.

We may now attempt to reconstruct the conditions which the Nøstvet folk found in eastern Norway. They lived in sheltered fjord areas, close to the shore. The climate was no longer subarctic, and the vegetation was lush. Oak forests grew right down to the shore, and the marine fauna must have been plentiful, but it seems unlikely that the inland forests were good hunting grounds. Contact with southern areas must have been by way of the western coast of Sweden, and impulses from southern

Scandinavian groups of hunters must have made themselves felt, but there are hardly any indications of a connection with the ancient Fosna hunters.

If we now leave the sheltered area near Oslo and turn to the outer coast of western Norway, where storms and the ocean have left their mark on land and cultures, we find abundant traces of a group of hunters who have always been regarded as part of the Nøstvet group. The best-known and richest traces of the western Norwegian variant of Nøstvet are in Bømlo – an archipelago open to the high sea, about halfway between Bergen and Stavanger.

Bømlo consists of one large island surrounded by hundreds of islets and skerries. Shores washed by the ocean give way to treeless moors, sheltered inlets and warm glens. Wherever one turns, the sea is near. To-day the land is bleak, but during the Atlantic period and in sub-boreal times, much of this island group was covered by forests.

We find traces of Stone Age man nearly everywhere in this ocean land. There are settlements on the open moors and in the more sheltered places; and remains have been discovered as high as eighty feet above sea-level, as well as below the present shore-line. Some of the sites are from the Early, others from the Late Stone Age; traces of a 'Stone Age' which, chronologically, belongs to the Bronze Age, have also been found.

The great wealth of finds is mainly accounted for by the favourable ecological conditions of this district. Even to-day, fishing is of the best. In summer, birds and eggs are easily obtainable, and in the past these islands were the haunt of numerous seals. But there is yet another fact to account for the number of the settlements – the local rock was outstandingly good.

The sites of the Early Stone Age are of the normal, open type, without any trace of houses or shelter. Nearly every suitable site in the area was inhabited during this period. In some of the settlements, the ground is entirely covered by worked stone – mostly flake-like refuse, though blocks, half-finished macrolithic tools and finished artifacts also abound. By far the most common raw material is greenstone; flint and other types of rock are rare. The most characteristic tool is the Nøstvet pick-like implement; pointed axes and flake axes too are common. The normal equipment also includes hammer-stones. Altogether, these Mesolithic settlements give the impression of predominantly macrolithic equipment. Tools such as small scrapers, burins, arrowheads, borers, etc. were obviously of lesser importance – a fact which clearly differentiates this from the Fosna culture.

Apart from the types of their tools, the Bømlo sites are remarkable chiefly for the tremendous amounts of stone refuse found there. As many as 1700 chippings per square metre have been registered, and practically all are of the same type of stone, a greenstone of very fine texture, extremely rare elsewhere.

This tremendous amount of waste and the remarkable number of unfinished artifacts, point to dwelling sites that were not visited merely during the hunting season; and the types of the tools also show that these are not solely hunting camps.

A simple explanation suggests itself: the people came to these islands to fetch raw material for their tools. One of the islets has the best deposit of fine-grained stone in the whole of western Norway. It is on the outermost fringe of the archipelago, out by the open Atlantic. Here, four miles from Bømlo, a large quarry and several small ones have been located. They were in use during the Mesolithic and Neolithic Ages. The island, Hespriholmen, is small – only about 800 feet long by 300 feet wide, and rising barely 100 feet above the sea.

The main quarry faces the ocean. It looks as though an enormous chunk had been bitten out of the almost vertical rock face. The open quarry is 100 feet broad by 35 feet high; its depth varies. More than 35,000 cubic feet of greenstone were quarried here. The working of the quarry began at the top, and as it

Plate 4

extended farther down the rock-face the sides grew steeper and broader so that the bottom of the quarry is wider than the top. The 'floor' is large and quite flat, forming a shelf about 20 feet above the present sea-level, 20 feet of sheer drop. Thus it is obvious that quarrying here must have stopped at a time when the sea-level was about 20 feet higher than it is to-day – that is, at some time during the Late Stone Age.

How these people were able to dislodge stone from the rock face, we do not know for certain. The presence of large fractures suggests that sledge-hammers may have been used; and traces that might be attributable to wedges have been discovered.

Work can have been carried on only during summer. There are, in fact, not many days in the year when one may safely land on the islet. It seems probable that the people paddled to the edge of the quarry and filled their hide boats with as much stone as they would hold. It is impossible to say how much this would be, but a boat-load can hardly have exceeded 3 cwt or so. As about 35,000 cubic feet (that is nearly 3000 tons) of greenstone were quarried, at least 20,000 boat loads must have been conveyed over this treacherous stretch of water – four miles of it, in part over the open sea – to the main island.

It is obvious that such amounts of greenstone catered for more than local needs. And this stone has turned up in finds in large parts of the coastal area of south-western Norway. It is an open question whether the quarry and the distribution of half-finished artifacts were the monopoly of groups of people who lived on the archipelago, or whether tribes from the whole of south-western Norway came to Bømlo to fetch greenstone. But the work of quarrying and transporting the stone was so exacting, so difficult, that one is disposed to imagine some form of specialization. Be that as it may – the quarry and the many 'workshop sites' would seem to show that the Nøstvet culture of western Norway was fully able to organize cooperative schemes during the Early and the Late Stone Ages.

CHAPTER II

The Neolithic Age and the First Farmers

THE LATE STONE AGE of Norway is a colourful, complex era. Impulses from without and stresses from within resulted in the growth of new and varied groups of hunter/fishers; the sub-arctic areas in the north saw the appearance of village-like settlements. Powerful groups of hunters trekked south, and found their way to the west coast of southern Norway. Active tribes of a hunting culture with its centre by the Skagerrak-Kattegat coast made the southern Norwegian hunting grounds their home. The natural resources of the mountains and forests were exploited more intensively than ever before. People found their way to practically every well-stocked lake or river, and to every good hunting district.

Clearly this great expansion of hunting groups in the various parts of the country was the result of the opportunities for fishing and hunting that existed practically everywhere. What may seem more surprising is the appearance of a farming society, with its characteristic pattern of economy and settlement, in certain parts of the country during the Neolithic Age. In this connection it should be borne in mind that the climate and the geological conditions of Norway allow of quite varied agriculture and stock-rearing in spite of the country's northerly latitude. Even though agriculture and stock-rearing were possible, the Neolithic peoples of Norway naturally stood less chance of developing a purely farming society than their contemporaries farther south in Europe. As one might expect, therefore, various local forms of 'mixed' culture arose.

This fact, that coastal hunters, reindeer-hunters, forest hunters and peasants lived during the same period of time – and in some areas even close together – adds interest to the Norwegian Neolithic complex of cultures. We may ask, for instance, which

Neolithic farming cultures, groups and impulses were strong enough to penetrate to the western, and northernmost outposts of Scandinavia? How, moreover, were such elements able to adapt themselves to such extreme conditions of climate and geo/ graphy?

PIONEER FARMERS: THE FUNNEL/BEAKER GROUP

Fig. 10

The earliest traces of farming in Norway come from the area by the Oslo Fjord. They may be dated partly by archaeological methods and partly by pollen analyses, both indicating an Early Neolithic date. The archaeological material is limited, though distinctive, and essentially the same as that of Neolithic finds

Plates 8, 9

from southern Scandinavia. We get complete series of polished chopping/axes and battle/axes, and some finds of a distinctly ritual character. The most characteristic implement is the large, thin/butted working axe of flint, well adapted to the task of clearing the forest. Typical too is a group of polygonal battle/ axes and double/edged axes. There are also some thick/butted flint axes of 'megalithic' type.

Compared with the wealth of material from southern Scan/ dinavia, the Norwegian finds are insignificant – one is tempted, in fact, to wonder if northern hunters could not have obtained these tools either by trading with farmers in the south, or by tak/ ing them as booty from raids on more prosperous parts.

But this is unlikely. For one thing, the 'new' finds and forms are almost entirely confined to the better agricultural areas of eastern Norway, where traces of Mesolithic or sub/Neolithic cultures are few or entirely lacking; these new people did not seek hunting districts, but areas with good soil and pasture.

Quite as important is the fact that the pattern of the occurrence of farmer material resembles that from the rest of the North, typologically and environmentally, and differs from that of the pure hunting cultures. We find votive offerings, grave goods

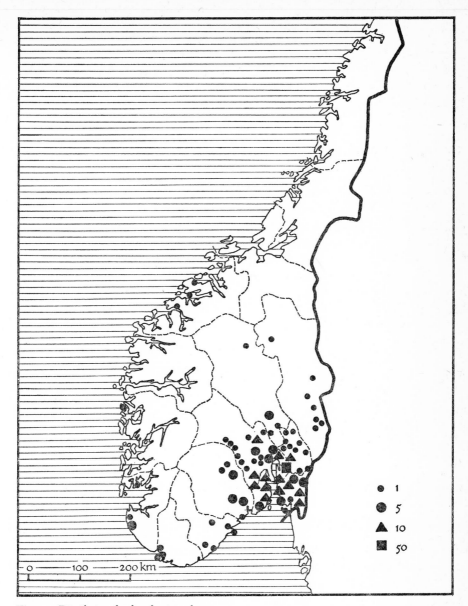

Fig. 10.   Distribution of earliest farming cultures

and hoards: the beliefs and customs of the farmer came to Norway early in the Neolithic Age. Undoubtedly these finds testify
to the presence of a branch of the so-called Funnel-Beaker
culture.

The finds from the beginning of the Neolithic Age show
that a culture based on farming had gained a foothold, but its
typical, huge stone graves seem to have been practically unknown. In Sweden, close to the Norwegian border, there are
many of these megalithic monuments, showing that a farming
society of southern Scandinavian type had flourished not far
away. But in Norway the farmers were too few for the true
megalithic culture, as represented by stone graves, to prosper.
The Norwegian burials from this period are flat graves, simple
in the extreme. The votive offerings, too, are simple, merely
axes buried in the earth or sunk in water or bogs.

Extensive botanical investigations add to our knowledge of
the first farming community of Norway. Especially the pollen
analyses from the Oslo area show that the land here was claimed
for agriculture at the same time as in Denmark. The methods
employed were also the same in both countries. With the transition to Early Neolithic, man had started to grapple with the
primeval forests of oak, lime, elm and ash, and his efforts left
their mark. Now trees and bushes that require light and air
could thrive, and herbage and shrubs – not least those that
provide fodder for domestic animals – were able to grow where
the dark forest had reigned supreme before.

These changes in the vegetation were certainly the result of
the fires started by these pioneers in their efforts to clear the
forest. In bogs, layers of charcoal mark the change in the vegetation; and in the level immediately above, evidence appears of
grain and of weeds: plants that can only have spread with the
farmers and their stock.

With their strong, thin-butted axes and by the use of fire,
these farmers thus penetrated the oak forests of the Oslo Fjord

district. They employed the same processes as the early farmers of Denmark, though it is natural enough that cultivation was not so widespread in Norway, and that the marks it left disappeared more quickly. This first settlement was the farthest-flung outpost of a cultural change that swept Europe early in the Neolithic Age. It lost much of its strength here in Norway during the transition to the Middle Neolithic; the farming culture stagnated, it seems, and it may even have declined.

Archaeological and botanical evidence both testify to such a decline. In most places, apparently, the forest again began to cover the fields and meadows; hunters again held the waste land almost alone.

As we saw above, the great stone graves of the megalithic culture hardly exist in Norway. The thick-butted megalithic chopping axes, the double-edged ritual axes and other megalithic tools are also rare. Nor are finds of later megalithic character concentrated in those areas where the first pioneer farmers had settled. Finds of burials and votive offerings are insignificant. From these facts we can only conclude that the Early Neolithic culture of the Funnel-Beaker invaders gradually declined. In the course of the Middle Neolithic the tracks of these pioneer farmers almost disappear; the first settlers cannot have kept up their way of life for more than a few generations after their arrival in Norway.

BRANCHES OF THE BATTLE-AXE CULTURES

Yet Norway did not lie deserted during the Middle Neolithic period. A succession of impulses swept the country, and it looks as if there were groups of people on the move in every part of it. In the main, this activity seems to have been due to the hunting tribes, but we can also find definite traces of groups whose way of life was shaped to some extent by stock-rearing and agriculture. Thus, even at such a time, when the hunting

Fig. 11

groups were expanding, agricultural and stock-rearing peoples in the east and the south made their presence felt.

The most important of these groups was the Swedish-Norwegian Boat-axe culture – but the Danish Battle-axe culture also played some part. These impulses gradually influenced the old haunts of the early pioneers by the Oslo Fjord; but they were powerful enough to leave their mark also on the favourable agricultural areas by the coast of south-western Norway, as well as on some districts lying to the north of the Dovre mountains.

The Boat-axe culture is represented by all the main elements typical of this group, including its characteristic battle-axe, its working axe and its pottery. The simple but distinctive manner of burial of this culture – in flat graves – was also practised here. As there are no local traditions on which the pottery, the axes, or the burial custom might have been modelled, the only possible conclusion is that immigrants brought the Boat-axe culture to Norway.

It is generally held that the economy of the Swedish-Norwegian Boat-axe people was based on stock-rearing, with some tilling of the soil. In Norway we find remnants of this culture mainly in areas particularly well suited to such a way of life, though many of these were also good hunting and fishing grounds, especially those near the sea. And in such places, typical hunters' settlements, their equipment much influenced by the Boat-axe culture, have been located. In other words, it looks as though the Boat-axe people of Norway did not devote their energies exclusively to agriculture. They had to adapt themselves to local conditions, like all the people who have ever lived in these parts. Pollen analyses would seem to confirm this theory, for neither the eastern Norwegian centre of the Battle-axe culture nor its 'colony' in south-western Norway has yielded botanical evidence that agriculture was practised here to any great extent during this phase. Only towards the end of the

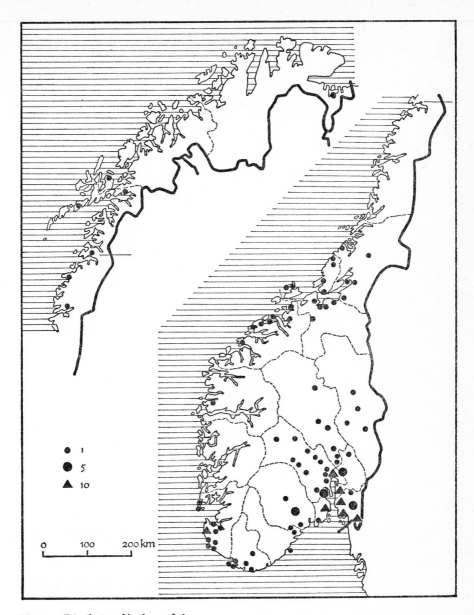

Fig. 11. Distribution of battle-axe finds

Neolithic, in fact, do the pollen remains again testify that stock⁄ rearing and husbandry were practised on such a large scale that we are justified in speaking of a significant expansion of agriculture. This being so, some romantic notions about the Boat⁄axe culture in Norway will have to be discounted. The traditional, dramatic picture of the incursion of the Boat⁄axe people – nomadic warriors on horseback, of the early, stormy period of the Indo⁄European tribes – bears, it now seems, little relation to the facts.

Even taking the most sober view of the Boat⁄axe culture, we shall find that it was a foreign element. Everything – tools, weapons, pottery and burial customs – is new and different; and there can be no doubt about the connection of this group with others in the North and elsewhere. We now see the Nor⁄ wegian branch as the farthest, the westernmost offshoot of a greater cultural complex which spread over large parts of Eur⁄ ope during the Middle Neolithic. As the Komsa and Fosna folk were the most distant and the last descendants of ancient hunt⁄ ers, so the Norwegian Battle⁄axe groups also appear as the outermost twig of a mighty tree whose roots were far distant.

THE PITTED WARE GROUP

At about the time when the Boat⁄axe people arrived in the country, another cultural group spread in southern Norway, the 'Pitted Ware culture', as it has been called. It is usually supposed that these people lived almost exclusively by hunting and fishing, but in Norway their life may have been less limited. They produced their own peculiar form of pottery; their tools were worked from blades and cylindrical cores; their arrows (and bows?) were also of a very distinctive kind. All these ele⁄ ments are often regarded as parts of one homogeneous culture, belonging to one group of people. Traces of this complex occur in Sweden, by the Skagerrak/Kattegat, and by the west coast

Fig. 12

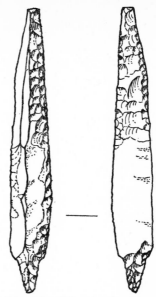

Fig. 12. Triangular flint arrowhead, Pitted Ware group. (Rogaland, western Norway). Length 10.5 cm.

of Norway, as far north as Bergen. Considerable remains have been found in Denmark also. The Pitted Ware types are most common by the coast, but settlements also occur far inland, in the mountains of Norway.

It is debatable – at least in the light of the Norwegian mate-rial – whether this Pitted Ware culture really was homogeneous, whether it spread by means of migration, and whether its people lived exclusively by hunting and fishing.

Within this cultural complex, there is a difference between those groups that fished off the weather-beaten shores of western Norway, and those that lived in the milder climate of Denmark and southern Sweden. They have certain important features in common – their flint technique, for instance, and the shape of their arrows – but there is nevertheless a great deal of difference between the two extremes of this culture.

Most of the Pitted Ware groups certainly lived mainly by hunting and fishing; but to all appearances they were in close contact with farmers, and in some places they seem to have been influenced by the Boat⁄axe people. In Norway, at least, we find Boat⁄axe pottery at some of their settlements; traces of a more settled way of life and of agriculture have also been found. One must suppose that a mixed culture developed, a culture which fused Boat⁄axe and Pitted Ware elements, while observ⁄ ing ancient local traditions. Excavations carried out on Krå⁄

Plate 11

kerøy, off the eastern shore of the Oslo Fjord and near the Swedish border, may serve to illustrate this.

These islands, with their sheltered inlets and forests of oak, would offer ideal conditions for people who lived mainly by hunting but also wished to raise stock and grow some food on the warm, sunny stretches between the rocky shore and the stony knolls. The fishing here is still good, and to this day elks inhabit the near⁄by forests; not many years ago, these waters were the haunt of seals.

Wherever they could make a hard across the foreshore in places sheltered against storms, people settled down, provided fresh water was at hand. They lived a little way above a shore which lay about 80 feet higher than the present coast⁄line, a Middle Neolithic level. In an area no bigger than 16 square miles, nearly thirty settlements have been found and partially excavated. All these settlements are small, none of them exceed⁄ ing 500–600 square feet in area – an indication that the people must have split into family groups. Another point of interest is the house foundations which have been found on some of the sites. They show that life here had assumed a settled form.

Let us turn to one of these sites for an illustration of the form of society which these people had adopted, their settlement pat⁄ tern and their means of livelihood. A sandy area, sloping down to the old shore, lies sheltered by hillocks. Three dwellings had stood by this inlet – one rectangular, and two smaller, almost oval huts. Together they covered about 600 square feet. The roofs were supported by posts, the walls were of wattle and daub. In the two huts, the floor was paved with stone; in the bigger house, stone had been used only for the foundations of the walls, which were also reinforced by sturdy posts.

The houses were destroyed by fire, and the burnt clay from the walls contains impressions of many kinds of seed, grain and chaff. Remains of wheat, barley and millet have been found. Thus during the latter part of the Middle Neolithic, the people grew some corn even away on these small islands where arable patches were few and small. Nor do they seem to have lacked domestic animals: just outside the settlement, where the sea once washed the shore, bones of cattle have been found; there was also the skeleton of a man. A clay sediment covered the bones, from which we may assume that they belong to the same period as the settlement.

There are not many sites that reflect a mixed culture so faith-fully. Some grain, a few domestic animals, but with the empha-sis on fishing and hunting – that is the pattern that prevailed in these parts right up to our own times.

This mixed culture, as mentioned earlier, seems to have some connection with the Pitted Ware group. The finds show, how-ever, that impulses from several quarters must have been at work. If we take a comprehensive view of the archaeological material from this densely settled island, we find that the majority of the flint types belong to the Pitted Ware culture. Thus not only the characteristic arrowheads, but also tools work-ed from cylindrical cores and small implements such as borers and knives are common. From the Boat-axe culture, it seems, the people of Kråkerøy adopted corded pottery, but much of the pottery must have been made locally. From the north they acquired the custom of using slate as a raw material, and the type of slender arrowheads made from it; the economic basis of life was mixed and the tools accorded with this. In fact one may ask whether anywhere or at any time a pure, unmixed 'cul-ture' ever occurred in Norway.

THE AGRICULTURAL REVOLUTION IN THE LATE
NEOLITHIC AGE

The Late Neolithic Age – the end of the pure Stone Age in
southern Norway – is an interesting period in the prehistory of
the country, though it has been little studied. What is certain
is that Neolithic groups then spread over large tracts of the
country. In fact, wherever stock-rearing and husbandry can
support life in the twentieth century, agriculture gained a firm
foothold during the last phase of the Stone Age.

Plate 6

Figs. 14, 15

The period is characterized by a tremendous number of stray
finds of flint daggers, flint sickles, flint axes, and socketed axes
made of local stone. The finds and forms are not peculiarly
Norwegian, agreeing as they do feature for feature with what is
characteristic of the last phase of the Stone Age in southern

Plate 12

Scandinavia. Offerings, hoards and graves – stone cists as well
as simple flat graves – have also been found, flat graves apparently being the most common form of burial.

Fig. 13

The distribution of the finds – some of them occur in areas
where Neolithic peoples settled early, some in other favourable
agricultural districts – reveals the force of this expansion as well
as its character. It was strongest where the geological formations
are predominantly Cambro-Silurian, and in other areas with
warm, fertile soil. An interesting point is that most of these
newly settled areas are practically devoid of finds from Mesolithic or sub-Neolithic hunting cultures. Thus we see that, towards the end of the Stone Age, most of the farmers chose to
cultivate land in places which had never attracted the hunters
or the fishermen. This applies first and foremost to parts of the
great inland forests of eastern Norway; but in western Norway,
too, the difference between the Late Neolithic expansion and
the sub-Neolithic settlements is often clearly defined. True, in
western Norway we can sometimes find traces of farmers and
hunters in the same place – but the rapid development of the
new way of life is most marked in the inner parts of this fjord

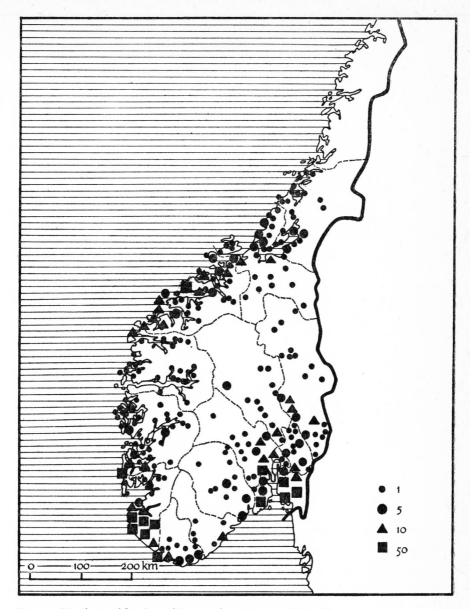

Fig. 13. Distribution of flint dagger finds in southern Norway and Trøndelag

Fig. 14. Flint
dagger, eastern
Norway. Length
26 cm.

landscape, where deep inlets cut their way between the steep, overhanging mountains. Here ecological conditions had been less favourable for the hunters fishermen than those by the open coast.

It is a debatable point whether this wave of settlement – impressive in scale, in many places – was due to immigration, or whether it was a purely internal expansion, the indirect result of impulses from outside. There is little in the archaeological finds and the form of the settlements to make one think immediately of a foreign origin; yet the difference between east and west in these Norwegian cultures is considerable. In the east, the type tool, dominating the finds completely, is the socketed stone axe; in the west, this type of axe is of secondary importance, and the flint dagger takes its place. The reason must be that western Norway received its impulses from Jutland, while Sweden served as the natural source for eastern Norway.

The finds illustrating this Late Neolithic expansion run into four figures, and the botanical material reflects it too, as we might expect. The botanical marks left by agriculture and stock-rearing are far clearer than they were in the pioneer phase, and they are no longer confined to the area by the Oslo Fjord. Inland, too, and on the south-west coast, Late Neolithic farmers made inroads into the primeval forests. Bogs in all these parts have well-defined charcoal strata showing that the people of this age, like the pioneers, made use of fire for clearing the woodland.

We learn from the archaeological finds, and from the traces left in the bogs and swamp, that at least in the most favourable places the land was not settled by isolated bands of people with their cattle, the way the pioneers had first practised agriculture by the Oslo Fjord a thousand years earlier. Instead, larger groups of farmers were looking for land. Wherever conditions have been studied, the resulting picture is the same: these farmers were numerous, and their settlement and cultivation of the land

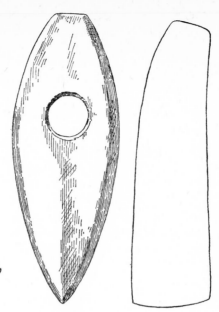

Fig. 15. Stone axe with hole for shaft, eastern Norway. Length 18.5 cm.

were completed in a relatively short space of time. The agricultural expansion in Norway at the end of the Stone Age can justifiably be called a 'Neolithic Revolution'.

THE HUNTER/FARMERS AT THE TRANSITION TO THE METAL AGE

Pollen analyses reveal large-scale forest clearance; archaeological finds multiply in the good agricultural districts; the evidence of the votive offerings, the burials and the tools – all contribute to an apparently quite unambiguous picture of Norway's Late Neolithic culture and form of settlement.

But this is not the whole story. We know that in many places the economy and way of life of the people depended greatly on local conditions, and that a mixed culture formed there towards the end of the Stone Age and during the Bronze Age.

This was the case particularly in western Norway, where some settlements of the time of transition to the early metal era

Plate 13

65

Fig. 16. Arrowheads of quartz and quartzite. Bordalshelleren, Vinje, Telemark, Hardanger moorlands. Lengths 2.5 and 3 cm. respectively

clearly reflect a life concerned with both hunting and agriculture. Large quantities of bones have been found on some of
these sites; those of cattle and sheep, and those of big game. On
the coast seal, deer and fish tempted the hunter/farmers during
the high season. Up in the mountains, reindeer bones left behind in the settlements of a people who were evidently not un-
acquainted with agriculture and stock-rearing show that the
natural resources of the hunting grounds were exploited (as,
indeed, they have always been by farmers in these parts). We
know positively from analyses of pollen, as well as from potsherds bearing impressions of grain, that these hunter/farmers of
coast and upland knew how to cultivate corn.

In the archaeological finds there is but little testifying to the
existence of the farmer. Fish-hooks, bodkins, harpoons of bone
and antler, scrapers and leaf-shaped arrows of quartzite, etc., all
point to hunting.

Fig. 16

We have proof, then, of a mixed culture and economy at the
transition to the metal era in many places. When the hunting
was good, the farmers left their land in search of seal, deer and
wild-fowl; they made for the coast where they could also fish.
Those who lived close to the reindeer moors naturally hunted
there. It is difficult to say which was the more important in their
way of life, hunting or farming. Climate and natural conditions
imposed their pattern as they must ever do in a country such as
Norway.

CHAPTER III

The Sub-Neolithic Cultures

THE COMBINED IMPULSES, migrations and innovations to which Norway was subjected during the Late Stone Age – coming from the south, the east and the north, to cross and recross, and to encounter older, local groups which continued to maintain their way of life – make a tangled skein where different cultural, economic and chronological groups cannot be distinguished clearly. What results is a motley picture consisting of Mesolithic heritage, new hunting cultures and a farming way of life.

In the north of Norway, the economic situation is not too complicated; for this part of the country was entirely uninfluenced by agriculture. But dating and distinguishing between the various groups of hunters is more involved than might be expected, seeing that the way of life was stable and the findings thus are directly comparable. Not the least difficult task is that of applying the conventional southern Scandinavian chronology to life in the far north; for there, the Stone Age lasted a very long time indeed, there was no Bronze Age, and the Iron Age was short. Concepts such as Hallstatt, La Tène and Roman Age make no kind of sense when applied to conditions in the two northernmost counties of Norway.

But the problems posed by northern Norway are quite fascinating. No other region in Scandinavia offers a comparable wealth of evidence on the hunter's way of life, lasting from the Neolithic to the Great Migrations. Conditions are ideal for the reconstruction of ways of settlement, methods of hunting and fishing, social structure and ecology. Moreover, this part of the country offers a unique opportunity for studying finds and monuments in a landscape unchanged since the Stone Age.

VILLAGE SETTLEMENTS BY THE VARANGER FJORD

The centre of the ancient Komsa culture, the coast of east Finn-mark from Alta to the Russian border, offers the best conditions for study.

In these parts, and especially by the Varanger Fjord, where the Arctic Ocean and the moorlands meet, the settlements are many and varied. On a stretch of shore about six miles long, high up the fjord, more than 250 houses have been found, lying in groups and representing several chronological and cultural phases, and some of them have been excavated.

Most of the houses belong to one of two types which have, however, much in common; for instance, both types huddle close together, forming a kind of village. They are datable with-in a period extending from the Early Neolithic to the end of the Bronze Age, but there are also groups of houses in this district that are of far later date.

Not only are the houses numerous, but many of them are well built, and often laid out in such a manner as to suggest a well-

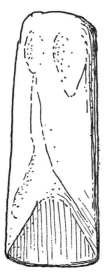

Fig. 17. Axe of polished slate, Sælneshøgda, Varanger. Length 10 cm.

ordered community. Practically all the sites, house foundations as well as the villages, are very rich in finds, and provide a relatively secure basis for dating. A fourfold chronological division of this material had thus won general acceptance.

'Period I' is a transition phase, marking a time when powerful cultural changes first made themselves felt by the Arctic coast. The people continued to use hard, often coarse stone; and the typical tanged arrowheads with an oblique edge, burins and other archaic small tools were still in use. But at the same time they started to work softer stones, tools were ground and polished, and new, heavy axes made their appearance. Whereas the Komsa hunters had lived in open camps, this transitional phase is represented by the remains of oval huts 10 to 13 feet across: low earthen walls suggest how they were built.

The next phase, 'Period II', has yielded more material. A few hundred yards from the site where the 'transitional' culture combining the ancient ways of the coast tribes with the new techniques and new mode of life can best be studied, lies Nordli, a large and populous settlement area of 'Period II', with abundant finds. The Mesolithic heritage is still noticeable. The old Komsa arrow, the burin, the curved knife, and certain archaic forms of scraper were still in use. But during this phase the old elements yield to the new, where raw material, form and technique are concerned.

A wealth of new types has appeared since 'Period I': large spear points, long arrowheads, knives, scrapers and crescent-shaped tools – all carefully hewn and retouched. This well-made, unpolished quartzite industry is supplemented by polished axes, chisels, knives, spearheads and arrowheads made ot slate and of greenstone. The polished items of 'Period II' are not very numerous, but they herald the technical revolution which was to take place during the next phase.

The most important innovation of 'Period II', however, is pottery. There are quantities of large, coarsely made, decorated

Fig. 18. Quartzite point, Nordli, Varanger Fjord. Length 7.5 cm.

Fig. 19. Slate knife, Nordli, Varanger Fjord. Length 18.5 cm.

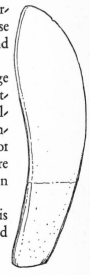

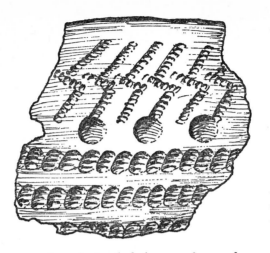

*Fig. 20.   Comb pottery,
Nordli, Varanger Fjord.
Height 8.7 cm.*

Fig. 20

pots; they obviously belong to the comb-pottery group. This is an important connection, for not only is it proof of strong impulses from the east – from Finland – but it also provides a means of dating the period to about 2000 BC.

From this 'Period II' group of settlements, so rich in finds, another few hundred yards take one to the great Karlebotn complex – with more than four score house foundations the most remarkable Stone Age site in the entire North. This village was built and occupied mainly during 'Period III'.

Plate 14

Fig. 21

The houses were built in two or three rows on a flat stretch of the shore, now 70 feet above sea-level. The village is open to the sea, while a steep slope provides shelter from the land side. The built-up area is some 550 yards long. The house foundations now appear as distinct depressions, enclosed by low walls. Many of them are so close together that they almost touch, but it seems obvious that this village site was planned. The houses vary somewhat in area, but none exceeds 300 square feet. The walls were of earth, and almost every house had an indoor hearth. Entry was from the sheltered landward side. Even if it seems too much to suppose that all the houses were occupied at

Fig. 21. Reconstruction of the village near Karlebotn, Varanger Fjord

one and the same time, we may assume that habitation was con⁄
tinuous in the settlement area.

The finds from the excavated houses are unusually plentiful
and varied. It is significant that quartzite and similar hard types
of stone were no longer in use. Now slate had become the most
common raw material. The village has yielded entire series of
long lances, slender arrowheads, strong knives, bodkins, etc.
Many of the tools are elegant in shape, and practically all are
carefully ground and polished. This village may be classified
as belonging to the 'slate culture', a term generally applied to
the Norwegian sub⁄Neolithic.

'Period III', unlike 'Period II', seems to have used very little,
if any pottery; and the last vestiges of Komsa influence on the
tools have disappeared. Here, on this site, Mesolithic elements

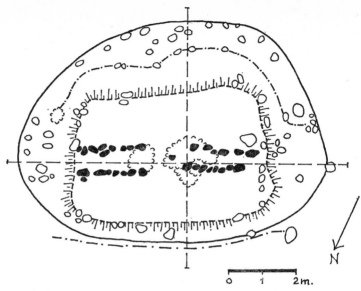

Fig. 22. House foundation with two hearths, Grasbakken, Varanger Fjord

are completely absent for the first time in northern Scandinavian prehistory.

The cultural, economic and chronological background of the Karlebotn village is fairly clear. This was a coastal culture that originated and developed in arctic and sub-arctic regions, houses and settlements of this type being unknown in the inland forests and mountains. Fishing and catching in the sea formed the basis of life; this work must have been carried out collectively. Even though each house can hardly have given shelter to more than one family unit, the very choice of the village form of settlement is significant. Even if we suppose no more than fifty houses to have been occupied at any one time, this was clearly a sizable village. At least 200–300 people lived on this shore; it seems improbable that any other place in northern Europe could have supported so large a group within so small an area, on fishing and catching alone.

In terms of southern Scandinavian chronology, the Karle-botn village is Late Neolithic; another settlement by the Va-ranger Fjord, about six miles east of Karlebotn, is more recent. This is Grasbakken, of 'Period IV'. Though technologically this period differs from the preceding phase, the settlement pat-tern is much the same.

Here again we have series of house foundations, grouped on dry stretches of flat land near the sea. Some of the houses are of the 'old' oval type, others are larger, rectangular, and built in a different manner. These new houses were built half below ground-level and had a long sunken approach on one side wall. They average 400 square feet in area, and almost all of them had two elongated hearths, built of stones placed on edge. Ap-parently low earthen benches skirted the walls.

The size of the houses, and the presence of two identical hearths, may imply that each sheltered two families. In any

Fig. 22

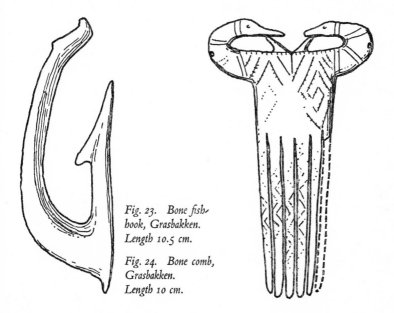

Fig. 23. Bone fish-hook, Grasbakken. Length 10.5 cm.

Fig. 24. Bone comb, Grasbakken. Length 10 cm.

Fig. 25. Bone harpoon, Gras- bakken. Length 16 cm.

Figs. 23–26

case, we gather from the size of the houses and from the num- ber of their foundations that this, too, was a large village – an organized community, where at least a couple of hundred people must have lived and worked.

Very large numbers of objects have been unearthed from the sites of the houses and in the big refuse heaps by the walls. These finds show clearly that the village dates from a period when bone and antler had largely replaced slate as the most important raw material. The latter, it is true, was still used, but the slate tools were smaller, the technique less accomplished, the types fewer; whereas the bone and antler tools are well-made and of many types. The quantity of finds yielded by this settlement is unparalleled. We have tools and equipment adapted to a num- ber of functions – most of them naturally associated with catch- ing and fishing. Harpoons, gaff-points, fish-hooks, fishing spears, daggers, knives, arrows, bodkins, chisels, scrapers, need- les, etc. – an assortment indicative of a varied life of fishing and catching, and of a society whose technical achievements were many and advanced. Much of the 'industrial design' practised here admirable, and not a few of the objects are decorated with all-over patterns. Some small animal sculptures attest a highly developed aesthetic sense.

Pottery once more came into use, an important point. There is no comb-pottery, but there are many examples of a ware con- taining asbestos and of pots with surface impressions made by textiles. This pottery testifies to a close contact with certain areas of Finland and Russia. Moreover, it provides a basis for dating to about 1000 BC – a clear confirmation that pure Stone Age hunting cultures flourished here when the life of the people of southern Norway was already much affected by impulses from the Bronze Age of northern Europe.

The copious implements of widely varying form and size found in the Varanger villages provide sufficient proof in them- selves of a specialized and highly developed system of hunting and catching economy. But the large amounts of refuse – bone and antler – tell us a good deal more about the means of livelihood and the hunting seasons of these people. By the Arctic Ocean, fishing and catching in the sea were, of course, of paramount importance. Fishing alone is represented by 20,000 recognizable finds, 80% of them cod-bones. Here we might point out that the Varanger district is northern Europe's second largest cod ground of historic times; the number of cod that make their way up the fjord during the months of April and May is colossal. We should thus be safe in assuming that the villages were inhabited during these two spring months.

While so much cod was caught, salmon was not fished at all. This fish, too, enters the fjord in large shoals which, however, do not arrive until June. The absence of salmon-bones must mean that the people were hunting elsewhere at that time of the year. There is further evidence to show that they moved away early in summer: no bones of young birds have been found, though there are plenty of remains of fully-fledged ones. More information on hunting and seasonal settlement is, however, provided by the bird remains. Bones of four species that spend only the winter in Norway have been found, birds that breed in Spitsbergen and other arctic regions and migrate to Norway in great numbers late in autumn. An abundance of their bones proves that there were people by the Varanger Fjord in winter. Large though fish and fowl loom on the refuse heaps, big game was more important still. Large quantities of seal bones have been found. They, too, add information about the seasonal settlement. The harp-seal, for instance, drops its young on the ice of the White Sea late in winter; and when, at the end of May and the beginning of June, the young are proficient swimmers, large herds of harp-seal enter the fjord. It is clear that the people were still in their villages during this season. Their harpoon points pierced for attaching a line, many of which have been found, were presumably used for seal-catching.

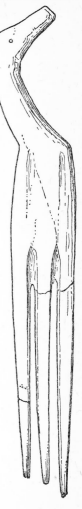

Fig. 26. Comb-shaped implement, the shaft formed like an animal's head, Grasbakken. Length 20 cm.

Judging from the bones found, whale seems to have been one of their most important quarries. Most of the bones come from small toothed whales, porpoises and white-fish, species that vary from 5 to 13 feet in length. Both whaling and sealing required efficient collaboration, sea-worthy boats, and good implements. The heavier lances and gaffs were probably used for whaling.

The only land animal hunted to any extent was the reindeer, the bones of hundreds of these having been found. Whether they were tame or wild cannot be ascertained, but is seems unlikely that people of so settled a life as these villagers should have moved with herds of tame reindeer all the year round – as reindeer keepers must – during their perpetual migrations. We may conclude that the Varanger Fjord villagers of the pre-Christian era had not yet learnt to tame the reindeer.

The bones and other archaeological finds call up a picture of a people who lived at the upper end of the great Varanger Fjord for most of the year. The ecology of the district made a settled life and a fairly highly developed social system possible. The main reason why man settled at this particular place throughout all phases of the Stone Age must have been the incidence of cod, seal, whale and wild reindeer, natural resources which were exploited to the full. The people's homes, their permanent domicile was here; here they built their winter houses, here they foregathered from the autumn until early summer. But then they would leave their villages in small groups and make for the open shore, where fishing, fowling and catching on islands and in inlets yielded richer returns, at this season, than their home-ground.

Some of the tools and pottery of certain of the Varanger periods show that the people were in close contact with inland tribes living to the east; but there is no particular reason to suppose that these villages were built by immigrants from the east, or that the tribes living here moved to and fro between coast and hinterland in the course of the year. Their manner of hunting is unthinkable without a great fund of experience, and their tools may be said to represent the acme of ancient traditions having their roots by the coast. Their form of life, in villages consisting of permanent houses, is also a coastal phenomenon well known from Siberia and from the more northerly part of the Norwegian littoral.

As to the problem of continuity or immigration, we are in the happy position of possessing important human skeletal material from the Varanger Fjord sites. Some of the human remains come from graves, others from the actual settlements. They consist of the bones of both children and adults; all the skeletons are from the last two periods, *i.e.* the time from about 1500 BC to the first century AD. Physical anthropologists have argued, from a study of this material, 'that it comes from a population of Nordic racial type, and one which lived within a small area'. They maintain, further, 'that it is not improbable that these people were isolated from related tribes farther south towards the end of the Stone Age, and that they later merged with immigrants of Lappish and East-Baltic type.' So we must conclude, it seems, that these villagers who lived close to the Russian arctic coast were of the same physical type as the people of southern Norway – a fact which may seem surprising.

THE SLATE COMPLEX

Many of the most important elements that characterize the different phases of settlement in Varanger occur over large parts of Fenno-Scandinavia. It is scarcely correct to speak of a homogeneous culture throughout this region, as some scholars have tended to do: conditions of climate and of ecology differ too widely within the area to make this plausible. None the less, the groups of hunters who lived here had certain techniques in common, which differed from those practised in, for instance,

77

Fig. 27. Slate
lance-point,
Lyngen, Troms.
Length 13.5 cm.

southern Scandinavia during the Neolithic and the Bronze
Ages.

Whilst northern Scandinavia and neighbouring areas to the
east are characterized by certain types of pottery – comb-pottery,
'asbestos' ware and textile-decorated wares – all the peoples with
whom we are here concerned also had this in common – that
they made extensive use of polished slate tools. The pottery types
in question are widespread in Finland, northern Russia, and
northern Norway and Sweden. Mountain, forest and coastal
settlements yielded examples of all three types. The impulses
reflected in these northern wares reached the country south of
Trondheim only sporadically, while the use of polished slate
tools extended farther south.

From the Varanger Fjord to south of Bergen – a distance of
about 1100 miles as the crow flies – slate as a raw material attained great importance, as did certain specialized tools made of
polished slate. Nor was this usage confined to the coast. Such
slate implements are typical forms in the Norwegian mountains
also, and to a still greater extent in the Swedish forests and
moorlands north of Uppland.

The term 'slate culture' is generally applied to this phenomenon, but 'slate complex' would undoubtedly be a more ap-
posite term. There is no reason to suppose that there was ever
one homogeneous 'culture' that covered the land from the Arctic Ocean to Bergen, from the shores of northern Norway to
the Gulf of Bothnia. Attempts have been made, moreover, to
trace a continuous connection between the slate 'culture' and
other groups of hunters in the circumpolar region. But proof
of such a direct cultural connection is difficult to find – at least
if we limit our interest to the recurrence of worked slate and the
tools typical of the slate complex. Still, the idea of a circumpolar
Stone Age culture is not without romantic appeal.

Various dates have been assigned to the slate complex. In
Varanger it seems that slate and the accompanying typical tools

Fig. 28. Slate knife, Finnmark. Length 10.5 cm.

Fig. 29. Slate dagger, the shaft formed like an animal's head, Varanger Fjord. Length 25 cm.

were introduced during 'Period II', around the year 2000 BC, and became prominent during 'Period III', a phase which seems to have extended into the Bronze Age in terms of southern Scandinavian chronology; but its use seems to have declined again during the latter phase.

Whether the chronological pattern is similar farther south is uncertain. It is unlikely that slate remained the main raw material after the beginning of the metal era, about the latter half of the second millennium BC. The countless variations of the slate-tool industry in its heyday do not seem to have outlasted the time when man learnt the use of metal. It appears that at this stage, quartz and quartzite once more assumed pride of place among the hard raw materials, and carefully chipped tools took the place of the polished slate implements.

We know very little of the last phase of the slate complex and of the nature of the groups of hunters who roamed large tracts of northern Scandinavia in the centuries preceding the Iron

79

Age. One thing is certain: the intensive exploitation of the vast hunting grounds continued far beyond the 'pure' Stone Age. This applies not least to the hunting grounds east of the Nor, wegian coast; these inland areas of Norway and Sweden are now being studied. Our preliminary findings there, and the finds from Finnmark, viewed against the background of the conditions which we know predominated in southern Scandi, navia, show that hunting cultures and a 'Stone Age' lived on wherever natural conditions made such a way of life profitable, while agriculture and a 'metal culture' gradually prevailed in areas with good soil.

SUB-NEOLITHIC HUNTERS IN THE MOUNTAINS OF SOUTHERN NORWAY

Turning our attention again to southern Norway, to the coun, try south of a line from Bergen to Oslo, we immediately realize that the hunter cultures of the Neolithic and later ages followed a different course from those of the north. Slate did not dominate the tool culture, the northern pottery types are unknown, and there was no village life; nor were tools of chipped quartzite used as extensively as in the far north. For all that, there were hunters living in the coastal regions, the mountains and the forests of southern Norway.

We have already noted the changing cultural pattern which resulted from the influence of the farmer culture. But even if we except these mixed groups and concentrate on the pure hunting tribes, there is an abundance of material from the entire Late Stone Age.

The mountains, once the haunts of Mesolithic reindeer-hunt,
Plates 15–17   ers, were exploited to a far greater extent by sub-Neolithic hunt, ers. Settlements were founded by practically every lake or river stocked with fish, in nearly every area providing good reindeer pasture. No longer did the people live only in open camps;

traces of houses, and finds by overhanging rocks or close to great boulders show that sheltered sites were in demand for habitation.

At least three main phases can be discerned among the mountain settlements. One is distinguished by the use of flint, and by certain favoured techniques: large blade arrows and flint cores. This group of settlements – as both the raw material and the form of the tools show – belongs to the Pitted Ware complex. One branch of this group we have already met in an earlier context: coastal hunters practising a little agriculture on the side, by the shores of the Oslo Fjord. But the mountain branch is obviously a different one, for it specialized in fishing and reindeer hunting. These mountain settlements containing flint tools are Middle Neolithic.

Plate 17

Another group of mountain hunters had connections with the slate complex. Settlements that have yielded finished and half-worked points, knives, needles, grinding-blocks, etc. provide clear evidence that these hunters were no casual visitors to the mountain moorlands of southern Norway, but had their regular hunting grounds here. They must have come from the north and the east; probably they came to the mountains at the same time as the Pitted Ware hunters took to hunting there. What happened when the tribes met, we do not know, but at least there is no evidence of any significant mixing of cultural elements.

The third main element – the latest, presumably, of the Stone Age peoples of the mountains between western and eastern Norway – used neither flint nor slate; following the fashion and developments elsewhere, particularly in the north, they made their tools from quartz and quartzite. Only a few of these have been found, mainly heart-shaped arrowheads; and the settlements are small. Possibly this modest complex was actually a branch of the coastal 'hunter/farmers'. That the finds are late is certain, but they cannot be really securely dated. The facts that slate and flint are almost entirely lacking, and that no definitely Neolithic forms occur among the finds, makes it unlikely that this group is of pure Stone Age date. Thus it is possible that these stone-using folk were the reindeer-hunters of the early metal era. A few radiocarbon analyses suggest a date in the last two centuries BC. If we consider this finding in connection with the other – early – datings available, we realize that hunters lived in the mountains of southern Norway for some six thousand years. No wonder that the archaeological problems are so many and so tangled.

THE SUB-NEOLITHIC PEOPLE OF THE WESTERN ISLANDS

Hunting in the mountains was a way of life which required adaptation not only to strange and perilous surroundings, but also to the ways and habits of a particular fauna. All the mountain peoples – the Mesolithic hunters, the 'flint folk', the 'slate folk' and the 'quartzite folk' – settled by rivers and lakes rich in fish, and along the routes followed by the reindeer during their annual treks. Hunting in the mountains called for knowledge and tools different from those required on the outer isles of western Norway, where life depended on seal, whale and cod.

So we cannot simply assume that the same people hunted in the mountains and fished in the sea. The people of the western islands had no cause to follow the long and perilous routes into the mountains, for there was food enough by the coast at all times of the year.

At the most favourable places, where narrow straits divide islands and headlands, and where the tidal variation is great, fishing has always been extremely good; there seal and whale can often be caught in quantity. It is in places like these that the sub-Neolithic settlements of south-western Norway occur, and many of the sites have yielded numerous finds. Some of these settlements point to an uninterrupted occupation from

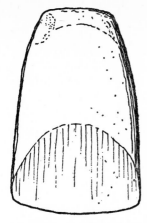

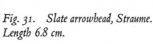

Fig. 30. Polished greenstone axe, Straume near Bergen. Length 8 cm.

Fig. 31. Slate arrowhead, Straume. Length 6.8 cm.

Mesolithic times onwards, and to a lively contact with the northern slate complex as well as with the southern and eastern Pitted Ware region.

An area of settlement which offers ideal conditions for studying this meeting between south and north, between ancient heritage and new impulses, is on Ramsvikneset in Straume, N. Hordland, among the islands off the coast near Bergen.

The figures give us some idea of the wealth of this settlement: a level about 30 inches thick and over 3000 square feet in area has yielded between 300 and 400 polished axes and chisels, more than 1000 arrowheads (mostly of slate) and quantities of other tools, as well as pottery.

Figs. 30–33

Even though no traces of houses, tents or other forms of shelter have been found, there can be little doubt that this was a fishing and catching camp of a relatively permanent type. Here the open sea is close at hand, yet conditions for hunting deer must also have been good. Animal bones found in the excavation provide evidence of fishing, whaling, and big-game hunting on land.

The cultural levels indicate two distinct periods. The earlier contains no pottery, and the typical tools are made from blades,

Fig. 33

Fig. 31

Fig. 30

Fig. 32

in veined quartz – a raw material with ancient traditions, but not found locally. Flint was used only to a limited extent. The most common form is a simple blade arrow; but slate points mostly small and thin, also occur. Axes, Mesolithic in character, have been found side by side with more 'modern', polished types, of oval or rectangular cross-section.

In the later level, slate tools predominate. Great numbers of points have been found, long, slender and beautifully made. Their edges are parallel, and the points needle-sharp. Lances, knives and needles occur, but not in such numbers. The quantity of small, well-made chisels and medium-sized axes of polished slate and greenstone, however, is striking.

This later level contained two types of pottery – the local, coarse variety, punch-decorated; and sherds from more distant parts. The latter ware is thinner, and the cord-decoration suggests an origin in the mixed culture established in eastern Norway in the Middle Neolithic period, the result of the meeting of the Boat-axe culture and the Pitted Ware complex.

This rich settlement on the islands west of Bergen is typical of the sub-Neolithic milieu of this coast. Life was fairly stationary here, based on an exploitation of the resources of those localities which nature has endowed with good fishing. The people had their roots in Mesolithic tradition, but they were ready and able to absorb new impulses from diverse sources, as regards both the choice of raw materials and new tool forms. This versatility is characteristic of their culture, and is of great archaeological interest; for two strong cultural currents met here, merged, and emerged in a new form. One of them came from the northern slate complex, the other spread up the coast from the south, presumably from the Pitted Ware complex, then in a phase of vigorous expansion. During the earlier period, a special technique of making tools from blades flaked off cylindrical blocks, and also the use of slender blade arrows with a tang, were derived from the south.

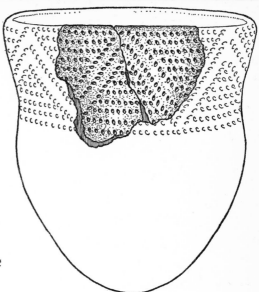

Fig. 32. Pot from Straume. Diameter at rim, 13.8 cm.

As we saw above, the pottery likewise shows a connection with the south – a connection continued into the later phase, when northern impulses were otherwise the stronger, as the large-scale use of slate indicates. The techniques and the forms are those which we know from northern Norway. But some specialized tools used for skinning, flenching and tanning – essential operations there – are not found in the Bergen district. Here the people used their own local tool, a chisel-like

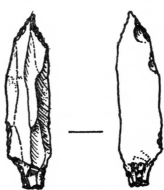

Fig. 33. Blade arrowhead of quartz. Length 4.7 cm. Ramsvikneset, Straume

85

implement, for such work. This intermingling of local forms with innovations from the north and the south does not suggest immigrations and sudden change. An ancient coastal culture, its roots in the Early Stone Age, was modified by the influences of expanding northern and southern groups rather earlier than 2000 BC. These impulses caused rapid changes in the industry, but neither type prevailed to the exclusion of the other. The terms, 'slate culture' and 'Pitted Ware culture' are equally misleading when applied to this area of western Norway. These rich settlements of wholly hunting tribes in western Norway were apparently deserted during the last phase of the Late Stone Age. It seems that human existence here, as in many other parts of southern and western Norway, was once again in a state of flux. Now agriculture became predominant, and left its mark on the form of settlement and the industry either directly or indirectly, while the slate complex and the Pitted Ware groups disappeared as formative factors.

Plate 18

Chapter IV

The Bronze Age

NO UNIFORM BRONZE AGE culture ever existed in Norway. On the contrary, a wide gulf separates the hunting
areas of the north from the southern agricultural districts. These
are the geographical and cultural extremes: on the one hand a
pure Stone Age culture, on the other a true Bronze Age way
of life – but between the two extremes there were many inter-
mediate stages.

In the ancient centres of the Neolithic 'agricultural expansion' a Bronze Age culture of the southern Scandinavian type
developed. The burial rites here, the cults, and the new tech-   Plates 19, 20
niques were all largely determined by more southerly Bronze Age
civilizations. The archaeological material from the Norwegian
Bronze Age is modest in quantity, except for one important
field: the ritual rock art of the period. To date, nearly five hundred zones have been located, yielding several thousand figures
all told. Through this form of art, important information about
other aspects of life has been handed down to us; for such things
as boats, carts, weapons and domestic animals are frequently
depicted.

The number of Bronze Age objects found is far less impres-
sive. The entire material hardly exceeds seven hundred finds,
and the datable burials with Bronze Age equipment total   Fig. 34
not more than a hundred. But there are hundreds of great earth
and stone barrows which, judging from their form and their
location, are probably of Bronze Age date.

The votive finds containing Bronze Age objects are fairly
numerous and often rich; this is also of importance for an
assessment of the cultural structure; it is significant, too, that
the composition of these offerings corresponds with that of
most Bronze Age centres of southern Scandinavia.

We must presume that the technical traditions of the Stone Age were still active even in the richest Bronze Age districts; but the people who lived in Norway during the Bronze Age were not unfamiliar with the casting of bronze – relatively advanced and complicated methods, as well as simple ones, certainly being practised locally. Even though these people lacked the ability to create their own local types and ornaments, they were well enough acquainted with their material to find a suitable raw material, namely soapstone, for the moulds which they needed.

Plate 31

Little is known of how far these bronze-using people penetrated into the hunting districts. How far north along the coast the new culture extended, is also uncertain. But even the densely wooded inland districts of eastern Norway have yielded graves and votive finds of types characteristic of the Bronze Age. Stray graves – certainly of Bronze Age type – have been found north of the Arctic Circle; bronze objects and rock art of the same period, certainly reflections of the Bronze Age culture, occur as far north as the 68th parallel. Even though no pure metal culture could thrive in such remote parts, these finds tell us a good deal about the degree of penetration of the first of the metal-using cultures.

There were three centres of the Bronze Age culture in Norway. The oldest and most clearly defined emerges as early as during the Early Bronze Age, in the fertile agricultural area of south-western Norway. The second main centre, where the new civilization gradually gained a foothold, is in the Oslo Fjord area, including adjacent inland districts. The Late Bronze Age, especially, is comparatively well represented here. The third main province comprises certain fertile tracts of central Norway, north of the Dovre mountains. This latter area borders on excellent hunting grounds, and accordingly saw great cultural conflicts; but even here we find all the elements of a true Bronze Age culture.

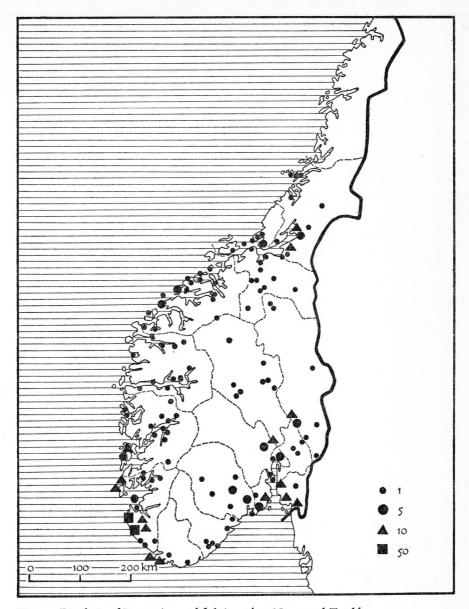

Fig. 34. Distribution of Bronze Age metal finds in southern Norway and Trøndelag

Plate 19 A close contact between a coastal district near Stavanger and Jutland is clearly shown by a group of monumental graves which are completely unrelated to the local Stone Age culture in either form or content. These graves are set up in conspicuous places, most often by the coast, in areas which were natural centres for agriculture, trade and sea-faring. The graves are, on the whole, constructed and furnished like those in the Bronze Age centres of southern Scandinavia. The burial chamber is long and often stone-covered, with a mound of earth on top. Such mounds can be up to 100 feet in diameter and 13–16 feet high. Occasionally the cists contain two bodies, and sometimes the square stones are carved with geometric patterns. The size of the graves and the amount of work that went into the building of the burial chamber testify to a social structure entirely different from that of the Stone Age here by the sea. The grave goods, wherever any are preserved, confirm the impression of a close contact with the important cultural centres beyond the Skagerrak. The choice of equipment follows fashions set farther south; the same applies to the forms, styles and sizes of the weapons and women's ornaments. Nothing is 'home-made', and none of the furniture of these chieftains' graves in any way reflects Stone Age traditions.

In the richer graves, the men were sometimes buried with a sword or a dagger. These are fine weapons, which undoubtedly enhanced the owner's social status in a society poor in metal. Lesser articles such as razors, tweezers, awls, buttons, etc. in the men's graves offer further proof of how the leading men in this south-western Norwegian Bronze Age province strove to follow fashion in every detail, presumably also in their clothing. Though no complete garment has been found, textile fragments provide sufficient evidence of garments made from woven wool.

The furniture of the women's graves also reflects the superior social position of those who were buried here. Their bronze or-

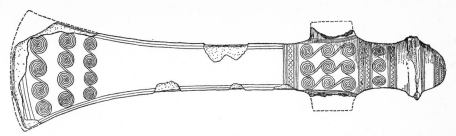

Fig. 35.   Ceremonial axe of bronze, Early Bronze Age, western Norway. Length 30 cm.

naments – arm-rings, belt clasps, neck-rings and brooches –
do not differ from the Scandinavian norm. Many of them must
certainly have been made in Danish workshops.

    The monumental graves and the occasionally very rich burial
offerings point to an upper stratum of society not merely with a
Bronze Age 'veneer', but truly of this culture – an impression
confirmed by the votive finds, which are informative not only by
virtue of the objects they comprise, but also by their ritual significance. As an example of such a find, showing a very clear
connection between peripheral and central areas, spiritually as
well as materially, we may instance an offering to a spring in
Etne between present-day Stavanger and Bergen.

    The find consists of three massive bronze axes decorated with
spirals, zigzags and other linear patterns. They can be dated to
the period 1200–1100 BC, and must have been particularly
valuable possessions. This find testifies to a custom common
among farming communities in many parts of Europe, and
springing from a belief in the strength of the axe and the power
of water.

    Axe-cults and sacrifices to water are conspicuous features of
the religion of the Bronze Age farmer. Bronze *lurer*, too, played
a like role; in this respect, again, the Norwegian Bronze Age
betrays the influence of southern Scandinavia. Men playing
lurer and others swinging axes are depicted in rock art, and there

Plate 22

Fig. 35

Fig. 48

91

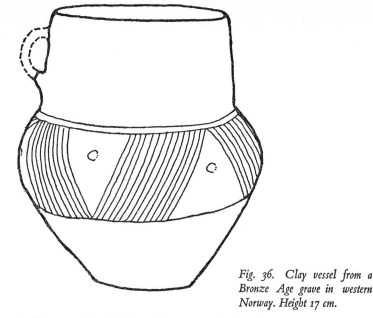

Fig. 36. Clay vessel from a Bronze Age grave in western Norway. Height 17 cm.

is often unmistakable evidence that bronze *lurer* were made and used in eastern and western Norway. Two magnificent examples found on Revheim in Stavanger, the very centre of the western Bronze Age province, provide valuable information in this respect.

These *lurer* were placed intact on a patch of marshy ground; in the course of time the swamp covered them several feet deep. Near the sacrificial site are characteristic examples of the rock art of the Bronze Age, carved on a sloping rock face. No doubt this was a hallowed locality where religious festivals were celebrated, probably with the object of procuring sunshine, rain and a good harvest. These *lurer* are composed of several tubes joined together. One *lur* curves to the left, and the other, curving to the right, forms a pendant piece. They are both 5 ft 10 in. long from the mouthpiece to the collar-like end. It is clear that these instruments, which were extremely valuable – their metal

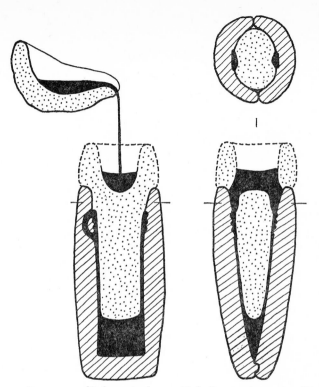

Fig. 37. Soapstone moulds for casting bronze, Early Bronze Age, western Norway. Length 36 cm.

Fig. 38. Bronze sword of the Hallstatt culture, western Norway. Length 71 cm.

content alone represented a fortune – were sacred: why else should they have been allowed to lie untouched until the swamp covered them?

About fifty such *lurer* remain from the Scandinavian Bronze Age, by far the greater part of them found in Denmark. Practically all lay in bogs and swamps, and they nearly always occur in pairs. The practice of using these great horns in religious ceremonies must have originated in Denmark, but the two *lurer* from Rogaland were made in Norway, as certain technical

Fig. 37
Plate 31

Fig. 36

Fig. 38

peculiarities show. They thus provide valuable information on the technical skill attained in this part of the country. Even difficult casting processes, we note, were mastered, as is also evidenced by moulds found in different parts of Norway; these are made of soapstone, a local stone which is easily worked and excellently suited for casting bronze. Moulds for axes, daggers and swords were also found, dating from both the Early and the Late Bronze Age. This is proof enough that people did not limit themselves to importing articles of bronze.

It is difficult to say whether the great burial mounds and the rich finds of metal are due to immigration into the agricultural districts by the coast, or whether the Bronze Age culture gained ground here as the result of local traditions merging with impulses from abroad. It is tempting to sketch a dramatic picture of merchant chieftains able, thanks to their metal weapons and their wealth, to settle in central areas offering superior economic possibilities. How it came about, we do not know; but the analogy between south-western Norway and Jutland is too striking to be explained in terms of mere occasional trading connections.

Little is known as yet about how much farther north along the coast and inland along the fjords the Bronze Age culture extended, or what forms it took there; but people are unlikely to have immigrated to these districts, even though a certain change of culture did take place. Unfortunately the region has not been studied systematically, but we do know of a number of cairns there, sometimes containing grave urns and burnt bones, some of which date from the Bronze Age. Stray finds of bronze objects occur, as well as examples of the typical rock art of the period. It is a fact, moreover, that certain settlements along the coast farther north, where people often lived in rock-shelters and caves, show a 'mixed culture', as discussed earlier (p. 66).

In a few places where natural conditions made for particularly good hunting, fishing and agriculture, the finds are more numerous and more composite; but there can be little doubt that the culture which we meet here had its roots in the Late Neolithic and had assimilated only a limited number of Bronze Age elements. Here the society of the Stone Age changed but slowly, and that at a time when the rest of Europe was on the threshold of the Iron Age.

THE STONE/BRONZE AGE OF EASTERN NORWAY

While the clearest traces of the Bronze Age in south/western Norway date from the earlier phase of the period, in eastern Norway they are later (*c.* 800–500 BC). Only then does the metal era begin in earnest there, and even districts far from the coast – parts that to/day still border on virgin forest and moun/ tains – yield bronze objects ranking among the best. But here again, we are faced with the same basic question: was this a Stone Age culture with certain Bronze Age elements – or did a really fundamental change take place, technically, ritually, and with regard to the settling of the land?

We may begin by stating that the new culture gained ground in some parts, while other districts adhered to the traditions of the Stone Age. But this is only what we would expect in so large an area of such varying ecology – one that includes large, open stretches of coast, inland forests, and vast mountain moor/ lands. Obviously a Bronze Age culture of the southern Scan/ dinavian type could never develop here in the wilds.

But burial rites, ceremonial sacrifices, pictorial magic, and the art of casting bronze entered into the lives of certain of the population of eastern Norway too. We are justified, therefore, in applying the term Bronze Age to their culture, although there was no large/scale expansion of these elements such as might reflect a major wave of immigration.

Graves are a dominant feature of the eastern Norwegian Bronze Age culture, and it is not so much the furniture as the

Plate 20

95

Plate 23

graves themselves that enable us to form an idea of the cultural level which they represent. These are cairns built over one or more stone cists, the length of a man. Sometimes the dead were inhumed, sometimes cremated. Most of the cairns are round, some are oblong. They vary in size, but a diameter of 65–100 feet and a height of 13–20 feet are not uncommon. They usually occupy dominant positions. Along the coast, we find them on treeless heights, often on bare headlands or islands – singly, or sometimes in groups.

Similar cairns occur inland along rivers and lakes. They are often set in commanding positions on hillocks, sometimes in comparatively lonely places. Like those by the coast, the graves tend to be large and well-built, but little furniture is preserved; it is therefore by their form and situation that we may date them.

The Bronze Age graves of eastern Norway, whether inland or on the coast, frequently lie by ancient highways; though these people did not always bury their chieftains where they worked the land and built their homes, the graves still testify to a way of life and a social system that must have been completely alien to a hunting community. Their social background is more stable, a society with a class system. To build graves, many of which contain more than 35,000 cubic feet of stone, on hills or far-off islands, required not only a material surplus but also considerable labour. In this, they differ greatly from the culture of the Norwegian Stone Age.

Plates 21, 25–31
Figs. 39, 40

Few metal objects have been found in eastern Norway, but what there is, is often magnificent, and the types are distinctive. Weapons predominate – daggers, swords, lances and axes – and there are also personal ornaments, of types common to the whole of Scandinavia. Some of the finds are hoards, others votive offerings. Their quality is high, even by southern Scandinavian standards. They come from the coast as well as from the more remote inland districts. As these finds invariably consist of

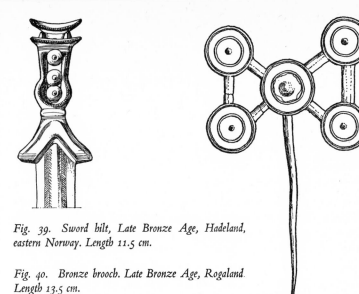

Fig. 39. Sword hilt, Late Bronze Age, Hadeland, eastern Norway. Length 11.5 cm.

Fig. 40. Bronze brooch. Late Bronze Age, Rogaland. Length 13.5 cm.

first-rate imported goods, their economic background can hardly have been stock-rearing and agriculture, for such produce was not of great value in overseas trade. Fur, therefore, must have been the source of their wealth. Many of the finds in fact come from districts close to excellent hunting grounds.

Most of the articles found in hoards and votive deposits in eastern Norway must have originated in Denmark during the last two phases of the Bronze Age. The most common are large, heavy neck-rings, ornate belt-boxes, sturdy brooches and clasps, often spectacle-shaped – all baroque in form, and decorated with the linear ornament characteristic of Scandinavian art in the Late Bronze Age. Quite a few finds, however, include articles made outside Scandinavia, such as the 'Wendel-rings', 'swan's-neck pins' and some swords of a Central European type.

Plates 26, 28

These collections of valuables contain scarcely a single object 'useful' to either hunter of farmer. Such articles as these were

97

'status symbols', pure and simple, and the character of the finds allows us to draw several interesting conclusions.

They show us, for one thing, that towards the end of the Bronze Age there was an economic surplus sufficient to allow of the amassing of valuables. Moreover, there are so many finds, and they are of so composite a nature, that the items contained in them cannot all have been obtained by way of occasional barter; it would seem that trade was better organized than that. The people who lived near the hunting grounds must have been in close touch with the farmers by the Oslo Fjord who, in turn, went by sea to the markets of southern Scandinavia in season. A third conclusion we may draw is that religious beliefs, as attested by many sacrificial deposits of women's adornments, must have been the same in the borderland of the eastern Norwegian wilds as in the agricultural villages of Denmark. Ideas and faith were common property. Many things suggest the cult of a goddess whose symbol was the neck-ring, and to whom the great hoards of female accoutrements were doubtless offered up.

THE ECONOMIC LIFE OF THE BRONZE AGE

Hunting produce must, as pointed out above, have been important when it came to paying for bronze weapons, tools and jewellery from abroad. Just how intensively the Norwegian hunting grounds were exploited early in the metal era, it is, however, difficult to determine. There is no problem where the far north is concerned – we know the rich hunters' villages by the coast well enough; but they had little if any contact with the Bronze Age provinces farther south. The religious, economic and social systems of the inhabitants of these settlements in Varanger and elsewhere north of the Arctic Circle had developed along lines different from those followed by the people of southern Norway. Therefore the finds and forms of the Arctic

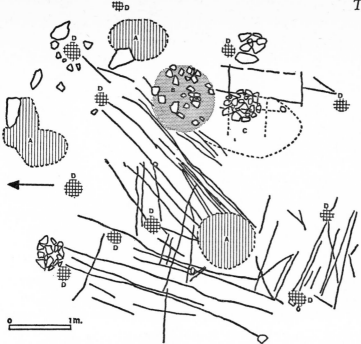

Fig. 41. Traces of a house foundation and of ploughed furrows, Østfold. A, depression; B, hearth; C, clay stratum; D, post-holes

coast cannot be used as a guide where the exploitation of the natural resources of the Bronze Age areas is concerned; there is, in fact, only scant evidence to show the importance of hunting and fishing in those parts where the Bronze Age people lived and worked. One or two facts are clear: for instance that caves and natural rock-shelters were frequently inhabited by hunters early in the metal era; and that the exploitation of the mountain moorlands continued unchanged. Investigation of the southern Norwegian hunting cultures of the early metal era has barely begun; as yet we get no more than a glimpse of that activity in the course of which the use of metal implements spread to the most remote provinces of the European Bronze Age culture.

Plate 13

Nor are we too well informed concerning the main lines of development in the more settled, agricultural way of life. We know little of what Bronze Age houses looked like. A few small, rectangular house foundations with low, earthen walls have been excavated in south-western Norway – that is all. But everything points towards permanent settlements, with houses and pasture-land, in the true Bronze Age districts. Recently, tilled fields from the Bronze Age were discovered in both eastern and western Norway, a discovery which shows that the cultivation of corn was of some importance.

There is one such site in the county of Østfold. On a farm-stead called Hunn, where fields, forest and fjord together make up the setting of one of Norway's most important groups of prehistoric sites, with a hill-fort, standing stones, burial mounds and traces of prehistoric fields have come to light. Between the topsoil and the sterile subsoil the vestiges of furrows crossing and recrossing could be clearly discerned. The burials and a house foundation above these traces of the plough enable us to date the fields to some time before the Iron Age.

Fig. 41

It is perhaps not so surprising that the people of eastern Norway, where there are large areas of easily worked land, began at so early a date to employ the methods of agriculture current in continental Europe at the time. More remarkable is the fact that traces of precisely the same process of tilling have come to light by the coast of western Norway, in an area bounded on one side by the ocean and by the mountains on the other. This evidence of corn-growing and of a well-developed agricultural system comes from Kvamsøy, about 150 miles north of Bergen. In this area, rich in settlements of Stone Age type, extensive traces of ard-furrows crossing and recrossing, like those at Hunn, have been unearthed. This field had been cleared on sandy soil, at a point where the shore widens into a plain. Ash, charcoal and scorched sand in the soil show that the forest and undergrowth had been burnt away before the field was ploughed.

But the field was exposed to wind and weather, and once the forest no longer provided shelter and the soil had been tilled, the wind played havoc. After a few years, drift-sand made cultivation impossible, and the people either moved away or changed their mode of life. Remains of six cultivated levels were found, indicating that for at least six seasons this field had been sown and reaped.

Perhaps these cultivated patches of land by the Oslo Fjord and in western Norway are our very best evidence of the great impact of the farming culture during Norway's metal era. Even in these places, at the uttermost limits of agriculture and of the Bronze Age, farmers settled and employed methods which had been developed abroad.

ROCK ART

By rock art we mean pictures hewn, incised or painted on rocky slopes, vertical rock faces or boulders of varying sizes. The subjects are human figures, animals, all kinds of inanimate objects, and also geometric patterns and non-figurative ornaments. Some of the pictures measure several yards, others merely a foot or so. Often the figures occur in groups, which may number several hundred. Single figures and very small groups have also been found.

Plates 32–39

Painted pictures are rare in the North – the paint may of course have been worn away by wind and weather – but a great number of hewn and incised pictures exist. It is these latter which are usually referred to as 'rock-carvings'.

Rock-carvings as such, regardless of their age, type of motif or cultural background, occur in Denmark, Norway and Sweden, but none have so far been found in Finland.

The Nordic rock-carvings have been known for a long time. The subject of exhaustive investigation, they have been interpreted and assessed in many ways. Most of the discussion about

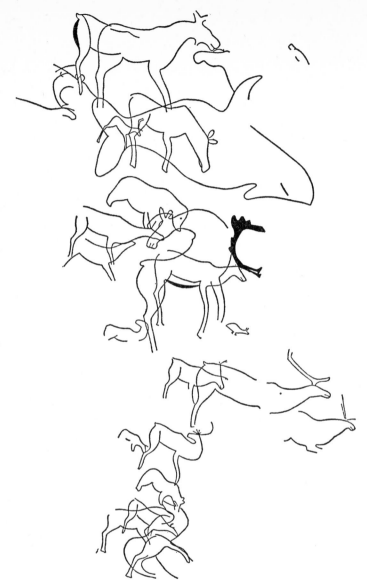

Fig. 42.   Group of pictures worked into a rock-face, Tysfjord, Nordland. Length of whale about 8 m.

Fig. 43.   Group of pictures hewn into a rock-face, Kalnes, Tune, Østfold. Over-all length about 4 m.

them has been concerned with the problems of dating and with the ideas that inspired them, but only rarely has an assessment of their artistic qualities been attempted. The fact that they embrace an 'impressionist' naturalism, a schematism that is more 'expressionist', a symbolic stereotyped form of art, and a purely non-figurative style tells us a good deal about the variations one can find in this form of art.

Nordic rock-carvings are traditionally divided into two main groups. This grouping is chiefly according to subject matter, style, geographical distribution and topographical location; but this is too hard and fast. It was often based on an over-simplified idea of the cultural conditions that gave rise to this art. True, the art of rock-carving does comprise two main phases, but we are now in a position to know that there is no firm dividing line between them, that there are many transitions of culture, chronology, geography and subject matter.

Figs. 42, 43   The two traditional groups are the northern, often designated 'arctic', and the southern, usually termed 'south Scandinavian rock-carvings'.

The choice of subjects and the location of the 'arctic' rock carvings have led most scholars to regard this group as the work of a wholly hunting culture. It was therefore assumed that the motifs derived exclusively from the activities of the hunter, and that this art thus expressed his world. Consequently, graphic art of the arctic group has, especially in Norway, also been called 'the hunters' art'. Particular importance has been attached to the fact that the great majority of these pictures represent game, and it has also frequently been pointed out that they most commonly occur in the good hunting districts, which even to-day lie far from human habitation. Here, large-scale hunting may have been engaged in, hordes of animals being chased to the edge of a precipice over which they plunged to their death.

These 'arctic carvings' have nearly always been dated to the Stone Age, some of them to the Mesolithic. This dating results from interpretations based partly on a study of style, partly on the position of such carvings in relation to the present sea-level. They have therefore often been called 'Stone Age carvings'. In other words, this group has been assigned to a period ending about the middle of the second millennium BC, according to the chronology of Scandinavian prehistory.

Here it must be stressed that many Nordic archaeologists held the orthodox view that in this part of the world the Stone Age – the true hunting culture – did not survive into the following phases, the Bronze Age and the Iron Age. This theoretical attitude has undoubtedly made it difficult to understand the art of the hunters. We must not forget that, in parts of Norway as well as of Sweden, people continued to live partly or even entirely by hunting: a Stone Age culture that survived into the metal ages. This must be borne in mind when assessing the background of rock art.

Fig. 44.   Deer from rock-carving at Ausevik, Sogn and Fjordane. Length about 65 cm.

Without going into details, we shall here consider some of the main points of the hunters' art.

Most of the pictures certainly do represent game; the most common being elks, reindeer and red deer. The bear is the only beast of prey depicted; this is because bears were also hunted for food. We occasionally find seals and whales, and fish such as halibut, flat fish and salmon. Sometimes human figures are shown, but they are comparatively rare. Boats are occasionally used as a motif, and we can distinguish between different types – a fact of chronological and cultural importance. In some zones, geometric designs are found: chequered patterns, spirals, crosses inscribed in circles, labyrinths and purely abstract linear patterns.

Plates 32, 37

Fig. 45.   Stylized deer from rock-carving at Vingen, western Norway. Length about 4 m.

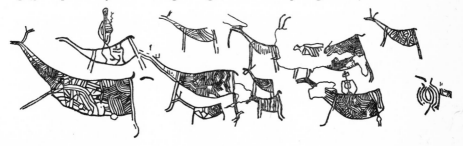

As a rule, no unity of composition can be discerned, but in certain cases it is clear from the arrangement of the pictures that the artist was at great pains to express some purpose or function by their relative placing.

Figs. 45, 47

The stylistic variations are great. There are some monumental pictures full of life and naturalism, while others, less supple in form, show bodies filled with a more or less irregular pattern of lines. In yet other pictures, the animal no longer belongs to zoology at all, but is well on the way towards becoming a pure symbol.

Figs. 42, 44
Plates 32, 33
Fig. 45
Plate 37

In addition to game from the forests, the mountains and the sea, human figures, inanimate objects and purely geometric patterns play a part in many zones of carvings. It is worth noting that some of these symbols do not belong to a pure hunting way of life, a true Stone Age culture. On the contrary, the spiral, the labyrinth, the sole of the foot, the cross inscribed in a circle and certain of the boats belong chronologically to the beginning of the metal era. Culturally, they must have come to the hunters from the beliefs and the ritual art of an agricultural people. In other words, the hunters' art is not pure, in so far as it is not entirely free from southern influence during the Bronze Age. We are thus confronted with a mixed milieu and a composite world of myth and religion.

Fig. 46

Plate 35

The geographical distribution of the hunters' art helps us to understand this, for such art is not as 'arctic' as the name would seem to imply. True, in Norway, where most of the carvings occur, there are many distinctive finds from Nordland and Troms, but Finnmark, the northernmost county of all, has yielded practically none. On the other hand, we encounter zones with many figures – examples of the hunters' art – farther south, in central Norway and along the coast between Bergen and Trondheim.

South of Bergen only a couple of 'hunters' figures' have been found, but when we turn to eastern Norway, we again come

Fig. 46. Dancing man from rock-carving at Ausevik, Sogn and Fjordane. Height 33 cm. (See fig. 47)

across zones of carvings spread over the whole region. In the Oslo Fjord area, for instance, animal carvings are numerous. So geographically, this is no arctic form. The art of the hunter shows a wide geographical distribution, in fact, and it occurs largely in those parts where a farming culture had started to make itself felt during the true Stone Age, areas under a particularly strong influence from southern Scandinavian culture during the Bronze Age.

Nor are the problems posed by the 'southern Scandinavian' carvings as simple as was thought. These pictures have usually been interpreted as the artistic expression of a farming culture, executed in the service of fertility magic. In choice of subject and in style they differ from the rock art of the hunters. As a rule, the figures are rather stereotyped, but they can and do vary greatly in size and proficiency. Plates 38, 39

Game is all but absent from these carvings of the farmers' culture, and boats dominate the choice of subject. In many of them the human figure plays an important part. Usually it is the man who is depicted, and in contrast to the hunters' art, his sex is usually greatly exaggerated. Domestic animals, for instance horses and oxen, are also common. Weapons such as spears, swords, axes, bows and arrows occur. The main implement used in cultivating the land – a primitive plough – is Fig. 43 Fig. 48

occasionally depicted, as are also carts and wagons. Geometric figures are often to be seen. The symbols used most in this so-called southern Scandinavian art include spirals, circles, labyrinths, cup-marks, grid patterns of various kinds, foot-sole symbols and various figures which are difficult to interpret.

The next point to consider is the distribution of the 'farmers' carvings'. Scholars have usually attached much importance to the fact that they are mainly found in southern Sweden, in parts of Norway and on the island of Bornholm. In Norway, they are most common in Østfold; some others have been found in Vestfold, on the Lista peninsula, in Rogaland, and scattered along the west coast. North of the Dovre mountains, too, there have been some very rich and varied finds of this type, mostly in certain districts of the Trondheim Fjord area. Rock-carvings which certainly belong to the 'farmers' art' occur north of the 66th parallel, near the Arctic Circle. In view of this distribution, the term 'southern Scandinavian' is as inadequate in defining this complex of carvings as 'arctic' is for the art of the hunters.

The distribution of the 'farmers' carvings' has naturally assumed some importance in the discussion of their cultural horizon. It has been stressed, for instance, that the carvings are found in places where agriculture began at an early date. Accordingly this art has been regarded as an expression of the farmers' world of myth. However, in areas which cannot possibly be described as fertile or easily cultivated, we find a number of zones of carvings containing a wealth of figures. This applies not least to Bohuslän in Sweden; here there are many monumental zones of carvings, yet they lie in poor and craggy pasture land. Conditions are the same in Østfold and Trøndelag, the two counties of Norway where this form of rock-carving was practised most widely. There are many typical 'farmers' carvings' here, and we find them mostly on rock faces close to heavy, clayey plains that were difficult to cultivate. Nor can one say that west-

Plate 24

Plate 39

Fig. 47. Pictorial frieze, with animals and linear patterns, Ausevik, Sogn and Fjordane. Length about 3.65 m.

ern Norway south of Trondheim, with its many fjords, is a typical agricultural region, or that the islands near the Arctic Circle make a first-class farming district. What farming culture there was in these areas was clearly very mixed. Stock-rearing, corn growing, hunting, fishing and catching all contributed to the food supply. We ought, therefore, to discontinue using the term 'farmers' carvings'; this term, used mainly in Norway, is misleading.

If we study the topographical location of these carvings, we discover yet another factor worth examining, namely that in certain areas, mainly in Norway, the 'hunters' carvings' are found side by side with those whose subjects stem from the farmers' sphere. This is less obvious in eastern Norway; but even here, often no more than a few miles separate zones of the one type of carving from those of the other. In some places in western Norway, the distance is even less, but it is in Trøndelag that we encounter really striking examples. There some of the most typical 'hunters' carvings' occur not merely in the same district, but often in the same locality; it is not even exceptional to find excellent carvings from the two different spheres on one rock face.

Clearly, therefore, the factor of geographical distribution provides no key to the difference between the two types of carving.

Nor is the topographical location always different, and it is evident that they were not always such worlds apart as has usually been maintained.

There are extreme instances, equally far apart in geography, in cultural context and in subject matter. But as we have seen, in some important areas where hunting was the natural mode of life the outlook and the beliefs of the farmer nevertheless made their appearance at an early date, during the Stone Age and the Bronze Age. In these areas, there were possibilities of con⁄tact between the two cultures, and this contact must have found expression in the forms of art and of spiritual life.

It may appear anomalous that the Bronze Age 'farmers' carv⁄ings' and the Stone Age 'hunters' carvings', in many cases at least, seem to be the artistic expression of peoples who not only lived at the same time, but who also were in close touch with each other. The idea that economic, cultural and artistic contrasts are contingent on differences of period has long been a tenet of archaeological research, and this must be the explana⁄tion of earlier chronological assessments, so often one⁄sided. Now, however, we know that the Norwegian hunters' Stone Age – or, rather, the hunters' culture – flourished at the time when the farmers' rock art was at its peak; and some of the hunters' art must also have been created during that period, the Bronze Age. Some of the oldest zones, however, may date from the *pure* Stone Age; this is indicated by the location of certain of the zones that lie by the ancient shore. However, the practice of carving ritual pictures on the rock seems to have died out on the approach of the Iron Age, to continue only sporadic⁄ally in some places in western Norway until the fourth or fifth century AD.

Rock art as practised by the hunters and the farmers is a ritual, a magic form of art. It was the farmer's aim to increase fertility, the seafarer's to ensure fair weather, the hunter's to gain power over his quarry. By creating an image of that which one

Fig. 48. Lur⁄players depicted on a Bronze Age rock⁄carving. Height about 97 cm. Lille Borge, Borge, Østfold

Fig. 48

wished to bring about, probably in connection with ritual ceremonies, good fortune would be ensured. Monumental pictures
of game are an expression of the hunter's desires, and figures of
men with exaggerated genitals express in a similarly simple way
the farmer's hopes of fertility. The geometric symbols and the
purely abstract pictures, on the other hand, are a more complicated reflection of the same magic train of thought. The great
number of such symbols is proof of the manifold variety of rock
art, and of the fact that this art reflects the thoughts and beliefs
of hunters and farmers, which added up to a colourful and
complex view of life.

CHAPTER V
The Iron Age

A T T H E T I ME of transition to the Iron Age, Norway under‚ went a change of culture as did the rest of the North – a crisis, one might well say. At all events, the archaeological ma‚ terial gives one the impression that the first phase of the metal era, the Bronze Age, came to an abrupt end. The contrast be‚ tween old and new is so sharp that one is tempted to imagine that the collapse was brought about by violent change.

Just what happened we do not know; but bronze disappear‚ ed, and no comparable wealth of iron filled the void. There are practically no votive offerings, no hoards from the beginning of the Iron Age; and the people no longer raised huge burial mounds. Nor is there anything to show that the custom of rock carving was kept up to any great extent.

Whilst the transition followed the same pattern throughout Scandinavia, the archaeological material reflecting this change and its effect is less, and still more fragmentary, in Norway than in the rest of Scandinavia. We must also bear in mind that it seems to have been largely limited to areas where agriculture was the most important way of life. Where people still obtained their livelihood by hunting, the change from bronze to iron did not make much difference. This is most easily seen in the north of Norway: the hunters' villages by the Varanger Fjord were not hit by any crisis.

THE PRE‚ROMAN PERIOD (FIFTH CENTURY BC–FIRST CENTURY AD)

Let us, however, turn our attention to those parts of Norway where the Scandinavian Bronze Age culture had either pre‚ vailed, or exerted a decisive influence. We shall find that there is little to learn about the first five centuries of the Iron Age except from what the graves can tell us.

On all main points these grave finds resemble those characteristic of the period throughout Scandinavia; and they show that it is incorrect, at any rate, to speak of a complete redistribution of the population. Both shores of the Oslo Fjord continued to be inhabited, as did the south coast and the coast further north almost as far as Bergen.

Practically all the material comes from flat graves containing cremation burials. Archaeological investigations are by no means complete, but although the evidence is scant, the types of grave and the nature of their contents are distinctive enough to warrant a few general conclusions. Thus the difference between eastern and western Norway, for instance, was as marked as it had been in the preceding era. The material shows that there was a continuity of habitation in the country as a whole, and it was still open to impulses from abroad.

Plates 40–42

The people buried their cremated dead in various ways. After the body had been burnt on the funeral pyre, charcoal, earth and bones were either cast haphazardly into a hollow in the ground, or placed in a vessel made of wood, bark or clay. Many of the graves were covered with stone slabs. An alternative practice, also common, was to collect only the burnt bones and inter them. This latter type of burial is most frequent in the west, where the urn was often placed in a small stone cist.

The cremation pits are usually less than twenty inches across at the top, tapering downwards to a depth of anything from eight to twenty inches. They are usually covered with stone slabs or placed beside a small boulder. Sometimes the grave and the ground around it were marked with a circle of small stones, or they were paved. Burial mounds or cairns over these cremation pits are practically unknown, though occasionally old barrows or cairns from the Bronze Age were re-used. The flat graves frequently lie close together, forming cemeteries, a practice most common in the areas east of the Oslo Fjord. One of their characteristic features is that children's graves occur side by side with those of adults; another is that the grave and such furniture as it contains do not vary, irrespective of the age and sex of the deceased. Actually, it seems that in some places this simple burial custom continued for many centuries to come. It does not differ from cremation as introduced during the Bronze Age, except in certain details, the result of new impulses from the south and the south-west.

The Early Iron Age graves contain little furniture. This paucity accords with normal practice in the North; but in Norway, it seems, this frugal tendency was more marked than in the central parts of Scandinavia. Undoubtedly many other cremation pits and urn burials, completely devoid of finds, belong to this first phase of the Iron Age – but as they contain nothing by which they may be dated, even their large number does not allow us to draw any conclusions.

The finds which do provide a basis for dating and a possibility of assessing the cultural contacts include pottery, iron and bronze brooches – some with a curved pin, others with a disc-shaped head – as well as a group of neck-rings with ornamented knobs, some iron fibulae, and buckles and belt-rings made of bronze and of iron. Especially worthy of note are sickles, curved knives and awls of iron. A couple of spear-points and swords are all the weapons that have come to light.

Plates 43, 44

Though meagre, this material includes datable finds from each of the first five centuries of the Norwegian Iron Age. The last part of this period is rather better represented than the earlier phases. Moreover, there is enough material, and it is sufficiently distinctive, to allow us to make certain fundamental deductions concerning the cultural contacts of the Iron Age. The characteristic brooches from the earlier part of the period, for instance, show not only a local variation, but one due to different Continental influences. While impulses from Bornholm and north-

*Fig. 49.   Clay face-urns from the transition period to the Early Iron Age. Bringsvær,
Fjære, East Agder. Heights 23 and 28 cm. respectively*

eastern Germany acted on eastern Norway, western Norway
was clearly influenced by north-western Germany and Jutland.
The connection between eastern Norway and the Oder/Vistula
region is also proved by pottery finds (simple face-urns) and
personal ornaments.

Fig. 49

This disparity continues into the second half of the period.
The eastern Norwegian province seems at that time to have
been subjected to a cultural influence from southern Sweden
and eastern Denmark, where La Tène impulses were much in
evidence. For example, there was the custom of placing sickles,
awls and curved knives in the graves – a practice common to
eastern Norway, western Sweden and eastern Germany.

The places that were settled during the first part of the Iron
Age lie along the coast from the Swedish border in the east, to
a little way south of Bergen in the west. The cultivated land
hardly formed a continuous belt, but then the distance between

its extremes is almost 400 miles. What is more, 'colonies' of farmers who were in touch with the coastal Iron Age districts also settled on good farming land by the inland rivers and lakes. In other words, quite a large area was inhabited by people whose culture was influenced by that of more central regions to the south. But we do not as yet know whether *all* the sites that have yielded finds from one or other of the centuries we are considering were continuously inhabited, or whether some of them were deserted for part of the time. This is a problem that still has to be solved.

Thus our picture of the first Iron Age culture is incomplete; we are unable to follow the development of habitation step by step. What is worse is that not a single farmhouse remains, no field, no trace of fortifications. It is only by their cemeteries, those artless cremation graves on the moraines and on sandy plains, that these farmers of the first phase of the Iron Age allow us a glimpse of their cultural level.

It is interesting to note that the changes in the pre-Roman Iron Age culture of parts of Norway kept in step with the development of the rest of northern Europe. This corroborates what the Neolithic and Bronze Ages have shown: that fundamental changes taking place on the southern shores of the Skagerrak and the Kattegat were reflected, though in a much feebler form, in the remoter regions to the north and west.

What impact the earliest Iron Age culture made on Norway is, however, an open question. Were the forests in the east, the huge mountain moorlands, the fjords and coastal districts of the west – which have yielded no Iron Age burials or other archaeological finds – completely deserted and depopulated? Or did hunting farmers (perhaps even 'true' hunters) continue to live here, without adopting a single feature of the new culture, and so leaving behind them no traces that we have yet been able to identify? The latter seems more likely; mountain and ocean continued to yield a good return.

The changes that occurred in Scandinavia at the beginning of the Iron Age have given rise to much speculation. One of the most important and well-founded arguments was based on studies of climate. We know that the climate of Scandinavia underwent a gradual change at this time. This must, it was claimed, have caused large tracts to be depopulated. The increase of humidity favoured fir and beech, but made it more difficult for mixed oak forests to thrive. For man with his livestock, it was argued, catastrophic conditions must have resulted: he had to move south, or perish. This may actually have happened in the most vulnerable areas. But it seems unlikely, on the whole, that conditions were so bad as to cause depopulation on a vast scale, and this is borne out by recent investigations, wherever such have been carried out.

We no longer believe these climatic changes to have been calamitous, but they did radically change the character of the Norwegian countryside. It was at this time that the forest disappeared from the outer coast, leaving the bleak landscape we see there to-day. More humid summers, more rain and snow in winter, brought the tree-line in the mountains down by some 600 feet. Such changes might ruin the farmer in exposed places, without affecting the hunter's lot to any extent. The lakes and rivers were still stocked with fish; in the now barer and bleaker mountains, the reindeer-hunter would prosper, while elk and fur-bearing animals continued to live in the forests. Cod, seal and whale came and went in the ocean in unchanged numbers.

THE ROMAN IRON AGE (CIRCA FIRST–FOURTH CENTURY AD)

It was during the first centuries of the Christian era that an Iron Age type of culture and a purely agricultural form of life at last became dominant in Norway. This was a period of growth; more land was settled than ever before, more contacts with the outside world established and maintained. A striking contrast indeed with the first phase of the Iron Age! Hardly a trace of agriculture from the earliest phase of the Iron Age survives north of Bergen; during the later phase, Iron Age culture penetrated to the districts north of the Arctic Circle. The former has yield-ed a mere hundred datable graves; burials of the Roman Iron Age number more than a thousand. In one and the same local-ity, large Roman Iron Age cemeteries sometimes succeed pitiful little clusters of a few graves from the first phase of the Iron Age. While that phase showed few signs of contact with abroad, entire sets of imported goods survive from the Roman Iron Age. We know little of the farmer's home, his way of life and his work, in the centuries before the Christian era; in the Ro-man Iron Age, our knowledge of these is, for the most part, really comprehensive, and we possess much information about the weapons in use at the time, about the runes, the social sys-tem and the technical innovations.

The reason for this expansion is not immediately obvious. Natural resources and climatic conditions remained largely un-changed. But two factors seem to have played a decisive part. In the first place, during the Roman Iron Age, man evidently learnt to smelt iron from the bog-ore found in so many areas in Norway, though this is a matter that has not been exhaustive-ly studied. Then there is abundant evidence of a lively contact with areas influenced by the culture of the Roman Empire. This connection enabled the people of Norway to sell their produce abroad in return for large-scale imports; it left its mark on cul-tural conditions everywhere in Iron Age Norway.

The burial customs and weapons, the apparel and adorn-ment, the luxury goods, and the arts and handicrafts – all these were shaped by the lively contact with southern Scandinavia and with other, more distant markets.

The burial rites were partly based on ancient, local traditions, partly modified by the influence of foreign practice. Cremation, as of old, continued on a large scale; the ashes were buried in

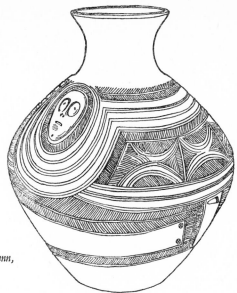

*Fig. 50.   Clay urn from Hunn,
Østfold. Height 28 cm.*

cremation pits as before. Where an urn was used, it may be better made and of a finer ware than before, but apart from this the changes were slight. These graves usually form large cem⁄eteries, some of which had been begun in the preceding period, and which are especially common in eastern Norway. An area between the river Glomma and the Swedish border, for instance, has yielded more than a thousand such graves, the majority of which seem to date from this period.

Some of these plain cremation burials are surrounded by a triangular, rectangular or circular stone edging. Graves of this kind frequently contain more than one burial, which suggests a ritual element in the burial ceremonies. Generally, however, the flat graves, poor in finds, give an unceremonious, matter⁄of⁄fact impression.

A contrast to these simple graves is provided by a new burial practice that was introduced, calling for more grave furniture

Fig. 50

and a more imposing monument. Often the dead were inhumed, but in these graves, too, cremation predominates. These variations do not, apparently, express any difference in beliefs or culture, for they were employed side by side.

Where, in this wealthy milieu, cremation was preferred, the burnt bones and the grave furniture were often interred in a bronze urn or a fine clay vessel. Regardless of whether such urns were used, or whether bones and gifts were merely placed on the ground, the grave is nearly always marked by a visible monument, be it a large, earthen mound, a cairn or an arrangement of standing stones. Where the dead were inhumed, either the grave was sunk into the ground, or a wooden coffin or stone cist was used. In these cases, too, a large monument usually marks the grave.

As a rule, the inhumation graves are furnished with a wide range of funerary gifts, often influenced by foreign fashion. In quantity and splendour, they do not always surpass the gifts accompanying the cremated dead, but they are often better preserved, and therefore call up a more complete picture.

Weapon-graves are a feature typical of the Norwegian Roman Iron Age. These warriors' graves are most common in eastern Norway, though traces of a warrior-caste have also been found along the west coast south of Trondheim, in the districts by the Trondheim Fjord, and even in the far north bordering on the territory of the Lapps. Throughout this period the weapons agree, in form and selection, with finds from the central areas of the Germanic lands. Many of them must have been imported, but not a few were certainly made by Norwegian smiths. The choice of arms and weapons, and the number of burial finds, vary somewhat in different phases of the Roman Iron Age; but everywhere the quality of the goods is excellent.

Fig. 51. Double-edged iron sword, Opland, eastern Norway. Length about 80 cm.

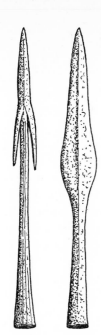

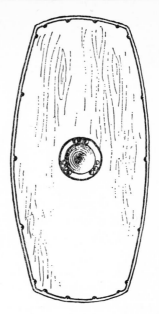

Fig. 52. Lance and spear from Lærdal, western Norway. Length of each 32 cm.

Fig. 53. Reconstruction of a shield from the Roman Iron Age, Hunn, Borge, Østfold. Length about 125 cm.

During the earlier part of the period, warriors were equipped with a short, broad, single-edged sword, one or two light spears – often barbed – and with a thin, wooden shield that had a conical boss to protect the hand. The single-edged sword, inspired by the Roman *gladius*, was later gradually replaced by the long, slim double-edged sword which had then become part of Roman equestrian equipment. There is clear proof of the close connection between the people here and related tribes in the south in the fact that this sword, the *spatha* of the Romans, became the most important weapon at an early date even in distant Norway.

Simultaneously the spear changed its form, following the southern model. A heavier, leaf-shaped lance, and a long, elegant spear with barbs now became an integral part of the equipment. Whether one lived north of the Arctic Circle, or fought on the frontiers of the Empire, one's arms were identical.

Plate 46

Plate 47
Fig. 51

Fig. 52

121

During this later phase shields were light, and either round

Fig. 53

or rectangular. Some were covered with leather, a few decorated with bronze mounts. In the finest weapons, the sword hilt and

Plate 51, *Fig. 54*

the shield boss were of bronze, or covered with silver sheet-foil. The spurs which often formed part of the warrior's equipment were also of bronze, sometimes covered with silver sheet-foil; stirrups, on the other hand, were unknown. Nor does the bow-and-arrow seem to have been used.

The warriors' graves of the Roman Age lie at strategic points along the coast, in the good agricultural districts inland, and near the routes to the hunting grounds – thus they not only reflect close contact with the southern, related tribes, but also show that the Iron Age farmer had conquered the wilds, and the merchant the far outposts.

Other evidence also testifies to internal expansion, and to

Plates 48–57

trade with the outside world. The numerous finds of imported articles, many in the luxury class, are at least as important as the warriors' graves in illustrating these aspects or Iron Age life. Among the imports, articles of bronze, personal ornaments and glass are conspicuous. Bronze vessels of various types were par-ticularly popular. Bowls, ladles, cauldrons and buckets made of bronze have been found in more than seventy Roman Age graves in Norway. A round-bellied cauldron, known in Scan-

Fig. 55

dinavia as *Østlandskjele* must have been especially highly prized, as examples of it were found at some eighty sites in Scandinavia, about half of them in Norway, and most of these in the eastern part. Early in Imperial times, they were turned out by Italic workshops; later they were also produced in Gaul. The distri-bution of the Scandinavian finds shows that, whether they came by way of the Rhine delta, or by more easterly routes, one of the export markets was eastern Norway.

Another, rather later, form of large bronze vessel was produc-

Plate 49
Fig. 56

ed in the Aquisgranum (Aix-la-Chapelle) district. This type, the *Vestlandskjele*, is low and wide. A goodly number of these

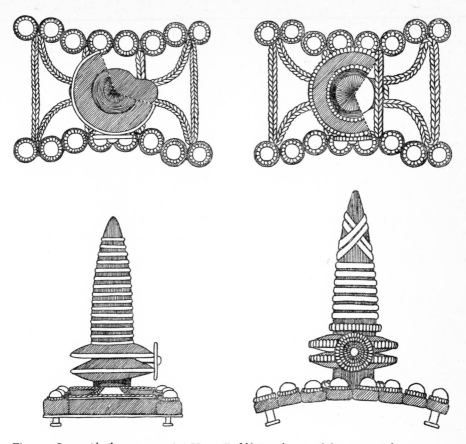

Fig. 54. Spurs with silver ornamentation, Hunn, Østfold. Lengths 5.5 and 6 cm. respectively

cauldrons came to western Norway by way of trade across the North Sea; the earliest example found in western Norway dates from the fourth century, though most of them are more recent. The production and sale of these later cauldrons went on for at least two hundred years, and contact between the Norwegian coast and western Europe was maintained into the Migration Period. It should be pointed out that bronze vessels of this type are practically unknown in Denmark and Sweden.

Plate 57

The frequent finds of glass conjure up the same kind of pic-ture of trade with Rome and her provinces; 250 objects of vari-ous types have come to light in Scandinavia, many of them in Norway. They include shallow bowls, drinking horns and – most numerous – tall beakers. The distribution of the glassware is the same as that of the other imported articles. It found its way to the coast, to the inland districts and also, though in lesser quantities, to the land north of the Dovre mountains: this fragile glass travelled distances of 1200 miles or more.

Weapons, bronze vessels, glass and imported jewellery – all these belonged of course to members of the upper classes. They account for only a small fraction of the total remains from this period in Norway. Alone they are enough, however, to tell us a great deal of what life was like in the different parts of the country: for instance, that there was a rich upper class; that trade with eastern and western Europe had attained the level of organized commerce; but above all, they furnish proof of the greatest exploitation yet of the ancient hunting grounds – for these provided produce that was bartered in trade with other countries.

Fig. 55.   Østlandskjele of bronze. Frøyshov, Udnes, Akers-hus. Diameter at widest point 28 cm.

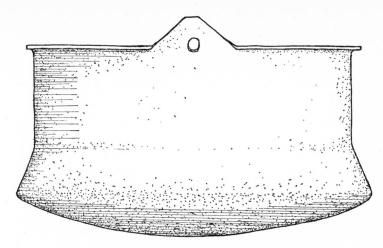

Fig. 56. Vestlandskjele *of bronze, Godøy, Møre, western Norway. Diameter at widest point about 30 cm.*

Let us choose four graves as typical of those furnished with articles purchased abroad in exchange for the surplus obtained from the mountains and the ocean. One is situated in the land bordering on the forest and the mountains of eastern Norway; one on the south-west coast, at a point convenient for voyages across the North Sea; one in the hunting and fishing country of the west coast, not far south of Trondheim; and one in the area north of the Arctic Circle.

The eastern Norwegian grave belonged to a cemetery some 75 miles north of Oslo, at Stabu, to the west of Mjøsa, Norway's largest lake. It was a typical warrior's grave, containing two swords, five spears and two shields. All the weapons are characteristic of the second century AD, and there can be little doubt that they were imported. One of the swords actually bears the initials SF in Roman letters on its double-edged blade, and is decorated with a bronze inlay representing Victory. This weapon certainly came from the cultural sphere of Rome. One

Plate 47

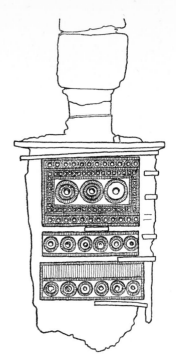

of the spears, too, is a rare piece. The shape is quite common – rather heavy and long – but on the blade a runic inscription, RAUNIJA (R?), had been pricked out. It numbers among the earliest of all runic inscriptions.

This is one of many weapon-finds from this area. Its capital value cannot be assessed; but it seems likely that this and similar finds in the district represent the returns of trapping in the near-by forests and mountains. The way to these hunting grounds was short, and access to the Oslo Fjord easy.

Some harbours on the south-west coast of Norway must have served as embarkation ports for boats crossing the North Sea. One of these was Avaldsnes, a little way south of the present-day town of Haugesund. The Avaldsnes district has yielded finds from practically all periods of Norwegian prehistory, including the Roman Age. One, a man's grave, is outstanding.

Plates 53, 54
Figs. 57–60

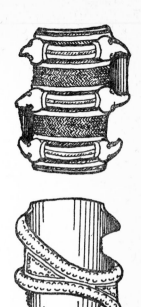

Figs. 57–60. Grave goods from Avaldsnes, Rogaland. 57, Roman bronze vessel. Height about 28 cm. 58, Detail of sword. Height of decorated part 6.7 cm. 59, Handle mounting from a Roman bronze cauldron. Diameter of mounting 5.7 cm. 60, Gold ring. Height 3.8 cm.

The body, fully clothed, was buried in an oak coffin. He was armed with excellent weapons: a shield, sword and two lances. The sword had a silver pommel, and the scabbard was leather-covered, sumptuously decorated with plates of silver, some of them gilt. The boss of the shield, tapering to a point, was of iron. It was partly covered with silver sheet-foil. The baldric apparently had a knob covered with gold sheet-foil. The grave furniture also included an arm-ring of gold, four gold finger-rings, a tin-plated bronze mirror, a pair of bronze scales, and thirty glass gaming pieces. A large hanging-bowl of bronze, a bronze bucket with a twisted handle and decorated with silver inlay, and a bronze sieve – all products of provincial Rome – add to the impression of wealth; a silver beaker and the rim mountings of a drinking horn complete the picture of a rich man. In no other Roman Iron Age burial in northern Europe has so much gold been found.

127

The reason why this and other rich graves occur in this area is that the sea-routes from the north and those for the south-west met here. Merchants bringing hunters' produce from the north called at Avaldsnes, and this was also the natural harbour for those coming from the west.

About 200 miles north of Avaldsnes, near the present-day fishing town of Ålesund, was another centre of commerce, hunting and sea-going, and it also has yielded rich finds from all periods of prehistory. Among the fourth- and fifth-century finds, one is more conspicuous than the rest. It comes from a monumental cairn on one of the outer islands, Godøy. This was a cremation burial; the ashes had been placed in a *Vest-landskjele*. The grave goods consist of two peerless beakers of beaten silver, probably of Scandinavian manufacture, a large arm-ring of gold weighing 10 ounces troy, a gold medallion, and the remains of bone arrows and a bone comb. The bronze cauldron, the silver beakers and the gold must, of course, represent a considerable capital: the find is typical of our series of rich men's graves with costly furniture brought from abroad.

Figs. 56, 61, 62

Plate 49

Fig. 61. Silver cup, Godøy, Møre, western Norway. Height 7 cm.

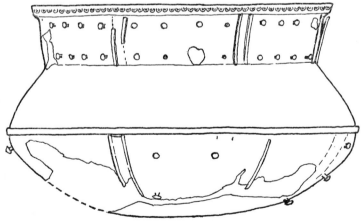

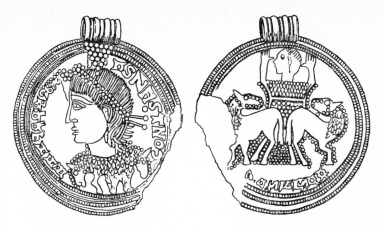

Fig. 62.   Copy of a Roman gold medallion, Godøy. Diameter about 4 cm.

This is interesting enough, but the medallion is even more so. It is a Scandinavian copy – probably Norwegian – of a Roman type. The original bore the portrait of Emperor Constans I (337–350). Constans' portrait on the obverse, and the imperial charioteer on the reverse, are distorted in the copy – so, naturally is the inscription – but not beyond recognition. The legend CONSTANSA, for instance, can be deciphered.

Roman emperors, as we know, would present kings and princes of other realms with gold medallions bearing their image, as a token of their respect. These medallions were in great demand, and some copies were made in Germanic lands. Thirteen have been found in the North, the majority of them in Norwegian graves. The medallion from the Godøy grave, far out by the open sea, not only provides a reliable date, the end of the fourth century, but it is also striking evidence that the great men of Norway were in close contact with the more central districts in Europe.

Fig. 62

Such graves, with their precious imported goods and splen﹑
did weapons, were confined to a leading class, unthinkable ex﹑
cept against a background of a population of humble hunters
and fishermen; but the traces left by the latter are sparse over
most of the country. In the area where Godøy lies, as it happens,
we can learn something about the hunters too. Here there is
evidence to show that, even though these people had left the
Stone Age behind, theirs was no true Iron Age culture. The
best example of the hunters' culture of the period is provided
by a find located only a couple of miles from Godøy.

In late Roman times, there was a settlement at the mouth of a
large cavern, Skjonghelleren, facing the sea. Whilst a single
object of iron and but few potsherds were found, it yielded
plenty of weapons and tools made from antler and bone. A
good deal of refuse too has survived. The find thus enables us
to reconstruct something of the culture and the hunting methods
it represents. The hunting equipment consisted mainly of a large
quantity of slender arrowheads of antler and bone, about eight
inches long. A strong bow must have been used to shoot these
arrows. Iron was not used; bone served the purpose well enough.
The spear points are of simple form, made from hollow bones,
polished and meticulously sharpened. There are no harpoons
and, oddly enough, no fish﹑hooks.

This was no mere seasonal hunting camp, as is shown by
spindle whorls of bone, personal ornaments made from teeth,
and a couple of antler spoons; women, it would seem, also lived
here.

The bone remains show that these cave﹑dwellers by the ocean
kept horses, cows, sheep and dogs. But even though they had
domestic animals, their diet consisted mostly of fish, fowl and
big game. Mammals such as seal, otter, red deer and reindeer
were hunted, but most of the bones are those of birds, no less
than 23 different species having been identified. Some of them
will have been caught in summer, but others are found in these

*Fig. 63. Bone
arrowheads,
Skjonghelleren,
Møre, western
Norway. Lengths
20 and 19.5 cm.*

parts only in winter. This again is evidence that the cavern must have been inhabited for the greater part of the year. Human re- mains occur among the refuse, suggesting that the dead were either 'buried' without much ado on the rubbish heap, or else that the cave-dwellers were cannibals. Similar conditions have been observed in other caves and rock-shelters by the coast, dat- ing from the Stone Age and the Iron Age – animal bones and human remains alike were cast on the refuse heap.

This find from Skjonghelleren is not without parallel, for there are other Iron Age caves and rock-shelters on the Nor- wegian coast. We have quite a number of instances of such sites where Iron Age people lived; their way of life was completely foreign to that suggested by the richly furnished graves. These must have been the people who procured the produce used for bartering on the markets from which the imported articles came. This is no 'Stone Age', but the cultural distinction can hardly have been great.

The trappers have left evidence of their activities in the number of high-quality foreign goods that survive even north of the Arctic circle. The conquest of the north began during the Ro- man Iron Age, and gathered momentum during the Migration Period. The area around Vestfjorden near Narvik is a classic example of this expansion of 'merchant farmers'. Stock-rearing is possible in these parts, but the district is more remarkable for its excellent hunting and fishing grounds. Here the sea cuts deep inland to Narvik and to the great moorlands of Sweden. In summer the reindeer trek from their moors in the east down to the shore; and elks and bears roam the mountains to this day. Some of the finest rock-carvings from the Stone Age and the Bronze Age occur here; and this area used to be one of the main strongholds of the culture of the Lapps. Vestfjorden's greatest claim to fame, however, is the tremendously profitable cod fish- ing which takes place here in winter.

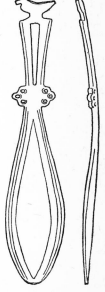

Fig. 64. Bone spoon from the Early Iron Age, Giseløy, Øksnes, Nordland. Length 15 cm.

The island of Steigen, which has yielded some of the clearest traces of the expansion from the south, lies at the centre of this district. Our knowledge of the local hunting population is still scanty; on the other hand, recent excavations have furnished a great deal of information about the Iron Age people who were making for the north. A grave found at the farm of Bø on this island is one of many proofs of this expansion.

The deceased in this grave had not been cremated, and he was well armed. Fragments of his clothing remain, showing that he was dressed in wool, not in fur. The weapons were international in type, and of superb quality; he was buried with a double-edged sword, two spears, arrowheads and a shield. The furniture also includes one pottery vessel and a plain gold finger-ring. The sword is of the normal *spatha* type, and it was thrust into a wooden sheath, covered with leather. The hilt is wound with horsehair, the boss is of bronze. A U-shaped ferrule decorates the sheath. The two iron spear points are the usual pair, one with strong barbs, the other heavier and broad.

The shield is rectangular with a bronze boss and handle. The boss had large knobs for fastening, and the top was covered with sheet-foil of silver-gilt. The body of the shield, made of wood, was painted red and blue, and decorated with bronze mouldings. The baldric was of leather, with bronze buckle and mountings. These grave goods suggest a date in the latter half of the third century; they are of high quality, and do not differ in any way from the norm among the wealthy throughout the Nordic-Germanic region at that time. North of the 68th parallel, on shores washed by the ocean, the good hunting and fishing had attracted people whose cultural affinities were with regions hundreds of miles farther south.

The cave-finds from the coast of western Norway point to a population of fishermen and catchers whose material and spiritual culture was not much affected by the common Germanic

Iron Age way of life. Were these people descended from the hunters of the Stone Age and of the beginning of the metal era? Impossible to say; but one thing is certain: stone was no longer used as a raw material. It had been discarded even in the remotest north of Norway.

Finnmark, in particular, offers plenty of traces of hunters from the first centuries of the Christian era, as from the ages that had gone before, but no systematic investigation has as yet been made. Once more, the most valuable information comes from the Varanger Fjord area. In this rich and stable hunting milieu, where the different cultural phases of the Stone Age were so well represented, extensive material remains also from this period. On the small island of Kjelmøy, some miles from the Russian border, parts of a settlement have been excavated. Here a great number of implements made from bone and antler have come to light; there are a very few traces of iron, and stone was not used.

Hundreds of tools were discovered in the Kjelmøy settlement. They include harpoons, gaffs, fish-hooks, arrowheads, knives. spear points, combs, spoons, potsherds and some implements of unknown function. The site has also yielded bones of no less than 41 animal species. The fare of these people was roughly the same as that which the Stone Age folk here had enjoyed, consisting largely of fish, fowl, seal, whale and reindeer.

The Kjelmøy find is no isolated case. The forms of some of the tools show that the people were in contact with coastal areas to the east and to the south during the Iron Age. Others show that Stone Age traditions had not been forgotten. What is ot especial interest, however, is the fact that the spoons, fish-hooks, harpoons and arrowheads typical of Kjelmøy occur in several finds from the 'Hunters' Iron Age' farther south on the Norwegian coast. The large series of distinctive bone arrows from Kjelmøy are identical in appearance with some of the forms from Skjonghelleren.

Fig. 65. Harpoon point made from antler, Kjelmøy, Finnmark. Length 8 cm.

Fig. 66. Bone fish-hook, Kjelmøy, Finnmark. Depth 9 cm.

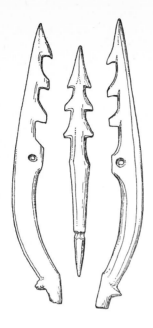

Fig. 67. Bone gaff (three-pronged fish spear), Kjelmøy. Length about 15 cm.

To go into questions of migrations and direct cultural connections would be beyond the scope of this book. Suffice it to say that the hunters of many parts of the coast had their roots in traditions and cultural impulses differing from those of the farming culture which flourished during the Roman Iron and Migration Ages. In spite of the spread of well-armed groups from the south, and uninfluenced by the strong cultural waves from the Continent, large groups of people lived in a 'Bone Age' culture here, dominated by ancient traditions of livelihood, of burial rites and of tools.

THE MIGRATION PERIOD (CIRCA AD 400–CIRCA 600)

The form of society which had developed in Norway during the Roman Iron Age seems to have remained stable during the centuries that followed. The archaeological evidence indicates no notable emigrations or immigrations in this part of the world.

134

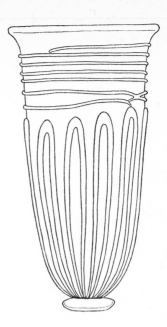

Fig. 68. Glass beaker from the Early Migration Age, Stange, Klepp in Rogaland. Height 19.5 cm.

On the contrary, growth within Norway, though powerful, would appear to have been relatively uneventful. New areas were settled, the ancient hunting grounds continued to be exploited. Burial rites remained substantially unchanged. In some parts of eastern Norway we see signs of a slowing-up of development, though impulses from the Continent were still acceptable. And in the west, foreign contacts were thriving, connections across the North Sea being clearly even stronger than during the Roman Iron Age. Imports such as bronze vessels, glass and, above all, gold found their way to Norway in greater quantities than to the rest of Scandinavia. Local crafts, styles and fashions did not, however, copy the foreigner slavishly. Technically and artistically the people showed more independence than their forebears in earlier phases of the Iron Age.

Fig. 68

A characteristic feature of the Norwegian Migration Period is the great number of house foundations and deserted farms. The larger groups enable us to study the manner of settlement and the economic basis of life in certain parts of the country in some detail. Most of the houses and farms lie in south-western Norway, in parts where development was particularly marked; here people even settled in places which had subsequently to be abandoned, and which have never been farmed since.

Fig. 69 The layout of most of the Iron Age farms is the same. Parcels of land, varying in size, were cleared around one or more houses. Here were the fields, and here the dead were buried. An enclosure bordering either on pastures or on the neighbouring farms surrounded the houses, fields and graves.

There is no trace in Norway of what might properly be called villages, the people living on more or less isolated farms. The number of houses on the farm might vary from one to five – long, rectangular buildings, with walls of earth and rubble. The average thickness of the walls must have been about three feet, while the height rarely exceeded five – but the variations are considerable. It is obviously impossible to find now how high the roofs, supported by two rows of posts, were, but they could have been pitched to a fair height, since the exterior width of the houses is usually about 27 feet.

Most of the houses sheltered people and their livestock. The farmers kept horses, cattle and sheep, and during winter most of the animals had to be fed indoors. Traces of interior dividing walls are rare, but it is usually possible to see that the animals were housed in the western part. Along the middle of the floor in the people's living-quarters, fires had been kindled, and most of the finds occur there. Cooking-pits were often sunk into the floor beside stone hearths.

Plate 58 The houses vary in size. The average length is from 65 to 100 feet, but some up to 300 feet long have been found. Thus a farm with several houses could be the home of a great number of people and animals. It seems natural to suppose that the occupants of such a farm would form an extended family, and

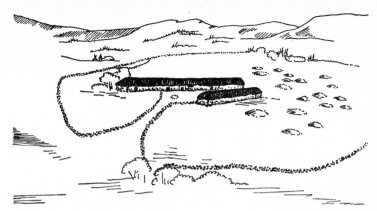

Fig. 69. Reconstruction of an Early Iron Age farm in the mountain heaths of Rogaland

that each branch of it would see to its own housekeeping, but that for other purposes they formed a closely-knit unit.

The area of enclosed, more or less cleared land varies from farm to farm. Where measurements are fairly reliable, the enclosure covers anything from 2 1/2 to 25 acres or so. It is usually surrounded by low stone walls, often with fenced paths leading up to the house. Some of the enclosed land must have been used for pasture, some cultivated. Stones that had been cleared away were heaped together. At several of the farms traces of the field remain, and these show that primitive ploughing was practised, at least to some extent.

There is usually a group of tumuli within the enclosure. The number naturally varies with the length of time the farm was occupied; but it seems that only a few of the people of the farm were buried with elaborate ritual.

Methods of clearing the land had apparently remained much the same as during the Stone and Bronze Ages. Pollen analyses, and traces of charcoal in the soil of the fields and under the walls of the houses, show that the forest was cleared by fire before houses were built or fields and meadows cultivated. Wheat, barley and oats were grown – but in most places stock-rearing was more important than corn growing.

The houses and farms of the Migration Period in south-western Norway are undoubtedly variants of a common Scandinavian system. There is clearly a connection between them and the great complexes of houses and farms on Gotland, Øland, Bornholm and Jutland of the same period and with similar buildings. But another Norwegian group of houses, also of the Early Iron Age, is more difficult to explain; both their origin and function are obscure. They do not seem to be farms, and they are without

Plate 59

parallel in the north. These complexes are arranged around a small, enclosed open space. The long houses, usually fifteen to twenty of them, lie close together, radiating from the centre. The gable ends facing the middle were either open or built of timber, while the other walls were built of earth and rubble. In most other respects the houses conform to the normal type, with hearths and with posts to support the roof. But one more divergence from the norm is that no signs of a byre-department remain. Enclosures and field complexes seem also to be lacking.

These sites lie in densely populated, prosperous areas. Their positions cannot be called strategic, yet the number of houses and the very compact way of building them call to mind a centre of power in the district in which each lies. Are they 'barracks' where the local merchant-chieftains could, on occasion, bring together the forces they required? When the North Sea was to be crossed, man-power was essential; when goods were conveyed to market, an escort was required. If we assume that each house held ten men, such camps must have housed a force comprising a couple of hundred.

To date, these radial complexes are known only from Rogaland and from northern Norway. Rogaland was a centre for merchant traffic going south to Jutland and western Europe during the Roman and Migration Ages, and it is thus natural enough that these circular camps should have been built there. And it is significant that similar camps have been found in northern Norway with its extensive hunting grounds, where we know that a ruling class from the south-west held sway at this time. People must have moved to the north during this period, from districts by the south coast; for these two widely separated regions had so much in common: burial customs, jewellery, pottery and peculiarities of dialect. The warrior grave from Bø in Steigen, which we cited to illustrate this movement towards the north during the Roman Iron Age, is only one of many pieces of evidence for this expansion, which in fact gained momentum during the Migration Age.

In this land bordering on the wilds, where much of the attraction of settlement lay in the prospect of being able to exploit native hunters of a different culture, a life in easily defended and well-manned camps would suggest itself naturally. True, the numerous northern Norwegian camps which have been explored seem to be more recent than those in Rogaland, but they must nevertheless be connected with the south, with the expansion of the Early Iron Age.

The demand for hunting produce caused not only a more intensive exploitation of the coast, and a trek towards the north, but also a fresh interest in the ancient hunting grounds of southern Norway's mountain moorlands. Iron Age types of settlements and tools appeared in the long valleys in the mountains. Considerable grave finds come from areas unsuited to agriculture; in such places, stock-rearing, hunting and iron-smelting must have been the means of supporting life. The graves sometimes illustrate this very clearly, for many of them contain a wealth of hunting equipment and well-wrought iron.

There is a settlement site, however, which illustrates this way of life still better. This is at Mogen, by the mountain lake of Møsvatn – not far from modern Rjukan in Telemark. This site

Plate 61

lies in the heart of the reindeer country, the lake is well stocked with fish, and bog-ore occurs locally. Here we have a house, 25 feet by 40, and a large midden. The side walls of the house, built of earth and rubble, were slightly curved. One of the end walls was of timber. Strong posts carried the roof, but the house was not partitioned. Several hearths were sunk into the stamped earth floor. The entrance was at the eastern end, and the refuse heap sprawled just outside. This house had been destroyed by fire. In the layers of the floor, a great number of objects were embedded: quantities of iron tools and weapons, finely deco-rated pottery, a few pieces of jewellery, and fragments of glass beakers. The number and quality of the iron objects is impres-sive; and since slag was also found, we know that those who lived here were self-supporting in this respect.

Apart from iron-smelting, these people clearly lived by hunt-ing. A great number of iron arrowheads tell us that they hunted big game, and the bones in the refuse give more specific infor-mation. Of the recognizable bones, 95% are those of reindeer, while domestic animals account for little more than 3%. It seems likely that reindeer were hunted not only for food, but also for the value of their hides. During the Middle Ages, reindeer hides ranked high among Norwegian fur exports. Probably this was so during earlier times too.

This site was not inhabited by a technically or economically backward mountain population, as is clearly shown by the amount of pottery, the well-designed iron objects and all the other equipment found, as well as by the construction of the house. This is no belated 'Stone Age'. On the contrary, it is a milieu similar to that of the wealthier farmers of southern Nor-way. Instead of reaping the harvest of their fields, these people reaped that of the mountain terrain.

The houses and farms, the furnaces for smelting iron, and the hunting camps of the Migration Period all fall into place to give us a picture of wealth, growth and diversified exploitation of the resources at hand. The burial customs are yet another reflection of the same conditions.

Various types of cremation and inhumation burials occur all over Norway, but western Norway has the highest percentage of grave finds from the fifth and sixth centuries. Plates 45, 60

Both types of burial may contain much grave furniture. The great stone cist graves are particularly impressive. They are of‑ ten several yards long, and sometimes lined with birch bark or bear‑skins. Where parts of the deceased's clothing remain, they show that the people were often clad in wool, silk and linen; the corpse was not infrequently covered with woollen blankets. The goods in many of the men's graves reflect that glory in battle which we already met with in the burials of the Roman Iron Age and the assortment of weapons and armour continues the tra‑ ditions and practices of that age. A double‑edged sword, two long spears, a shield, and sometimes a bow‑and‑arrow – these were the usual requisites for battle. Sometimes the grave goods include a belt with metal mounts, to hold the man's tinder‑ box, knife, awl, tweezers and other personal effects. Occasion‑ ally a small pair of scales testifies that a merchant was buried here; the many finds that include gold currency suggest the same thing. Plate 60

There are no Norwegian Migration Period burials of the 'princely' class, but some of them are so richly furnished that they stand out far above those of the 'middle classes'. The Snar‑ temo finds, from the county of West Agder in south‑eastern Norway, provide the best examples of graves of leading families, economically and socially. The site in question lies between coast and hinterland, and a thriving economy must have de‑ veloped there as the result of seafaring, agriculture and hunting. Plate 62

Two of the graves in this group are more opulent than the rest. They yielded, for instance, two double‑edged swords, their pommels, hilts and scabbards richly decorated with gold and silver in the style characteristic of the period. The strap-tags and various mounts are in the same ornate style. Four gold rings, two glass beakers, five bronze vessels and a pair of scales, complete with a set of weights, testify to foreign trade and wealth. Quite a few textile fragments were also found.

In form and in the quality of the furniture, the women's graves do not differ much from the men's; but jewellery, not weapons, indicates the social status. Typical of current fashion are the large, cruciform brooches and the ornate 'relief-brooches' of silver, as well as numerous smaller pins, buckles, rings and hooks. In some districts it was usual to 'set a lavish table' for the dead, men and women alike, with a great number of eating and drinking vessels – a tradition from the Roman Iron Age. The production of glass and of bronze cauldrons and dishes did not cease after the collapse of the Western Empire, and in Norway they were as highly prized as ever. It is particularly in western Norway that they formed part of the furniture of the graves of the rich. Some two hundred grave finds from the Migration

Plates 64, 65, 69

Plate 69
Figs. 56, 68

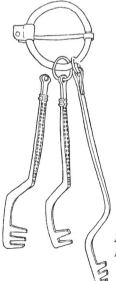

Fig. 70. *Key-ring with keys, bronze. Ullensvang, western Norway. Length of longest key 15 cm.*

*Fig. 71. Gold bracteate from Etne in Hor,
daland. Diameter 7 cm.*

Period have yielded glass and bronze vessels, but the native
products of clay and wood predominate. Clearly, the produc,
tion of Norwegian pottery increased greatly at this time, for the
finds run into four figures, and comprise both fine ware and
coarse. Some of the pots continue the traditions of Roman Iron
Age pottery, others – a large group of bucket,shaped pots – are
made from a ware consisting largely of asbestos and talc. The
latter are often profusely decorated, and seem to have grown out
of the northern Norwegian traditions of the early metal era.

Some of the richer men's and women's graves contain per,
sonal ornaments whose form is a mixture of older, Roman
trends and the contemporary Scandinavian style. The numerous
gold bracteates (amulets bearing a picture on one side) are par,
ticularly interesting in this connection. Originally, the Emperor's
portrait on Roman coins and medallions was imitated; but very
soon Scandinavian taste gained the upper hand. Naturalistic
features were stylized – the portrait of the foreign Emperor, for

Plates 68, 69

Plate 66
Fig. 71

143

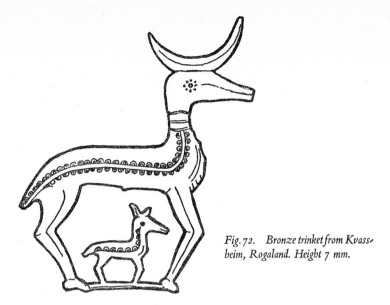

Fig. 72. Bronze trinket from Kvass-
heim, Rogaland. Height 7 mm.

instance, was changed entirely – and often magic symbols and
runes were added, to increase the 'power' of the medallion.

Altogether, the Migration Period was a creative era, an era
of new styles; artistic talents were combined with technical mastery. Gold, silver and bronze objects that have been preserved
speak volumes. Casting, repoussé, chasing, engraving, granu-
lation work, filigree – all these techniques were mastered. It
seems obvious that only specialists supplying an ever-increasing
demand could have produced the precious metals or the pottery
of this age. This was a time of mounting wealth, when the leading families had contacts over the entire Germanic area, and so
specialist craftsmen could work and prosper. It was a time when
foreign impulses no longer prevailed exclusively, and artists
were freer to express their creative urge in a more native style.
This is why we find, during the Migration Age, such an almost incredible flowering of pictorial and decorative art. It is
to be seen in sheet-metal work, some of it highly schematized,

Plates 62–67,
Figs. 70–73

Fig. 72

Fig. 73

Fig. 73. Thin gold plate with a highly stylized repoussé representation of a love scene, Rogaland. Height about 15 cm.

but relatively realistic, as well as in a more intricate and subtle form of animal ornamentation, often carved. These pictures, highly stylized as they are, suggest beasts crawling, running, fighting. Many kinds of myth and cultic ideas must surely underlie this intricate pictography.

The spiritual milieu of the time, its myths and taboos, are expressed more tangibly in runic inscriptions. Runes and runic magic were already known during the Roman Iron Age, but it was not until the Migration Period that the alphabet became so common that a fair amount of material has been preserved.

Runes came to Norway from the south. They were developed by Germanic peoples, through contact with cultures possessing an alphabet. How and when this happened we do not know, but the similarity with Mediterranean alphabets, such as the Greek and the Roman, is so great as to suggest their ultimate origin. The earliest inscriptions date from the third century AD,

Plate 71

145

and include some Norwegian finds. Most inscriptions in the earliest runic alphabet come from Scandinavia; but the majority of Germanic tribes will have used the runes in the same way, with the same kind of meaning and implications. This com, mon Germanic alphabet had 24 runes, and the inscriptions show that the language was harmonious: from Norwegian con, texts we have names such as WidugastiR, WagigaR, Hadu, laikaR, HagustaldaR and Agilamundo. Some of the inscrip, tions are pregnant with witchcraft, and menacing; the art of making runes was clearly the prerogative of a group of men who combined the dignity of chieftaincy with that of priest, hood. A personal reference, as it were, is contained in some: the pronoun I (*ek*) followed by a word – *erilaR* – not a name, but signifying one of the élite who mastered the magic of runes. This word seems cognate with the title *jarl* (earl) of later Saga times.

The fact that mastery of the runes was a symbol of social sta, tus confirms what we might conclude from the delight in the ornate, the numerous hoards of gold, the great number of richly furnished graves: during the Roman Iron Age and the Migra, tion Period, the difference between the social classes must have been great.

HILL-FORTS But whether there were highly organized groups within society, such as tribal units, we still do not know. Though there is a marked difference in the archaeological material as between one part of the country and another, particularly as between the east and the west, it is not clear whether this distinction was merely geographical, or also social. One group of finds, however, it is tempting to interpret as evidence of a form of organization embracing more than mere family groups, namely the hill-forts which are scattered over most of the country south of the Arctic Circle. Eastern Norway has particularly many – over two hundred. In plan and construction they hardly vary, and their siting too seems to follow strict rules. They are always on steep hills, preferably such as allowed them to be approached from one side only. At the point where access was easiest, one or more ramparts were built, usually dry walled. Many such ramparts are very large, with low stone walls several hundred yards in length.

The forts are so situated that one can usually see from one to the next, and in populous areas they could form a defensive net, work. Most hill-forts stand in or near ancient settlements, especially in those areas which were greatly affected by the growth and development of the Roman Iron and Migration Ages. Some, however, are found in sparsely populated places, far from modern habitation. They are most likely ancient frontier posts and road blocks.

Very few hill-forts have been excavated. The finds, though scarce, and the situation of the forts – close to Early Iron Age settlements – suggest a date within this period. It seems that the third and fourth centuries were times of unrest in eastern Norway, when such forts would be required; in the west, it was during the next two centuries that defence against assault was called for. Since warrior graves abound, warlike expansion seems to have been the rule during these two spans of time, and such expansion would presumably need to be backed by some form of strong social organization.

For the extensive foreign traffic of the Roman Iron and Migration Ages, good, sea-worthy boats were needed. The art of navigation left its mark here and there among graves and votive offerings, and we even have remains of some boat-houses. The burials are the least informative; for though the ritual reflects an association with the sea, the simple boat burials of the time tell us little about boat or ship construction. A votive find containing the remains of two boats is more important; it comes from a bog at Kvalsund, near Ålesund on the west coast. This find enables us to reconstruct the method of ship-building in use at the end of the Migration Period.

BOATS
AND
SHIPS
Plate 70

147

The largest of these boats was about 60 feet long. It was man-
ned by the pairs of oars, and probably rigged for sailing. It was
strongly constructed, and the eight strakes were in part lashed,
in part nailed to the ribs. This Kvalsund boat had a true keel –
an important point; it is altogether a far more sea-worthy vessel
than the older Scandinavian ships from Hjortspring in Denmark and Nydam in Schleswig. A boat like this could be sailed
across the open North Sea and over the treacherous coastal waters of northern Norway. Sea-worthy vessels for shorter voyages
were also in use. The smaller boat from Kvalsund, a light and
slender rowing boat, 33 feet long and built of the very best materials, is a good example. A different group of finds with which
archaeology is becoming familiar reflects other aspects of the

Plate 70

seafaring of the Migration Period: large boat-houses, elliptical
in shape, in which ships were laid up during the winter. They
could measure up to 100 feet along the major axis, 27 along the
minor one. Their walls, built of earth and rubble and panelled
on the inside, were low; the roof rested on the walls, without
support from posts. The resulting construction was roomy
enough to house large ships with tall prows. Not only do these
boat-houses tell us a good deal about the type of ship in use, but
their excellent planning testifies to an art of building more varied
than the farmhouses might lead one to expect. There are ruins
of hundreds of such boat-houses along the Norwegian coast.
Though some were undoubtedly built during the Viking Age
and the Middle Ages, others are of Early Iron Age date. The
investigations now being carried out are expected to yield valuable results in the near future, providing us with information
on an important aspect of the coastal culture of western Norway
which, by the end of the Migration Period, had grown so strong
both in numbers and in navigational skill that a large-scale
expansion became possible. This expansion manifested itself in
the subsequent military and colonizing activities of the Late
Iron Age.

THE LATE IRON AGE (CIRCA AD 600–CIRCA 1000)

About AD 600, a further change took place in Norway – a great and fundamental change in many respects. The language was transformed, beliefs were substantially modified, and this in turn had its effect upon burial practice; methods of fighting changed, and arms and armour took new forms, as did fashions in general. Technical innovations abound and the permanently inhabited districts grew and were added to. Another feature of this new era is that imports and impulses from what had once been the provinces of Rome had long since ceased to have any significance.

Plates 73, 75
Fig. 74

From an archaeological point of view, the most interesting features of this process are the changes in technology, ritual and social organization.

Once again the burials supply the most valuable information. For some reason, grave finds from the first half of the period –

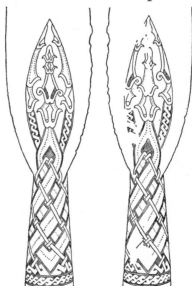

Fig. 74. Ornamented lance-point of iron, found about 3300 feet above sea-level, Lærdal, Sogn and Fjordane. Total length 51 cm.

up to the year 800 – are comparatively few, while the next two hundred years or so are strikingly well represented. Burial prac-tice, however, did not completely change during these four centuries, nor did the grave furniture alter greatly.

There are thousands of Late Iron Age graves spread over the whole country, from Finnmark in the north to the southern tip of Norway. Of the grand total of some 200,000 prehistoric sites and monuments the majority are grave mounds, and of these a large proportion date from the Late Iron Age, especially from its last phase, the Viking Age. Late Iron Age mounds were usually built of earth and rubble. They are circular in plan, domed, and tend to stand out more in the landscape than those from the Early Iron Age. Especially in eastern Norway the mounds from this, the last phase of prehistory, are very conspic-uous, sometimes measuring up to 100 feet in diameter and 13–20 feet in height. Large cemeteries dating from this period are the exception; the mounds are usually found in small groups, representing the deceased of one farm or one family.

Both inhumation and cremation were practised. As in earlier periods, there seems to have been no fundamental difference of background between the two forms of burial: in this respect, tradition continued unchanged. But there are other important features of the burial rites which are new. Cinerary urn burials were not common any more. The production of pottery had practically stopped, and bronze vessels were no longer import-ed. For this reason, the custom of providing the dead with eating and drinking vessels of pottery, glass and bronze ceased.

On the other hand, the amount of tools, driving and riding tackle, and weapons among the grave furniture increased. The lavishness of the grave furniture is often astounding, and it re-flects not only the glory of battle, but also many aspects of every-day life. Regardless of whether the deceased was a small farmer or a member of the chieftain class, his weapons, and the tools of his trade or the symbols of his status in life accompanied him

Plate 72

in death. For this reason, the evidence for the tool industry of the Late Iron Age is far more complete than for the following four of five centuries.

During the Merovingian Age, and to an even greater extent during the Viking Age, women's graves, too, were generously equipped with objects reflecting both work and pleasure. Often the deceased received not only her jewellery, brooches and the like, but also her weaving implements and various household utensils. Great as is the contrast between the grave of the Oseberg queen and those of women from small farms, the principle is the same – to the next world one travelled in one's finest array, but ready and equipped for work.

Domestic animals, most often a dog and a horse, are common in the graves of the period. This is a new feature, well in keeping with the idea of the grave as an image of the world of the living. The fact that horses are common may be taken to reflect not only social status, but also their use for military purposes and travel. The same is true of the remains of boats and ships which have been found in Late Iron Age graves on some parts of the coast. The true 'Viking ships' from Oseberg, Tune and Gokstad do not stand alone – there are a number of other funerary ships, of which little except the iron nails remains. It seems likely that ship burial, like the practice of furnishing the dead with tools and domestic animals, is east Scandinavian in origin, but it was most widely employed in Norway, where it flourished in the graves of people in all walks of life.

The great increase in the archaeological material testifies to a geographical expansion of equal extent. As early as during the Roman Iron Age, there was a permanent Iron Age population north of the Arctic Circle. During the Migration Period, people moved from the established settlements to new places; and during the Merovingian Age, the northern limit of the Iron Age culture reached present-day Tromsø. At the end of the Iron Age, West Finnmark had been incorporated into the Iron

Age territory, and grave finds show conclusively that this an/
cient home of hunters now housed scattered settlements of peo/
ple who had come from the south. Though the Lapps were
more numerous than the newcomers, the latter kept their cul/
ture intact, and no doubt regarded themselves as a ruling class.
Their Lappish neighbours are represented by some inhum/
ation burials in stone cists, the grave goods including bronze
ornaments of Finnish or Russian origin. Little else is known
about the early prehistory of the Lapps, but it is certain that they
had arrived in northern Norway by the time the 'Norwegians'
settled there during the Late Iron Age.

The salient points of Norwegian Late Iron Age culture are
the same, irrespective of what part of the country we study. The
cultural unity was amazingly strong. The explanation must be
sought in the ships – the vessels developed during earlier periods
were perfected during the Late Iron Age. They enabled this
unity to be maintained over great distances.

We have more than seven thousand grave finds from the
Norwegian Late Iron Age, and a little over 75% of these are
men's graves. Less than 20% of the material – and this applies
to men's and women's graves alike – comes from the first two
centuries of the period. These figures illustrate the growth and
development that took place during the last two centuries of
Norwegian prehistory. We can only guess at the total number
of items from all these graves, but it must exceed 100,000, for
even the common farmer was buried with many gifts. A burial
rite with sacrifices of all kinds of equipment requires a high
standard of living. Iron must have been used freely by all, and
the quantities of tools, jewellery and weapons are amply sufficient
to have supported a class of specialist artisans.

In keeping with the Iron Age traditions of Norway, the
weapons from the last phase of the era, too, are striking. More
than 3000 swords are preserved, and rather fewer spears, axes
and shields. In one important respect the selection of weapons

Plate 75

in the graves differs from that of earlier times: though the sword and the spear were still obligatory, the axe also became a common weapon in the course of the Late Iron Age. Bows and arrows seem to have become more popular, but they are not a regular part of the equipment of the graves. Naturally the details of the weapons changed somewhat during the Late Iron Age, but the 'standard set' remained the same throughout the period.

The great demand for weapons caused the art of forging iron to reach a level that has never been equalled. Some of the equipment was no doubt imported, but most of it was certainly made by Norwegian smiths, from local bog-ore. The centres for this bog-ore smelting were in certain inland districts of Norway – many smelting sites have been found, and iron deposits are common there.

METAL-SMITHS

The trade of the smith was widely practised during the Late Iron Age, and he was a highly respected member of the community. This is shown by the fact that rather more than 10% of the men's graves contain the tools of this craft, totalling more than 1000 items. Some of these graves contain so many tools for forging and for more delicate operations, that we can feel fairly sure that the men buried here were specialists who not only made the weapons but also decorated them. One grave may serve as an illustration: it was excavated in the central part of a region that has yielded many traces of iron-smelting, Morgedal in Telemark. The grave in question contained almost 200 different objects of iron; no fewer than 25 are various tools of the smith's trade, including heavy tongs and hammers, smaller chisels, files, and more specialized tools for drawing wire and forging nails. There is also equipment for smelting and casting metal, probably silver. In fact, the complete equipment of a very well-assorted smithy was buried with its owner.

Fig. 75

The rest of the grave furniture makes it abundantly clear that this man followed the armourer's trade. There are no fewer than

four swords, all of one type, four spears, three with sockets elab-
orately ornamented with inlaid copper and silver wire, seven
strong axes, two shield buckles and a number of knives and
arrows. In addition, there were as many as seven horse-bits, and
several locks. It seems likely that this smith, like so many of
fellows, was buried with all his tools, and with a selection of
the masterpieces wrought by him. He probably mastered all the
different aspects of his trade, and we may take it that his output
was large enough to supply a considerable area. His home was
in a district of scattered farms, where the economy was based
mainly on stock-rearing. In a region such as this, ready access
to raw material and the great demand for well-forged weapons
would favour the development of a class of professional smiths.

WOOD-
WORKING

The specialized crafts of the time also included woodwork.
Grave finds from the Late Iron Age include examples of wood-
carving, carpentry and boat-building. That this was the work
of specialists, no one who has seen, for instance, the rich graves
from Gokstad and Oseberg, would doubt; in corroboration we
can cite any number of scraping-irons, plane-irons, carpenters'
axes, drills, saw blades, awls, chisels, etc. Occasionally such
tools occur in complete sets, together with weapons, which were
an obligatory part of the funerary gifts, whatever the deceased's
trade may have been.

FARMING
IMPLEMENTS

But the majority of the tools from the period are in some way
or other connected with farming. Considerably more than 1000
grave finds include at least one agricultural implement. Most of
them are sickles, scythes, and iron shoes for hoes; but the quantity of iron ploughshares, too, is appreciable. During the Late
Iron Age, sickles and scythes were in common use as far north
as Tromsø, more than 200 miles beyond the Arctic Circle. The
number of scythes and sickles found in the graves is a reliable
indication of the quality of the land, and of the relative importance of agriculture and stock-rearing. About 1000 sickles have
come to light, and nearly 300 scythes. The fact that ploughshares

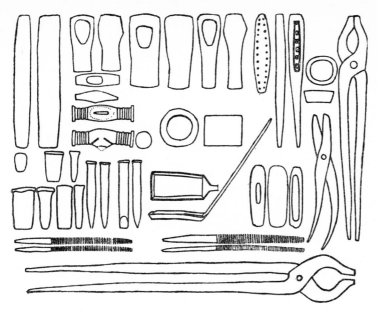

Fig. 75. The tools of a Viking Age smith, found in a grave at Morgedal, Telemark. Length of large tongs 62 cm.

are also fairly numerous shows that agriculture must have at-tained quite a high standard during the Iron Age. Such objects occur in the counties of Nordland and Troms, showing that some, at least, of the arable land of these northern districts was being farmed regularly.

In a country such as Norway, where distances are immense, communications would of course present special problems. During the long winter, the inland districts are deep in snow, and the coast is battered by storms. The varied burial customs of the Late Iron Age afford glimpses of traffic on sea and land. More than a hundred boat burials give us a fair picture of the standard of seafaring. But the clearest picture of travel during

COMMUNICA-
TIONS

the period is furnished by finds of horse gear. No fewer than 1200 graves have yielded the remains of harness; various types of horse-bits predominate – there are over a thousand of them. We have fewer stirrups and spurs; but the most splendid of all metal finds from the Late Iron Age is a golden spur from Rød in Rygge, in the county of Østfold. It is decorated with animal ornaments in the Jellinge style, executed in filigree.

Plate 74

On land people did not travel only on horseback, for we know that carts and sledges were used. The Oseberg find provides the best-known examples: a large four-wheeled wagon, three beautifully carved sledges and an ordinary working sledge. That horses were used as draught animals also appears, for fifteen were interred with the queen. Her food-supply was ensured by the provision of an ox, flour, grain and other comestibles.

The rich and highly differentiated tool industry typical of the period naturally grew out of ancient traditions. Some of the shapes occur for the first time in the find of La Tène origin; and it seems likely that the types of tools used, and their basic forms, were adopted in Scandinavia very early in the Iron Age; but only when the burial ritual of the Late Iron Age prescribed so large and varied a selection of grave goods, do the burials offer a comprehensive picture of what was actually in use. Together with other finds – weapons, jewellery, hoards of precious metals, etc. – this material shows the Late Iron Age to have been a period of tremendous spiritual and material activity. A result of this was yet another expansion of settled land in Norway. But the homeland had grown too small – adventurous pioneers now settled in the Faroes, the British Isles and Iceland. Among the most important factors making possible such an expansion at home and abroad, were no doubt the high technical standard which had been attained, the good supply of iron, and the social system under which it became customary not only for the leading classes, but also for the large mass of farmers, to be well armed.

Incursions into lands beyond the perilous wagers demanded sea-going ships that were well-nigh perfect, and this requirement had been reached in the open ships of the Late Iron Age. With a craft like the Gokstad ship, one could sail with comparative ease to the White Sea or to Ireland. But the account of the expeditions of Viking times falls outside the scope of this volume.

The great geographical contrasts in culture and economy so characteristic of the Stone Age, the Bronze Age and part of the Early Iron Age seem to have diminished greatly during the Merovingian and Viking Ages. There were still local groups, and the difference between eastern and western Norway remained substantial; but the ancient competing cultural trends that had met and so often crossed each other no longer made themselves felt in the same way. Impulses from the north, from arctic regions, no longer threatened to upset the cultural pattern which had been established farther south in Norway. All traces of a pure, local hunting culture had disappeared south of the North Cape.

In fact, during the Late Iron Age, Norway became Norwegian, and it was then that the modern northern frontier of European culture was drawn.

Select Bibliography

Abbreviations

AA   *Acta Archaeologica*
BMÅ   *Bergen Museums Årbok*
DNVS   *Det norske videnskapsakademi, skrifter*
FFT   *Finska förnminnesforeningens Tidsskrift*
SMÅ   *Stavanger Museums Årbok*
UBÅ   *Universitetet i Bergen. Årbok.*
UOÅ   *Universitetets Oldsaksamlings Årbok.*

General Works

BRÖGGER, A. W.: *Kulturgeschichte des norwegischen Altertums*, Oslo 1926.
CLARK, GRAHAME: *The Mesolithic Settlements of Northern Europe*, Cambridge 1936.
GJESSING, G.: *Norges steinalder*, Oslo 1945.
HAGEN, A.: *Vårt folks historie*, vol I, Oslo 1962.
HOUGEN, B.: *Fra seter til gård*, Oslo 1947.
SHETELIG, H.: *Préhistoire de la Norvège*, Oslo 1926.
SHETELIG, FALK and GORDON: *Scandinavian Archaeology*, Oxford 1937.

Studies on Special Subjects:

CHAPTER I

BØE, J. AND A. NUMMEDAL: *Le Finmarkien*, Oslo 1936.
FREUNDT, E. A.: Komsa – Fosna – Sandarne, *AA XIX*, 1948.
HAGEN, A.: Mesolitiske Jegergrupper i norske høgfjell, *UOÅ*, 1960–61, Oslo 1963.
JUKO, K.: Die Askolakultur, *FFT* 57, Helsinki 1956.
ODNER, K.: *Komsakulturen i Nesseby og Sør-Varanger* (English Summary), 1965.

CHAPTER II

HAFSTEN, U.: Pollen–Analytical Investigations on the History of Agriculture in the Oslo and Mjøsa Regions, *Viking,* vol 21, 1958.

HAGEN, A.: Jordbrukspionerer i steinalderen (English Summary), *Viking*, 1960.
HINSCH, E.: Traktbegerkultur – Megalitkultur (English Summary), *UOÅ*, 1951–53. Oslo 1955.
— Yngre steinalders stridsøkskultur i Norge (English summary), *UBÅ*. Bergen 1954.
MALMER, M.: *Jungneolitische Studien*, Lund 1962.

CHAPTER III

BAKKA, E.: Ramsvikneset. *A Subneolithic Dwelling-place in Western Norway*. Manuscript.
BØE, J.: *Til høgfjellets forhistorie* (French summary), Bergen 1942.
GJESSING, G.: *Yngre steinalder i Nord-Norge*, Oslo 1942.
— Circumpolar Stone Age, *Acta Arctica* 1944.
MARTENS I. and A. HAGEN: *Arkeologiske undersøkelser langs elv og vann* (German Summary), Oslo 1960.
SIMONSEN, P. *et al.*: *Varangerfunnene I–III* (English Summary), Tromsø 1960–63.

CHAPTER IV

BØE, J.: *Felszeichnungen im westlichen Norwegen*, Bergen 1932.
GJESSING, G.: *Nordenfjelske ristninger og malninger av den arktiske gruppe*, Oslo 1936.
HAGEN, A.: Europeiske impulser i østnorsk bronsealder, *Viking* 1954.
— *Rock Carvings in Norway*, Oslo 1965.
MARSTRANDER, Sv.: *Østfolds jordbruksristninger* (English summary), Oslo 1963.

CHAPTER V

ARBMAN, H.: *The Vikings*, London and New York 1961.
BLINDHEIM, CH.: Smedgraven fra Bygland i Morgedal (English summary), *Viking* 1962.
BRÖGGER, G.W.: The Prehistoric Settlement of Northern Norway, *BMÅ* 1932.
BRÖGGER G. W. AND H. SHETELIG: *The Viking Ships*, Oslo 1951.

FETT, P.: Arms in Norway between 400 and 600 AD, *BMÅ* 1938/39.
GRIEG, S.: *Gjermundbufunnet*, Oslo 1947.
HAGEN, A.: *Studier i jernalderens gårdssamfunn* (English summary), Oslo 1953.
HERTEIG, A.: *Bidrag til jernalderens bosetningshistorie på Toten* (German summary), Oslo 1955.
HINSCH, E.: Førromersk jernalder i Norge, *FFT*, Helsingfors 1951.
— Naust og hall i jernalderen (French summary), *UBÅ* 1960.
HOUGEN, B.: *The Migration style of Ornament in Norway*, Oslo 1936.
— *Snartemofunnene. Studier i folkevandringstidens ornamentikk og Tekstilhistorie* (German summary), Oslo 1935.
LUND, H. E.: Håløygske (nord-norwegische) Häuptlings-Zentren und Hofanlagen ('tunanlegg') vom Steigen-Typus aus älteren und jüngeren Eisenzeit, *Praehistorische Zeitschrift Vol. XLI*, 1964, p. 97.
PETERSEN, J.: *De norske vikingesverd*, Christiania 1919.
— *Vikingetidens redskaper* (English summary), Oslo 1951.
SJØVOLD, TH.: *The Iron Age Settlement of Arctic Norway*, I, Oslo 1962.
SLOMANN, W.: Folkevandringstiden i Norge, *SMÅ* 1955.
— *Sætrangfunnet*, Oslo 1959.
SOLBERG, O.: *Eisenzeitfunde aus Ostfinmarken*, Christiania 1909.

Sources of Illustrations

Grateful acknowledgment is made to the following persons and institutions who have kindly provided photographs and permission to reproduce them in the plates:
Universitetets Oldsaksamling, Oslo, 2, 6–10, 12, 15, 19, 21–23, 25, 27–31, 37, 40–48, 50, 51, 55–58, 62, 63, 66, 67, 69, 72, 74; Historisk Museum, Bergen, 3, 4, 14, 18, 20, 34, 35, 49, 53, 54, 59, 70, 71; Studio Pan, Oslo, 26, 52, 64, 65, 68, 73, 75; Ragnar Utne, Fredrikstad, 1, 5, 13, 16, 24, 32, 33, 36, 38, 39, 61; E. Johansen, Fredrikstad, 11; Photo Berthau, Fredrikstad, 17.
The majority of the line drawings are the work of Mrs Bente Odner. Mr. A. Noll Sørensen drew Fig. 5 and Mrs Mary Storm Figs. 49 and 55.

5

6

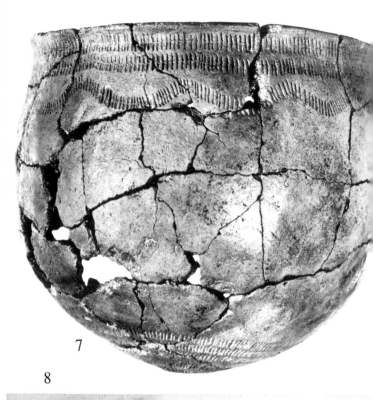

7

8

9

10

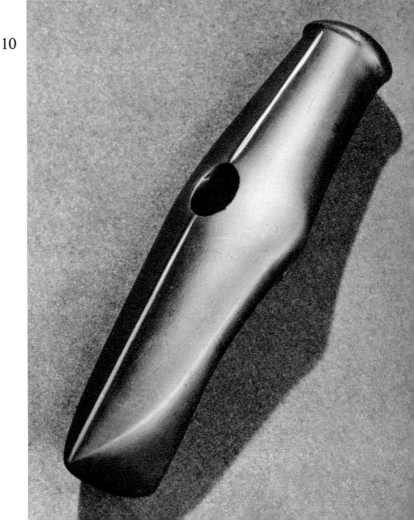

12

13

14

15

17

18

21

22

23

25

26

27

28

29

30

31a   31b

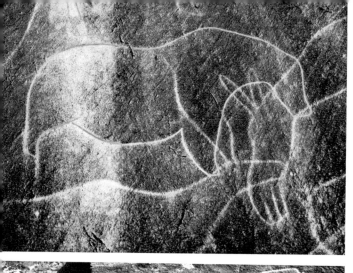

32

33

34

35

36

37

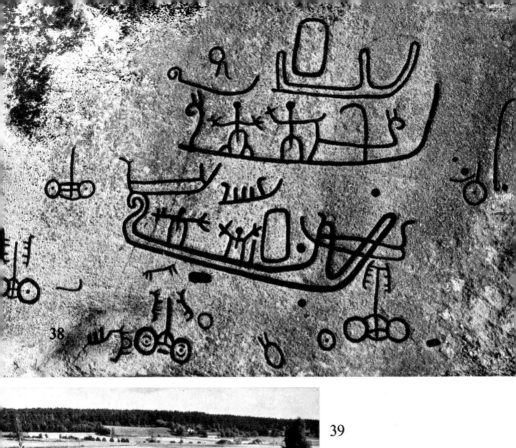

38

39

40

41

42

43

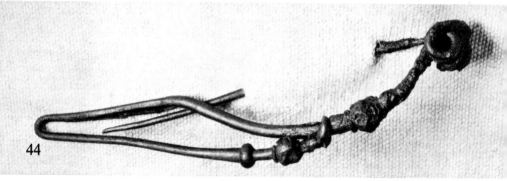

44

45

46

47

48

49

50

51

52

53

54

55

56

57

60

61

62

63

64

65

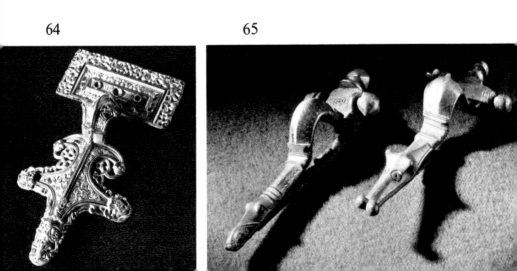

67

68

70

71

72

73

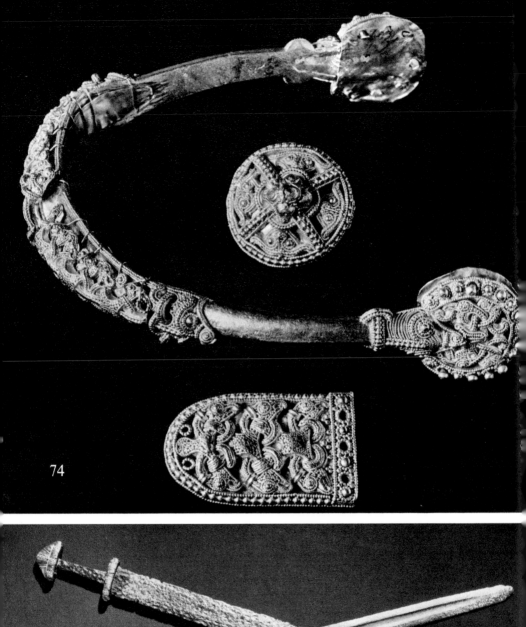

74

75

Notes on the Plates

1 Terrain typical of Stone Age settlements in the southern Norwegian mountains (Hardanger moorlands).

2 Fosna landscape, Tverrvåg, Frøya, South Trøndelag. It is in such terrain that most of the Fosna sites on the western Norwegian coast have been located.

3 Mount Komsa, Alta, Finnmark. On the hills to the left, the first sites from the 'Komsa culture' were found and excavated by Anders Nummedal.

4 The greenstone quarry on the island of Hespriholmen, Bømlo, western Norway. The quarry is about 100 feet broad by 35 feet high, and was in use during the Mesolithic and Neolithic Ages.

5 Dwelling site of the Fosna reindeer hunters, near the Hardanger glacier, 4700 feet above sea-level. The site is situated on a little island, and must be dated to about 5000 BC.

6 Flint dagger, Late Neolithic. Eklo, Værdalen. Nord-Trøndelag. Length about 30 cm.

7 Clay vessel from a boat-axe grave, Borgebund, Råde, Østfold. Height about 17 cm. The vessel was found together with a typical battle-axe of stone and two working axes of flint and stone.

8 Early Neolithic weapons from eastern Norway. The double-edged axe on the right is about 20 cm. long.

9 Early Neolithic polygonal battle-axe, Sarpsborg, Østfold.

10 Eastern Norwegian boat-axe. Lake Fiskum, Buskerud. Length about 20 cm.

11 Coastal house foundations of the mixed Pitted Ware culture, Kråkerøy near Fredrikstad, Østfold. The site is on sandy ground, sloping down to the shore, sheltered by hillocks.

12 Cist grave from the end of the Stone Age, Spydeberg, Østfold. Only a few grave cists of this type from the Neolithic Age have been excavated in Norway.

13 A rock-shelter in a western Norwegian mountain valley, Valldal in Røl-dal, Hardanger. At the transition to the metal era, this shelter was used by people of a mixed hunting/farming culture.

14 The site of the Karlebotn village by the Varanger Fjord in Finnmark. The foundations of more than eighty huts from the end of the Stone Age have been found on this flat stretch of coast.

15 Implements of slate and quartz, from eastern Norwegian mountain sites.

16 A mountain lake with sub-Neolithic dwelling sites along the shores. Grasvatnet, Nordland.

17 House foundation from the Pitted Ware group, excavated on the shore of a mountain lake near Haukelidseter, Telemark. About 9 × 15 ft.

18 Sub-Neolithic burial in a rock-shelter on the coast of western Norway, Grønhelleren, Solund, Sogn and Fjordane. The skeleton of a young man was found together with remains of three other skeletons in a thick layer of bones and implements from the settlement site.

19 Bronze Age burial mounds by the coast of south-western Norway. Vanse, West Agder. Diameter about 100 ft.

20 Bronze Age burial cairn by the sea-shore. Mølen, Brunlanes, Vestfold. Diameter about 100 ft. On this treeless height several similar cairns are located.

21 Bronze Age dagger from the Vestby stone cist. Length 33.5 cm.

22 Bronze collar from a woman's grave. Diameter about 15 cm. Vigrestad, Hå, Rogaland.

23 Stone cist with a bronze dagger. Middle Bronze Age, Vestby, Akershus. The three-feet-long cist was covered by a round cairn set in a commanding position on a hillock near the Oslo fjord.

24 Eastern Norwegian landscape, with Bronze Age carvings on a rock in the foreground. Skjælin, Skjeberg, Østfold.

25 Gold arm-ring and toilet accessories from the eastern Norwegian Bronze Age.

26 A woman's ornaments from the Late Bronze Age, eastern Norway. Many things suggest the cult of a goddess to whom the great hoards of female accoutrements were offered up.

27 Bronze Age weapons and pottery. Eastern Norway.

28 Hoard from the Late Bronze Age, Nystad Gjerpen, Telemark, near the eastern Norwegian coast. Most of the articles found in this and similar hoards must have originated in Denmark during the last two phases of the Bronze Age.

29 Two horned animals from a rich Late Bronze Age hoard, Lunner, Hadeland, eastern Norway.

30 X-ray of one of the horned animals.

31 Mould of soapstone. Vanse, West Agder. The number of soapstone moulds for axes, daggers and swords found in different parts of Norway proves that people were well enough acquainted with difficult casting processes. Length about 15 cm.

32 Bear, elk and reindeer. Chiselled pictures from the rich hunting and fish-
    ing district of Tysfjord, Nordland. These naturalistic renderings, part of
    a substantial group of rock art, are typical of the 'arctic' style.

33 Naturalistic picture of a reindeer, about 1.80 m. long. Rock carving at
    Bøla, near Lake Snåsa, North Trøndelag.

34 Running deer from the Ausevik group. Length 115 cm. In this western
    Norwegian fjord area surrounded by rugged mountains, hunting on a
    large scale must have been carried on in the Stone and Bronze Ages.

35 Stylized stag and geometric patterns. Part of a group of rock-carvings con-
    taining about 350 figures, at Ausevik near Florø, Sogn and Fjordane.
    Length of the stag 55 cm.

36 Stylized picture of a bull elk, about 2 m. long, hewn in a rock on Åskollen
    near Drammen on the west side of the Oslo Fjord.

37 A whale and elks, with strange stylized figures. Skogerveien, Drammen.
    Length of the whale about 2 m.

38 Ships, carts and men. Part of a rock-carving with stylized figures at Begby,
    Borge, Østfold.

39 An eastern Norwegian landscape with a Bronze Age rock-carving. Bak-
    kehaugen, Ingedal, Østfold.

40 Early Iron Age graves at Gunnarstorp, Skjeberg, Østfold. More than 200
    cremation graves, forming a large cemetery, have been excavated at this
    site.

41 Early Iron Age cremation grave at Gunnarstorp, Skjeberg, Østfold.

42 A typical grave from the pre-Roman Iron Age: a stone cist containing
    pottery and burnt bones. Frivoll, East Agder.

43 Iron sickel from the pre-Roman period. Eastern Norway.

44 Early Iron Age fibula. Length 10.5 cm. Grave-find from Ås, Sande, Vestfold.

45 Ship-setting of stones with a Migration Period cremation grave. The standing stones increase in height towards each end. A similar ship-setting and three circles are near by. Over-all length of the ship-setting about 80 ft. Istrehågan, Tjølling, Vestfold.

46 Weapons from an early Roman Iron Age grave near Mjøsa, in the interior of eastern Norway. Ile, Furnes, Hedmark. Length of the sword 40 cm.

47 Part of the furniture from a rich Roman Iron Age grave, Stabu, Toten, eastern Norway. Length of the sword 71 cm. Warrior graves are most common in the eastern part of the country, though traces of a Roman Age 'warrior caste' are to be found also along the west coast and even in the far north bordering on the territory of the Lapps.

48 Bronze cauldron, a so-called *Østlandskjele*, from a third-century AD grave at Toten, Oppland. This type of imported cauldron must have been especially highly prized in eastern Norway.

49 The Godøy find. A so-called *Vestlandskjele*, which was used as an urn for the deceased's charred bones, two silver cups, a gold arm-ring and a gold medallion. Godøy. Giske, near Ålesund, Møre and Romsdal. Fourth century. Diameter of the bronze cauldron about 35 cm.

50 Roman bronze bucket, from a grave-find at Tune, Østfold. Height about 25 cm. Second century AD.

51 Spurs with silver ornamentation, found in a well-equipped warrior's grave at Hunn, Borge, Østfold. Second century AD. Height 5.5 and 6 cm. respectively.

52 Brooches ornamented with gold and silver. Second to third century. Eastern Norway.

53 Bronze vessels and gaming pieces of glass from the Avaldsnes grave. The Avaldsnes district near Haugesund has yielded finds from practically all periods of Norwegian prehistory.

54 Gold finger-ring from the Avaldsnes find. An arm-ring, weighing about 19 ounces, and three other finger-rings were found in the same grave. In no other Roman Iron Age burial in Northern Europe has so much gold been found.

55 Gilded bronze brooch with filigree ornamentation. Late Roman Iron Age. Skalberg, Sandar, Vestfold.

56 Gold pendant, or 'berlock', from the second century, found in a woman's grave at Fevang, Sandar, Vestfold. Height 3 cm.

57 Glass bowls found in a woman's grave with a number of imported goods, among them a cauldron, ladle and bowl of bronze and two gold finger-rings. Store-Dal, Skjeberg, Østfold. Second century AD.

58 The remains of a long-house from a Migration Age farm. Length about 100 ft. Åseral, West Agder.

59 A complex of long-houses and graves, near the south-western coast of Norway. Leksaren in Varhaug, Rogaland. Complexes of this type are known only from Rogaland and from northern Norway.

60 Stone cist with pottery. Typical inhumation grave from the Migration Age (sixth century AD) in south-west Norway. Skreros, Vegusdal, East Agder.

61 Settlement site from the Migration Age, excavated in the mountains near Rjukan, Telemark. Length of the house about 40 ft.

62 Sword-hilt and clasp from one of the richest Norwegian burial finds dating from the Migration Age (sixth century AD). Snartemo, Lyngdal, West Agder.

63 Gold scabbard-mounts from eastern Norway. Norway was rich in gold from the Roman to the Migration Age. This group of scabbard-mounts includes pieces which rank among the finest examples of the goldsmith's art.

64 Square-headed brooch of silver-gilt, decorated with niello, coloured stones and filigree. On the reverse of the plate there is an indecipherable runic inscription. Length 17.8 cm. Fonnås, Rendal, Hedmark. Sixth century AD.

65 Bronze brooches, Vang, Hedmark. These two bronze pins from the interior of eastern Norway are characteristic examples of the applied art of the Migration Age. They terminate in the typical highly individual animal-heads.

66 Gold hoard from Sletner, Eidsberg, Østfold, About AD 500.

67 A large buckle for a baldric, found in a chieftain's grave at Åker near Hamar, Hedmark. It is of silver gilt, decorated with niello, gold and garnets. End of the sixth century AD.

68 Wooden box and pottery vessel from eastern Norway. Fifth to sixth century AD.

69 Sixth-century grave goods from a richly furnished woman's grave, found in a barrow in Ommundrød, Hedrum, Vestfold.

70 Reconstruction model of a boat-house excavated at Karmøy, Rogaland. In it is shown a reconstruction of the Kvalsund ship from Sunnmøre, Møre and Romsdal. Migration Age.

71 Runic inscriptions and rock-carvings, Kårstad in Nordfjord, Sogn and Fjordane.

72 A Viking Age grave mound, typical for eastern Norway. Asker near Oslo.

73 Spearheads of iron, from the Merovingian Age. Both are richly decorated with incised lines. Length 42.5 and 51 cm., respectively.

74 Spur and strap-mountings of gold, decorated with a fantastic filigree design. Rød, Værne Kloster, Rygge, Østfold.

75 Viking swords. Steinsvik, Lødingen, Nordland (ninth century) and eastern Norway (tenth century).